C000137978

Not For Tourists™ Guide to BOSTON

Not For Tourists Inc New York **2004-2005**

Published and designed by:
Not For Tourists, Inc.
NFT.—Not For Tourists. Guide to BOSTON 2004-2005
www.notfortourists.com

Concept by
Jane Pirone

Information Design
Jane Pirone
Rob Tallia
Scot Covey
Diana Pizzari

Editor
Jane Pirone

Managing Editors
Rob Tallia
Diana Pizzari

City Editors
Harold T Kelly Jr
Tim Moran

Writing and Editing
Cathleen Cueto
Harold T Kelly Jr
Brendan Lynch
Tim Moran
Diana Pizzari
Rob Tallia

Research
Annie Holt
Sherry Wasserman

Editorial Interns
Shilpa Raman
Mirjana Rutter
Christopher Salyers

Research Interns
Munira Ahmed
Lauren E. Fonda
Sharyn Jackson

Graphic Design/Production
Alexandra Anderson
Scot Covey
Matthew Knutzen
Ran Lee
James Martinez
Amy Oh
Christopher Salyers
Nick Trotter

Proofing
Jack Schieffer

Contributors
Richard Beresis
Jessica Dixon-Streeter
Nancy Howell
Brian G. Lewandowski
Sarah Pascarella

Printed in China
ISBN# 0-9740131-4-5 $14.95
Copyright © 2004 by Not For Tourists, Inc.

Every effort has been made to ensure that the information in this book is as up-to-date as possible at press time. However, many details are liable to change—as we have learned. The publishers cannot accept responsibility for any consequences arising from use of this book.

Dear NFT User:

Thank you for buying the ultimate user's manual to Boston. In your hands you hold a book that contains thousands of business listings and descriptions of scores of local features that make Boston a unique, terrific city. Whether you live in Boston (or Cambridge, or Somerville, or Brookline …), work in Boston, or just find yourself in Boston a lot, we trust that this book will help you use and get the most out of the city.

Part of what makes Boston fascinating is that every aspect of life in Boston co-exists with its opposite. Modernity flourishes while history endures. Town and Gown are mutually suspicious, but need one another. Upper-class patricians rub shoulders with working-class heroes. Love lives with hate in the heart of many Red Sox fans. The ugliness of the Big Dig is a stone's throw from some of the prettiest urban parks in the nation.

To help you navigate all this quirkiness, we had to make this book easy to use. Like Boston (and by implication, like you), this book is smart. It's packed with great maps. It is unusually comprehensive. It celebrates knowledge, design and practicality. It understands that Boston is a city of neighborhoods, each of which has its own particular character, filled in its nooks and crannies with plenty to see and do.

In short, this book is wicked cool. But this book can only be the ultimate Boston user's manual to the extent that you, the NFT user, can trust it. So, if you have something to say about what you see in this book, please send us your feedback. Know of a great new place to eat? Tell us. Has a phone number changed? Let us know. E-mail us through our website: www.notfortourists.com.

Here's hoping you find what you need.

Harry, Diana, Rob, and Jane

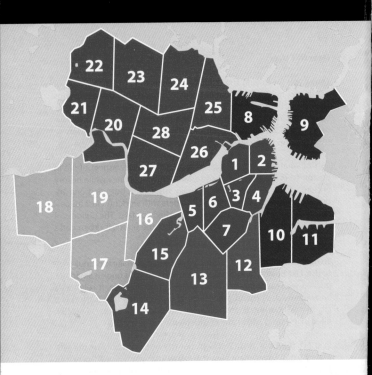

Boston Area Driving Map
and Downtown Boston Map
foldout, last page

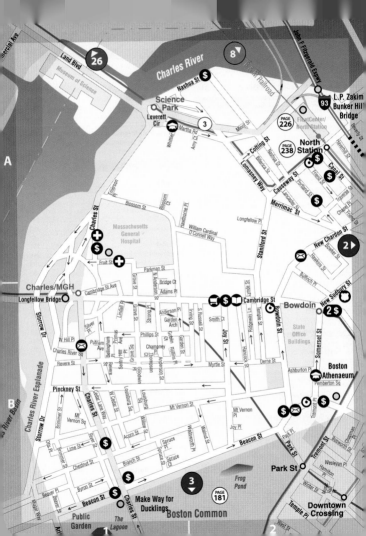

Map 1

Boston's newest landmark is the Leonard P. Zakim Bunker Hill Bridge, a wide name befitting the world's widest cable-stayed bridge. On Beacon Hill, cobblestones and gas lamps reflect the neighborhood's colonial history (where the State House is now, John Hancock once fed cows). Between the Zakim and Beacon Hill lies the West End, formerly a bustling working-class neighborhood but now a charmless tract dominated by high-rise apartment buildings.

Banks

- **Cambridge Trust** · 65 Beacon St
- **Citizens** · 1 Center Plaza
- **Fleet** · 104 Canal St
- **Fleet** · 125 Nashua St
- **Fleet** · 161 Cambridge St
- **Fleet** · 200 Portland St
- **Fleet** · 243 Charles St
- **Fleet** · 3 Center Plaza
- **Fleet** · 45 Charles St
- **Sovereign Bank** · 1 Beacon St
- **Sovereign Bank** · 125 Causeway St
- **Sovereign Bank** · 27 Beacon St
- **Sovereign Bank** · 67 Beacon St

Donuts

- **Dunkin' Donuts** · 10 Beacon St
- **Dunkin' Donuts** · 106 Cambridge St
- **Dunkin' Donuts** · 111 Causeway St

Hospitals

- **Massachusetts Eye and Ear Infirmary** · 243 Charles St
- **Massachusetts General Hospital** · 55 Fruit St

Landmarks

- **Boston Athenaeum** · 10 1/2 Beacon St
- **FleetCenter** · 150 Causeway St
- **Leonard P Zakim Bunker Hill Bridge** · Causeway St & I-93
- **Longfellow Bridge** · Cambridge St & Charles St
- **Make Way for Ducklings** · Charles St & Beacon St
- **Massachusetts General Hospital** · 55 Fruit St

Libraries

- **West End** · 151 Cambridge St

Police

- **District A-1** · 40 New Sudbury St

Post Offices

- 136 Charles St
- 25 New Chardon St
- 24 Beacon St

Schools

- **Boston Children's School** · 8 Whittier Pl
- **Suffolk University** · 8 Ashburton Pl

Supermarkets

- **Stop & Shop** · 181 Cambridge St

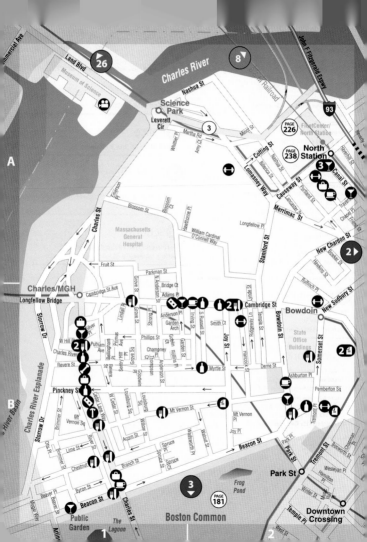

Map 1

Charles Street is home to two high-quality food markets: Deluca's (near Beacon Street) and Savenor's (toward Cambridge Street). For intimate dining, consider Lala Rokh or the Hungry i, or for a splurge, The Federalist. Istanbul Cafe has moved to Brighton; Buzzy's Roast Beef has moved into the afterlife (Heaven? Hell? Purgatory? Difficult to say).

Bars

- **21st Amendment** · 150 Bowdoin St
- **Beacon Hill Pub** · 149 Charles St
- **Boston Beer Works** · 112 Canal St
- **Cheers** · 84 Beacon St
- **Hill Tavern** · 228 Cambridge St
- **Hurricane O'Reilly's** · 150 Canal St
- **Sullivan's Tap** · 168 Canal St
- **The Four's** · 166 Canal St

Coffee

- **Cafe Mosaic** · 276 Friend St
- **Capital Coffee House** · 122 Bowdoin St
- **Starbucks** · 1 Charles St
- **Starbucks** · 222 Cambridge St

Copy Shops

- **Copy Clone** · 31 Mt Vernon St
- **Copy Cop** · 1 Beacon St
- **Ikon Document Services** · 3 Center Plaza
- **Kinko's** · 2 Center Plaza

Gyms

- **Basketball City** · 35 Lomasney Way
- **Beacon Hill Athletic Club** · 261 Friend St
- **Beacon Hill Athletic Club** · 3 Hancock St
- **Boston Sports Club** · 1 Bulfinch Pl
- **Fitcorp** · 1 Beacon St

Hardware Stores

- **Charles Street True Value Hardware** ·
  54 Charles St

Liquor Stores

- **Beacon Capitol Market** · 32 Myrtle St
- **Beacon Hill Wine & Spirits** · 63 Charles St
- **Charles Street Liquors** · 143 Charles St
- **Fine Wine Cellars** · 9 Beacon St
- **Jobi's Liquors** · 170 Cambridge St
- **Simmons Liquor Store** · 210 Cambridge St

Movie Theaters

- **Museum of Science Omni Theater** · Science Park

Pet Shops

- **Fi-Dough** · 103 Charles St

Restaurants

- **75 Chestnut** · 75 Chestnut St
- **Cafe Podima** · 156 Cambridge St
- **The Federalist** · 15 Beacon St
- **Figs** · 42 Charles St
- **Harvard Gardens** · 316 Cambridge St
- **Hungry i** · 71 1/2 Charles St
- **King & I** · 145 Charles St
- **Lala Rokh** · 97 Mt Vernon St
- **Ma Soba** · 156 Cambridge St
- **New York Soup Exchange** · 3 Center Plaza
- **Panificio** · 144 Charles St
- **Upper Crust** · 20 Charles St

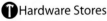Shopping

- **Black Ink** · 101 Charles St
- **Deluca's Market** · 11 Charles St
- **Hilton's Tent City** · 272 Friend St
- **Savenor's Market** · 160 Charles St

Video Rental

- **Fred's Video Beacon Hill** · 63A Charles St
- **Mike's Movies** · 248 Cambridge St

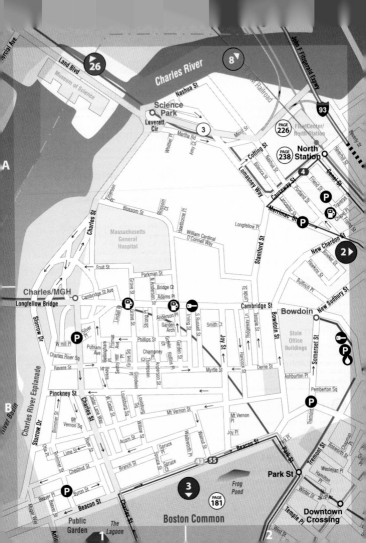

Ah, Storrow. Every Storrow Drive interchange is dangerous and difficult to navigate, so exercise extreme caution. Just remember: if you think Storrow Drive is wretched, imagine how wretched traffic would be around here if Storrow didn't exist. Of all bad Boston parking areas, Beacon Hill might have the worst parking of them all—but since it's near all four T lines, why drive at all?

Subway
- ■ • Bowdoin
- ■ • Charles/MGH
- ■ ■ • Downtown Crossing
- ■ ■ • North Station
- ■ ■ • Park St
- ■ • Science Park

Bus Lines
- **4** • North Station—World Trade Center Via Federal Courthouse
- **43** • Ruggles Station—Park & Tremont Streets
- **55** • Jersey & Queensberry—Copley Sq or Park & Tremont Streets

Car Rental
- **Avis** • 3 Center Plaza
- **Dollar** • 209 Cambridge St

Car Washes
- **Professional Auto Detailers** • 1 Center Plaza

Gas Stations
- **Exxon** • 239 Cambridge St
- **Gulf** • 296 Cambridge St
- **Mobil** • 150 Friend St

Parking

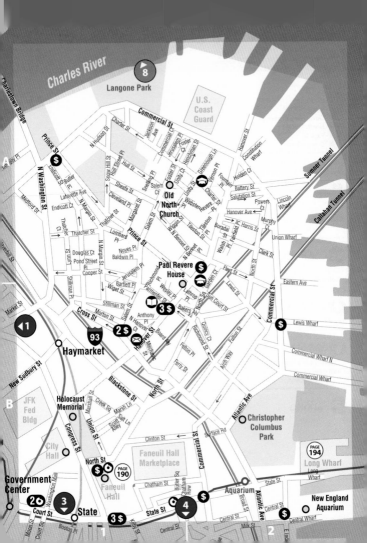

Charles River

Langone Park **8**

U.S. Coast Guard

Charlestown Bridge

Commercial St

Charter St
Jackson Ave
Commercial Wharf

Prince St
N Washington St
N Hudson St

$

Butler
Snow Hill St
Hull St
Sheafe St
Salem St
Foster St
Jerusalem Pl
Henchman St
Greenough Ln
Vernon Ct
Fountain
Constitution Wharf

Medford St
N Margin St
Lafayette Ave
Endicott St
Cleveland Pl
Margaret St
Sheafe St
Unity St
Webster Ave
Charter St
Salutation St
Powers Ct
Lincoln Wharf

Sumner Tunnel

Old North Church

Hanover Ave
Boradal
Harris St
Union Wharf

Endicott Ct
Thatcher Ct
Thatcher St
Lombard
N Bennet St
Tileston St
Walsh
Hartland
Clark St

Callahan Tunnel

Prince St
Noyes Pl
Baldwin Pl
Fleet St
Eastern Ave

Douglas Ct
Pond Street Pl
Cooper St
Jerusalem Pl
Bartlett Pl

Paul Revere House **$**

Garden Ct
Lewis St
Commercial St
Eastern Ave

Stillman St
Bartlett Pl
Wiget St
Richmond St
Parmenter St
Wesley Pl
Lathrop
N Court St
Lewis Wharf

Cross St
Morton St
Stillman St
N Hanover Ct
Anthony
Hanover St
Bakers Al
Quincy St
Richmond St
3 $

2 $

93

Haymarket
Hanover St
Board
Marshall
Fulton St
Commercial Wharf N

Blackstone St
North St
Richmond St
Felton Pl
Arch Way
Commercial Wharf

Terry St

New Sudbury St

B

JFK Fed Bldg

Holocaust Memorial

Creek Sq
Marsh Ln
Scott Alley
North St

Clinton St
Atlantic Ave

Congress St
Union St
Marshall
Salt Ln
Riley

Christopher Columbus Park

City Hall

Faneuil Hall Marketplace

Commercial St
Surface Rd

Long Wharf

PAGE 194
Long Wharf

Government Center

North St **$**
PAGE 190

Chatham St
Butler Sq
Chatham Row

Aquarium
Broad St

New England Aquarium

2 Court St

3

State

3 $
State St
Kilby St
Central St
Milk St

4

$

$

Atlantic Ave
Central Wharf

Central St

1   **2**

Map 2

The North End is distinctly Italian, down to the flag on the "Welcome to the North End" sign near the entrance to the Callahan. The demolition of the Central Artery and the resultant open spaces will finally reconnect the North End with the Faneuil Hall area. Faneuil Hall Marketplace may be a tourist trap, but it's very much used by locals, particularly those that work in the office buildings nearby.

$ Banks

- **Century Bank** · 275 Hanover St
- **Citizens** · 28 State St
- **Citizens** · 315 Hanover St
- **Citizens** · 53 State St
- **Fleet** · 2 Atlantic Ave
- **Fleet** · 260 Hanover St
- **Fleet** · 283 Causeway St
- **Fleet** · 4 Commercial St
- **Fleet** · 48-50 Salem St
- **Fleet** · 60 State St
- **Fleet** · 64-66 Cross St
- **Sovereign Bank** · 1 Union St
- **Sovereign Bank** · 287 Hanover St
- **Sovereign Bank** · Central Wharf

Donuts

- **Dunkin' Donuts** · 1 Congress St
- **Dunkin' Donuts** · 100 City Hall Plaza
- **Dunkin' Donuts** · 111 State St
- **Dunkin' Donuts** · 2 City Hall Sq

Landmarks

- **Christopher Columbus Park** · Atlantic Ave
- **City Hall** · 1 City Hall Plaza
- **Faneuil Hall** · Congress St & North St
- **Holocaust Memorial** · Congress St & Union St
- **New England Aquarium** · Central Wharf
- **Old North Church** · 193 Salem St
- **Paul Revere House** · 19 North Sq

Libraries

- **North End** · 25 Parmenter St

Post Offices

- · 217 Hanover St

Schools

- **Eliot Elementary School** · 16 Charter St
- **St John School** · 9 Moon St

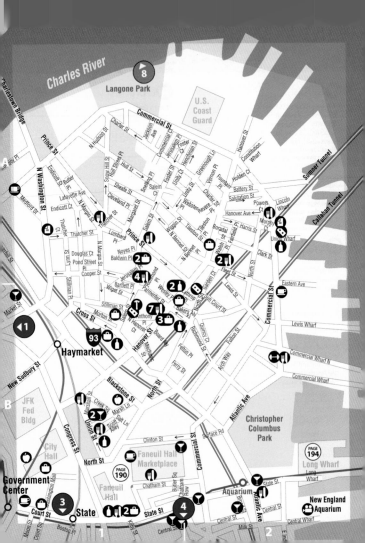

The taverns around Haymarket can serve as a refuge from inclement weather or general Faneuil Hall craziness. Foodies should acquaint themselves with Haymarket's farmer's market. Predictably, the North End has an insane number of good Italian restaurants, bakeries, and grocers. The food court in Quincy Market isn't a bad place to grab take-away lunches, but steer clear in April and May (high season for school field trips).

Bars

- **Bell in Hand Tavern** · 45 Union St
- **Black Rhino** · 21 Broad St
- **Black Rose** · 160 State St
- **Grand Canal** · 57 Canal St
- **Green Dragon Tavern** · 11 Marshall St
- **Ned Devine's** · Faneuil Hall Marketplace
- **The Office** · 5 Broad St
- **Tia's on the Waterfront** · 200 Atlantic Ave

Coffee

- **Causeway Cafe** · 239 Causeway St
- **Starbucks** · 2 Atlantic Ave
- **Starbucks** · 63-64 Court St
- **Starbucks** · Quincy Market

Copy Shops

- **Harborside Copy** · 338 Commercial St
- **Sir Speedy Printing Center** · 77 N Washington St

Farmer's Markets

- **City Hall Plaza** · City Hall Plaza at Cambridge St
- **Haymarket** · Blackstone St

Gyms

- **Beacon Hill Athletic Club** · 85 Atlantic Ave

Hardware Stores

- **Salem Street True Value** · 89 Salem St

Liquor Stores

- **Cirace's Liquor** · 173 North St
- **Federal Wine & Spirits** · 29 State St
- **Hanover Liquors** · 363 Hanover St
- **Martignetti Liquors** · 64 Cross St
- **Waterfront Beer & Wine** · 450 Commercial St
- **Wine Bottega** · 341 Hanover St
- **Wine Cave** · 33 Union St

Movie Theaters

- **Simons IMAX Theatre** · Central Wharf

Restaurants

- **Antico Forno** · 93 Salem St
- **Billy Tse** · 240 Commercial St
- **Boston Sail Loft** · 80 Atlantic Ave
- **Bricco** · 241 Hanover St
- **Caffe Paradiso** · 255 Hanover St
- **Cosi** · 53 State St
- **Daily Catch** · 323 Hanover St
- **Galleria Umberto** · 289 Hanover St
- **Green Dragon Tavern** · 11 Marshall St
- **L'Osteria** · 104 Salem St
- **La Famiglia Giorgio's** · 112 Salem St
- **La Summa** · 30 Fleet St
- **Lucca** · 226 Hanover St
- **Mamma Maria** · 3 North Sq
- **McCormick & Schmick's** · Faneuil Hall Marketplace
- **Pinang** · Faneuil Hall Marketplace
- **Pizzeria Regina** · 11 1/2 Thatcher St
- **Prezza** · 24 Fleet St
- **Sage** · 69 Prince St
- **Sel de la Terre** · 255 State St
- **Taranta** · 210 Hanover St
- **Theo's Cozy Corner** · 162 Salem St
- **Trattoria a Sacalinatella** · 253 Hanover St
- **Union Oyster House** · 41 Union St

Shopping

- **Bova's Bakery** · 134 Salem St
- **Brooks Brothers** · 75 State St
- **Dairy Fresh Candies** · 57 Salem St
- **Green Cross Pharmacy** · 393 Hanover St
- **Holbrows Flowers** · 100 City Hall Plaza
- **Maria's Pastry Shop** · 46 Cross St
- **Mike's Pastry** · 300 Hanover St
- **Modern Pastry** · 257 Hanover St
- **Monica's Salumeria** · 130 Salem St
- **Newbury Comics** · 1 Washington Mall
- **Rand McNally** · 84 State St
- **Salumeria Italiana** · 151 Richmond St
- **Salumeria Toscana** · 272 Hanover St

Video Rental

- **Beantown Video** · 372 Commercial St
- **North End Video** · 292 North St
- **Video Cinema** · 62 Salem St

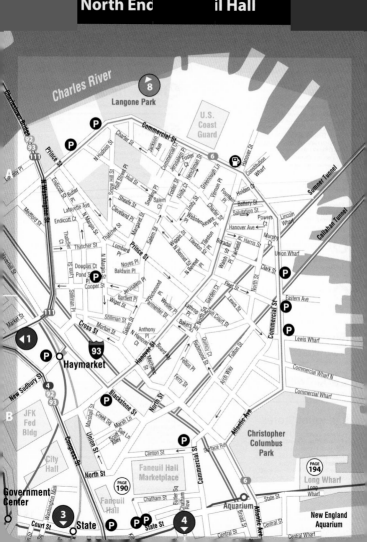

Charles River

Langone Park
8

U.S. Coast Guard

Commercial St

Charlestown Bridge

Prince St

92
93
111

Le Roy Pl

Charter St

N Hudson St

Jackson Ave

Commercial Ct

Jerusalem Ct

Foster Ct

Greenough Ln

Hancock Ct

Vernon Pl

Fountain Ct

Holden Ct

Constitution Wharf

6

Hanover Ave

Sumner Tunnel

Hull St

Snelling Pl

Foster St

Union St

Unity St

Charter St

Webster Ave

Fleet St

Battery St

Salutation St

Powers Ct

Lincoln Wharf

Callahan Tunnel

Endicott St

Butler

Lafayette Ave

Cleveland Pl

Salem St

Margaret St

Wiget Ct

N Bennet St

Revere St

Tileston St

Hanover Ave

Murphy Pl

Harris St

Wash

Fairfield

Union Wharf

Medford St

Endicott Ct

Thatcher

Thatcher St

Sheafe St

Lombard

Prince St

Noyes Pl

Baldwin Pl

Tileston St

Clark St

Eastern Ave

Thatcher St

Stillman St

Thatcher

Unity St

Douglas Ct
Pond St
Cooper St

Jerusalem Pl

Bartlett Pl

Parmenter St

Richmond Pl

Wesley Pl

N Hanover Ct

N Bennet St

Garden Ct

North St

Lathrop Pl

Salem Court St

Lewis St

P

Clark St

Commercial St

Market St

111

Cross St

Stillman St

Morton St

Wiget St

Anthony Pl

N Hanover Ct

Bakers Al

Board

Mechanic

P

Haymarket
93

New Sudbury St

4
92
93

B

JFK Fed Bldg

City Hall

Government Center

11

Blackstone St

Union St

Marshall St

Creek Sq

Marsh Ln

Scott Alley
Salt Ln

Hanover St

Richmond St

Lewis Wharf

Commercial Wharf N

Commercial Wharf

Dunley Ct

Fulton St

Clinton St

Pelton Pl

Ferry St

Atlantic Ave

Surface Rd

Arch Way

Christopher Columbus Park

North St

Cambridge St

Washington Mall

Court St

3
State

Faneuil Hall Marketplace
PAGE
190

Faneuil Hall

Chatham St

Butler Row

Chatham Row

State St

P P
4

6

Aquarium

State St

Broad St

Central St

Atlantic Ave

Central St

PAGE
194

Long Wharf

Long Wharf

New England Aquarium

Your best transportation option in the North End is your own feet. If you're taking the T to the North End, get off at Haymarket or North Station. Street parking is difficult, but there are plenty of garages on the Faneuil Hall side of the Artery. The garage at Parcel 7 on Blackstone Street is handy and validates parking for some businesses in the North End.

Subway

- ■ · **Aquarium**
- ■ ■ · **Haymarket**
- ■ ■ · **State**

Bus Lines

- **4** · North Station—World Trade Center via Federal Courthouse
- **6** · Boston Marine Ind Park—South Station/ Haymarket Station
- **92** · Assembly Sq Mall—Downtown via Sullivan Sq Station, Main St
- **93** · Sullivan Sq Station—Downtown via Bunker Hill St & Haymarket Station
- **111** · Woodlawn or Broadway & Park Ave— Haymarket Station via Mystic River/Tobin Bridge

Gas Stations

· **Mobil** · 420 Commercial St

P Parking

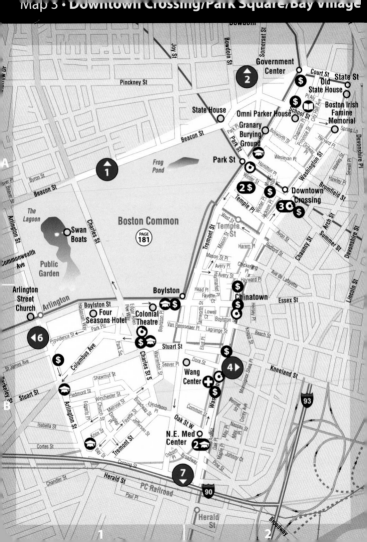

Map 3 · Downtown Crossing/Park Square/Bay Village

Downtown Crossing is a congested beehive, but city shopping districts are supposed to be this way, aren't they? Emerson College's move from Back Bay a few years ago helped make the Theater District more vibrant. Unlike its tonier relative Beacon Hill, the tiny 19th-century enclave Bay Village has practically no commercial space, making it refreshingly serene after a snowstorm.

Banks

- **Citizens** · 73 Tremont St
- **Fleet** · 1 Summer St
- **Fleet** · 11 Winter St
- **Fleet** · 157 Stuart St
- **Fleet** · 58 Winter St
- **Fleet** · 6 Tremont St
- **Fleet** · 630 Washington St
- **Fleet** · 710 Washington St
- **Fleet** · 80 Boylston St
- **Sovereign Bank** · 30 Winter St
- **Sovereign Bank** · 600 Washington St
- **Sovereign Bank** · 61 Arlington St
- **Sovereign Bank** · 769 Washington St

Donuts

- **Dunkin' Donuts** · 127 Tremont St
- **Dunkin' Donuts** · 417 Washington St
- **Dunkin' Donuts** · 426 Washington St
- **Dunkin' Donuts** · 630 Washington St
- **Dunkin' Donuts** · 750 Washington St
- **Dunkin' Donuts** · 8 Park Plaza
- **Honey Dew Donuts** · 426 Washington St

Hospitals

- **Tufts-New England Medical Center** · 750 Washington St

Landmarks

- **Arlington Street Church** · 351 Boylston St
- **Boston Irish Famine Memorial** · School St & Washington St
- **Colonial Theatre** · 106 Boylston St
- **Four Seasons Hotel** · 200 Boylston St
- **Granary Burying Ground** · Tremont St & Park St
- **Old State House** · 206 Washington St
- **Omni Parker House** · 60 School St
- **State House** · Beacon St & Park St
- **Swan Boats** · Arlington St & Boylston St
- **Wang Center** · 270 Tremont St

Libraries

- **Kirstein Business** · 20 City Hall Ave

Schools

- **Boston High School** · 152 Arlington St
- **Boston Renaissance Charter School** · 250 Stuart St
- **Emerson College** · 120 Boylston St
- **Josiah Quincy Elementary School** · 885 Washington St
- **Josiah Quincy Upper School** · 900 Washington St
- **New England School of Law** · 154 Stuart St
- **Suffolk University Law School** · 120 Tremont St

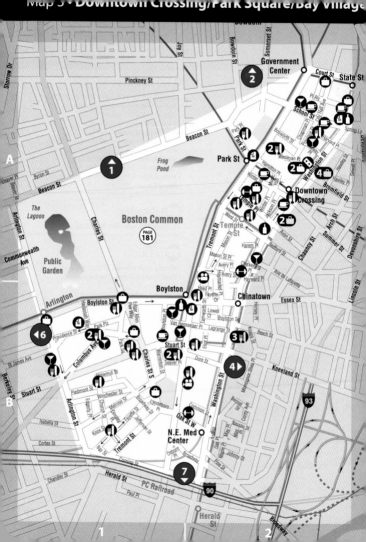

Map 5 • Downtown Crossing/Park Square/Bay Village

Stop into Filene's Basement once in a while—you never know what might have turned up. Celebrate your purchase upstairs by noshing on the unique, eponymous Chacarero. Scoff if you like about the number of chain restaurants in this area, but some of them (like Legal's and McCormick's) offer very good food and service. This area also boasts Dedo, Aujourd'hui and, across the Common, No. 9 Park.

Bars

- **Felt** · 533 Washington St
- **MJ O'Connor's** · 27 Columbus Ave
- **Parker's Bar** · 60 School St
- **Pravda 116** · 116 Boylston St
- **The Littlest Bar** · 47 Province St
- **The Tam** · 222 Tremont St
- **Whiskey Park** · 64 Arlington St

Coffee

- **Filene's Cafe** · 426 Washington St
- **Starbucks** · 12 Winter St
- **Starbucks** · 143 Stuart St
- **Starbucks** · 240 Washington St
- **Starbucks** · 27 School St
- **Starbucks** · 62 Boylston St

Copy Shops

- **Copy Cop** · 260 Washington St
- **Emerson College Print Copy Center** · 201 Tremont St
- **Kinko's** · 125 Tremont St
- **Sir Speedy Printing Center** · 20 Province St

Gyms

- **Crunch Fitness** · 17 Winter St
- **Sports Club LA** · 2 Avery St
- **Wang YMCA of Chinatown** · 8 Oak St W

Liquor Stores

- **Foerster's Market & Liquors** · 78 Boylston St
- **Merchants Wine & Spirits** · 6 Water St
- **Wine Cellar** · 497 Washington St

Movie Theaters

- **Loews Boston Common** · 175 Tremont St
- **Wang Center** · 270 Tremont St

Restaurants

- **Aujourd'hui** · 200 Boylston St
- **Buddha's Delight** · 3 Beach St
- **Chacarero** · 426 Washington St
- **Davio's** · 75 Arlington St
- **Dedo** · 69 Church St
- **Dominic's** · 255 Tremont St
- **Emperor's Garden** · 690 Washington St
- **Finale** · 1 Columbus Ave
- **Herrera's Mexican Grille** · 11 Temple Pl
- **Jacob Wirth** · 31-37 Stuart St
- **Krystal's Cafe** · 12 Church St
- **Legal Sea Foods** · 25 Park Sq
- **Locke-Ober** · 3 Winter Pl
- **Mantra** · 52 Temple Pl
- **McCormick & Schmick's** · 34 Columbus Ave
- **No 9 Park** · 9 Park St
- **Penang** · 685 Washington St
- **Pho Pasteur** · 123 Stuart St
- **Pigalle** · 75 S Charles St
- **Rock Bottom Brewery** · 115 Stuart St
- **Sam LaGrassa's** · 44 Province St
- **Silvertone Bar & Grill** · 69 Bromfield St
- **Teatro** · 177 Tremont St
- **Tequila Mexican Grill** · 55 Bromfield St

Shopping

- **Beacon Hill Skate Shop** · 135 Charles St S
- **Bromfield Camera & Video** · 10 Bromfield St
- **City Sports** · 11 Bromfield St
- **Filene's** · 426 Washington St
- **Filene's Basement** · 426 Washington St
- **H & M** · 350 Washington St
- **HMV** · 24 Winter St
- **LJ Peretti** · 2 1/2 Park Sq
- **Lotus Designs** · 482A Columbus Ave
- **Macy's** · 450 Washington St
- **Marshall's** · 350 Washington St
- **Old Town Camera** · 226 Washington St
- **Shreve, Crump & Low** · 330 Boylston St
- **Staples** · 25 Court St
- **TJ Maxx** · 350 Washington St

Video Rental

- **Kung Fu Video** · 365 Washington St

Map 3 • Downtown Crossing/Park Square/Bay Village

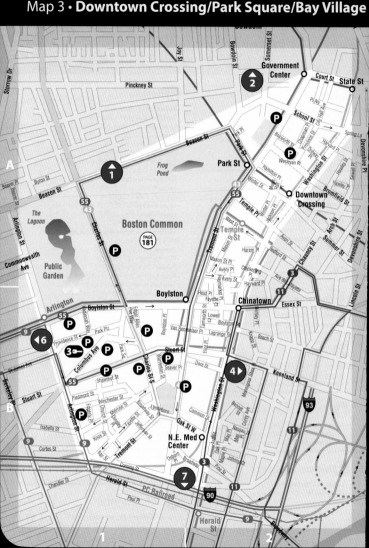

This area is well served by the T and buses, and now that the Silver Line is operational, there's less reason than ever to drive around here. Note that Tremont Street runs in only one direction until it intersects with, uh, Tremont Street, and that Washington Street north of West Street in Downtown Crossing is a pedestrian mall closed to traffic.

Subsection

Subway

- ■ ■ · **Arlington**
- ■ ■ · **Boylston**
- ■ ■ · **Chinatown**
- ■ ■ · **Downtown Crossing**
- ■ ■ · **Government Center**
- ■ ■ · **N.E. Medical Center**
- ■ ■ · **Park St**

Bus Lines

- **3** · Boston Marine Ind Park—South Station/ Haymarket Station
- **9** · City Point—Copley Square via Brodway Station
- **11** · City Point—Downtown Bayview Route
- **43** · Ruggles Station—Park & Tremont Streets
- **55** · Jersey & Queensberry—Copley Sq or Park & Tremont Streets

Car Rental

- **Budget** · 24 Park Plaza
- **Dollar** · 26 Park Plaza
- **Hertz** · 30 Park Plaza

Parking

The Financial District is (unsurprisingly) the heart of Boston's banking and mutual fund industries and home to its largest concentration of skyscrapers. (One Lincoln Place is the newest member of the high-rise club.) When (if) the Dig is completed, Chinatown Gate will become the centerpiece of a new park.

Banks

- **Asian American Bank & Trust** · 68 Harrison Ave
- **Banknorth** · 15 Broad St
- **Boston Federal Savings Bank** · 75 Federal St
- **Boston Private Bank & Trust** · 10 Post Office Sq
- **Century Bank** · 24 Federal St
- **Century Bank** · 280 Atlantic Ave
- **Citizens** · 1 Financial Center
- **Citizens** · 40 Summer St
- **Citizens** · 6 Ave De Lafayette
- **Citizens** · 77 Franklin St
- **Eastern Bank** · 101 Federal St
- **Eastern Bank** · 265 Franklin St
- **Fleet** · 0 Post Office Sq
- **Fleet** · 1 Financial Center
- **Fleet** · 1 Post Office Sq
- **Fleet** · 100 Federal St
- **Fleet** · 125 High St
- **Fleet** · 175 Federal St
- **Fleet** · 30 Rowes Wharf
- **Fleet** · 65 Franklin St
- **Fleet** · 730 Atlantic Ave
- **Fleet** · 79 Summer St
- **General Bank** · 21 Milk St
- **One United Bank** · 133 Federal St
- **Sovereign Bank** · 125 Summer St
- **Sovereign Bank** · 160 Federal St
- **Sovereign Bank** · 300 Congress St
- **Wainwright Bank & Trust** · 63 Franklin St

Donuts

- **Dunkin' Donuts** · 10 Winthrop Sq
- **Dunkin' Donuts** · 101 Summer St
- **Dunkin' Donuts** · 16 Kneeland St
- **Dunkin' Donuts** · 176 Federal St
- **Dunkin' Donuts** · 265 Franklin St
- **Dunkin' Donuts** · 70 E India Row
- **Dunkin' Donuts** · 750 Atlantic Ave

Landmarks

- **Boston Harbor Hotel** · 70 Rowes Wharf
- **Chinatown Gate** · Beach St & Hudson St
- **Customs House Tower** · 3 McKinley Sq
- **Dreams of Freedom** · 1 Milk St
- **Federal Reserve** · 600 Atlantic Ave
- **Filene's Basement** · 426 Washington St
- **Old South Meeting House** · 310 Washington St
- **Old State House** · 206 Washington St
- **South Station** · Atlantic Ave & Summer St

 Post Offices

- 25 Dorchester Ave
- 90 Devonshire St
- 7 Ave De Lafayette

Supermarkets

- **Super 88** · 73 Essex St

Sundries / Entertainment

Although there are plenty of worthwhile restaurants in Chinatown, you might consider Emperor's Garden (Map 3) for dim sum, Taiwan Cafe for the real deal, Penang (Map 3) for picky relatives, or Ocean Wealth for seafood. For late-night bites, remember that neighbors News and South Street Diner serve late. Some of Boston's top restaurants, including Radius, Julien, and Meritage, call the Financial District home.

Map 4

Bars

- **Elephant & Castle** · 161 Devonshire St
- **JJ Foley's** · 21 Kingston St
- **Jose McIntyre's** · 160 Milk St
- **Les Zygomates** · 129 South St
- **Mr Dooley's Boston Tavern** · 77 Broad St
- **News** · 150 Kneeland St
- **Times Restaurant and Bar** · 112 Broad St
- **Trio** · 174 Lincoln St

Coffee

- **Bean & Leaf Company** · 20 Custom House St
- **Boston Coffee Exchange** · 32 Summer St
- **Peet's Coffee & Tea** · 176 Federal St
- **Starbucks** · 1 Federal St
- **Starbucks** · 1 Financial Ctr
- **Starbucks** · 1 International Pl
- **Starbucks** · 10 High St
- **Starbucks** · 101 Federal St
- **Starbucks** · 211 Congress St

Copy Shops

- **Copy Cop** · 1 International Pl
- **Copy Cop** · 101 Summer St
- **Copy Cop** · 13 Congress St
- **Copy Cop** · 155 Milk St
- **Copy Cop** · 230 Congress St
- **Copy Cop** · 77 Milk St
- **Copy Cop** · 85 Franklin St
- **Kinko's** · 10 Post Office Sq
- **Sir Speedy Printing Center** · 76 Batterymarch St

Gyms

- **Boston Sports Club** · 1 Devonshire St
- **Boston Sports Club** · 10 Franklin St
- **Fitcorp** · 100 Summer St
- **Fitcorp** · 125 Summer St
- **Fitness International** · 1 International Pl
- **Langham Hotel Health Club** · 250 Franklin St
- **Rowes Wharf Health Club & Spa** · 70 Rowes Wharf
- **Wellbridge Health and Fitness Center** · 695 Atlantic Ave

Hardware Stores

- **Hardware Outlet Co** · 51 High St

Pet Shops

- **Aqua World** · 20 Tyler St

Restaurants

- **Chau Chow City** · 83 Essex St
- **Country Life Vegetarian** · 200 High St
- **Good Life** · 28 Kingston St
- **J Pace & Son** · 2 Devonshire Pl
- **Julien** · 250 Franklin St
- **Les Zygomates** · 129 South St
- **Meritage** · 70 Rowes Wharf
- **Milk Street Cafe** · 50 Milk St
- **New Shanghai** · 21 Hudson St
- **News** · 150 Kneeland St
- **Ocean Wealth** · 8 Tyler St
- **Peach Farm** · 4 Tyler St
- **Peking Tom's** · 25 Kingston St
- **Pho Hoa** · 17 Beach St
- **Radius** · 8 High St
- **Sakurabana** · 57 Broad St
- **Shabu-Zen** · 16 Tyler St
- **South Street Diner** · 178 Kneeland St
- **Sultan's Kitchen** · 72 Broad St
- **Taiwan Cafe** · 34 Oxford St
- **Vault** · 105 Water St

Shopping

- **Chinese American Company** · 38 Kneeland St

Video Rental

- **Shang Hai Video** · 15 Hudson St
- **Top Ten Video Music (Chinese)** · 219 Harrison Ave
- **Universe Video (Chinese)** · 5 Knapp St

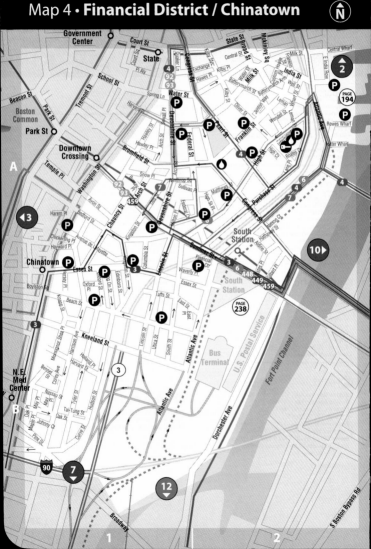

Map 4 • **Financial District / Chinatown**

The Financial District suffers mightily from the Dig. If you're not familiar with this area, check up on traffic changes before you head out. Currently, Kneeland Street is the primary feeder onto I-93 South and I-90 West; for I-93 North, aim for South Station and get onto Atlantic Avenue. If you don't absolutely need to drive around here, don't, especially during rush hour.

Subway

- ■ ■ · **Chinatown**
- ■ ■ · **Downtown Crossing**
- ■ ■ · **Park St**
- ■ · **South Station**
- ■ ■ · **State**

Bus Lines

- **3** · Boston Marine Ind. Park—South Station/ Haymarket Station
- **4** · North Station—World Trade Center Via Federal Courthouse
- **6** · Boston Marine Ind. Park—South Station/ Haymarket Station
- **7** · City Point—Otis & Summer Streets via Northern Ave. & South Station
- **92** · Assembly Sq Mall—Downtown via Sullivan Sq Station, Main St
- **93** · Sullivan Sq Station—Downtown via Bunker Hill St & Haymarket Station
- **448** · Marblehead—Haymarket, Downtown Crossing or Wonderland
- **449** · Marblehead—Haymarket, Downtown Crossing or Wonderland
- **459** · Marblehead—Haymarket, Downtown Crossing or Wonderland

Car Rental

- **Enterprise** · 1 International Pl

Car Washes

- **Eddie's Professional Auto Detailers** · 1 International Pl
- **Soft-Touch Professional Car Care** · 152 Congress St

Parking

Map 5 • **Back Bay (West) / Fenway (East)**

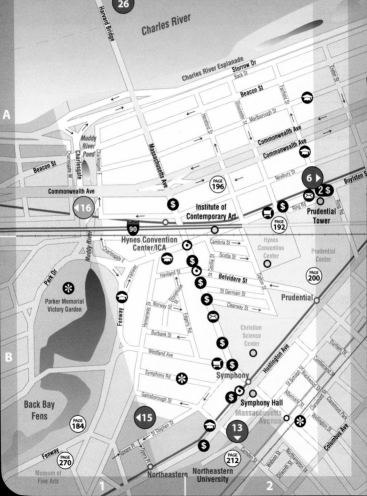

Map 5

Traffic on Mass Ave! MassPIRG on Newbury Street! Berklee students between classes! This area is fraught with minor perils, but that's because there's a lot going on. The striking group of buildings that comprises the Christian Science Center, together with the Pru and 111 Huntington (the "Daily Planet"), looks great at night. The long, Soviet-looking structure facing the Mother Church on Mass Ave is Church Park, a luxury apartment building.

Banks

- **Compass Bank** · 184 Massachusetts Ave
- **Fleet** · 133 Massachusetts Ave
- **Fleet** · 161 Massachusetts Ave
- **Fleet** · 221 Massachusetts Ave
- **Fleet** · 285 Huntington Ave
- **Fleet** · 346 Huntington Ave
- **Fleet** · 800 Boylston St
- **Fleet** · 855 Boylston St
- **Fleet** · 90 Massachusetts Ave
- **Sovereign Bank** · 279 Massachusetts Ave
- **Sovereign Bank** · 799 Boylston St

Donuts

- **Dunkin' Donuts** · 1108 Boylston St
- **Dunkin' Donuts** · 153 Massachusetts Ave
- **Dunkin' Donuts** · 283 Huntington Ave

Landmarks

- **Christian Science Center** · 175 Huntington Ave
- **Hynes Convention Center** · 900 Boylston St
- **Institute of Contemporary Art** · 955 Boylston St
- **Prudential Tower** · 800 Boylston St
- **Symphony Hall** · 301 Massachusetts Ave

Post Offices

- 207 Massachusetts Ave
- 800 Boylston St

 Schools

- **Berklee College of Music** · 1140 Boylston St
- **Boston Conservatory** · 8 The Fenway
- **City on a Hill Charter School** · 320 Huntington Ave
- **Kingsley Montessori School** · 30 Fairfield St
- **Newman Preparatory School** · 245 Marlborough St

Supermarkets

- **Trader Joe's** · 899 Boylston St
- **Whole Foods Market** · 15 Westland Ave

Community Gardens

- **Richard Parker Memorial Victory Garden** · The Fenway at Boylston St
- **Symphony Road Garden** · 56 Symphony Rd
- **Wellington Common** · Southwest Corridor at Wellington St

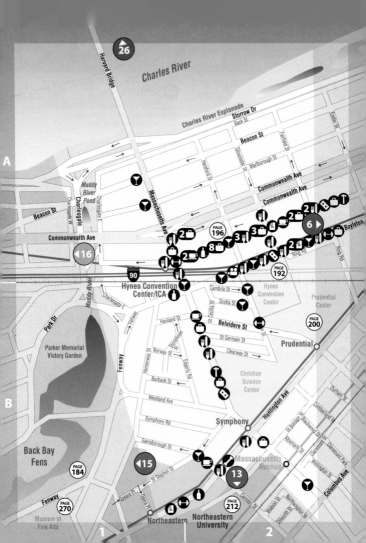

Trident Booksellers and Cafe is a terrific spot for brunching and browsing. Get earthy (or drink) at Other Side Cosmic Cafe. Beer drinkers who can handle Tufnel-level stereo volume and a touch of attitude should try Bukowski's. Also try Clio or Cafe Jaffa (depending on your budget for the evening). Berklee students often sit in at Wally's, joining more established musicians to play live jazz most nights of the week.

 Bars

- **Blue Cat Cafe** · 94 Massachusetts Ave
- **Bukowski's** · 50 Dalton St
- **Crossroads** · 495 Beacon St
- **Dillon's** · 955 Boylston St
- **Kings** · 10 Scotia St
- **Lir** · 903 Boylston St
- **Our House East** · 52 Gainsborough St
- **Sonsie** · 327 Newbury St
- **The Last Drop** · 421 Marlborough St
- **Top of the Hub** · 800 Boylston St
- **Wally's Café** · 427 Massachusetts Ave

 Coffee

- **Bodhi Cafe** · 335 Newbury St
- **Espresso Royale** · 286 Newbury St
- **Espresso Royale** · 44 Gainsborough St
- **Starbucks** · 151 Massachusetts Ave
- **Starbucks** · 350 Newbury St

Copy Shops

- **Copy Cop** · 815 Boylston St
- **Gnomon Copy** · 325 Huntington Ave
- **Mail Boxes Etc** · 304 Newbury St
- **Sir Speedy Printing Center** · 827 Boylston St

 **Gyms**

- **Boston Fitness & Swim Club** · 39 Dalton St
- **Boston Sports Club** · 361 Newbury St
- **YMCA** · 316 Huntington Ave

Hardware Stores

- **Economy Hardware** · 219 Massachusetts Ave

Liquor Stores

- **Bauer Wine & Spirits** · 330 Newbury St
- **Costello's** · 1084 Boylston St
- **Huntington Wine & Spirits** · 301 Huntington Ave

 Movie Theaters

- **Institute for Contemporary Art** · 955 Boylston St

Pet Shops

- **Dr Weiner's Pet Care Center** · 272 Huntington Ave

Restaurants

- **Bangkok City** · 167 Massachusetts Ave
- **Bangkok Cuisine** · 177A Massachusetts Ave
- **Betty's Wok & Noodle Diner** · 250 Huntington Ave
- **Cactus Club** · 939 Boylston St
- **Cafe Jaffa** · 48 Gloucester St
- **Capital Grille** · 359 Newbury St
- **Ciao Bella** · 240A Newbury St
- **Clio** · 370A Commonwealth Ave
- **Island Hopper** · 91 Massachusetts Ave
- **L'Espalier** · 30 Gloucester St
- **Lir** · 903 Newbury St
- **Other Side Cosmic Cafe** · 407 Newbury St
- **Shanti: Taste of India** · 277B Huntington Ave
- **Sonsie** · 327 Newbury St
- **Tapeo** · 266 Newbury St
- **Trident Booksellers and Cafe** · 338 Newbury St
- **Vinny T's** · 867 Boylston St

Shopping

- **Allston Beat** · 348 Newbury St
- **Army Barracks** · 328 Newbury St
- **Back Bay Bicycle** · 336 Commonwealth Ave
- **Blades Board & Skate** · 349A Newbury St
- **Boston Beat** · 279 Newbury St
- **CD Spins** · 324 Newbury St
- **Daddy's Junky Music** · 159 Massachusetts Ave
- **Deluca's Market** · 239 Newbury St
- **Economy Hardware** · 219 Massachusetts Ave
- **John Fluevog** · 306 Newbury St
- **Johnson Artist Materials** · 355 Newbury St
- **JP Licks** · 352 Newbury St
- **Mars Records** · 299 Newbury St
- **Matsu** · 259 Newbury St
- **Newbury Comics** · 332 Newbury St
- **Orpheus** · 362 Commonwealth Ave
- **Sweet & Nasty** · 90A Massachusetts Ave
- **Trident Booksellers and Cafe** · 338 Newbury St
- **Utrecht Art Supply Center** · 333 Massachusetts Ave
- **Virgin Megastore** · 360 Newbury St

 Video Rental

- **Blockbuster** · 235 Massachusetts Ave
- **Hollywood Video** · 899 Boylston St

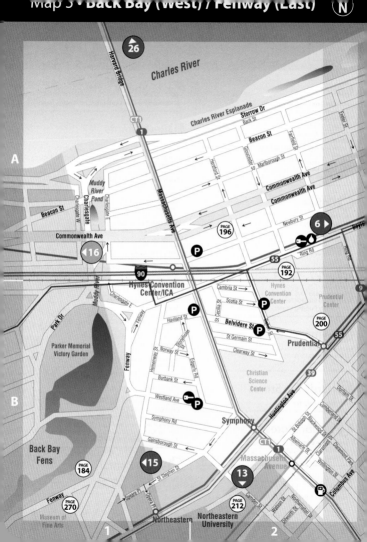

Traffic is always nasty on Mass Ave during the week. On weekends it becomes a parking lot, so avoid driving around here on Saturdays and Sundays if at all possible. (At least this area isn't perpetually under construction.) And remember: there's no left turn from Boylston Street onto Mass Ave. Few spots in Boston make it so easy for traffic cops to fill their quotas.

Subway

- ■ · **Hynes Convention Center/ICA**
- ■ · **Massachusetts Avenue**
- ■ · **Prudential (E)**
- ■ · **Symphony (E)**

Bus Lines

- ⓒⓉⓘ · Central Square, Cambridge—BU Medical Center/BU Medical Campus
- ❶ · Harvard/Holyoke Gate—Dudley Station via Mass. Ave. & BU Medical Center
- ❾ · City Point—Copley Square via Brodway Station
- ㉠⓪ · Forest Hills Station—Back Bay Station via Huntington Ave
- ㊺ · Jersey & Queensberry—Copley Sq or Park & Tremont Streets

⊝ Car Rental

- · **Avis** · 41 Westland Ave
- · **Enterprise** · 800 Boylston St

◌ Car Washes

- · **Bradford Auto "Park & Wax"** · 800 Boylston St

⊕ Gas Stations

- · **Sunoco** · 584 Columbus Ave

ⓟ Parking

Map 6 • **Back Bay (East) / South End (Upper)**

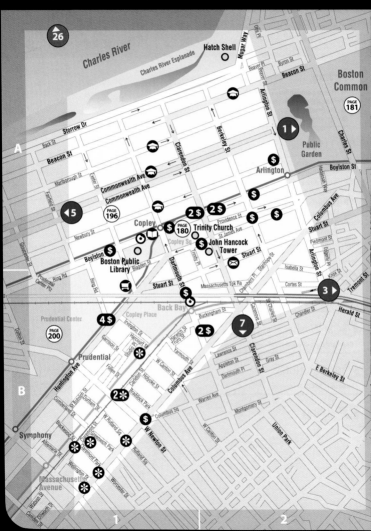

This area features the 'top' of Newbury Street, whose mix of locals, tourists, and international students and slackers have helped local businesses weather the recession. Also here are the boulevards inspired by 19th-century Paris, Trinity Church, the Hancock Tower, and some of Boston's larger hotels. Diverse architecture in an attractive setting makes Copley Square a popular brown-bag lunch spot.

Banks

- **Citizens** · 426 Boylston St
- **Citizens** · 535 Boylston St
- **Citizens** · 607 Boylston St
- **Fleet** · 101 Huntington Ave
- **Fleet** · 110 Huntington Ave
- **Fleet** · 130 Dartmouth St
- **Fleet** · 145 Dartmouth St
- **Fleet** · 210 Berkeley St
- **Fleet** · 31 St James Ave
- **Fleet** · 465 Columbus Ave
- **Fleet** · 557 Boylston St
- **Fleet** · 6 Newbury St
- **Fleet** · 699 Boylston St
- **Fleet** · 745 Boylston St
- **Sovereign Bank** · 100 Huntington Ave
- **Sovereign Bank** · 111 Huntington Ave
- **Sovereign Bank** · 200 Clarendon St
- **Sovereign Bank** · 575 Boylston St
- **Wainwright Bank & Trust** · 155 Dartmouth St

Donuts

- **Dunkin' Donuts** · 145 Dartmouth St
- **Dunkin' Donuts** · 715 Boylston St

O Landmarks

- **Boston Public Library** · 700 Boylston St
- **Hatch Shell** · Esplanade
- **John Hancock Tower** · 200 Clarendon St
- **Trinity Church** · 206 Clarendon St

Libraries

- **Boston Public Library** · 700 Boylston St

Post Offices

- 390 Stuart St

Schools

- **Commonwealth School** ·
  151 Commonwealth Ave
- **Fisher College** · 118 Beacon St
- **Learning Project Elementary School** ·
  107 Marlborough St
- **Snowden International High School** ·
  150 Newbury St

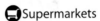 Supermarkets

- **Shaw's** · 53 Huntington Ave

Community Gardens

- **Blackwood/Claremont Garden** ·
  Southwest Corridor at Claremont St
- **Braddock Park Garden** ·
  Southwest Corridor at Braddock Park
- **Follen Street Garden** ·
  Southwest Corridor at Follen St
- **Greenwich/Cumberland Garden** ·
  Southwest Corridor at Greenwich Pk
- **Harcourt/West Canton Garden** ·
  Southwest Corridor at W Canton St
- **Titus Sparrow Park Gardens** ·
  W Rutland Sq at Columbus Ave
- **Wellington Green** · Wellington St & Columbus Ave
- **Worcester Street Community Garden** ·
  Worcester St at Columbus Ave

Map 6

Newbury Street has plenty to offer if you're willing to help subsidize shopkeepers' high rents. The shops at the Prudential and Copley Place are particularly convenient to public transportation. In bad weather, remember that the Pru has Boston's largest branch of Barnes & Noble and that Copley Place's cinema focuses on the "smaller" movies. Shaw's Supermarket is a welcome addition to this area (good riddance to the old Star Chamber).

Bars

- **Anchovies** · 433 Columbus Ave
- **Clery's** · 113 Dartmouth St
- **Saint** · 90 Exeter St
- **The Rattlesnake** · 384 Boylston St
- **Vox Populi** · 755 Boylston St

Coffee

- **Coffee and More** · 261 Dartmouth St
- **Starbucks** · 10 Huntington Ave
- **Starbucks** · 165 Newbury St
- **Starbucks** · 441 Stuart St
- **Starbucks** · 443 Boylston St
- **Starbucks** · 755 Boylston St
- **Torrefazione Italia** · 85 Newbury St

Copy Shops

- **Copy Cop** · 601 Boylston St
- **Kinko's** · 187 Dartmouth St
- **Printing Plus** · 31 St James Ave
- **Pro Print** · 410 Boylston St

Farmer's Markets

- **Copley Square** · Copley Sq at St James Ave

Gyms

- **Boston Sports Club** · 561 Boylston St
- **Fitcorp** · 800 Boylston St
- **HealthWorks Fitness Center** · 441 Stuart St
- **Metropolitan Fitness** · 209 Columbus Ave

Hardware Stores

- **Parks Paint & Hardware** · 233 Newbury St

Liquor Stores

- **Best Cellars** · 745 Boylston St
- **Boston Wine Cellars** · 474 Columbus Ave
- **Clarendon Wine** · 563 Boylston St

Movie Theaters

- **Loews Cineplex Copley Place** · 100 Huntington Ave

Pet Shops

- **Petcentric Spa** · 248B W Newton St

Restaurants

- **33** · 33 Stanhope St
- **Abe & Louie's** · 793 Boylston St
- **Bangkok Blue** · 651 Boylston St
- **Bomboa** · 35 Stanhope St
- **Brasserie Jo** · 120 Huntington Ave
- **Charlie's Sandwich Shoppe** · 429 Columbus Ave
- **Claremont Cafe** · 535 Columbus Ave
- **Fire & Ice** · 31 St James Ave
- **Geoffrey's Cafe Bar** · 160 Commonwealth Ave
- **George, An American Tavern** · 384 Columbus Ave
- **Grill 23 & Bar** · 161 Berkeley St
- **Grillfish** · 162 Columbus Ave
- **House of Siam** · 542 Columbus Ave
- **Jae's** · 520 Columbus Ave
- **Legal Sea Foods** · 800 Boylston St
- **Mistral** · 223 Columbus Ave
- **Osushi** · 10 Huntington Ave
- **Pho Pasteur** · 119 Newbury St
- **Rouge** · 480 Columbus Ave

Shopping

- **Anthropologie** · 799 Boylston St
- **Brooks Brothers** · 46 Newbury St
- **Chocolate Truffle** · 31 St James Ave
- **City Sports** · 480 Boylston St
- **Crate & Barrel** · 777 Boylston St
- **E6 Apothecary** · 167 Newbury St
- **Hempest** · 207 Newbury St
- **International Poster Gallery** · 205 Newbury St
- **Kitchen Arts** · 161 Newbury St
- **Lindt Master Chocolatier** · 704 Boylston St
- **Lord & Taylor** · 760 Boylston St
- **Louis Boston** · 234 Berkeley St
- **Marshall's** · 500 Boylston St
- **Neiman Marcus** · 5 Copley Pl
- **Saks Fifth Avenue** · 800 Boylston St
- **Tannery** · 400 Boylston St
- **Teuscher Chocolates of Switzerland** · 230 Newbury St
- **Tweeter Etc** · 350 Boylston St
- **Winston Flowers** · 131 Newbury St

Video Rental

- **City Video** · 240 Newbury St
- **Videosmith** · 275 Dartmouth St
- **Videosmith** · 465 Columbus Ave

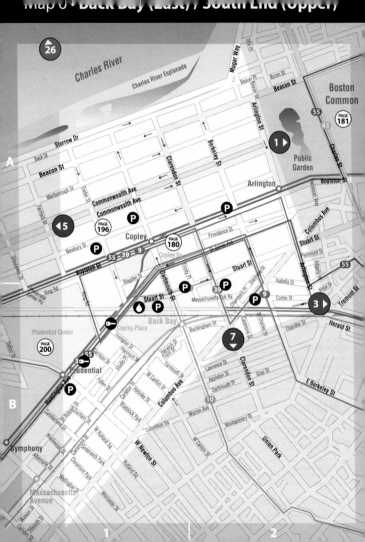

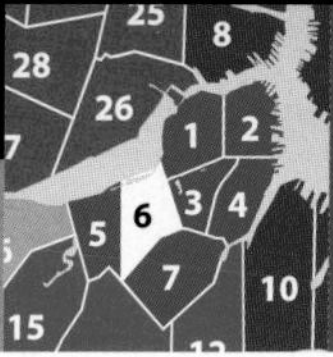

In Boston, jaywalking is a time-honored pastime. Perhaps nowhere is this more true than in this area. So, both drivers and pedestrians should be careful, especially around the Pru. Back Bay is generally well served by public transportation, even though (somewhat unusually) no buses actually run down Comm Ave. Street parking? Good luck.

Subway

- **Arlington**
- **Copley**
- **Back Bay**

Bus Lines

- 9 • City Point—Copley Square via Brodway Station
- 10 • City Point—Copley Squre via Andrew Station & BU Medical Area
- 39 • Forest Hills Station—Back Bay Station via Huntington Ave
- 43 • Ruggles Station—Park & Tremont Streets
- 55 • Jersey & Queensberry—Copley Sq or Park & Tremont Streets

Car Rental

• **Dollar** • 110 Huntington Ave
• **Hertz** • 120 Huntington Ave

Car Washes

• **Dr Detail Car Cleaning** • 100 Huntington Ave

Parking

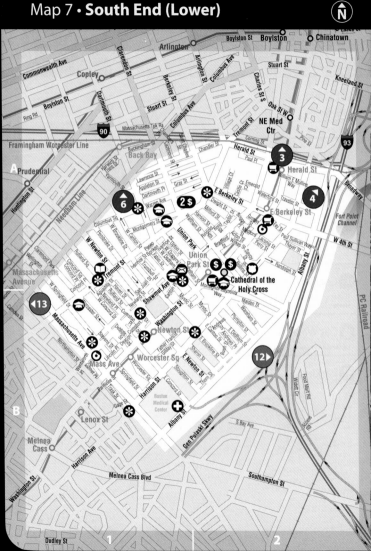

Map 7 • **South End (Lower)**

The South End is America's largest Victorian neighborhood, has the city's largest gay population, and is perhaps the most ethnically and economically diverse area in Boston. The South End continues to see new residential and commercial development. With gentrification comes new names for neighborhoods, so of course the area south of Washington Street has been dubbed "SoWa" (goofy, but less risible than renaming Downtown Crossing "the Ladder District").

Banks

- **Citizens** · 1355 Washington St
- **Fleet** · 539 Tremont St
- **Fleet** · 557 Tremont St
- **Mercantile Bank** · 1320 Washington St

Donuts

- **Dunkin' Donuts** · 1138 Washington St
- **Dunkin' Donuts** · 616 Massachusetts Ave

Hospitals

- **Boston University Medical Center** · 715 Albany St

Landmarks

- **Cathedral of the Holy Cross** · 1400 Washington St

Libraries

- **South End** · 685 Tremont St

Police

- **District D-4** · 650 Harrison Ave

Post Offices

- 59 W Dedham St

Schools

- **Cathedral Elementary School** · 595 Harrison Ave
- **Cathedral High School** · 74 Union Park St
- **Joseph J Hurley Elementary School** · 70 Worcester St
- **William Blackstone Elementary School** · 380 Shawmut Ave
- **William McKinley School** · 90 Warren Ave

 Supermarkets

- **Foodie's Urban Market** · 1421 Washington St
- **Ming's Supermarket** · 1102 Washington St
- **Super 88** · 50 Herald St

Community Gardens

- **Berkeley Street Community Garden** · Berkeley St & Tremont St
- **Dartmouth Park** · Dartmouth St at Warren Ave
- **Harrison Urban Garden** · Harrison Ave at E Brookline St
- **Northampton Community Garden** · Northampton St at Harrison Ave
- **Rutland Green** · 74 Rutland St
- **Rutland's Haven** · 21 Rutland St
- **Rutland/Washington Streets Garden** · Washington St & Rutland St
- **Unity Towers** · W Dedham St & Shawmut Ave
- **Warren/Clarendon Garden** · Warren Ave at Clarendon St
- **West Springfield Community Garden** · 106 W Springfield St

Map 7 • **South End (Lower)**

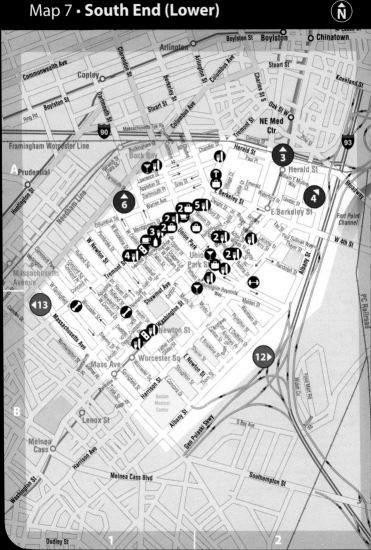

Map 7

The South End may not have many dive bars or "Irish" pubs, but it definitely has serious food. Four relative newcomers in close proximity along Tremont Street are worth examining: B&G Oysters, The Butcher Shop, Nightingale, and Perdix. Along Washington Street, Mike's City Diner serves up a great breakfast with prices that haven't yet been Tremontized. And if you've never had Ethiopian food before, try the Addis Red Sea.

Bars

- **Delux Cafe** · 100 Chandler St
- **Donovan's Tavern** · 1505 Washington St
- **Waltham Tavern** · 298 Shawmut Ave

Coffee

- **Francesca's** · 564 Tremont St
- **Starbucks** · 627 Tremont St

Gyms

- **Mike's Gym** · 560 Harrison Ave

Hardware Stores

- **Warren Hardware** · 470 Tremont St

Liquor Stores

- **Wine Emporium** · 607 Tremont St

Pet Shops

- **Paws** · 169 W Springfield St
- **The Pet Shop Girls** · 472 Shawmut Ave

Restaurants

- **Addis Red Sea** · 544 Tremont St
- **Aquitaine** · 569 Tremont St
- **B&G Oysters** · 550 Tremont St
- **Caffe Umbra** · 1395 Washington St
- **Delux Cafe** · 100 Chandler St
- **Dish** · 253 Shawmut Ave
- **Emilio's** · 536 Tremont St
- **flour bakery & cafe** · 1595 Washington St
- **Franklin Cafe** · 278 Shawmut Ave
- **Garden of Eden** · 571 Tremont St
- **Hamersley's Bistro** · 553 Tremont St
- **Masa** · 439 Tremont St
- **Metropolis Cafe** · 584 Tremont St
- **Mike's City Diner** · 1714 Washington St
- **Morse Fish** · 1401 Washington St
- **Nicole's** · 639 Tremont St
- **Nightingale** · 578 Tremont St
- **Joe V's** · 1 Union Park
- **Perdix** · 560 Tremont St
- **Pho Republique** · 1415 Washington St
- **Red Fez** · 1222 Washington St
- **Sister Sorel** · 645 Tremont St
- **Thai Village** · 592 Tremont St
- **Tremont 647** · 647 Tremont St
- **Union Bar and Grille** · 1357 Washington St

Shopping

- **Aunt Sadie's** · 18 Union Park St
- **Community Bicycle Supply** · 496 Tremont St
- **Earthbound** · 607A Tremont St
- **Lionette's** · 577 Tremont St
- **Posh** · 557 Tremont St
- **The Butcher Shop** · 552 Tremont St
- **Tommy Tish** · 102 Waltham St

Video Rental

- **Mike's Movies** · 630 Tremont St
- **South End Video** · 1636 Washington St

Map 7

Street parking north of Washington Street is a disaster, a situation compounded by the paucity of parking lots and garages. Visitors to the South End should strongly consider using the Silver Line (particularly to go to any spot on or near Washington Street). You think that parking is bad now? Just wait until The Atelier (on Tremont Street at Berkeley Street) opens...

Subway

- ■ ■ • **NE Med Center**
- ■ ■ • **Herald St**
- ■ • **E Berkeley St**
- ■ • **Union Park St**
- ■ • **Newton St**
- ■ • **Worcester Sq**
- ■ • **Mass Ave**
- ■ • **Lenox St**
- ■ • **Melnea Cass Blvd**

Bus Lines

- **CT1** • Central Square, Cambridge—BU Medical Center/BU Medical Campus
- **CT3** • Beth Israel Deaconess Medical Center—Andrew Station via BU Medical Center
- **1** • Harvard/Holyoke Gate—Dudley Station via Mass Ave & BU Medical Center
- **8** • Harbor Point/Umass—Kenmore Station via South End Medical Area
- **9** • City Point—Copley Square via Brodway Station
- **10** • City Point—Copley Squre via Andrew Station & BU Medical Area
- **43** • Ruggles Station—Park & Tremont Streets
- **47** • Central Sq, Cambridge—Broadway Station via South End Medical Area

P Parking

For many Bostonians, Charlestown means little more than the Navy Yard and the Bunker Hill Monument, a perspective that many residents of Charlestown just might share. This area is dominated by low-slung homes, industrial buildings along the Mystic River, and plenty more hills than just Bunker Hill. Charlestown's best asset may be the views of downtown Boston across the water.

$ Banks

- **Citizens** · 5 Austin St
- **Co-Operative Bank** · 201 Main St

Donuts

- **Dunkin' Donuts** · 11 Austin St

O Landmarks

- **Bunker Hill Monument** · Monument Sq
- **Charlestown Navy Yard** ·
  Constitution Rd & Warren St
- **Tobin Memorial Bridge** · Route 1
- **Warren Tavern** · 2 Pleasant St

Libraries

- **Charlestown** · 179 Main St

Schools

- **Bunker Hill Community College** ·
  250 New Rutherford Ave
- **Charlestown High School** · 240 Medford St
- **Clarence R Edwards Middle School** · 28 Walker St
- **Harvard-Kent Elementary School** ·
  50 Bunker Hill St

Community Gardens

- **Charlestown Sprouts** · Medford St at Terminal St
- **Pier 6 Garden** · 1st Ave & 8th St

Map 8 · **Charlestown**

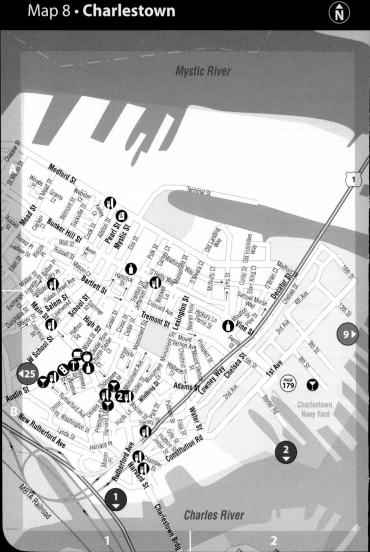

Charlestown doesn't offer much for fine food and drink, but its standouts compete well with their rivals across the harbor. Olives has finally started to take reservations for smaller groups, and Meze Estiatorio is helping affirm that "fine Greek food" isn't always an oxymoron. For a change of pace, try the North African cuisine at Tangierino.

Bars

- **Ninety Nine** · 29 Austin St
- **Sullivan's Pub** · 85 Main St
- **Tavern on the Water** · 1 Pier 6 at E 8th St
- **Warren Tavern** · 2 Pleasant St

Coffee

- **The Coffee Shop** · 1 Thompson Sq

Copy Shops

- **Printing Plus** · 151 Pearl St

Farmer's Markets

- **Charlestown** · Main St & Austin St

Hardware Stores

- **Aubuchon Hardware** · 5 Austin St

Liquor Stores

- **Bunker Hill Liquors** · 200 Bunker Hill St
- **Charlestown Liquors** · 10 Thompson Sq
- **McCarthy Brothers Liquors** · 9 Moulton St

Restaurants

- **Brothers** · 156 Bunker Hill St
- **Figs** · 67 Main St
- **Ironside Grill** · 25 Park St
- **Jenny's Pizza** · 320 Medford St
- **Meze Estiatorio** · 100 City Sq
- **Ninety Nine** · 29 Austin St
- **Olives** · 10 City Sq
- **Paolo's Trattoria** · 251 Main St
- **Souper Salad** · 126 High St
- **Tangierino** · 83 Main St
- **Warren Tavern** · 2 Pleasant St

Video Rental

- **Blockbuster** · 5 Austin St

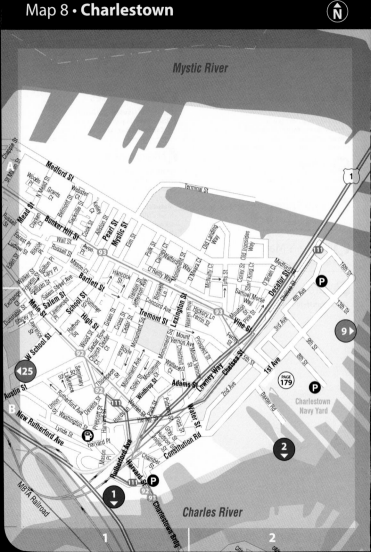

Map 8 · **Charlestown**

N

Mystic River

A

Medford St

Woods
Pl
Mead Grants
Ct

Webster St
Belmont St
Sackville St
Kelley Ct
Alston St
Pearl St
Mystic St
Elm St

Chappie St
St Main St

Russell
St

Mead St
Claden St
Bunker Hill St
Wall St
Russell St
Avon St
Look St
Cook St

Forrest St
Bigoe St
Eden St
Ludlow St
Walker St
Exchange Ct
Franklin St
Bolton St
Sullivan St
Cary Pl
Mason St

Terminal St

Polk St
Carney Ct
Walford St
O'Reilly Way
Monument St
Old Landing Way

Corey St
Starr King Ct
O'Meara Ct
McNulty Ct
Tufts St

Old Ironsides Way

Medford St
O'Brien Ct
Decatur St

16th St

13th St

Hancock St
Bartlett St
Salem Street Ave
School St
Lawnwood St
High St
Hatfen St
Salem St
Sommer St
Trenton St
Jefferson Ave
Boswell Ct
Hickory Ln
Concord St
Warren Row
Ferrin St
Lexington St

Samuel Morse Way
Moulton St

4th Ave

9th St

8th St

Main St
Lawrence St
Stacey St
Dunstable St

Tremont St

Wood St
Cleaver Row
Cedar St
Soley St
Monument Ct
Green St
Cross St
Bogle St
Thompson St
Church Ct
Mount Vernon Ave
Monument Sq
Mount Vernon St
Prospect St
Chestnut St

Vine St
Farm St
Pine St

3rd Ave

1st Ave

W School St
Seminary St
Lawrence St
Rutherford Ave Devens St
Prescott St
Harvard St
Winthrop St
Monument St
Adams St
Lowney Way
Chelsea St

PAGE
179

Charlestown
Navy Yard

Austin St
Union St
Washington St
Lynde St
Warren St
Putnam St
Harley St
Hurd St
Water St
Foss St
Gray St
Sullivan Pl
2nd Ave

Baxter Rd

B
New Rutherford Ave

Harvard Pl

Harvard Ave
Mason St
Hudson St
Porter St
Chamber St
Constitution Rd

MBTA Railroad

Charles River

1

2

Map 8

Charlestown is underserved by public transportation. The Orange Line stops that serve Charlestown are at Sullivan Square and Bunker Hill Community College, neither of which is near the Navy Yard or City Square. From downtown Boston to these points, consider using the 92 bus or the 93 bus. Or, if it's warm, consider taking the City Water Taxi from Long Wharf.

Bus Lines

- **92** • Assembly Sq Mall—Downtown via Sullivan Sq Station, Main St
- **93** • Sullivan Sq Station—Downtown via Bunker Hill St & Haymarket Station
- **111** • Woodlawn or Broadway & Park Ave— Haymarket Station via Mystic River/Tobin Bridge

Gas Stations

• **Shell** • 1 Rutherford Ave

Ⓟ Parking

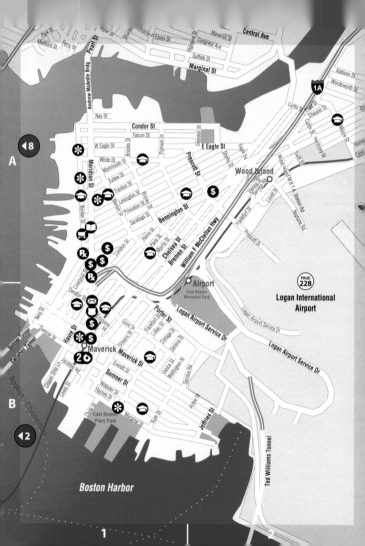

The portion of East Boston nearest to the airport is defined largely by Central Square (close to the tunnels, thereby attracting the larger stores), Maverick Square (a curious rectangle catering to East Boston's large Latino community), and unattractive Day Square. The general feel is one of a small, blue-collar North Shore town, fitting for what was once the international headquarters of the clipper ship industry.

Banks

- **Citizens** · 26 Central Sq
- **East Boston Savings Bank** · 1 Bennington St
- **East Boston Savings Bank** · 10 Meridian St
- **East Boston Savings Bank** · 294 Bennington St
- **Fleet** · 3-11 Porter St
- **Fleet** · 47 Maverick Sq

Donuts

- **Dunkin' Donuts** · 13-15 Maverick Sq
- **Honey Dew Donuts** · 14 Maverick Sq

Libraries

- **East Boston** · 276 Meridian St

Pharmacies

- **CVS** · 210 Border St
- **Walgreens** · 1 Central Sq

Police

- **District A-7** · 69 Paris St

Post Offices

- 50 Meridian St

Schools

- **Dante Alighieri Elementary School** · 37 Grove St
- **Donald McKay Elementary/Middle School** · 122 Cottage St
- **East Boston Central Catholic School** · 69 London St
- **East Boston High School** · 86 White St
- **Hugh Roe O'Donnell Elementary School** · 33 Trenton St
- **James Otis Elementary School** · 218 Marion St
- **Patrick J Kennedy Elementary School** · 343 Saratoga St
- **Samuel Adams Elementary School** · 165 Webster St
- **St Mary Star of the Sea Elementary School** · 58 Moore St
- **Umana/Barnes Middle Scool** · 312 Border St

Supermarkets

- **Shaw's** · 246 Border St

Community Gardens

- **Eagle Hill Memorial Community Garden** · 343 Border St
- **Joseph Ciampa Garden** · Marginal St & Cottage St
- **O'Donnell Elementary School Garden** · 33 Trenton St
- **Shore Plaza East Garden** · 520 Border St
- **Winthrop Street Garden** · 25 Winthrop St

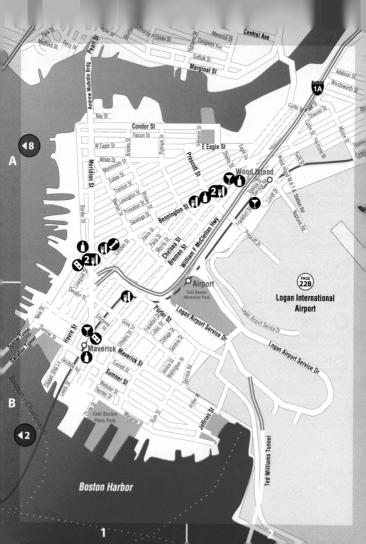

East Boston isn't on the top of many "where to dine" lists. Uncle Pete's has good barbecue, and Santarpio's Pizza has its fans—draw your own conclusions. Plenty of storefronts sell pupusas and other Central American favorites. If a pleasant place to have a drink is what you're looking for, get back on the Blue Line.

Bars

· **Lobby Bar** · 267 Frankfort St
· **Pony Lounge** · 411 Chelsea St
· **Trainor's Cafe** · 129 Maverick St

Liquor Stores

· **Castillo Liquors** · 228 Meridian St
· **Clipper Ship Wine & Spirits** · 17 Maverick Sq
· **Day Square Liquor** · 288 Bennington St
· **Neptune Liquors** · 1 Neptune Rd

Pet Shops

· **Golden Fins Imports** · 55 Bennington St

Restaurants

· **Cafe Belo** · 254 Bennington St
· **Cafe Italia** · 150 Meridian St
· **La Terraza** · 19 Bennington St
· **Nana Cora's** · 295 Bennington St
· **Santarpio's Pizza** · 111 Cheslea St
· **Topacio** · 120 Meridian St
· **Uncle Pete's Hickory Ribs** · 309 Bennington St

Video Rental

· **Blockbuster** · 184 Border St
· **Maverick Audio & Video** · 25 Maverick Sq

The obvious route into East Boston from almost anywhere in Boston is the Callahan Tunnel. Be sure to stay in the right lane and take the first exit out of the tunnel, which dumps you onto Porter Street in front of Santarpio's. Bang a right on Chelsea Street to get to Maverick Square, or double back (legally, please) to get to Central Square.

Subway
- ■ · **Maverick**
- ■ · **Airport**
- ■ · **Wood Island**

Bus Lines
- **112** · Wellington Station—Wood Island Station via Central Ave, Mystic Mall & Admiral's Hill
- **116** · Wonderland Station—Maverick Station via Revere St
- **117** · Wonderland Station—Maverick Station via Revere St
- **120** · Orient Heights Station—Maverick Station via Bennington St
- **121** · Wood Island Station—Maverick Station via Lexington

🚗 Car Rental
- **Airways Rent A Car** · 161 Orleans St
- **National** · 6 Tomahawk Dr

💧 Car Washes
- **Squikee Clean** · 452 Bremen St

⛽ Gas Stations
- **Getty** · 331 Bennington St
- **Mobil** · 470 Meridian St
- **Shell** · 52 Meridian St

🅿 Parking

With the exception of the area immediately around the Artery, this area will probably see more change in the next five years than any other in Boston. Fort Point, which already hosts the largest artist community in New England, will continue to develop. The quarter-mile-long Boston Convention and Exhibition Center, now scheduled to open to exhibitors in 2005, should spur additional development along the waterfront.

$ Banks

- **Citizens** · 441 W Broadway
- **Eastern Bank** · 470 W Broadway
- **Fleet** · 332 Congress St
- **Fleet** · 460 W Broadway
- **Mt Washington Bank** · 430 W Broadway

Donuts

- **Dunkin' Donuts** · 268 Summer St
- **Dunkin' Donuts** · 330 Congress St
- **Dunkin' Donuts** · 482 W Broadway
- **Dunkin' Donuts** · 75 Old Colony Ave

Landmarks

- **Boston Tea Party Ship & Museum** · Congress St Bridge
- **Children's Museum** · 300 Congress St

Libraries

- **Washington Village** · 1226 Columbia Rd

Police

- **District C-6** · 101 W Broadway

Post Offices

- 444 E 3rd St

Schools

- **James Condon Elementary School** · 200 D St
- **Michael J Perkins Elementary School** · 50 Burke St
- **Patrick F Gavin Middle School** · 215 Dorchester St
- **South Boston High School** · 95 G St
- **St Augustine's School** · 209 E St

Community Gardens

- **Foster's Nook Community Garden** · Athens St at F St

Map 10 · **South Boston (West) / Fort Point** Ⓝ

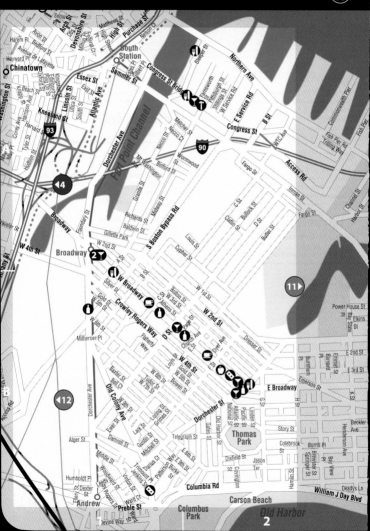

Map 1

Martini-and-music mavens should check out Lucky's, which is fun even for those not aspiring to post-modern hipsterdom. Most dining spots along the waterfront rely on old glory, not fabulous food, to bring in customers. As Fort Point develops, expect intrepid restaurateurs to arrive.

Bars

- **Baggot Inn** · 110 Dorchester St
- **Blackthorn Pub** · 471 W Broadway
- **Lucky's** · 355 Congress St
- **Shenanigans** · 332 W Broadway
- **The Cornerstone** · 16 W Broadway
- **The Quiet Man** · 11 W Broadway

Coffee

- **Jake's Coffee Shop** · 402 W Broadway
- **Revefort Coffee House** · 218 W Broadway

Farmer's Markets

- **South Boston** · 444 W Broadway

Hardware Stores

- **Josephs Brothers Hardware** · 369 Congress St

Liquor Stores

- **Al's Liquors** · 226 W Broadway
- **Donoghue's Liquors** · 341 W Broadway
- **New Bay View Liquors** · 108 Dorchester St
- **Old Colony Wine** · 259 Dorchester Ave

Restaurants

- **Amrheins** · 80 W Broadway
- **Barking Crab** · 88 Sleeper St
- **Lucky's** · 355 Congress St
- **Salsa's Mexican Grill** · 118 Dorchester St

Video Rental

- **Blockbuster** · 267 Old Colony Ave
- **Knapp Video** · 470 W Broadway

The opening of the Ted Williams Tunnel—the big transportation news in this area—slashes the time it takes to get to Logan Airport for anyone coming from points south or west. To get to Fort Point by bus, take the 4 bus from North Station or the 7 bus from South Station. The Silver Line will connect the new convention center with downtown Boston and the airport.

Subway

- ■ · **South Station**
- ■ · **Broadway**
- ■ · **Andrew**

Bus Lines

- CT3 · Beth Israel Deaconess Medical Center—Andrew Station via BU Medical Center
- **3** · Boston Marine Ind. Park—South Station/Haymarket Station
- **4** · North Station—World Trade Center via Federal Courthouse
- **5** · City Point—McCormack Housing via Andrew Station
- **6** · Boston Marine Ind. Park—South Station/Haymarket Station
- **9** · City Point—Copley Square via Broadway Station
- **10** · City Point—Copley Squre via Andrew Station & BU Medical Area
- **11** · City Point—Downtown Bayview Route
- **47** · Central Sq, Cambridge—Broadway Station via South End Medical Area

Car Rental

· **Hertz** · 164 Northern Ave

Car Washes

· **Super Shine Auto Wash** · 39 Old Colony Ave

Gas Stations

· **Exxon** · 79 W Broadway
· **Shell** · 302 W Broadway

Parking

Map 11 · **South Boston (East)**

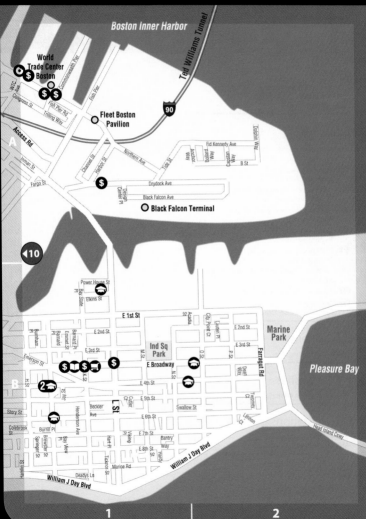

Boston Inner Harbor

World
Trade Center
Boston

WTC Ave
Congress St
Trilling Way
Commonwealth Pier
Fish Pier
Fid Kennedy Ave

Ted Williams Tunnel

90

Access Rd

Inman St

Fargo St

Channel St

Harbor St

Northern Ave

Tide St

A

Dolphin Way

Boating Way

Anchor Way

Capstan Way

B St

Drydock Ave

Design Center Pl

Black Falcon Ave

Black Falcon Terminal

Fleet Boston
Pavilion

◄10

Power House St

Bay State Pl

Elkins St

E 1st St

Acadia St

E 2nd St

Cdg Point Ct

Camden St

Burnham Pl

Barnard Pl

Emmet St

Barnard St

E 2nd St

E 3rd St

M St

N St

Ind Sq
Park

E Broadway

O St

E 3rd St

P St

Marine
Park

Farragut Rd

Emerson St

K St

H St

L St

2

E 4th St

Cutler
Ct

E 5th St

Swallow St

Dean
Way

Twomey
Ct

Lennon
Ct

Pleasure Bay

Story St

Colebrook St

N Quincy St

Beckler
Ave

Henderson Ave

Burrill Pl

Brewster St

Springer St

Bay View

E 6th St

Viking
Pl

Hart Pl

E 7th St

Bantry
Way

E 8th St

Trinity

Marine Rd

Teaxton St

Deadys Ln

William J Day Blvd

Head Island Cswy

William J Day Blvd

B

1

2

Predominantly residential South Boston, filled with classic triple-deckers, is still very much the most Irish neighborhood in this most Irish of American cities. The Boston Marine Industrial Park, a city development initiative, is home to Legal Sea Foods' seafood processing center (located on Seafood Way, of course) and the Black Falcon Terminal, one of America's most popular cruise ship ports.

Banks

- **First Trade Union Bank** · 10 Drydock Ave
- **First Trade Union Bank** · 753 E Broadway
- **Fleet** · 636 E Broadway
- **Mt Washington Bank** · 708 E Broadway
- **Sovereign Bank** · 1 Seaport Ln
- **Sovereign Bank** · 2 Seaport Ln
- **Sovereign Bank** · 200 Seaport Blvd

Donuts

- **Dunkin' Donuts** · 200 Seaport Blvd

Landmarks

- **Black Falcon Terminal** · 1 Black Falcon Ave
- **Boston World Trade Center** · 200 Seaport Blvd
- **Fleet Boston Pavilion** · 290 Northern Ave

Libraries

- **South Boston** · 646 E Broadway

Schools

- **Gate of Heaven School** · 609 E 4th St
- **Joseph P Tynan Elementary School** · 650 E 4th St
- **Oliver Hazard Perry Elementary School** · 745 E 7th St
- **South Boston Harbor Academy** · 7 Elkins St
- **St Brigid's School** · 866 E Broadway
- **St Peter's School** · 518 E 6th St

Supermarkets

- **Stop & Shop** · 713 E Broadway

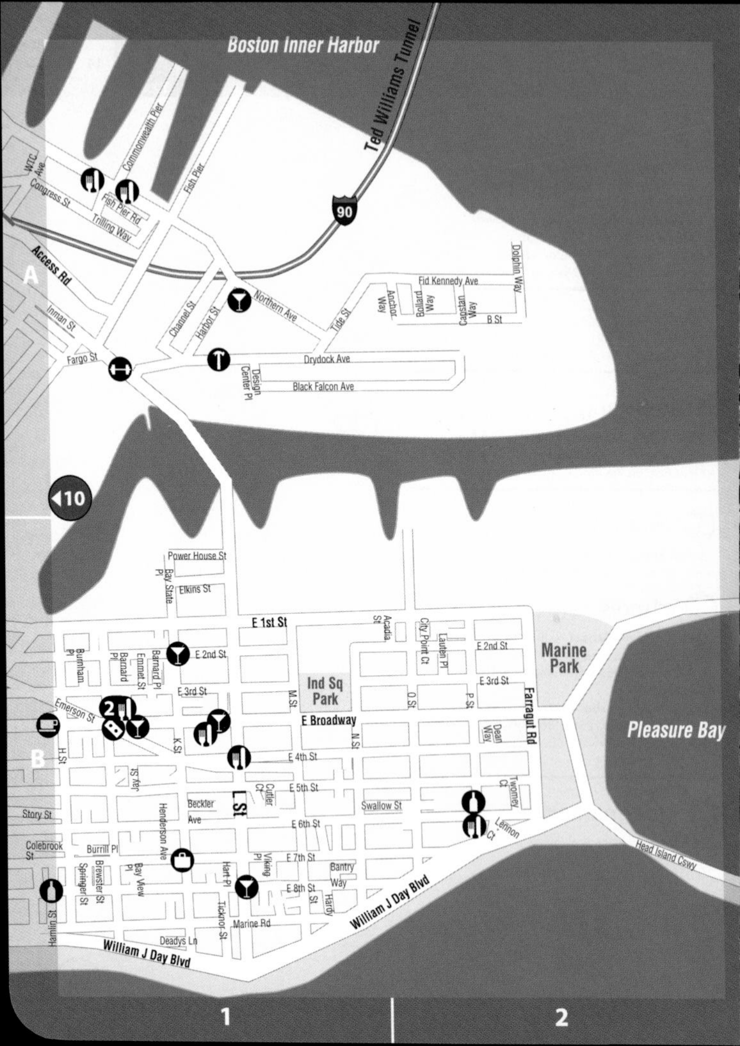

Map 11 · **South Boston (East)**

Boston Inner Harbor

Ted Williams Tunnel

WTC Ave
Congress St
Fish Pier Rd
Trilling Way
Commonwealth Pier
Fish Pier

Access Rd

90

A

Inman St

Fargo St

Channel St
Harbor St
Tide St
Northern Ave

Fid Kennedy Ave
Dolphin Way
Design Center Pl
Drydock Ave
Black Falcon Ave

B St
Barnard Way W
Blackjack Way
Quicksand Way

10

Power House St
Bay State Pl
Elkins St

E 1st St

Burnham Pl
Barnard Pl
Emmet St
Barnard Pl
E 2nd St
Acadia St
City Point Ct
E 2nd St
Laiden Pl
Marine Park

E 3rd St
Ind Sq Park
O St
E 3rd St
Pleasure Bay

N St
Farragut Rd

2 1
K St
E Broadway
Dean Way
P St

Emerson St
H St
E 4th St
Cutter St

Story St
Beckler Ave
E 5th St
Swallow St
L St
Twohey Ct
Lennon Ct

Colebrook St
Spanger St
Hatch St
Burrill Pl
Henderson Ave
Bay View
Brewster St
E 6th St
E 7th St
Viking Pl
Bantry Way

Deadys Ln
Tudor St
Marine Rd
E 8th St
Hardy St
William J Day Blvd

William J Day Blvd

Head Island Cswy

1   **2**

Map 11

As an established residential community, South Boston has a number of places to get a bite or a drink, but little variety—subs and pubs still dominate. If you're not a pub person, you're probably better off elsewhere. North of the channel at the Marine Industrial Park, there's a lot of fresh seafood, but no place to eat it in. Those interested in the noble science of zymurgy brewing should take a free tour at the Harpoon Brewery.

Bars

- **Boston Beer Garden** · 734 E Broadway
- **Corner Tavern** · 645 E 2nd St
- **Harpoon Brewery** · 306 Northern Ave
- **L Street Tavern** · 658 E 8th St
- **Playwright** · 658 E Broadway

Coffee

- **Java House** · 566 E Broadway

Gyms

- **Boston Athletic Club** · 653 Summer St

Hardware Stores

- **Backstage Hardware & Theatre Supply** · 21 Drydock Ave

Liquor Stores

- **Adams Liquors** · 474 E 8th St
- **Jimmy's Korner** · 143 P St

Restaurants

- **Aura** · 1 Seaport Ln
- **Boston Beer Garden** · 734 E Broadway
- **Cafe Porto Bello** · 672 E Broadway
- **Farragut House** · 149 P St
- **No-Name Restaurant** · 15 Fish Pier Rd
- **Playwright** · 658 E Broadway
- **Red's Eastside Grill** · 81 L St

Shopping

- **Miller's Market** · 336 K St

Video Rental

- **Hub Video** · 613 E Broadway

Map 11 · **South Boston (East)**

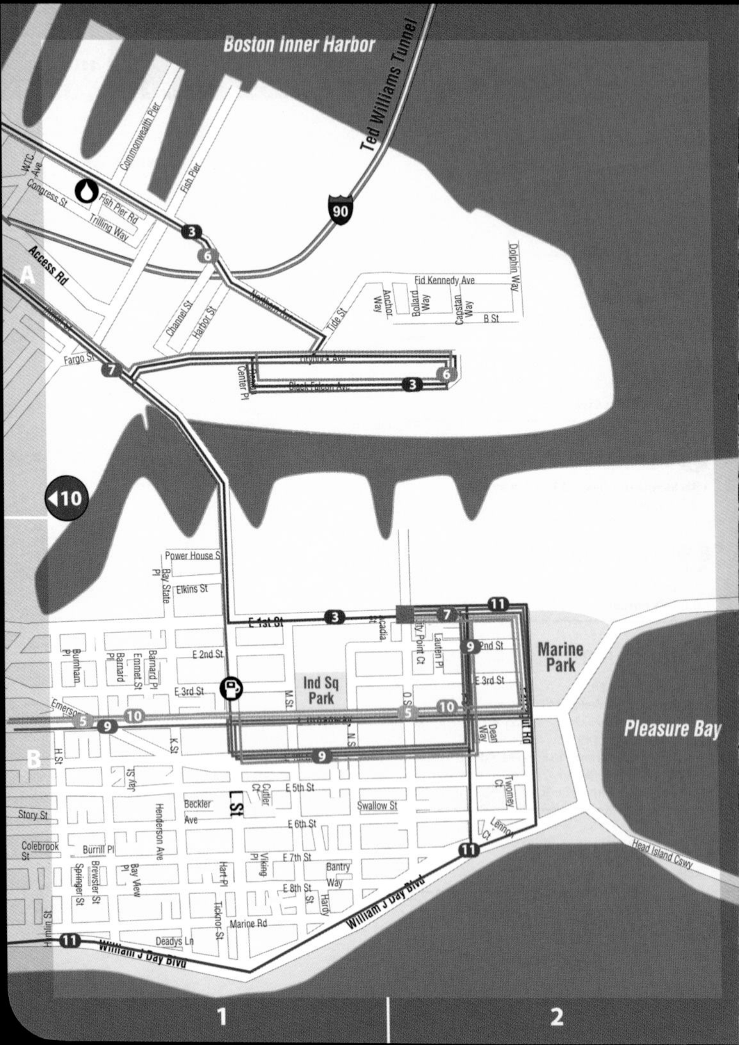

N

Boston Inner Harbor

Ted Williams Tunnel

VFW Pkwy
Congress St
Trilling Way
Fish Pier Rd

Access Rd

A

90

3

6

Fid Kennedy Ave.
Dolphin Way

Bolman Way
Ramp
Captain Way
B St

Channel St
Harbor St
Tide St
Anchor Way

Fargo St

7

6

3

Terminal Ave.

Seal Harbor St

10

Power House St

Bay State Pl
Elkins St

E. 1st St.

3

7

11

Burnham
Barnard Pl
Emmet St.
Barnard Pl

E. 2nd St.

Bay Point Ct

E 2nd St

9

Laurel Pt

Marine
Park

E 3rd St

Ind Sq
Park

M St.

O St.

Emerson St

E. 3rd St.

P

B

5

10

9

5

10

Pleasure Bay

H St.

K St.

N St.

9

Drum Way

Story St

L St.

Beckler Ave

E. 5th St.

Swallow St

Twohig Ct

Colebrook St

Burrill St

Cutter St

E. 6th St.

Levine Ct

Springer St
Brewster St

Bay View

E. 7th St.

Vinling St

Bantry Way

11

Head Island Cswy

Henderson Ave

Hart Pl

E. 8th St.

Hardy St

Tadorn Rd

Marine Rd

11

Deadys Ln

William J Day Blvd

William J Day Blvd

1

2

For the most part, parking in this area is bad, and the concentration of commercial space along Broadway prompts a lot of nettlesome double-parking on weekends. This area is connected to the Red Line by buses running from the Broadway T stop (the 9 bus) and the Andrew T stop (the 10 bus).

Bus Lines

3 · Boston Marine Ind. Park—
South Station/Haymarket Station

5 · City Point—McCormack Housing via
Andrew Station

6 · Boston Marine Ind. Park—
South Station/Haymarket Station

7 · City Point—Otis & Summer Streets via
Northern Ave. & South Station

9 · City Point—Copley Square via
Broadway Station

10 · City Point—Copley Square via
Andrew Station & BU Medical Area

11 · City Point—Downtown Bayview Route

Car Washes

· **Mr Perfection** · 1 Seaport Ln

Gas Stations

· **Exxon** · 607 E 3rd St

71

Map 12 • Newmarket / Andrew Square

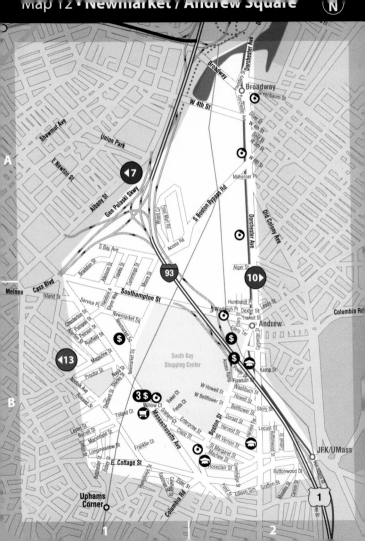

Map 13 12 14

Map

At the cast-off crossroads where Roxbury, Dorchester, and South Boston meet lie Newmarket, Boston's primary fresh produce and food-processing cluster, and South Bay Shopping Center, a bland collection of big box retailers. Nearby are Suffolk County jail and a sizeable number of self-storage facilities. In Andrew Square, only the building above the T stop inspires any confidence.

$ Banks

- **Asian American Bank & Trust Company** · 101 Allstate Rd
- **Citizens** · 60 Newmarket Sq
- **Fleet** · 65 Rear Boston Rd
- **Fleet** · 8 Allstate Rd
- **Mt Washington Bank** · 501 Southampton St
- **Sovereign Bank** · 7 Allstate Rd

Donuts

- **Dandy Donuts & Deli** · 220 Dorchester Ave
- **Dunkin' Donuts** · 22 W Broadway
- **Dunkin' Donuts** · 256 Boston St
- **Dunkin' Donuts** · 510 Southampton St
- **Dunkin' Donuts** · 8B Allstate Rd
- **Watermark Doughnut** · 370 Dorchester Ave

Schools

- **Monsignor Ryan High School** · 11 Mayhew St
- **Roger Clap Elementary School** · 35 Harvest St
- **St Mary's Elementary School** · 52 Boston St

Supermarkets

- **Super 88** · 101 Allstate Rd

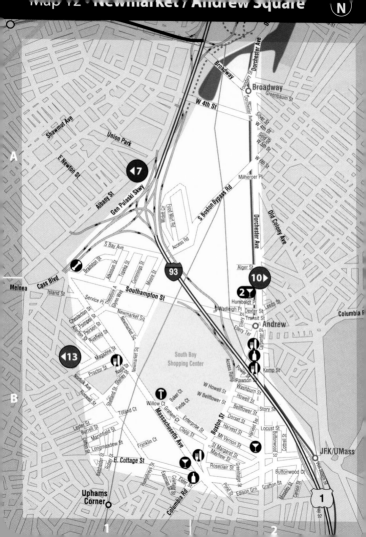

Map 72 • Newmarket / Andrew Square

There simply aren't more than a couple of options in this area. Hopefully, Cafe Polonia will stick around as long as Victoria has. Boston Brisket in Newmarket is a likely supplier of the gray corned beef you might be dining on around St. Patrick's Day. Since the smallest amount they'll sell is a 15-pound slab, however, don't stop by looking for a sandwich…

Bars

- **Aces High** · 551 Dorchester Ave
- **Dot Tavern** · 840 Dorchester Ave
- **Killarney Tavern** · 1295 Massachusetts Ave
- **Sports Connection Bar** · 560 Dorchester Ave

Hardware Stores

- **Home Depot** · 5 Allstate Rd

Liquor Stores

- **Andrew Square Liquors** · 605 Dorchester Ave
- **Cape Verdean Liquors** · 690 Columbia Rd

Pet Shops

- **Skipton Kennel & Pet Center** · 70 Southampton St

Restaurants

- **224 Boston Street** · 224 Boston St
- **Baltic Deli & Cafe** · 632 Dorchester Ave
- **Cafe Polonia** · 611 Dorchester Ave
- **Victoria** · 1024 Massachusetts Ave

Map 1

This largely commercial and industrial area isn't well served by public transportation. If you need to get to South Bay Shopping Center without driving, take the 10 bus from Andrew Square.

Subway

- ■ · **Broadway**
- ■ · **Andrew**
- ■ · **JFK/UMass**

Bus Lines

- **CT3** · Beth Israel Deaconess Medical Center— Andrew Station via BU Medical Center
- **3** · Boston Marine Ind Park— South Station/Haymarket Station
- **5** · City Point—McCormack Housing via Andrew Station
- **8** · Harbor Point/Umass—Kenmore Station via South End Medical Area
- **9** · City Point—Copley Square via Broadway Station
- **10** · City Point—Copley Square via Andrew Station & BU Medical Area
- **11** · City Point—Downtown Bayview Route
- **16** · Forest Hills Station—Andrew Station or UMASS via Columbia Rd
- **17** · Fields Corner Station—Andrew Station via Uphams Corner & Edward Everett Sq
- **18** · Ashmont Station—Andrew Station via Fields Corner Station
- **47** · Central Sq, Cambridge—Broadway Station via South End Medical Area
- **171** · Dudley Station—Logan Airport via Andrew Station

Commuter Rail

· **Uphams Corner**

Car Rental

· **Enterprise** · 230 Dorchester Ave
· **U-Haul** · 985 Massachusetts Ave

Gas Stations

· **Sunoco** · 110 Dorchester Ave
· **Telly's Service Center** · 150 Southampton St

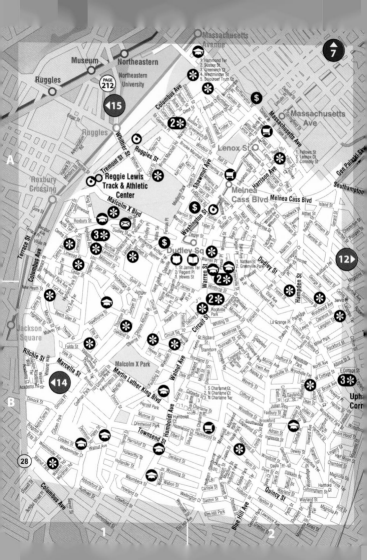

Roxbury has some attractive middle-class pockets and plenty of schools and park space, but much of this area suffers from urban blight. Commercial activity is centered around Dudley Square. Roxbury is experiencing some creep from Northeastern and other schools nearby as students look east for cheaper housing.

Banks

- **Citizens** · 2343 Washington St
- **Fleet** · 114 Dudley St
- **Fleet** · 1762 Washington St

Donuts

- **Dunkin' Donuts** · 1131 Tremont St
- **Dunkin' Donuts** · 1350 Tremont St
- **Dunkin' Donuts** · 2360 Washington St

O Landmarks

- **Reggie Lewis Track & Athletic Center** · 1350 Tremont St

Libraries

- **Dudley** · 65 Warren St

Police

- **District B-2** · 135 Dudley St

Post Offices

- · 55 Roxbury St

Schools

- **Boston Latin Academy** · 205 Townsend St
- **Carter Development Center** · 396 Northampton St
- **David A Ellis Elementary School** · 302 Walnut Ave
- **George Lewis Middle School** · 131 Walnut Ave
- **Henry Dearborn Middle School** · 35 Greenville St
- **Henry L Higginson Elementary School** · 160 Harrishof St
- **James P Timilty Middle School** · 205 Roxbury St
- **John Winthrop Elementary School** · 35 Brookford St
- **Nathan Hale Elementary School** · 51 Cedar St
- **Phillis Wheatley Middle School** · 20 Kearsarge Ave
- **William Monroe Trotter Elementary School** · 135 Humboldt Ave

Supermarkets

- **Foodie's Urban Market** · 333 Martin Luther King Blvd
- **People's Tropical Food** · 1830 Washington St
- **Tropical Foods** · 2101 Washington St

Community Gardens

- **Allan Crite Garden** · 107-125 Cedar St
- **Back to the Roots Garden Club** · John Eliot Square Housing
- **Bartlett and Lambert Streets Garden** · Bartlett St & Lambert Ave
- **Bessie Barnes Memorial Park and Garden** · 25 Warwick St
- **Cabot Street Garden** · Cabot St
- **Centre Place Garden** · 66 Centre St
- **Hawthorne Youth & Community Center Garden** · 6 Fulda St
- **Highland 400 Garden** · 22 Linwood St
- **James E Small, Sr Garden** · 15 Kearsarge Ave
- **Jardin de la Amistad** · 403 Dudley St
- **Lenox-Kendall Community Garden** · Tremont St at Lenox St
- **Leyland St Community Garden and Tot Lot** · 6 Leyland St
- **Leyland Street Garden Extension** · 20 Leyland St
- **Leyland Street Sitting Park** · 3 Leyland St
- **Magazine Street Garden** · 27 Magazine St
- **Margaret Wright Memorial Garden** · 61 Fort Ave
- **Paige Academy Garden** · 42 Highland St
- **Phyllis Wheatley School Garden** · 20 Kearsarge Ave
- **Rosie's Place** · 889 Harrison Ave
- **Saranac/New Castle Garden** · Southwest Corridor at Northampton St
- **Savin-Maywood Garden** · 54 Savin St
- **Sealy Memorial Garden** · 10 Highland St
- **St Joseph's Community Gardens** · Regent St & Hulbert St
- **The Food Project Lot #1** · Langdon St at George St
- **The Food Project Lot #2** · W Cottage St & Brook Ave
- **United Neighbors of Lower Roxbury** · 69 Warwick St
- **Wakullah Street Garden** · 19 Wakullah St
- **Waldren Road Park** · 7 Waldren Rd
- **Warren Gardens** · Warren Ave at Circuit St
- **Warren Place Garden** · 17 Warren Pl

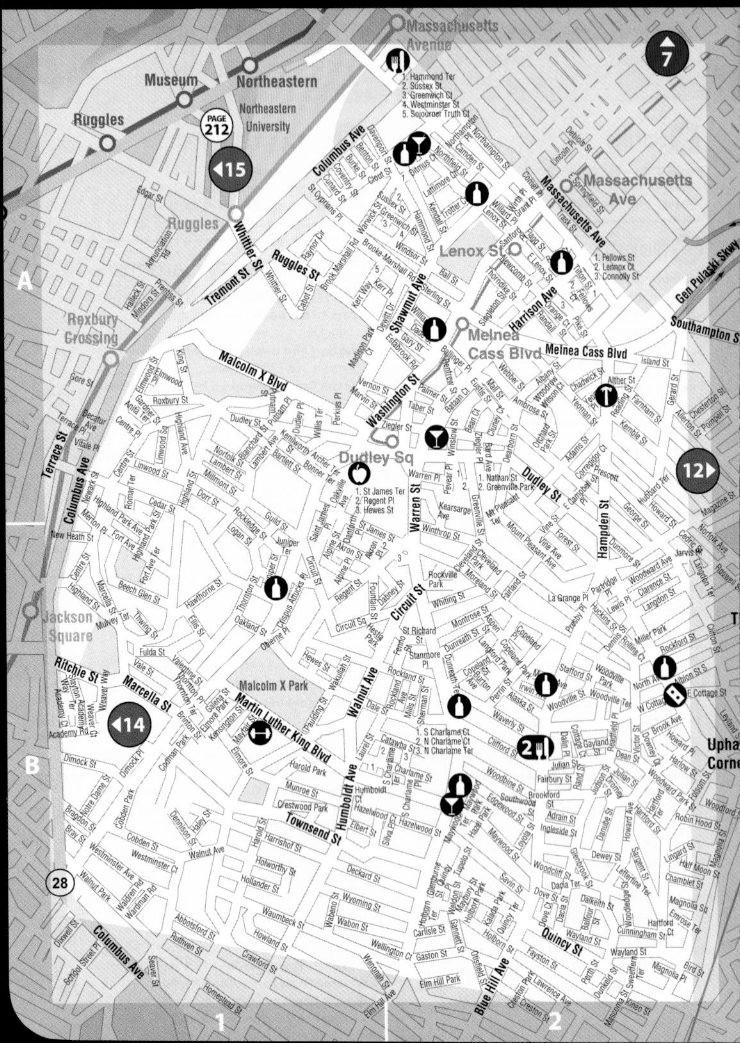

Map 13 • **Roxbury**

N

7

Museum

Northeastern

Ruggles

Northeastern
University

PAGE
212

15

Ruggles

Columbus Ave

1. Hammond Ter
2. Sussex St
3. Greenwich St
4. Westminster St
5. Sojourner Truth Ct

Massachusetts
Avenue

Whittier St

Tremont St

Ruggles
Ruggles St

Massachusetts
Ave

Massachusetts
Ave

Roxbury
Crossing

Lenox St

Shawmut Ave

1. Fellows St
2. Lenox Ct
3. Connolly St

Harrison Ave

Gen Pulaski Skwy

Southampton St

Malcolm X Blvd

Roxbury St

Washington Ave

Melnea
Cass Blvd

Melnea Cass Blvd

Terrace St

Columbus Ave

Dudley Sq

Warren St

Dudley St

1. St James Ter
2. Regent Pl
3. Hewes St

12

Hampden St

1. Nathan St
2. Greenville Park

Jackson
Square

Circuit St

Rockville
Park

Ritchie St

Marcella St

14

Malcolm X Park

Martin Luther King Blvd

Walnut Ave

Humboldt Ave

1. S Charlame Ct
2. N Charlame Ct
3. N Charlame Ter

Upham
Corner

28

Townsend St

Columbus Ave

Blue Hill Ave

Quincy St

1

2

Roxbury is home to Merengue, a Dominican oasis that apparently caters the clubhouse at Fenway Park, and Bob the Chef's, which has been running a popular Sunday jazz brunch for many years. Otherwise, dining around here is mostly uninspired.

Bars

- **Biarritz Lounge** · 177 Dudley St
- **C&S Tavern** · 380 Warren St
- **Slades Bar & Grill** · 958 Tremont St

Farmer's Markets

- **Dudley Town Common** · Dudley St & Washington St

Gyms

- **Roxbury Family YMCA** · 285 Martin Luther King Blvd

Hardware Stores

- **Hampden Supply Co** · 101 Hampden St

Liquor Stores

- **Blue Hill Liquors** · 108 Blue Hill Ave
- **Brothers Liquors** · 616 Shawmut Ave
- **Caribbean Liquors** · 527 Dudley St
- **Folgers Liquors** · 2665 Washington St
- **Garden Liquors** · 276 Warren St
- **Hollywood Liquors** · 950 Tremont St
- **Liquor Land** · 874 Harrison Ave
- **Simon's Liquor** · 2169 Washington St
- **Warren Liquors** · 368 Warren St

Restaurants

- **Bob the Chef's** · 604 Columbus Ave
- **Breezeway Bar and Grill** · 153 Blue Hill Ave
- **Merengue** · 156 Blue Hill Ave

Video Rental

- **J&B Videos** · 537 Dudley St

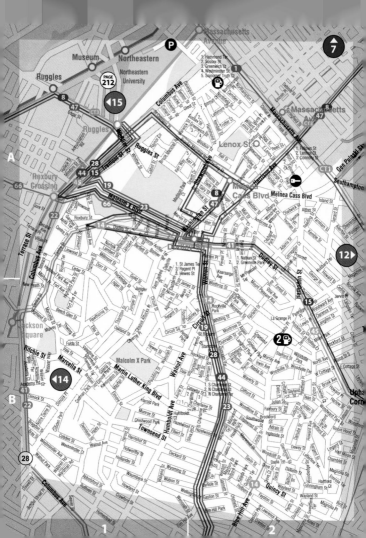

Each of the three "CT" express buses passes through this area. The CT1 bus runs between Dudley Square and Harvard Square; the CT2 bus follows a bizarre route from Ruggles to Sullivan Square; and the CT3 bus connects Dudley Square to Logan Airport. Traffic in Roxbury gets nasty when school lets out in the early afternoon.

Subway

- **Mass Ave**
- **Ruggles**
- **Roxbury Crossing**
- **Jackson Square**
- **Northeastern** (E)
- **Museum** (E)
- **Ruggles** (E)
- **Mass Ave**
- **Lenox St**
- **Melnea Cass Blvd**
- **Dudley Square**

Car Rental

- **Enterprise** • 839 Albany St

Gas Stations

- **Exxon** • 67 Blue Hill Ave
- **Sunoco** • 785 Tremont St
- **Whole Gas** • 67 Blue Hill Ave

Parking

Bus Lines

- CT1 • Central Square, Cambridge—BU Medical Center/BU Medical Campus
- CT2 • Beth Israel Deaconess Medical Center—Andrew Station via BU Medical Center
- 1 • Harvard/Holyoke Gate—Dudley Station via Mass. Ave. & BU Medical Center
- 8 • Harbor Point/Umass—Kenmore Station via South End Medical Area
- 14 • Roslindale Sq—Heath St via Dudley Station, Grove Hall & American Legion Hwy
- 15 • Kane Sq or Fields Corner Station—Ruggles Station via Uphams Corner
- 19 • Fields Corner Station—Ruggles Station via Grove Hall & Dudley
- 22 • Ashmont Station—Ruggles Station via Talbot Ave & Jackson Sq
- 23 • Ashmont Station—Ruggles Station via Washington St
- 28 • Mattapan Station—Ruggles Station via Dudley Station
- 41 • Centre & Eliot Streets—JFK/Umass Station via Dudley Station, Centre St & Jackson Sq Station
- 44 • Jackson Sq Station—ruggles via Seaver St & Humboldt
- 45 • Franklin Park Zoo—Ruggles Station via Blue Hill Ave
- 47 • Central Sq, Cambridge—Broadway Station via South End Medical Area
- 66 • Harvard Square—Dudley Station via Allston & Brookline

Map 14 · **Jamaica Plain**

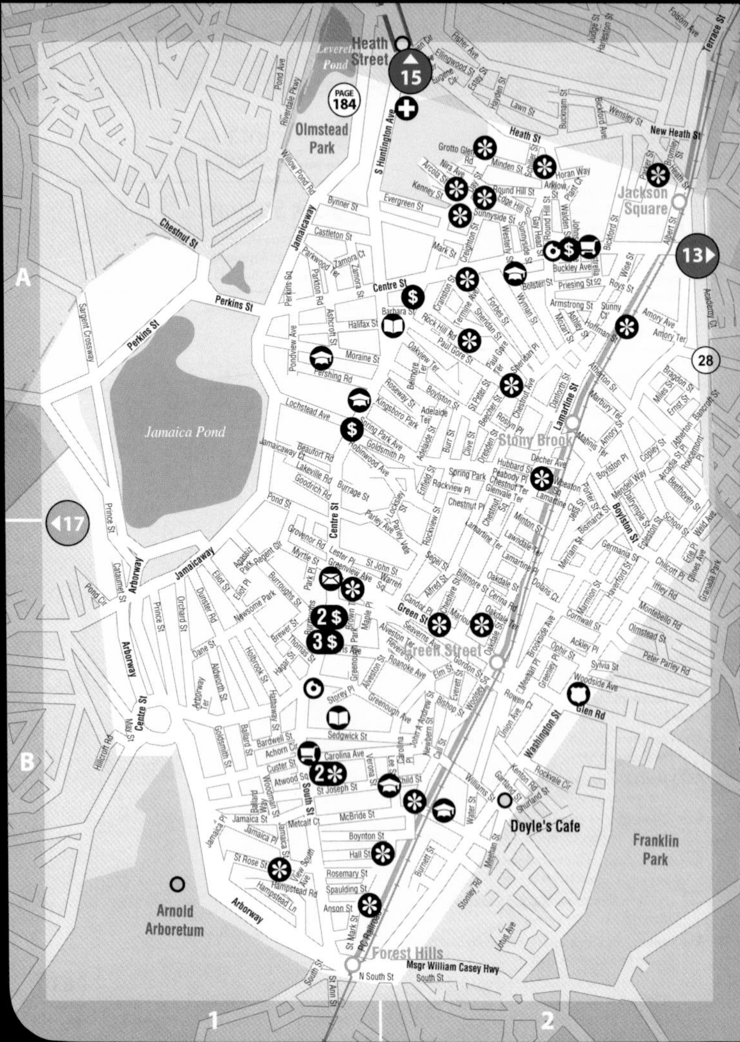

Leverett Pond

Heath Street

PAGE 184

Olmstead Park

Chestnut St

Heath St

New Heath St

Jackson Square

13

28

Perkins St

Centre St

Jamaica Pond

Stony Brook

17

Green Street

2

3

2

Doyle's Cafe

Franklin Park

Arnold Arboretum

Forest Hills

Msgr William Casey Hwy

1

2

The proximity of the Emerald Necklace and the diversity of its residents help foster a vibe in Jamaica Plain that's more relaxed than in many other parts of the city. Although some Cambridge residents think JP is closer to Providence than to downtown, its arboreal pleasantness and cheaper housing attract residents who don't mind living at the bottom of the E train and the Orange Line.

Banks

- **Boston Private Bank & Trust** · 401 Centre St
- **Citizens** · 696 Centre St
- **Fleet** · 315 Centre St
- **Fleet** · 677 Centre St
- **Hyde Park Cooperative Bank** · 733 Centre St
- **People's Federal Savings Bank** · 725 Centre St
- **Roxbury Highland Bank** · 515 Centre St
- **Wainwright Bank & Trust** · 687 Centre St

Donuts

- **Dunkin' Donuts** · 315 Centre St
- **Dunkin' Donuts** · 757 Centre St

Hospitals

- **VA Boston-Jamaica Plain Campus** ·
  150 S Huntington Ave

O Landmarks

- **Arnold Arboretum** · 125 Arborway
- **Doyle's Cafe** · 3484 Washington St

Libraries

- **Connolly** · 433 Centre St
- **Jamaica Plain** · 12 Sedgwick St

Police

- **District E-13** · 3345 Washington St

Post Offices

- · 655 Centre St

Schools

- **English High School** · 144 McBride St
- **James Curley Elementary School** ·
  40 Pershing Rd
- **John F Kennedy Elementary School** · 7 Bolster St
- **Louis Agassiz Elementary School** · 20 Child St
- **Mary E Curley Middle School** · 493 Centre St

Supermarkets

- **Harvest Co-op Market** · 57 South St
- **Stop & Shop** · 301 Centre St

Community Gardens

- **60 Paul Gore Street Garden** · 60 Paul Gore St
- **Agassiz Community Orchard and Garden** ·
  20 Child St
- **Anson Street Garden** ·
  Southwest Corridor & Anson St
- **Arcola/Day Sitting Park** · Arcola St & Day St
- **Bowditch School Building Garden** · 82 Green St
- **Bromley Heath Gardens** · Bromley Heath Housing
- **Edward M Berke Memorial Garden** · St Rose St
- **Farnsworth House Garden** · 90 South St
- **Forbes Street Community Garden** · 19 Forbes St
- **Hall/Boynton Garden** ·
  Southwest Corridor & Hall St
- **Hennigan School Garden** ·
  Grotto Glen Rd & Day St
- **Lamartine and Hubbard Streets Garden** ·
  Southwest Corridor & Lamartine St
- **McBride/Boynton Street Garden** ·
  Southwest Corridor & McBride St
- **Nira Avenue Garden** · 10 Nira Ave
- **Oakdale Terrace Garden** · Oakdale Ter
- **Paul Gore/Beecher Community Garden** ·
  Paul Gore St & Beecher St
- **Roundhill/Day Streets Community Garden** ·
  66 Roundhill St
- **Southwest Corridor Community Farm** ·
  Lamartine St at Hoffman St
- **Starr Lane Park** · 17 Starr Ln
- **Walden Street Garden** · 13 Walden St

Map 14 • **Jamaica Plain**

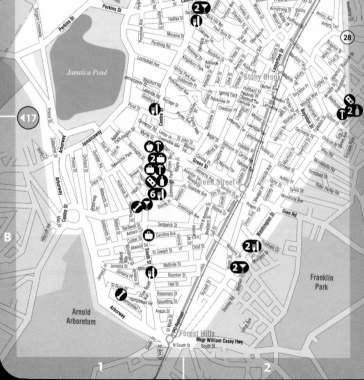

Map 14

The Brendan Behan Pub and the Milky Way Lounge, both neighborhood faves, are located near each other on Centre Street. Closer to the Forest Hills T stop are Doyle's Cafe (serving since 1882) and the Midway Cafe. JP's restaurant scene continues to develop in interesting ways—the uninitiated should consider Wonder Spice Cafe, Ten Tables or Arbor to start their investigations.

Bars

- **Brendan Behan Pub** · 378 Centre St
- **Costello's Tavern** · 723 Centre St
- **Doyle's Cafe** · 3484 Washington St
- **Midway Cafe** · 3496 Washington St
- **Milky Way Lounge and Lanes** · 405 Centre St

Farmer's Markets

- **Jamaica Plain** · 677 Centre St

Hardware Stores

- **Ace Hardware** · 656 Centre St
- **True Value** · 3121 Washington St
- **Yumont Hardware** · 702 Centre St

Liquor Stores

- **Blanchard Liquors** · 741 Centre St
- **Chauncy Liquor Mart** · 3100 Washington St
- **Egleston Liquors** · 3086 Washington St

Pet Shops

- **Centre Pet** · 765 Centre St
- **The Cat's Meow** · 62 St Rose St

Restaurants

- **Arbor** · 711 Centre St
- **Bukhara** · 701 Centre St
- **Centre Street Cafe** · 699 Centre St
- **Doyle's Cafe** · 3484 Washington St
- **El Oriental de Cuba** · 416 Centre St
- **Jake's Boss BBQ** · 3492 Washington St
- **James's Gate** · 5 McBride St
- **JP Seafood Cafe** · 730 Centre St
- **Purple Cactus Burrito & Wrap** · 674 Centre St
- **Tacos El Charro** · 349 Centre St
- **Ten Tables** · 597 Centre St
- **Wonder Spice Cafe** · 697 Centre St

Shopping

- **Boomerangs** · 716 Centre St
- **CD Spins** · 668 Centre St
- **Ferris Wheels Bicycle Shop** · 64 South St
- **JP Licks** · 659 Centre St

Video Rental

- **Columbus Video** · 1967 Columbus Ave
- **Video Underground** · 389 Centre St
- **Videosmith** · 672 Centre St

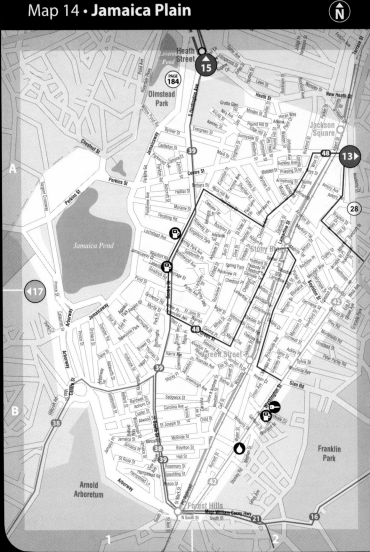

Map 14 · **Jamaica Plain**

Parking is easier to find here than in most other parts of the city. To get to JP from Back Bay, consider taking the 39 bus instead of the Orange Line. The 39 bus runs down the middle of Centre Street, supplanting the extension of the E train that ran along this route until the mid-1980s.

Subway

- **· Jackson Square**
- **· Stony Brook**
- **· Green St**
- **· Forest Hills**
- **· Heath St** (E)

Bus Lines

16 · Forest Hills Station—Andrew Station or UMASS via Columbia Rd

21 · Ashmont Station—Forest Hills Station via Morton St

38 · Wren St—Forest Hills Station via Centre & South Streets

39 · Forest Hills Station—Back Bay Station via Huntington Ave

42 · Forest Hills Station—Ruggles Station via Washington Station & Dudley

48 · Jamaica Plain Loop Monument—Jackson Sq Station via Green St

Car Rental

· **Enterprise** · 3430 Washington St

Car Washes

· **Jamaica Plain Car Wash** · 3530 Washington St

Gas Stations

· **Citgo** · 561 Centre St
· **Hatoff's** · 3440 Washington St
· **JP Metro Auto Service** · 525 Centre St

Map 15 • Fenway (West) / Mission Hill

Map 1

Longwood is home to a number of nationally prominent medical institutions, including Dana-Farber, Children's Hospital and the Brigham. There are plenty of students in this area—Harvard Medical, the Massachusetts College of Art and Wentworth Institute of Technology are all here, as is Northeastern, whose full-time enrollment of 16,000 students makes it only the second-largest school on this side of the river.

Banks

- **Citizens** · 1628 Tremont St
- **Fleet** · 1614 Tremont St
- **Fleet** · 1643 Tremont St
- **Fleet** · 300 The Fenway
- **Fleet** · 333 Longwood Ave
- **Fleet** · 360 Huntington Ave
- **Sovereign Bank** · 58 Forsyth St
- **Sovereign Bank** · 6 Francis St

Donuts

- **Dunkin' Donuts** · 115 Forsyth St
- **Dunkin' Donuts** · 1420 Boylston St
- **Dunkin' Donuts** · 1631 Tremont St
- **Mike's Donuts** · 1524 Tremont St

Hospitals

- **Brigham and Women's Hospital** · 75 Francis St
- **Children's Hospital** · 300 Longwood Ave
- **Dana-Farber Cancer Institute** · 44 Binney St

Landmarks

- **Isabella Stewart Gardner Museum** ·
  280 The Fenway
- **Mission Church Basilica** · 1545 Tremont St
- **Museum of Fine Arts** · 465 Huntington Ave

Libraries

- **Parker Hill** · 1497 Tremont St

Post Offices

- 1575 Tremont St

Schools

- **Boston Latin School** · 78 Ave Louis Pasteur
- **David Farragut Elementary School** ·
  10 Fenwood Rd
- **Harvard Medical School** · 25 Shattuck St
- **James Hennigan Elementary School** ·
  200 Heath St
- **Manville School** · 3 Blackfan Cir
- **Massachusetts College of Art** ·
  621 Huntington Ave
- **Massachusetts College of Pharmacy and Health Sciences** · 179 Longwood Ave
- **Northeastern University** · 360 Huntington Ave
- **Simmons College** · 300 The Fenway
- **Wentworth Institute of Technology** ·
  550 Huntington Ave

Supermarkets

- **Star Market** · 33 Kilmarnock St
- **Stop & Shop** · 1620 Tremont St

Community Gardens

- **Lawn Street Garden** · 59 Lawn St
- **Mission Hill Community Garden** · 742 Parker St
- **Tobin Community Center Garden Club** ·
  1481 Tremont St

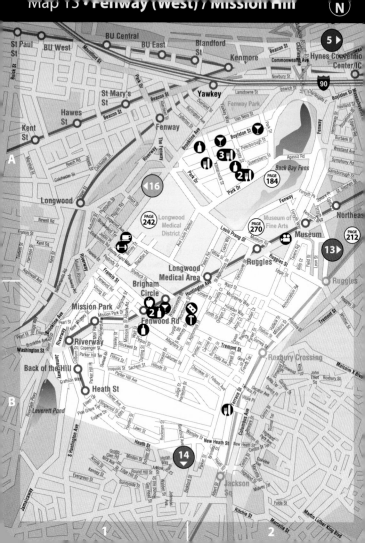

Map 13 • Fenway (West) / Mission Hill

Map 15

Tucked inside the Fenway are some good restaurants that reflect the low-key character of this neighborhood, including Brown Sugar and Buteco. In short proximity along Boylston Street are Sophia's, Machine, The Ramrod, and The Baseball Tavern—a little something for everyone.

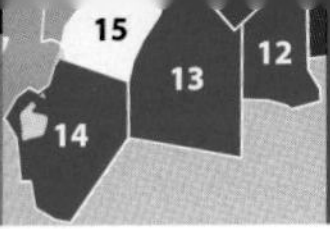

Bars

- **Flann O'Brien's** · 1619 Tremont St
- **Sophia's** · 1270 Boylston St
- **The Baseball Tavern** · 1306 Boylston St

Coffee

- **Red Bean Coffee Roasters** · 350 Longwood Ave

Farmer's Markets

- **Mission Hill** · Huntington Ave & Tremont St

Gyms

- **Fitcorp** · 350 Longwood Ave

Hardware Stores

- **AC Hardware** · 1562 Tremont St

Liquor Stores

- **Bradley Liquors** · 1383 Boylston St
- **Brigham Liquors** · 732 Huntington Ave
- **Jersey Street Liquors** · 48 Queensberry St
- **Michel's Wine & Spirits** · 750 Huntington Ave
- **Tremont Liquors** · 1623 Tremont St

Movie Theaters

- **Museum of Fine Arts** · 465 Huntington Ave

Restaurants

- **Brown Sugar Cafe** · 129 Jersey St
- **Buteco** · 130 Jersey St
- **El Pelon Taqueria** · 92 Peterborough St
- **Linwood Grill & BBQ** · 81 Kilmarnock St
- **Mississippi's** · 103 Terrace St
- **Rod Dee II** · 94 Peterborough St
- **Sorento's** · 86 Peterborough St

Video Rental

- **Bangkok Video (Thai)** · 142 Smith St

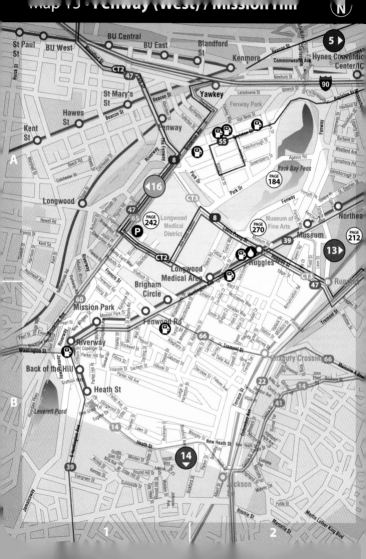

In an ideal world, a tram line would run down the middle of Boylston Street. This would ease the game-day crunch on the Green Line and provide better access to the Fens and the area around the intersection of Park Drive and Brookline Avenue. Trying to park around here on game day? Arrive early and bring Mr. Jackson. Don't count on street parking in the Fenway neighborhood itself.

Subway

- ■ **Northeastern** (E)
- ■ **Museum of Fine Arts** (E)
- ■ **Longwood Medical Area** (E)
- ■ **Brigham Circle** (E)
- ■ **Fenwood Rd** (E)
- ■ **Mission Park** (E)
- ■ **Riverway** (E)
- ■ **Back of the Hill** (E)
- ■ **Heath** (E)
- ■ Roxbury Crossing

Bus Lines

- **CT2** · Sullivan Station—Ruggles Station via Kendall/MIT
- **CT3** · Beth Israel Deaconess Medical Center— Andrew Station via BU Medical Center
- **8** · Harbor Point/Umass—Kenmore Station via South End Medical Area
- **8** · Roslindale Sq—Heath St via Dudley Station, Grove Hall & American Legion Hwy
- **22** · Ashmont Station—Ruggles Station via Talbot Ave & Jackson Sq
- **39** · Forest Hills Station—Back Bay Station via Huntington Ave
- **41** · Centre & Eliot Streets—JFK/Umass Station via Dudley Station, Centre St & Jackson Sq Station
- **47** · Central Sq, Cambridge—Broadway Station via South End Medical Area
- **60** · Chestnut Hill—Kenmore Station via Brookline Village & Cypress St
- **65** · Brighton Center—Kenmore Station via Washington St, Brookline Village
- **66** · Harvard Square—Dudley Station via Allston & Brookline

Commuter Rail

· Yawkey

Car Washes

· **Athens Shell** · 525 Huntington Ave

Gas Stations

- · **Exxon** · 1420 Boylston St
- · **Mobil** · 1301 Boylston St
- · **Mutual Gas** · 1325 Boylston St
- · **Mutual Gas** · 1600 Tremont St
- · **Texaco** · 1241 Boylston St
- · **Texaco** · 525 Huntington Ave
- · **Texaco** · 914 Huntington Ave
- · **US Gas** · 634 Huntington Ave

Parking

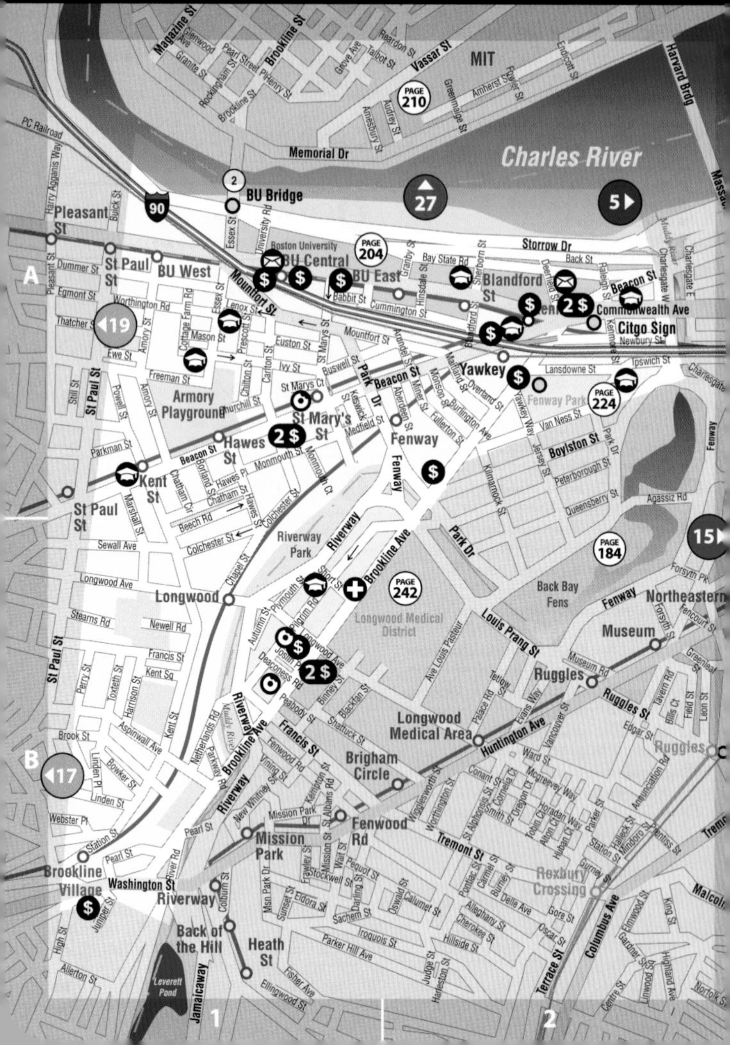

Map 10 • **Kenmore Square / Brookline (East)**

Maravia St
Brookline St
Vassar St
Pearl St
Beacon St
Talbot St
Cherry St
Pilgrim St
Granite St
Pine St
Tufts St
Sydney St
MIT
Harvard Bridg

PC Railroad

Memorial Dr

Charles River

PAGE 210

PAGE 204

2 BU Bridge

90

Pleasant St
St Paul St
BU West
St Paul St
Dummer St
Egmont St
Thatcher St

Mountfort St
Boston University
BU Central
BU East

Storrow Dr
Back St
Bay State Rd

27

5

Blandford
Commonwealth Ave
Citgo Sign
Newbury St
Beacon St

2

19

Ewe St
Freeman St
Worthington Rd
Mason St
Pratt St
Lenox St
Prescott St

Cummington St
Rabbit St
Mountfort St
Euston St
Ivy St

Yawkey
Lansdowne St
Tipswich St

Armory Playground
Churchill St

Chilton St
St Marys Ct
St Mary's St

Beacon Dr
Maitland St
Miner St

Fenway Park

PAGE 224

2

Hawes St
Beacon St
St Mary's St

Fenway
Van Ness St

Boylston St

Kent St
St Paul St
Sewall Ave

Chatham St
Beech Rd
Colchester St

Queensberry St
Agassiz Rd

15

Riverway Park
Riverway

Park Dr

Back Bay Fens

Fenway
Northeastern
Museum

PAGE 184

Longwood

PAGE 242

Louis Prang St

Longwood Medical District

Ruggles

Stearns Rd
Newell Rd
Francis St
Kent Sq

2

Longwood Medical Area

Huntington Ave

Ruggles St

Ruggles

17

Brook St
Aspinwall Ave
Kent St

Brigham Circle

Tremont St

Webster Pl

Fenwood Rd

Roxbury Crossing

Brookline Village

Washington St
Riverway

Mission Park

Columbus Ave

Back of the Hill
Heath St

Leverett Pond
Jamaicaway

1
2

Kenmore Square is dominated by Boston University and, between April and October, by visitors to Fenway Park (take the tour). The Citgo sign, which has suffered recently from cold winters, is scheduled to get some much-needed TLC. Riverway Park is a peaceful, often overlooked link in the Emerald Necklace.

Banks

- **Brookline Savings Bank** · 1016 Beacon St
- **Brookline Savings Bank** · 160 Washington St
- **Citizens** · 435 Brookline Ave
- **Citizens** · 560 Commonwealth Ave
- **Fleet** · 1024A Beacon St
- **Fleet** · 201 Brookline Ave
- **Fleet** · 410 Brookline Ave
- **Fleet** · 540 Commonweath Ave
- **Fleet** · 660 Beacon St
- **Fleet** · 700 Commonwealth Ave
- **Fleet** · 771 Commonwealth Ave
- **Fleet** · 775 Commonwealth Ave
- **Mercantile Bank** · 61 Brookline Ave
- **Sovereign Bank** · 350 Longwood Ave
- **Sovereign Bank** · 552 Commonwealth Ave

Donuts

- **Dunkin' Donuts** · 1008 Beacon St
- **Dunkin' Donuts** · 350 Longwood Ave
- **Dunkin' Donuts** · 457 Brookline Ave

Hospitals

- **Beth Israel Deaconess Medical Center** ·
  330 Brookline Ave

Landmarks

- **BU Bridge** · Essex St & Mountfort St
- **Citgo Sign** · Commonwealth Ave & Beacon St
- **Fenway Park** · 4 Yawkey Way

Post Offices

- 775 Commonwealth Ave
- 11 Deerfield St

Schools

- **Ansin Religious School of Ohabei Shalom** ·
  1187 Beacon St
- **Boston Arts Academy** · 174 Ipswich St
- **Boston University** · 1 Sherborn St
- **Fenway High School** · 174 Ipswich St
- **Ivy Street School** · 200 Ivy St
- **Kids Are People Elementary School** ·
  656 Beacon St
- **New England Hebrew Academy** · 9 Prescott St
- **New England School of Photography** ·
  537 Commonwealth Ave
- **The Winsor School** · 103 Pilgrim Rd

Map 16 · **Kenmore Square / Brookline (East)**

The strip of bars and clubs along Lansdowne Street and Brookline Avenue continues to pull in crowds of nightlife enthusiasts—Sox fans when there's a game in town, and students, well, always. Great Bay has made a splash with top-drawer seafood at the Hotel Commonwealth. But, with few exceptions, if you seek service and sobriety go elsewhere.

Bars

- **An Tua Nua** · 835 Beacon St
- **Atlas Bar & Grill** · 3 Lansdowne St
- **Audubon Circle** · 838 Beacon St
- **Boston Billiard Club** · 126 Brookline Ave
- **Cask'n Flagon** · 62 Brookline Ave
- **Jillian's** · 145 Ipswich St
- **PJ Kilroy's** · 822 Beacon St
- **Who's on First?** · 19 Yawkey Way

Coffee

- **Espresso Royale** · 736 Commonwealth Ave
- **Starbucks** · 595 Commonwealth Ave
- **Starbucks** · 775 Commonwealth Ave
- **Starbucks** · 874 Commonwealth Ave

Copy Shops

- **Kinko's** · 534 Commonwealth Ave

Gyms

- **Boston Sports Club** · 201 Brookline Ave
- **City Gym & Aerobic Center** · 542 Commonwealth Ave
- **Gold's Gym** · 71 Lansdowne St

Hardware Stores

- **Economy Hardware** · 1012 Beacon St

Liquor Stores

- **Wine Press** · 1024 Beacon St

Movie Theaters

- **AMC Theatres Fenway 13** · 201 Brookline Ave

Restaurants

- **Ankara Cafe** · 472 Commonwealth Ave
- **Audubon Circle** · 838 Beacon St
- **BB Wolf** · 109 Brookline Ave
- **Boston Beer Works** · 61 Brookline Ave
- **Cafe Belo** · 636 Beacon St
- **Chef Chang's House** · 1004 Beacon St
- **Great Bay** · 500 Commonwealth Ave
- **India Quality** · 484 Commonwealth Ave
- **Sol Azteca** · 914A Beacon St

Shopping

- **Bed Bath & Beyond** · 401 Park Dr
- **Boston Bicycle** · 842 Beacon St
- **Economy Hardware** · 1012 Beacon St
- **Guitar Center** · 750 Commonwealth Ave
- **Nuggets** · 486 Commonwealth Ave
- **Ski Market** · 860 Commonwealth Ave
- **Staples** · 401 Park Dr
- **Tweeter Etc** · 874 Commonwealth Ave

Video Rental

- **Beacon Video Stop** · 1038 Beacon St
- **Blockbuster** · 532 Commonwealth Ave

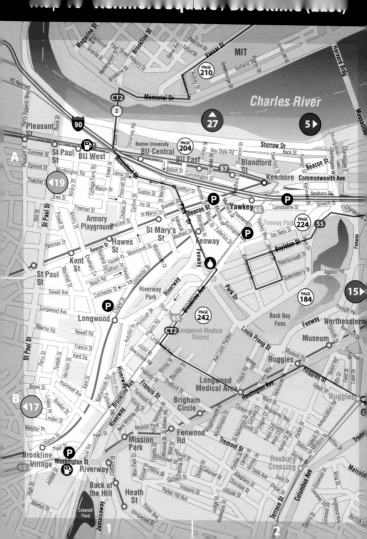

Map 1

The Kenmore Square T stop is a major-league mess on game days, so avoid it unless you're part of the throng heading to Fenway Park. B train riders might find the 57 bus to be the better choice to head into Kenmore Square at these times. Parking around BU presents its own problems, but it does get (a little) easier to park the further west you go along Comm Ave.

Subway
- ■ · **Kenmore**
- ■ · **Blandford St** (B)
- ■ · **BU East** (B)
- ■ · **BU Central** (B)
- ■ · **BU West** (B)
- ■ · **St Paul St** (B)
- ■ · **St Mary's St** (C)
- ■ · **Hawes St** (C)
- ■ · **Kent St** (C)
- ■ · **St Paul St** (C)
- ■ · **Fenway** (D)
- ■ · **Longwood** (D)
- ■ · **Brookline Village** (D)

Bus Lines
- **C T2** · Sullivan Station—Ruggles Station Via Kendall/MIT
- **55** · Jersey & Queensberry—Copley Sq or Park & Tremont Streets
- **57** · Watertown Yard—Kenmore Station via Newton Corner & Brighton Center
- **65** · Brighton Center—Kenmore Station via Washington St, Brookline Village

🌢 Car Washes
· **Advance Auto Detailing** · 401 Park Dr

🅿 Gas Stations
· **Gulf** · 25 Washington St
· **Mobil** · 850 Commonwealth Ave

🅿 Parking

Map 17 Coolidge Corner / Brookline Hills

Map 17

Essentials

Welcome to the heart of Brookline. Most of the "action" in residential, well-heeled Brookline is concentrated around Beacon Street, Washington Street and Harvard Street; the rest of this area is even more sedate. Brookline Hills offers some good views of the Boston area.

Banks

- **Banknorth** · 1641 Beacon St
- **Brookline Co-Operative Bank** · 264 Washington St
- **Brookline Savings Bank** · 1340 Beacon St
- **Compass Bank** · 1299 Beacon St
- **Fleet** · 1319 Beacon St
- **Sovereign Bank** · 1 Harvard St

Donuts

- **Dunkin' Donuts** · 1316 Beacon St
- **Dunkin' Donuts** · 1671 Beacon St
- **Dunkin' Donuts** · 20 Boylston St
- **Dunkin' Donuts** · 265 Boylston St
- **Dunkin' Donuts** · 8 Harvard St

Hospitals

- **Franciscan Children's Hospital** · 30 Warren St

Libraries

- **Brookline Main Library** · 361 Washington St

Police

- **Brookline Police Department** · 350 Washington St

Post Offices

- 1295 Beacon St
- 207 Washington St

Schools

- **Amos A Lawrence School** · 194 Boylston St
- **Boston Graduate School of Psychoanalysis** · 1581 Beacon St
- **Brookline High School** · 115 Greenough St
- **Israeli Complementary School** · 50 Sewall Ave
- **John D Runkle School** · 50 Druce St
- **Maimonides School** · 34 Philbrick Rd
- **Pierce School** · 50 School St
- **St Mary of the Assumption School** · 67 Harvard St
- **William H Lincoln School** · 19 Kennard Rd

Supermarkets

- **Star Market** · 1717 Beacon St
- **Stop & Shop** · 155 Harvard St
- **Trader Joe's** · 1309 Beacon St
- **Whole Foods Market** · 15 Washington St

Map 17 · **Coolidge Corner / Brookline Hills**

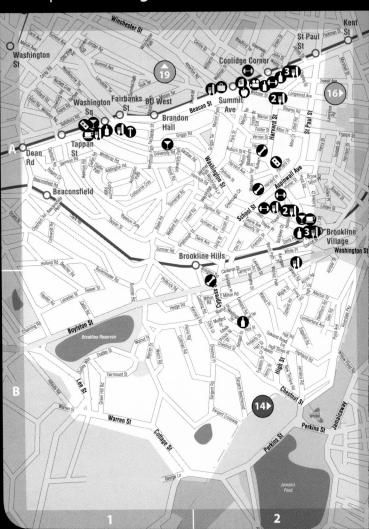

The Coolidge Corner Movie Theatre, which is the only operating Art Deco theater in the Boston area, shows a varied slate of new and vintage films. For the most part, food and drink options in this area are pretty basic. Matt Murphy's deserves the attention it gets for successfully putting good food into a good pub, and B&D Deli continues to draw a crowd.

Bars

- **Anam Cara** · 1648 Beacon St
- **Matt Murphy's Pub** · 14 Harvard St
- **The Last Drop** · 596 Washington St

Coffee

- **Starbucks** · 15 Harvard St
- **Starbucks** · 1655 Beacon St

Copy Shops

- **Kinko's** · 1370 Beacon St

Farmer's Markets

- **Brookline** · Centre St at Beacon St

Gyms

- **Beacon Hill Athletic Club** · 279 Washington St
- **Fitness Connection** · 310 Harvard St
- **Fitness Unlimited** · 62 Harvard St
- **Studio Elle** · 1318 Beacon St

Hardware Stores

- **Connelly Hardware** · 706 Washington St

Liquor Stores

- **Best Cellars** · 1327 Beacon St
- **Foley's Liquor Store** · 228 Cypress St
- **Food Center Liquors** · 10 Harvard Sq
- **Gimbel's Liquors** · 1637 Beacon St
- **London Wine** · 1300 Beacon St

Movie Theaters

- **Coolidge Corner Movie Theatre** · 290 Harvard St

Pet Shops

- **Bone Appetit Bakery** · 397 Washington St
- **Brookline Grooming & Pet Supplies** · 146 Harvard St
- **Gill's Tropical Fish & Pet Supply** · 361 Boylston St

Restaurants

- **Anna's Taqueria** · 1412 Beacon St
- **B&D Deli** · 1653 Beacon St
- **Baja Betty's Burritos** · 3 Harvard Sq
- **Boca Grande** · 1294 Beacon St
- **Cafe Mirror** · 362 Washington St
- **Cafe St Petersburg** · 236 Washington St
- **Fajitas & 'Ritas** · 48 Boylston St
- **Fugakyu** · 1280 Beacon St
- **Lucy's** · 242 Harvard St
- **Matt Murphy's Pub** · 14 Harvard St
- **Pho Lemon Grass** · 239 Harvard St
- **Seoul Kitchen** · 349 Washington St
- **Tsunami** · 10 Pleasant St
- **Village Fish** · 22 Harvard St
- **Village Smokehouse** · 1 Harvard St
- **Washington Square Tavern** · 714 Washington St

Shopping

- **Flip Side Records** · 1410 Beacon St

Video Rental

- **Hollywood Video** · 111 Harvard St
- **Movieworks** · 1658 Beacon St

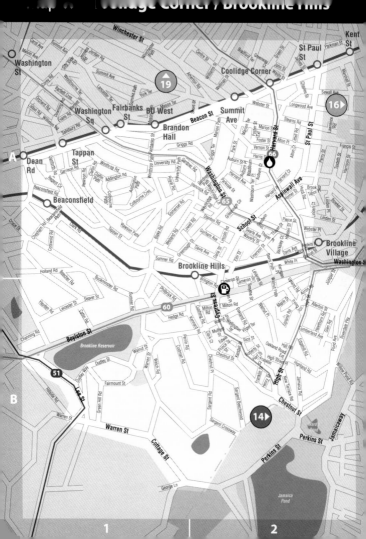

Map 1

With very few exceptions, Brookline completely prohibits overnight street parking, even for residents (generally, street parking is permitted only for two hours). So, if you're visiting Brookline, do yourself a favor and take the T. If you are already in Brookline, note that the 66 bus along Harvard Street is the best way to get to Harvard Square, and the 65 bus takes you over to Brighton Village.

Subway

- ■ · **Kent St** (C)
- ■ · **St Paul St** (C)
- ■ · **Coolidge Corner** (C)
- ■ · **Summit Ave** (C)
- ■ · **Brandon Hall** (C)
- ■ · **Fairbanks St** (C)
- ■ · **Washington Sq** (C)
- ■ · **Tappan St** (C)
- ■ · **Dean Rd** (C)
- ■ · **Brookline Village** (D)
- ■ · **Brookline Hills** (D)
- ■ · **Beaconsfield** (D)

Bus Lines

- **51** · Cleveland Circle—Forest Hills Station via Hancock Village
- **60** · Chestnut Hill—Kenmore Station via Brookline Village & Cypress St
- **65** · Brighton Center—Kenmore Station via Washington St, Brookline Village
- **66** · Harvard Square—Dudley Station via Allston & Brookline

Car Washes

· **Scrubadub Auto Wash** · 143 Harvard St

Gas Stations

· **Mobil** · 345 Boylston St

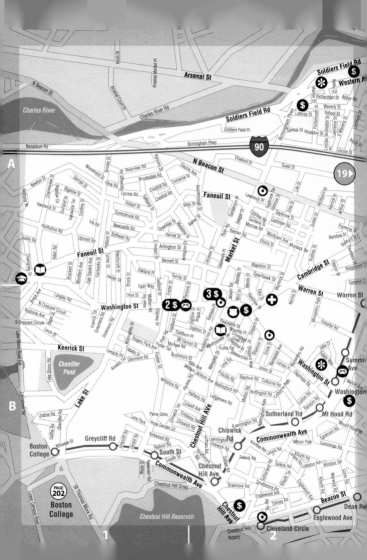

Brighton has been a primarily residential neighborhood since the 19th century. Today, it attracts young families and graduate students seeking a little more peace and quiet than can be found in, say, next-door Allston. At night, sleepy Brighton gets sleepier still. Cleveland Circle, the last stop on the C train, was designed by Frederick Law Olmstead to be a grand terminus for Boston's first streetcar line.

Banks

- **Citizens** · 1380 Soldiers Field Rd
- **Citizens** · 35 Washington St
- **Citizens** · 414 Washington St
- **Fleet** · 315 Washington St
- **Fleet** · 350 Chestnut Hill Ave
- **Fleet** · 5 Chestnut Hill Ave
- **Mercantile Bank** · 423 Washington St
- **People's Federal Savings Bank** · 435 Market St
- **Sovereign Bank** · 30 Birmingham Pkwy
- **Sovereign Bank** · 415 Market St

Donuts

- **Dunkin' Donuts** · 1955 Beacon St
- **Dunkin' Donuts** · 214 N Beacon St
- **Dunkin' Donuts** · 235 Washington St
- **Dunkin' Donuts** · 350 Washington St

Hospitals

- **St Elizabeth's Medical Center** · 736 Cambridge St

Libraries

- **Brighton** · 40 Academy Hill Rd
- **Faneuil** · 419 Faneuil St

Police

- **District D-14** · 301 Washington St

Post Offices

- 409 Washington St
- 1558 Commonwealth Ave

Schools

- **Our Lady of the Presentation School** · 634 Washington St

Community Gardens

- **Charles River Community Garden** · 1450 Soldiers Field Rd
- **Commonwealth Tenants Association Garden** · 35 Fidelis Way

Map 18 · Brighton

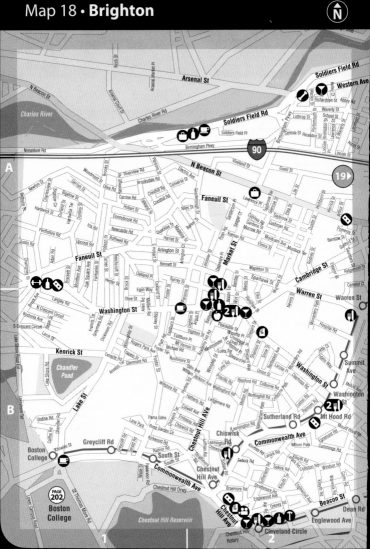

Although there are a number of businesses in and around Cleveland Circle, there's very little out here to make a special trip for. Rowdier Brighton residents are probably heading into Allston or down to Cleveland Circle for their nights out; quieter residents are probably heading over to Brookline.

Bars

- **Boyne** · 458 Western Ave
- **CitySide** · 1960 Beacon St
- **Green Briar** · 304 Washington St
- **Joey's** · 416 Market St
- **Mary Ann's** · 1937 Beacon St
- **Soho** · 386 Market St

Coffee

- **Espresso Royale** · 2201 Commonwealth Ave
- **Greenhouse Cafe** · 425 Washington St
- **Starbucks** · 1660 Soldiers Field Rd

Copy Shops

- **Flash Printing & Copy** · 370 Chestnut Hill Ave
- **Kinko's** · 252 Washington St

Farmer's Markets

- **Brighton** · 5 Chestnut Hill Ave

Gyms

- **YMCA** · 615 Washington St

Hardware Stores

- **Cleveland Circle Hardware** · 1920 Beacon St

Liquor Stores

- **Dorr's Liquor Mart** · 354 Washington St
- **Martignetti Liquors** · 1650 Soldiers Field Rd
- **Oak Square Liquors** · 610 Washington St
- **Reservoir Wines & Spirits** · 1922 Beacon St

Movie Theaters

- **National Amusements Circle Cinema** · 399 Chestnut Hill Ave

Pet Shops

- **Toureen Kennels & Grooming Salon** · 505 Western Ave

Restaurants

- **Bamboo** · 1616 Commonwealth Ave
- **Bangkok Bistro** · 1952 Beacon St
- **Bluestone Bistro** · 1799 Commonwealth Ave
- **Devlin's** · 332 Washington St
- **Green Briar** · 304 Washington St
- **Harry's Bar & Grill** · 1430 Commonwealth Ave
- **Jasmine Bistro** · 412 Market St
- **Soho** · 386 Market St
- **Tasca** · 1612 Commonwealth Ave

Shopping

- **CompUSA** · 205 Market St
- **Staples** · 1660 Soldiers Field Rd

Video Rental

- **Blockbuster** · 358 Chestnut Hill Ave
- **Brighton Video** · 596 Washington St
- **Hollywood Video** · 103 N Beacon St
- **Viper Video** · 1620 Commonwealth Ave

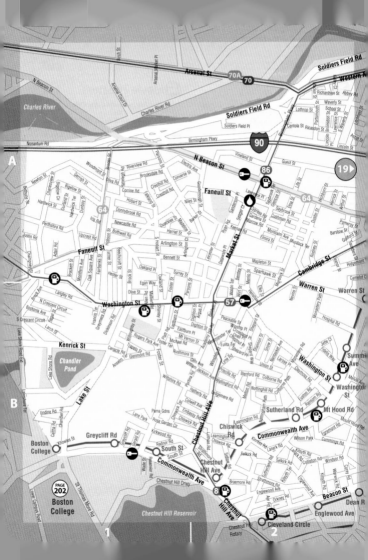

If you're a Brighton resident who doesn't live near Comm Ave or Beacon Street, you have practically no access to the T at all. Know that the 57 bus connects Brighton Village with Kenmore Square, and that the 86 bus connects Brighton Village to Harvard Square and Somerville. Predictably, as you get closer to Cleveland Circle, Brighton's already wretched parking gets even worse.

Map

Subway

- **Warren St** (B)
- **Summit Ave** (B)
- **Washington St** (B)
- **Mt. Hood Rd** (B)
- **Sutherland Rd** (B)
- **Chiswick Rd** (B)
- **Chestnut Hill Ave** (B)
- **South St** (B)
- **Greycliff Rd** (B)
- **Boston College** (B)
- **Englewood Rd** (C)
- **Cleveland Circle** (C)

Bus Lines

- **57** · Watertown Yard—Kenmore Station via Newton Corner & Brighton Center
- **64** · Oak Square—Central Sq, Cambridge or Kendall/MIT
- **70** · Cedarwood, N Waltham or Watertown Sq—University Park via Central Sq
- **70A** · Cedarwood, N Waltham or Watertown Sq—University Park via Central Sq
- **86** · Sullivan Sq Station—Cleveland Circle via Harvard/John

 ## Car Rental

- **Merchants Rent A Car** · 12 Wirt St
- **Rent A Wreck** · 2022 Commonwealth Ave
- **U-Haul** · 240 N Beacon St

 ## Car Washes

- **Scrubadub Auto Wash** · 235 Market St

Gas Stations

- **Exxon** · 433 Washington St
- **Gulf** · 1650 Commonwealth Ave
- **Gulf** · 1927 Beacon St
- **Gulf** · 195 N Beacon St
- **Gulf** · 455 Washington St
- **Mobil** · 1550 Commonwealth Ave
- **Shell** · 332 Chestnut Hill Ave
- **Sunoco** · 602 Washington St

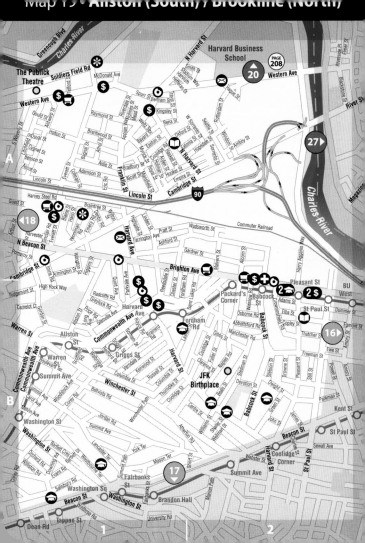

Map 19 • Allston (South) / Brookline (North)

Map 1

Harvard has been purchasing land in Allston for years, and it now owns more land in Boston than it owns in Cambridge. We're assuming that what Harvard eventually develops on its newest tract, which lies mostly south of Cambridge Street, will look nicer than the MBTA railyards that are there now. Most of the remainder of this area is dominated by younger people seeking rents cheaper than those up Comm Ave.

Banks

- **Asian American Bank & Trust** · 230 Harvard Ave
- **Century Bank** · 300 Western Ave
- **Citizens** · 1065 Commonwealth Ave
- **Citizens** · 370 Western Ave
- **Citizens** · 60 Everett St
- **Fleet** · 1237 Commonwealth Ave
- **Fleet** · 881 Commonwealth Ave
- **Fleet** · 957 Commonwealth Ave
- **People's Federal Savings Bank** · 229 N Harvard St
- **Sovereign Bank** · 171 Harvard Ave

Donuts

- **Dunkin' Donuts** · 1020 Commonwealth Ave
- **Dunkin' Donuts** · 179 Brighton Ave
- **Dunkin' Donuts** · 209 N Harvard St
- **Dunkin' Donuts** · 210 Harvard Ave
- **Dunkin' Donuts** · 60 Everett St
- **Twin Do-Nuts** · 501 Cambridge St

Hospitals

- **Arbour-HRI Hospital** · 227 Babcock St

O Landmarks

- **John F Kennedy Birthplace** · 83 Beals St
- **The Publick Theatre** · 1400 Soldiers Field Rd

Libraries

- **Coolidge Corner** · 31 Pleasant St
- **Honan-Allston** · 300 N Harvard St

Post Offices

- 47 Harvard Ave
- 117 Western Ave

Schools

- **Another Course to College School** · 989 Commonwealth Ave
- **Bay Cove Academy** · 156 Lawton St
- **Beacon High School** · 74 Green St
- **Congregation Kehillath Israel Religious School** · 384 Harvard St
- **Edward Devotion School** · 345 Harvard St
- **Media and Technology Charter School** · 1001 Commonwealth Ave
- **Michael Driscoll School** · 64 Westbourne Ter
- **Torah Academy** · 11 Williston Rd

Supermarkets

- **Shaw's** · 1065 Commonwealth Ave
- **Shaw's** · 370 Western Ave
- **Stop & Shop** · 60 Everett St
- **Super 88** · 1 Brighton Ave

Community Gardens

- **Christian Herter Community Garden** · 1155 Soldiers Field Rd
- **Penniman Road Community Garden** · 30 Penniman Rd

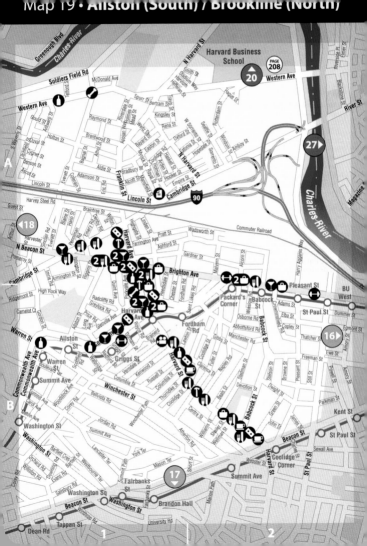

Map 19 • Allston (South) / Brookline (North)

Map 19

With the Rat long gone, the Paradise is the rock standard-bearer on this side of the river (note that the Paradise Lounge now serves up some mean pizzas). Other tried-and-true rock-and-beer joints include The Avenue and Harper's Ferry. Sunset Grill & Tap does indeed have a lot of taps and some decent food to boot.

Bars

- **The Avenue Bar & Grille** · 1249 Commonwealth Ave
- **Harper's Ferry** · 156 Brighton Ave
- **Kinvara Pub** · 34 Harvard Ave
- **Model Cafe** · 7 N Beacon St
- **Our House** · 1277 Commonwealth Ave
- **Paradise Rock Club & Lounge** · 969 Commonwealth Ave
- **Sunset Grill & Tap** · 130 Brighton Ave
- **Tonic** · 1316 Commonwealth Ave
- **Wonder Bar** · 186 Harvard Ave

Coffee

- **Peet's Coffee & Tea** · 285 Harvard St
- **Starbucks** · 277 Harvard St
- **Starbucks** · 473 Harvard St

Copy Shops

- **Commonwealth Copy** · 500 Lincoln St

Gyms

- **Boston Sports Club** · 15 Gorham St
- **HealthWorks Fitness Center** · 920 Commonwealth Ave
- **Wellbridge Health and Fitness Center** · 1079 Commonwealth Ave

Hardware Stores

- **Aborn True Value** · 438 Harvard St
- **Economy Hardware** · 140 Harvard Ave
- **Model Hardware** · 22 Harvard Ave

Liquor Stores

- **Blanchard Liquors** · 103 Harvard Ave
- **Brookline Liquor Mart** · 1354 Commonwealth Ave
- **Hurley's** · 1441 Commonwealth Ave
- **Mall Discount Liquors & Wines** · 525 Harvard St
- **Marty's Liquors** · 193 Harvard Ave
- **Wine Shop** · 370 Western Ave

Movie Theaters

- **Allston Cinema** · 214 Harvard Ave

Pet Shops

- **Petco** · 304 Western Ave
- **The Pet Shop** · 165 Harvard Ave

Restaurants

- **Anna's Taqueria** · 446 Harvard St
- **Brown Sugar Cafe** · 1033 Commonwealth Ave
- **Buddha's Delight** · 404 Harvard St
- **Cafe Belo** · 181 Brighton Ave
- **Cafe Brazil** · 421 Cambridge St
- **Coolidge Corner Clubhouse** · 307 Harvard St
- **El Cafetal** · 479 Cambridge St
- **Istanbul Cafe** · 1414 Commonwealth Ave
- **Rubin's** · 500 Harvard St
- **Saigon** · 431 Cambridge St
- **Spike's Junkyard Dogs** · 108 Brighton Ave
- **Sunset Grill & Tap** · 130 Brighton Ave
- **V Majestic** · 164 Brighton Ave
- **Zaftigs Delicatessen** · 335 Harvard St

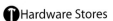 Shopping

- **Berezka International Food Store** · 1215 Commonwealth Ave
- **Bob Smith's Wilderness House** · 1048 Commonwealth Ave
- **CD Spins** · 187 Harvard St
- **City Sports** · 1035 Commonwealth Ave
- **Economy Hardware** · 140 Harvard Ave
- **Herrell's Ice Cream** · 155 Brighton Ave
- **In Your Ear** · 957 Commonwealth Ave
- **International Bicycle Center** · 89 Brighton Ave
- **JP Licks** · 311A Harvard St

Video Rental

- **Allston Video & Goods (Chinese)** · 141 Brighton Ave
- **Blockbuster** · 481 Harvard St
- **Bostonian Video** · 145 Brighton Ave
- **Cinemasmith** · 283 Harvard St
- **Jin Video (Korean)** · 16 Harvard St
- **Korean Book & Video Renting Store (Korean & Japanese)** · 156 Harvard Ave
- **Videosmith** · 1266 Commonwealth Ave

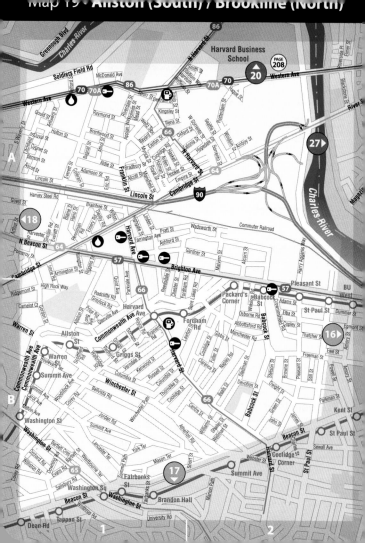

The B train has too many damn stops. Period. The whole point of a tram is to move people efficiently, which the B train simply can't do. Worse, there's no way to drive from Allston into Cambridgeport without hitting the traffic that's a permanent fixture on the Western Avenue Bridge and the River Street Bridge. Still worse, parking in Allston isn't much better than parking in Brookline or Brighton.

Subway

- **St. Paul St** (B)
- **Pleasant St** (B)
- **Babcock St** (B)
- **Packard's Corner** (B)
- **Fordham Rd** (B)
- **Harvard Ave** (B)
- **Griggs St** (B)
- **Allston St** (B)
- **Warren St** (B)
- **Summit Ave** (B)
- **Washington St** (B)

Bus Lines

- **57** · Watertown Yard—Kenmore Station via Newton Corner & Brighton Center
- **64** · Oak Square—Central Sq, Cambridge or Kendall/MIT
- **65** · Brighton Center—Kenmore Station via Washington St, Brookline Village
- **66** · Harvard Square—Dudley Station via Allston & Brookline
- **70** · Cedarwood, N Waltham or Watertown Sq—University Park via Central Sq
- **70A** · Cedarwood, N Waltham or Watertown Sq—University Park via Central Sq
- **86** · Sullivan Sq Station—Cleveland Circle via Harvard/John

Car Rental

- **Adventure Rent-A-Car** · 139 Brighton Ave
- **Budget** · 95 Brighton Ave
- **Enterprise** · 292 Western Ave
- **Enterprise** · 996 Commonwealth Ave
- **Ferris Service Station** · 455 Harvard St
- **U-Save Auto & Truck Rental** · 25 Harvard Ave

Car Washes

- **Allston Car Wash** · 434 Cambridge St
- **Shield System Cloth Car Wash** · 360 Western Ave

Gas Stations

- **Exxon** · 198 Western Ave
- **Gulf** · 226 Harvard Ave

Map 20 · **Harvard Square / Allston (North)**

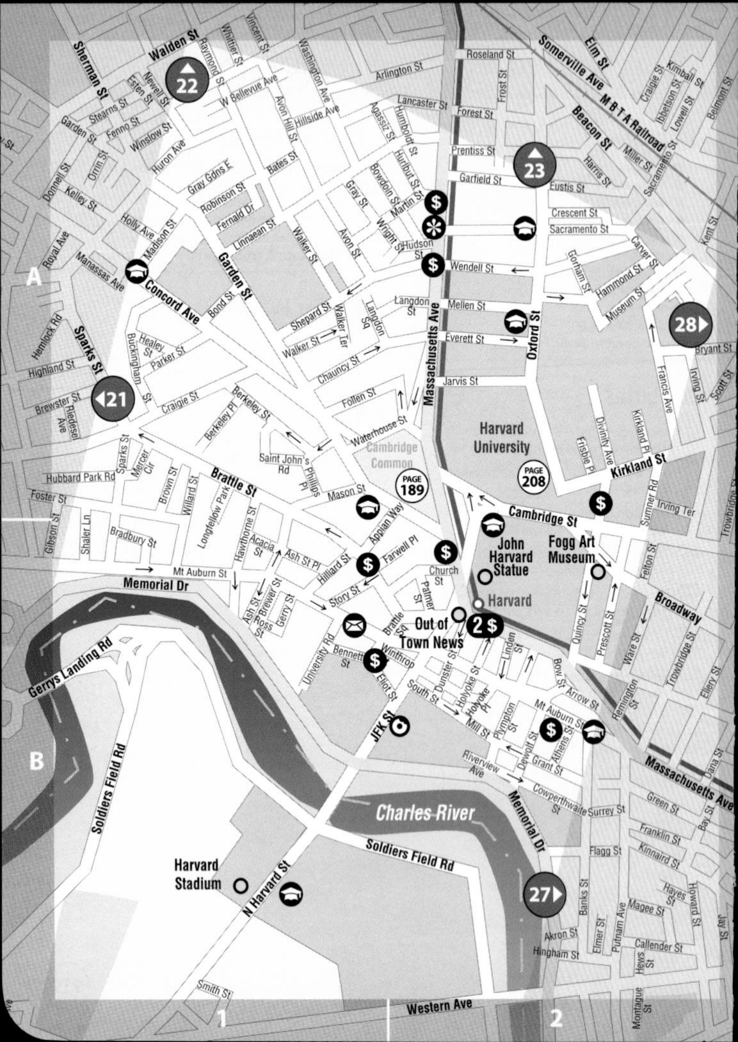

Like all vibrant neighborhoods, Harvard Square changes with time. Many long-timers bitterly resent the "mallification" of this area (having an Abercrombie where The Tasty and The Wursthaus used to be is indeed unsettling), but the fundamental character of Harvard Square remains, anchored by Out of Town News, street kids and competent buskers. And who's responsible for One Western Avenue in Allston? Yikes.

 Banks

· **Cambridge Savings Bank** ·
  1374 Massachusetts Ave
· **Cambridge Trust** · 1336 Massachusetts Ave
· **Cambridge Trust** · 1720 Massachusetts Ave
· **Fleet** · 1414 Massachusetts Ave
· **Fleet** · 1663 Massachusetts Ave
· **Fleet** · 28 Eliot St
· **Fleet** · 45 Quincy St
· **Fleet** · 67 Mt Auburn St
· **Wainwright Bank & Trust** · 44 Brattle St

 Donuts

· **Dunkin' Donuts** · 65 JFK St

 Landmarks

· **Fogg Art Museum** · 32 Quincy St
· **Harvard Stadium** · Soldiers Field Rd
· **John Harvard Statue** · Harvard Yard
· **Out of Town News** · 0 Harvard Sq

 Post Offices

· 125 Mt Auburn St

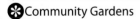 **Schools**

· **Boston Archdiocesan Choir School** ·
  29 Mt Auburn St
· **Harvard Business School** · Soldiers Field Rd
· **Harvard University** · 1350 Massachusetts Ave
· **Lesley University** · 29 Everett St
· **Maria L Baldwin School** · 28 Sacramento St
· **Radcliffe College** · 10 Garden St
· **St Peter's School** · 96 Concord Ave

Community Gardens

· **Sacramento Street Garden** ·
  Sacramento St at Massachusetts Ave

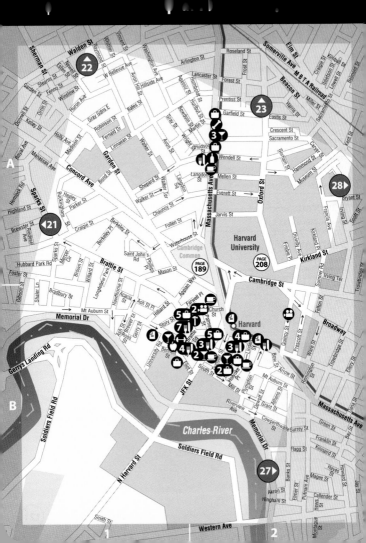

This area has some delightful restaurants, including expensive Rialto, less expensive Cambridge, 1, and even less expensive Grendel's. Bibliophiles will doubtlessly enjoy the 25+ bookstores. Beyond books, Harvard Square is a great place to shop for records and ice cream, but puzzlingly, not videos or liquor. What's up with this? If you just have to buy beer or wine in Harvard Square, go to Cardullo's.

Bars

- **Cambridge Common** · 1667 Massachusetts Ave
- **John Harvard's Brew House** · 33 Dunster St
- **Noir** · 1 Bennett St
- **Redline** · 59 JFK St
- **Shay's Lounge** · 58 JFK St
- **Temple Bar** · 1688 Massachusetts Ave
- **West Side Lounge** · 1680 Massachusetts Ave

Coffee

- **Peet's Coffee & Tea** · 100 Mt Auburn St
- **Starbucks** · 1662 Massachusetts Ave
- **Starbucks** · 31 Church St
- **Starbucks** · 36 JFK St

Copy Shops

- **Gnomon Copy** · 1304 Massachusetts Ave
- **Gnomon Copy** · 99 Mt Auburn St
- **Kinko's** · 1 Miffin Pl

Farmer's Markets

- **Cambridge/Charles Square** · 1 Bennett St

Gyms

- **Wellbridge Health and Fitness Center** · 5 Bennett St

Hardware Stores

- **Dickinson Brothers True Value** · 26 Brattle St

Liquor Stores

- **Harvard Wine** · 1664 Massachusetts Ave

Movie Theaters

- **Brattle Theatre** · 40 Brattle St
- **Harvard Film Archive** · 24 Quincy St
- **Loews Cineplex Harvard Square** · 10 Church St

Pet Shops

- **Cambridge Pet Care Center** · 1724 Massachusetts Ave

Restaurants

- **9 Tastes** · 50 JFK St
- **Border Cafe** · 32 Church St
- **Brother Jimmy's BBQ** · 96 Winthrop St
- **Caffe Paradiso** · 1 Eliot Sq
- **Cambridge, 1** · 27 Church St
- **Casablanca** · 40 Brattle St
- **Chez Henri** · 1 Shepard St
- **Finale** · 30 Dunster St
- **Greenhouse Coffee Shop** · 3 Brattle St
- **Grendel's Den** · 89 Winthrop St
- **Harvest** · 44 Brattle St
- **Hi-Rise Bread Company** · 56 Brattle St
- **John Harvard's Brew House** · 33 Dunster St
- **Mr & Mrs Bartley's Burger Cottage** · 1246 Massachusetts Ave
- **Pho Pasteur** · 36 Dunster St
- **Rialto** · 1 Bennett St
- **Shilla** · 57 JFK St
- **UpStairs on the Square** · 91 Winthrop St
- **Veggie Planet** · 47 Palmer St

Shopping

- **Alpha Omega** · 57 JFK St
- **Black Ink** · 5 Brattle St
- **Bob Slate** · 1288 Massachusetts Ave
- **Cardullo's Gourmet Shoppe** · 6 Brattle St
- **City Sports** · 16 Dunster St
- **Crate & Barrel** · 48 Brattle St
- **Harvard Coop** · 1400 Massachusetts Ave
- **Herrell's Ice Cream** · 15 Dunster St
- **Leavitt & Pierce** · 1316 Massachusetts Ave
- **Newbury Comics** · 36 JFK St
- **Nini's Corner** · 1394 Massachusetts Ave
- **Nomad** · 1741 Massachusetts Ave
- **Out of Town News** · 0 Harvard Sq
- **Planet Records** · 54B JFK St
- **Staples** · 57 JFK St
- **Stereo Jack's** · 1686 Massachusetts Ave
- **Tannery** · 11A Brattle St
- **Tess** · 20 Brattle St
- **Tweeter Etc** · 104 Mt Auburn St
- **Twisted Village** · 12B Eliot St

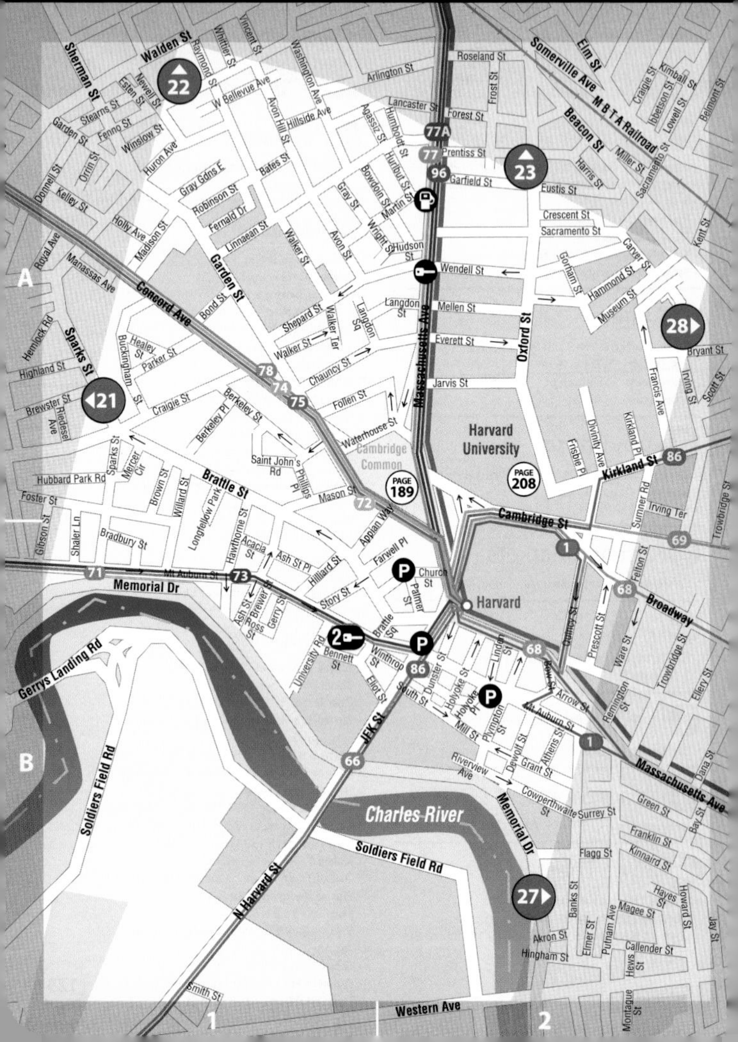

Map 20 • Harvard Square / Allston (North)

Sherman St

Walden St

▲ 22

Elm St

Somerville Ave M B T A Railroad

Roseland St

Frost St

Beacon St

Craigie St

Kimball St

Robinson St

Lowell St

Hubbard St

Kent St

Stearns St

Fenn St

Winslow Ave

W Bellevue Ave

Arlington St

Lancaster St

Forest St

77A

77

Prentiss St

96

Garfield St

Miller Ave

Harris St

Hollis Ave

Garden Gdns E

Bates St

Martin St

Wright St

Hudson St

Eustis St

Crescent St

Sacramento St

▲ 23

Huron Ave

Robinson Dr

Fernald Dr

Linnaean St

Avon St

Gorham St

Hammond St

Museum St

A

Kelley St

Holly Ave

Madison St

Garden St

Shepard St

Walker St

Wendell St

Langdon St

Mellen St

Everett St

Jarvis St

Oxford St

Francis Ave

Irving Ave

Scott St

28 ▶

Bryant St

Manassas Ave

Hemlock Rd

Highland St

Sparks St

◀ 21

Brewster St

Kirkland St

86

Divinity Ave

Frisbie Pl

Sumner Rd

Irving Ter

Trowbridge St

Buckingham St

Healey St

Parker St

78

74

75

Chauncy St

Follen St

Harvard
University

PAGE
208

Hubbard Park Rd

Foster St

Mercer Cir

Berkeley St

Berkeley Pl

Saint John's Rd

Waterhouse St

Cambridge
Common

PAGE
189

Cambridge St

1

69

Broadway

68

Shaler Ln

Bradbury St

Gibson St

71

Brattle St

Longfellow Park

Hawthorne St

Acacia St

Ash St

Hilliard St

Mason St

72

Appian Way

Farwell Pl

Church St

P

Palmer St

Story St

Harvard

Prescott St

Ware St

Wendell St

Memorial Dr

73

Story St

Brewster St

Gerry's St

Bennett St

2

University Rd

Winthrop St

86

JFK St

P

P

Mt Auburn St

Arrow St

1

Eliot St

Dunster St

Holyoke St

Plympton St

P

Bow St

Mill St

DeWolfe St

Grant St

Cowperthwaite St

Surrey St

Green St

Gerry's Landing Rd

66

Riverview Ave

Franklin St

Kinnaird St

Soldiers Field Rd

Charles River

Memorial Dr

Soldiers Field Rd

27 ▶

Akron St

Hingham St

Banks St

Putnam Ave

Magee St

Callender St

N Harvard St

Smith St

Western Ave

B

1

2

Driving and street parking in the immediate vicinity of Harvard Square are difficult, so it's handy that this is a genuine public transportation hub. If you come to this area often, check the routes of the many buses that pass through the underground Harvard Station bus depot. Maybe someday Harvard will fund a rail connection in Allston.

Subway
■ · **Harvard**

Bus Lines

- **1** · Harvard/Holyoke Gate—Dudley Station via Mass Ave & BU Medical Center
- **66** · Harvard Square—Dudley Station via Allston & Brookline
- **68** · Harvard/Holyoke Gate—Kendall/MIT via Broadway
- **69** · Harvard/Holyoke—Lechmere Station via Cambridge St
- **71** · Watertown Square—Harvard Station via Mt Auburn St
- **72** · Huron Ave—Harvard Station via Concord Ave
- **73** · Waverley Sq—Harvard Station via Trapelo Road
- **74** · Belmont Center—Harvard Station via Concord Ave
- **75** · Belmont Center—Harvard Station via Concord Ave
- **77** · Arlington Heights—Harvard Station via Massachusetts
- **77A** · North Cambridge—Harvard Station Local
- **78** · Arlmont Village—Harvard Station via Park Circle
- **86** · Sullivan Sq Station—Cleveland Circle via Harvard/Johnston Gate
- **96** · Medford Square—Harvard Station via George St & Davis Sq

Car Rental

- **Alamo** · 1663 Massachusetts Ave
- **Avis** · 1 Bennett St
- **Thrifty** · 110 Mt Auburn St

Gas Stations

- **Gulf** · 1725 Massachusetts Ave

Parking

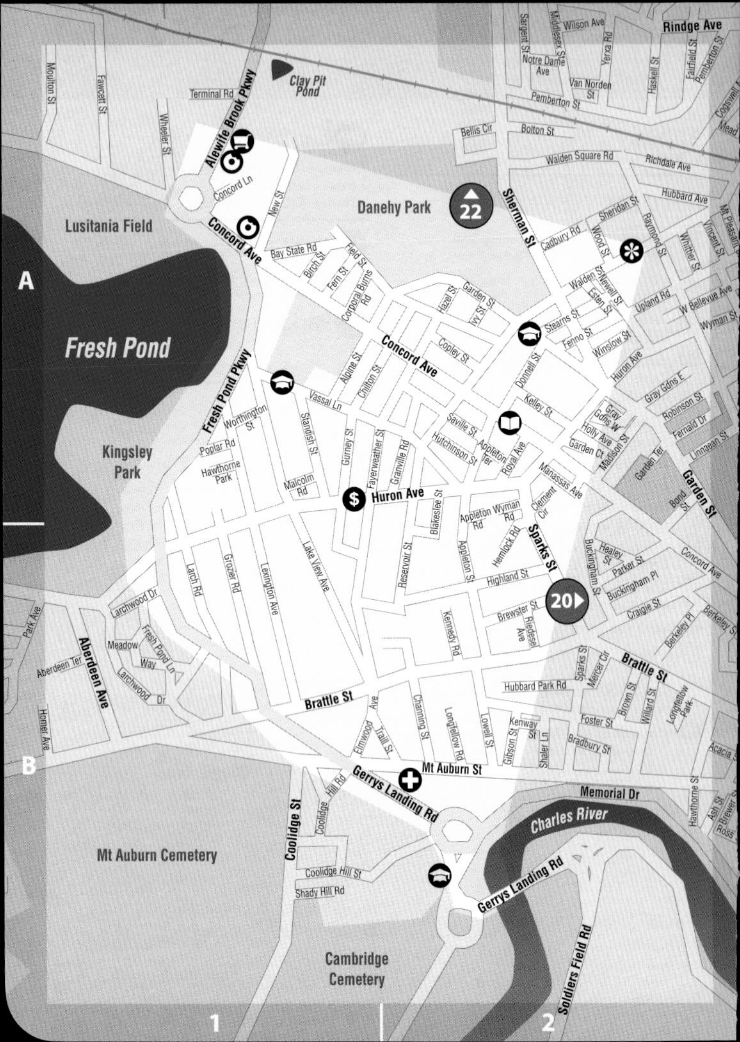

Map 21 · **West Cambridge**

N

Rindge Ave

Moulton St
Fawcett St
Wheeler St

Terminal Rd
Clay Pit Pond

Concord Ln

New St

Alewife Brook Pkwy

Concord Ave

Sargent St
Wilson Ave
McKinley Ave

Notre Dame Ave
Van Norden St
Pemberton St

Bellis Cir
Bolton St

Walden Square Rd
Richdale Ave
Hubbard Ave

Sherman St

22

Danehy Park

Cadbury Rd
Sheridan St

Sherman St
Cogswell Ave
Harvey St

Lusitania Field

Bay State Rd

Field St
Biron St
Concord Burns

Fern St

Garden St
Hurd St

Walden St
Chester St

Upland Rd
W Bellevue Ave
Wyman St

Concord Ave

Copley St

Stearns St
Donnel St
Fenno St

Winslow St

Fresh Pond

Agassiz St
Clifton St
Vassal Ln

Gurney St
Fayerweather St
Granville Rd

Kelley St

Seville St
Hutchinson St
Agassiz Ter
Royal Ave

Holly Ave
Garden Ct
Garden Outlook

Gray Gdns E
Robinson St
Fernald Dr

Linnaean St

Gadne Ter

Garden St

Fresh Pond Pkwy

Worthington St
Poplar Rd

Hawthorne Park

Slamesh St

Lake View Ave

Larch Rd

Griswold Rd

Lexington Ave

$

Huron Ave

Malcolm Rd

Reservoir St
Blackstone St

Appleton Wyman Rd
Rd

Clement St
Manassas Ave

Sparks St

Healey St
Channing St
Parker St
Buckingham Pl
Craigie St

Concord Ave
Berkeley St
Berkeley Pl

20

Kingsley Park

Park Ave
Aberdeen Ave
Home Ave

Larchwood Dr
Meadow Way
Larchwood Dr

Fresh Pond Ln

Appleton St
Hemlock Rd

Highland St

Kennedy Rd

Brewster St
Frederick
St

Brattle St

Sparks St
Manassas Cir
Scott St
Brown St
Willard St

Acacia St

Brattle St

Hubbard Park Rd

Foster St
Kenway
Gibson St
Lowell St
Sibley Ln
Berkeley St

Bradbury St

Channing Ave
Tyall St

Elmwood Ave

Coolidge St

Mt Auburn St

Gerrys Landing Rd

✚

Memorial Dr

Coolidge Hill Rd

Coolidge Hill St

Shady Hill Rd

Mt Auburn Cemetery

Charles River

Gerrys Landing Rd

Soldiers Field Rd

Cambridge Cemetery

A

B

1

2

Map 21

With its trees, sizeable lots and nice homes, West Cambridge is a very pleasant place to live for those who can afford it. Quiet streets provide respite from the urban bustle that characterizes the rest of Cambridge. Otherwise, it's boring, and the walk to either Harvard Square and Porter Square can seem pretty long during a Nor'easter…

Banks

· **Cambridge Trust** · 353 Huron Ave

Donuts

· **Dunkin' Donuts** · 201 Alewife Brook Pkwy
· **Dunkin' Donuts** · 517 Concord Ave

Hospitals

· **Mount Auburn Hospital** · 330 Mt Auburn St

Libraries

· **Boudreau** · 245 Concord Ave

Schools

· **Buckingham Browne & Nichols School** ·
  80 Gerrys Landing Rd
· **Cambridge Montessori School** · 161 Garden St
· **John M Tobin School** · 197 Vassal Ln

 Supermarkets

· **Whole Foods Market** · 200 Alewife Brook Pkwy

Community Gardens

· **Corcoran Park Garden** · Walden St at Lincoln Way

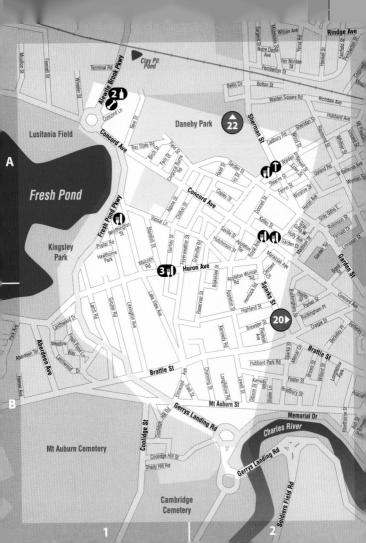

There aren't many options for entertainment or shopping in this predominantly residential area, and although there are decent places to eat, there's nothing here worth making a special trip for.

Hardware Stores

· **Masse Hardware** · 249 Walden St

Liquor Stores

· **Kappy's Liquors** · 215 Alewife Brook Pkwy
· **Mall Discount Liquors & Wines** ·
  202 Alewife Brook Pkwy

Pet Shops

· **Pet Supply Outlet Store** · 211 Alewife Brook Pkwy

Restaurants

· **Aspasia** · 377 Walden St
· **Full Moon** · 344 Huron Ave
· **Hi-Rise Bread Company** · 208 Concord Ave
· **Il Buongustaio** · 370 Huron Ave
· **Real Pizza** · 359 Huron Ave
· **Tokyo** · 307 Fresh Pond Pkwy
· **Trattoria Pulcinella** · 147 Huron Ave

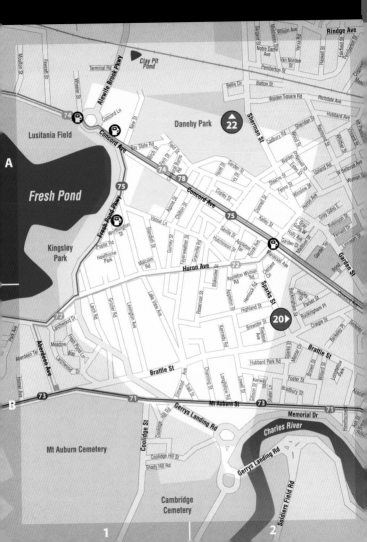

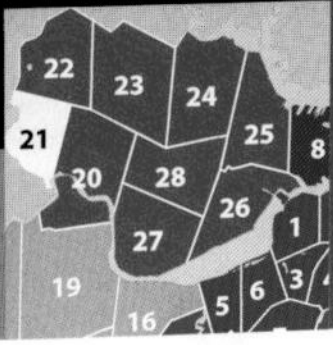

Map 21

Got a car with a Cambridge sticker? You're set. No car? You're screwed. Car, but no sticker? Still screwed. Have fun.

Bus Lines

- **71** • Watertown Square—Harvard Station via Mt Auburn St
- **72** • Huron Ave—Harvard Station via Concord Ave
- **73** • Waverley Sq—Harvard Station via Trapelo Road
- **74** • Belmont Center—Harvard Station via Concord Ave
- **75** • Belmont Center—Harvard Station via Concord Ave
- **78** • Arlmont Village—Harvard Station via Park Circle

Gas Stations

- **Citgo** • 199 Concord Ave
- **Gulf** • 260 Lexington Ave
- **Shell** • 603 Concord Ave
- **Sunoco** • 515 Concord Ave

Map 22 • **North Cambridge / West Somerville**

Davis Square's popularity grew in the 1990s as younger types seeking a cool but still somewhat affordable neighborhood moved in. The rush has passed, but Davis Square is still enjoyed by residents and passers-through alike. Traditionally working-class North Cambridge and West Somerville now attract a number of Tufts students and young professionals seeking a balance of convenience and (relatively) cheaper housing.

Banks

- **Atlantic Bank** · 2067 Massachusetts Ave
- **Century Bank** · 2309 Massachusetts Ave
- **Wainwright Bank & Trust** ·
  174 Alewife Brook Pkwy

Donuts

- **Hub Donuts** · 199 Alewife Brook Pkwy

O Landmarks

- **Cambridge School of Culinary Arts** ·
  2020 Massachusetts Ave
- **Somerville Theatre** · 55 Davis Sq

Libraries

- **O'Neill** · 70 Ridge Ave

Post Offices

- 58 Day St

Schools

- **Benjamin Banneker Charter School** ·
  21 Notre Dame Ave
- **Cambridge Friends School** · 5 Cadbury Rd
- **Cambridge School of Culinary Arts** ·
  2020 Massachusetts Ave
- **M E Fitzgerald School** · 70 Ridge Ave
- **Matignon High School** · 1 Matignon Rd
- **North Cambridge Catholic High School** ·
  40 Norris St
- **Powder House Community School** ·
  1060 Broadway
- **St John the Evangelist's School** · 122 Ridge Ave
- **Tufts University** · 205 Packard Ave

✴ Community Gardens

- **Don McMath Park Community Garden** ·
  Pemberton St & Sherman St
- **Whittemore Avenue Garden** · Whittemore Ave

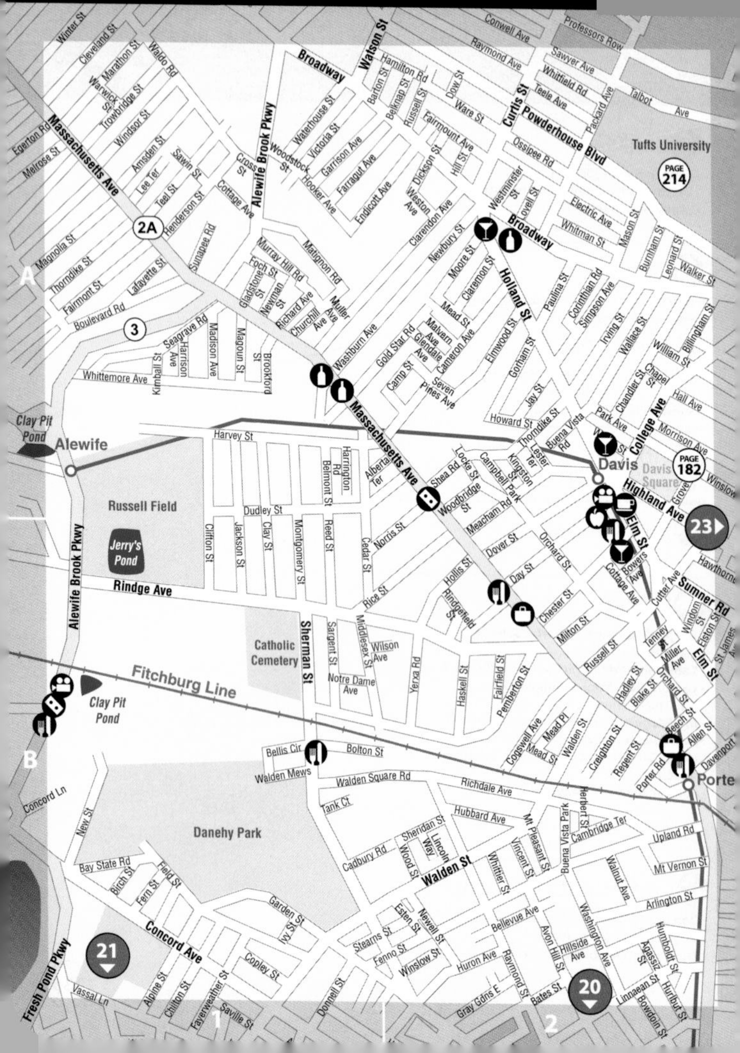

Map 22 • **North Cambridge / West Som**

Tufts University

PAGE 214

Winter St
Cleveland St
Marathon St
Vernon St
Trowbridge St
Windsor St
Cottage Ave
Aberdeen St
Seven St
Teel St
Henderson St

Conwell St
Broadway
Watson St
Hamilton Rd
Raymond Ave
Professors Row
Sawyer Ave
Whitfield Rd
Teele Ave
Talbot Ave

Egerton Rd
Massachusetts Ave
Melrose St

Barton St
Wallace St
Victoria Ave
Woodstock St
Garrison Ave
Farnount Ave
Hooker Ave
Endicott Ave

Curtis St
Powderhouse Blvd
Ossipee Rd

Magnolia St
Thorndike St
Fairmont St
Boulevard Rd

2A

Murray Hill Rd
Loomis St
Richard Ave
Churchill Ave
Miller St
Washburn Ave

Broadway
Newbury St
Moore St
Claremont St
Mead St
Gold Star Rd
Elmwood St

Electric Ave
Whitman St
Lowell St
Westminster
Paulina St

Burnham St
Walker St
William St

3

Whittemore Ave
Kimball Ave
Madison Ave
Brookford St
Magoun St

Melvin Ave
Gladding Ave
Carre St
Pines St
Sevan St

Corinthian Rd
Simpson Ave
Irving St
Wallace St

Chandler St
Chapel St
Hall Ave

Clay Pit Pond
Alewife

Harvey St
Massachusetts Ave
Howard St
Gorham St
Thorndike St
Buena Vista

College Ave
Morrison Ave

Harrington
Belmont St
Shea Rd
Locke St
Campbell Rd
Kingston St

Davis
Davis Square
Highland Ave
Elm St
Winslow

PAGE 182

23

Russell Field
Dudley St
Jackson St
Clay St
Montgomery St
Reed St
Nortis St
Cedar St
Woodbine St
Meacham Rd
Dover St
Orchard St
Day St
College Ave

Sumner Rd
Hawthorne

Jerry's Pond

Rice St
Hollis St
Rindge Ave
Chester St
Milton St

Russell St
Hadley St
Tenney St
Blake St
Miller St
Elm St

Fairfield St
Pemberton St
Pennsylvania St

Conwell St
Mead Pl
Creighton St

Cornell St
Porter Rd
Regent St
Allen St
Davenport

Porte

Fitchburg Line
Clay Pit Pond

Catholic Cemetery
Sherman St
Sargent St
Middlesex St
Wilson Ave
Notre Dame Ave
Haskell St

Bellis Cir
Bolton St
Walden Mews
Walden Square Rd
Richdale Ave

Herbert St
Cambridge Ter
Upland Rd

Concord Ln
Danehy Park

Tank Ct
Cadbury Rd
Sheridan Way
Lincoln Way
Wood Sq
Hubbard Ave
Mt Pleasant St
Vincent St
Whittier St

Buena Vista Park
Walnut Ave
Mt Vernon St

New St
Bay State Rd
Field St
Birch St
Stearns St
Fenno St
Winslow St
Garden St
Newell St
Bellevue Ave
Avon Hill St
Hillside Ave
Arlington St
Agassiz St

21

Concord Ave
Huron Ave
Gray Gdns E
Bates St

20

Vassal Ln
Copley St
Saville St
Dunster St
Gray Gdns E
Linnaean St
Hurlbut St

Fresh Pond Pkwy

1   2

Johnny D's Uptown continues to book an interesting assortment of live acts, and should be checked out by any music lover. Across the street, live music is occasionally on the bill at the Somerville Theatre, which also shows good late-run movies. Redbones has great barbecue and an expansive beer selection.

Bars

- **Johnny D's Uptown** · 17 Holland St
- **PJ Ryan's** · 239 Holland St
- **Redbones** · 55 Chester St

Coffee

- **Someday Cafe** · 51 Davis Sq

Farmer's Markets

- **Somerville** · Day St and Herbert St

Liquor Stores

- **Buy Rite Liquors** · 2440 Massachusetts Ave
- **Norton Beverage** · 2451 Massachusetts Ave
- **Teele Square Liquors** · 1119 Broadway

Movie Theaters

- **Loews Cineplex Fresh Pond** ·
  168 Alewife Brook Pkwy
- **Somerville Theatre** · 55 Davis Sq

Restaurants

- **Cafe Barada** · 2269 Massachusetts Ave
- **Elephant Walk** · 2067 Massachusetts Ave
- **Jasper White's Summer Shack** ·
  149 Alewife Brook Pkwy
- **Jose's** · 131 Sherman St
- **Redbones** · 55 Chester St

Shopping

- **Bicycle Exchange** · 2067 Massachusetts Ave
- **Daddy's Junky Music** · 2238 Massachusetts Ave

Video Rental

- **Blockbuster** · 180 Alewife Brook Pkwy
- **Palmer Video** · 2368 Massachusetts Ave

Tufts University

PAGE 214

Davis Square

PAGE 182

Russell Field

Jerry's Pond

Clay Pit Pond

Clay Pit Pond

Fitchburg Line

Catholic Cemetery

Danehy Park

Walden St

Concord Ave

Porte

Rindge Ave

Sherman St

Notre Dame Ave

Alewife

Remember that the 77A bus will take you down Mass Ave to Harvard Square, but not on weekends—for that, you'll have to look for the 77 bus. Parking around here is a lot saner than in other parts of Cambridge and Somerville but, predictably, tightens up the closer you get to Davis Square.

Subway

- ■ **Porter**
- ■ **Davis**
- ■ **Alewife**

Bus Lines

- **74** • Belmont Center—Harvard Station via Concord Ave
- **75** • Belmont Center—Harvard Station via Concord Ave
- **77** • Arlington Heights—Harvard Station via Massachusetts
- **77A** • North Cambridge—Harvard Station Local
- **78** • Arlmont Village—Harvard Station via Park Circle
- **79** • Arlington Heights—Alewife Station via Massachusetts Ave
- **83** • Rindge Ave—Central Sq, Cambridge via Porter Square Station
- **87** • Arlington Center or Clarendon Hill—Lechmere Station
- **88** • Clarendon Hill- Lechmere Station via Highland Ave
- **89** • Clarendon Hill- Sullivan Sq Station via Broadway
- **90** • Davis Square—Wellington Station via Sullivan Square Station
- **96** • Medford Square—Harvard Station via George St & Davis Sq
- **350** • North Burlington—Alewife Station via Burlington

Car Rental

- • **U-Haul** • 2480 Massachusetts Ave

Car Washes

- • **Cambridge Car Wash** • 2013 Massachusetts Ave

Gas Stations

- • **Jack's Gas** • 2535 Massachusetts Ave
- • **Massachusetts Avenue Firestone** • 2480 Massachusetts Ave
- • **Mobil** • 2615 Massachusetts Ave

Parking

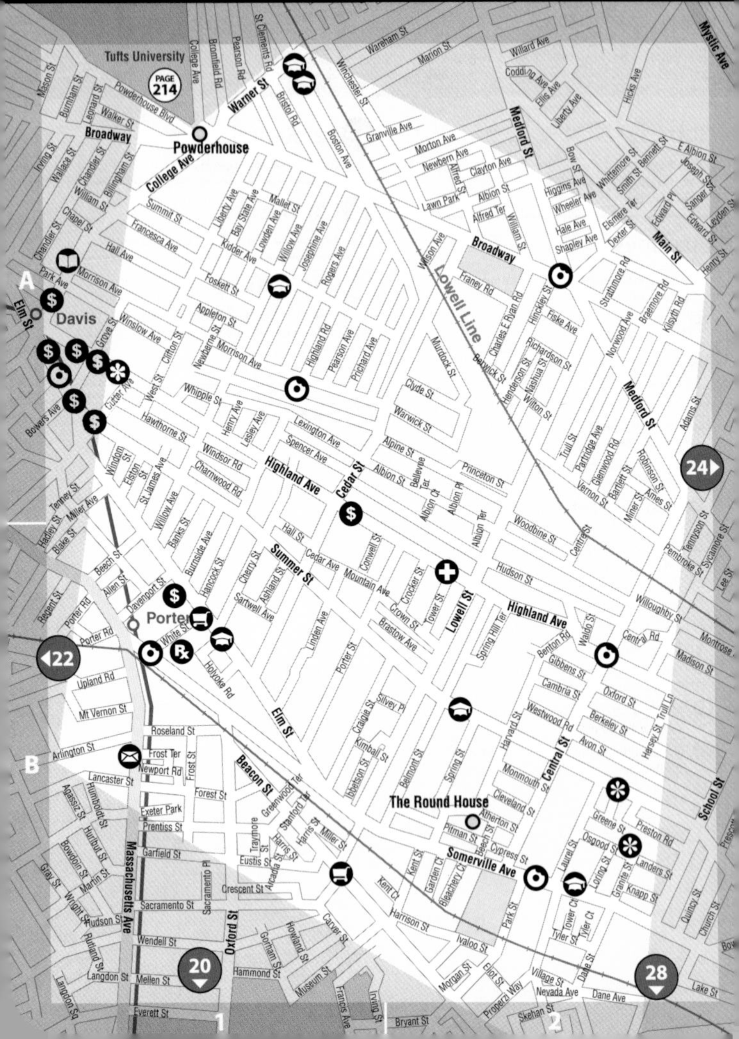

Map 23 • **Central Somerville / Porter Square**

Tufts University
PAGE
214

Broadway

Powderhouse

College Ave

Davis

Porter

The Round House

Somerville Ave

Massachusetts Ave

Lowell Line

Broadway

Highland Ave

Highland Ave

A

B

22

24

20

28

1

Porter Square is often forgotten, stuck as it is between its neighbors on the Red Line, Harvard Square and Davis Square. Still, there's a good mix here of decent places to live and things to do, and the location is pretty convenient to many other parts of town. Away from Porter Square and the eastern edge of Davis Square is the dense, hilly core of residential Somerville.

Banks

- **Cambridge Savings Bank** · 53 White St
- **Central Bank** · 399 Highland Ave
- **Citizens** · 212 Elm St
- **East Cambridge Savings Bank** · 285 Highland Ave
- **Middlesex Federal Savings** · 1 College Ave
- **Sovereign Bank** · 403 Highland Ave
- **Wainwright Bank & Trust** · 250 Elm St
- **Winter Hill Bank** · 5 Cutter Ave

Donuts

- **Dunkin' Donuts** · 1 White St
- **Dunkin' Donuts** · 154 Highland Ave
- **Dunkin' Donuts** · 244 Elm St
- **Dunkin' Donuts** · 504 Broadway
- **Dunkin' Donuts** · 519 Somerville Ave
- **Russ' Donuts** · 2 Highland Rd

Hospitals

- **Somerville Hospital** · 230 Highland Ave

O Landmarks

- **Powderhouse** · College Ave & Broadway
- **The Round House** · 36 Atherton St

Libraries

- **Somerville West** · 40 College Ave

Pharmacies

- **CVS** · 35 White St

Post Offices

- · 1953 Massachusetts Ave

Schools

- **Benjamin G Brown School** · 201 Willow Ave
- **John F Kennedy School** · 85 Elm St
- **St Anthony's School** · 480 Somerville Ave
- **St Catherine's of Genoa School** · 192 Summer St
- **St Clement's Elementary School** · 589 Boston Ave
- **St Clement's High School** · 579 Boston Ave

Supermarkets

- **Star Market** · 275 Beacon St
- **Star Market** · 49 White St

Community Gardens

- **Avon Street Garden** · 117 Summer St
- **Bikeway Garden** · 393 Highland Ave
- **Osgood Garden** · Osgood St

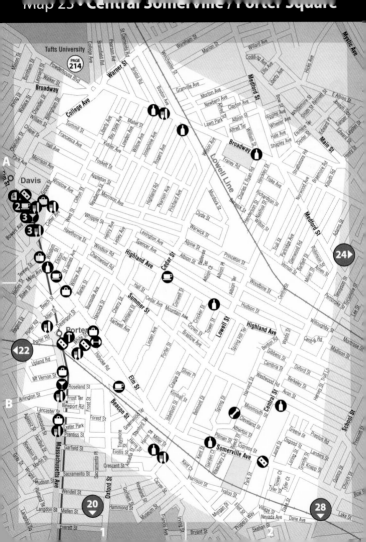

Map 23 · Central Somerville / Porter Square

In this area, the closer you are to the Red Line, the better your choices. For a slice of Japan in 02140, check out the Porter Exchange (next to the Porter T stop) and its Japanese supermarkets and food stalls. Hamburgerologists owe themselves a trip to R.F. O'Sullivan's.

Bars

- **Christopher's** · 1920 Massachusetts Ave
- **Joshua Tree** · 256 Elm St
- **Sligo Pub** · 237A Elm St
- **The Burren** · 247 Elm St

Coffee

- **Cafe Rossini** · 278 Highland Ave
- **Carberry's Bakery & Coffee House** · 187 Elm St
- **Diesel Cafe** · 257 Elm St
- **Starbucks** · 260 Elm St
- **Starbucks** · 729 Somerville Ave

Copy Shops

- **Sir Speedy Printing Center** · 260 Elm St

Gyms

- **HealthWorks Fitness Center** · 36 White St

Hardware Stores

- **Tags Ace Hardware** · 29 White St

Liquor Stores

- **Ball Square Fine Wines & Liquors** · 716 Broadway
- **Blue Label Liquors** · 2 Carter St
- **City Side Liquors** · 594 Somerville Ave
- **Crowley's Liquors** · 152 Boston Ave
- **Downtown Wine & Spirits** · 225 Elm St
- **Seven Hills Wine & Spirits** · 288 Beacon St
- **Somerville Wine & Spirits** · 235 Highland Ave
- **Woody's Liquors** · 523 Broadway

Pet Shops

- **Big Fish, Little Fish** · 55 Elm Pl

 Restaurants

- **Anna's Taqueria** · 236 Elm St
- **Anna's Taqueria** · 822 Somerville Ave
- **Blue Fin** · 1815 Massachusetts Ave
- **Christopher's** · 1920 Massachusetts Ave
- **Diva Indian Bistro** · 246 Elm St
- **Kaya** · 1924 Massachusetts Ave
- **Out of the Blue** · 382 Highland Ave
- **RF O'Sullivan's** · 282 Beacon St
- **Rosebud Diner** · 381 Summer St
- **Savannah Grill** · 233 Elm St
- **Sound Bites** · 708 Broadway

Shopping

- **Ace Wheelworks** · 145 Elm St
- **Bob Slate** · 1975 Massachusetts Ave
- **CD Spins** · 235 Elm St
- **City Sports** · 1815 Massachusetts Ave
- **Disc Diggers** · 401 Highland Ave
- **Nuggets** · 46 White St

Video Rental

- **Blockbuster** · 1 Porter Sq
- **City Video** · 23 White St
- **Hollywood Express** · 238 Elm St
- **Massive Video** · 519 Somerville Ave

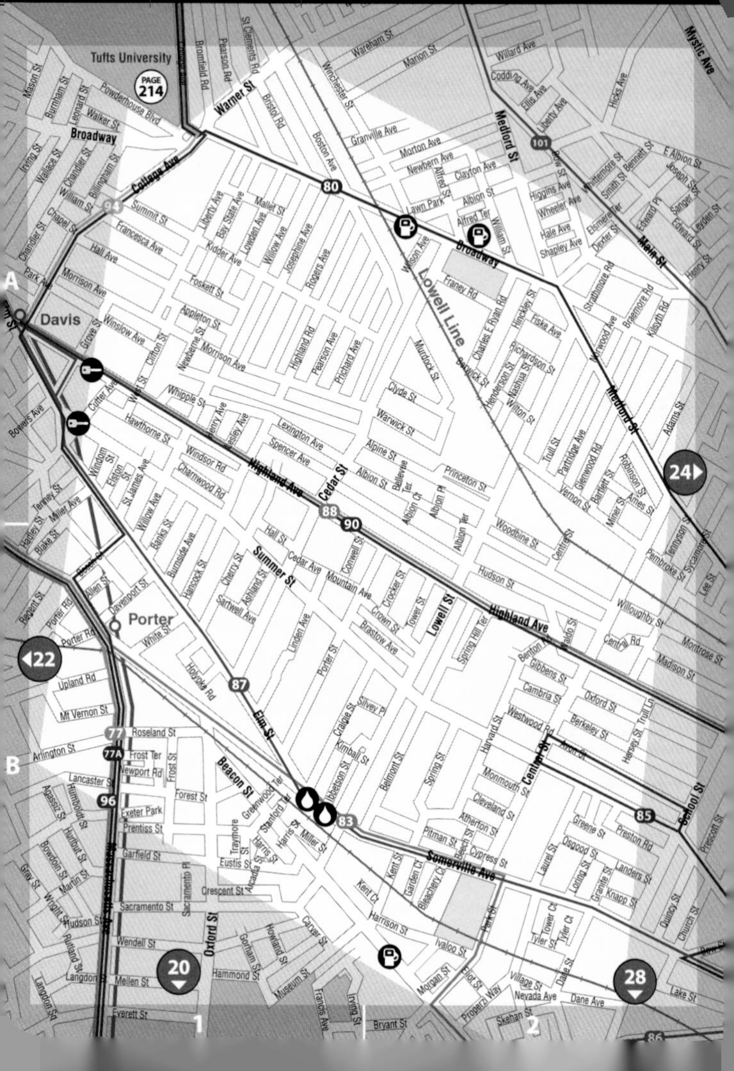
Tufts University
PAGE 214
Mason St
Burnham St
Leonard St
Powderhouse Blvd
Walker St
Broadway
Irving St
Wallace St
Chandler St
Billingham St
William St
Chapel St
College Ave
Summit St
Francesca Ave
Hall Ave
Park Ave
Morrison Ave
Davis
Grove St
Winslow Ave
Clifton St
Bowers Ave
Cutter Ave
West St
Whipple St
Hawthorne St
Windom St
Erston St
St James Ave
Willow Ave
Banks St
Terney St
Miller Ave
Hadley St
Blake St
Beech St
Allen St
Davenport St
Porter
White St
Regent St
Porter Rd
22
Upland Rd
Mt Vernon St
Arlington St
Roseland St
Frost Ter
Newport Rd
Frost St
Lancaster St
Agassiz St
Humboldt St
Forest St
Exeter Park
Prentiss St
Hurlbut St
Bowdoin St
Martin St
Garfield St
Gray St
Wright St
Hudson St
Sacramento St
Crescent St
Sacramento Pl
Eustis St
Traymore St
Rutland St
Wendell St
Oxford St
Gorham St
Howland St
Langdon Sq
Langdon St
Mellen St
Hammond St
Everett St
Museum St
Francis Ave
Irving St
Bryant St
Massachusetts Ave
1
2
20
Bromfield Rd
Pearson Rd
St Clements Rd
Warner St
Bristol Rd
Winchester St
Wareham St
Marion St
Granville Ave
Boston Ave
Morton Ave
Newbern Ave
Alfred St
Clayton Ave
Albion St
Alfred Ter
Lawn Park
William St
Wilson Ave
Broadway
Liberty Ave
Bay State Ave
Mallet St
Lowden Ave
Kidder Ave
Willow Ave
Josephine Ave
Rogers Ave
Foskett St
Appleton St
Newberne St
Morrison Ave
Highland Rd
Pearson Ave
Prichard Ave
Lowell Line
Franey Rd
Murdock St
Berwick St
Clyde St
Warwick St
Henry Ave
Wesley Ave
Windsor Rd
Charnwood Rd
Lexington Ave
Spencer Ave
Alpine St
Bellevue Ter
Albion St
Albion Ct
Albion Pl
Albion Ter
Princeton St
Highland Ave
Cedar St
Hall St
Summer St
Cedar Ave
Mountain Ave
Conwell St
Crocker St
Crown St
Tower St
Lowell St
Brastow Ave
Cherry St
Ashland St
Sartwell Ave
Burnside Ave
Hancock St
Linden Ave
Porter St
Holyoke Rd
Elm St
Beacon St
Greenwood Ter
Stanford Ter
Harris St
Arcadia St
Miller St
Ibbetson St
Kimball St
Craigie St
Silvey Pl
Belmont St
Spring St
Spring Hill Ter
Woodbine St
Hudson St
Highland Ave
Willard Ave
Codding Ave
Ellis Ave
Liberty Ave
Medford St
Hicks Ave
Mystic Ave
Vinal Ave
Higgins Ave
Wheeler Ave
Hale Ave
Shapley Ave
Whitemore St
Smith St
Bennett St
Elsmere Ter
Dexter St
E Albion St
Joseph St
Sanger St
Edward Pl
Edward St
Leyden St
Henry St
Main St
Strathmore Rd
Braemore Rd
Kilsyth Rd
Charles E Ryan Rd
Hinckley St
Fiske Ave
Richardson St
Nashua St
Henderson St
Wilton St
Norwood Ave
Medford St
Adams St
Trull St
Partridge Ave
Glenwood Rd
Bartlett St
Robinson St
Vernon St
Miner St
Ames St
Central St
Tennyson St
Sycamore St
Pembroke St
Lee St
Willoughby St
Waldo St
Benton Rd
Gibbens St
Cambria St
Central Rd
Montrose St
Madison St
Oxford St
Berkeley St
Westwood Rd
Harvard St
Avon St
Hersey St
Trull Ln
Monmouth St
Central St
Cleveland St
Atherton St
School St
Prescott St
Pitman St
Beech St
Cypress St
Somerville Ave
Greene St
Preston Rd
Osgood St
Landers St
Knapp St
Granite St
Loring St
Laurel St
Kent St
Garden Ct
Bleachery Ct
Kent Ct
Harrison St
Carver St
Ivaloo St
Park St
Tower Ct
Tyler Ct
Tyler St
Dane St
Quincy St
Church St
Morgan St
Eliot St
Properzi Way
Village St
Nevada Ave
Dane Ave
Skehan St
Lake St
28
24
A
B
80
94
88
90
87
101
77
77A
96
83
85
86

Thanks largely to the Red Line, Porter Square is well served by public transportation. To get from Porter Square to North Station during rush hour in a hurry, consider taking the commuter rail instead of the subway. Metered parking is (relatively) easy to find along Mass Ave, but more difficult to locate across the line in Somerville.

Subway
■ • Porter

Bus Lines
- 77 • Arlington Heights—Harvard Station via Massachusetts
- 77A • North Cambridge—Harvard Station Local
- 80 • Arlington Center—Lechmere Station via Medford Hills
- 83 • Rindge Ave—Central Sq, Cambridge via Porter Square Station
- 85 • Spring Hill—Kendall/MIT Station via Summer St & Union
- 86 • Sullivan Sq Station—Cleveland Circle via Harvard/John
- 88 • Clarendon Hill- Lechmere Station via Highland Ave
- 90 • Davis Square—Wellington Station via Sullivan Square Station
- 94 • Medford Square—Davis Sq Station via W Medford & Medford
- 96 • Medford Square—Harvard Station via George St & Davis Sq
- 101 • Malden Center Station— Sullivan Square Station

Car Rental
- **Aardvark Auto Rental** • 378 Highland Ave
- **Enterprise** • 377 Summer St

Car Washes
- **Lechmere Auto Wash** • 664 Somerville Ave
- **Somerville Car Wash** • 680 Somerville Ave

Gas Stations
- **Gulf** • 225 Beacon St
- **Shield Service Station** • 620 Broadway
- **Sunoco** • 541 Broadway

Map 24 · **Winter Hill / Union Square**

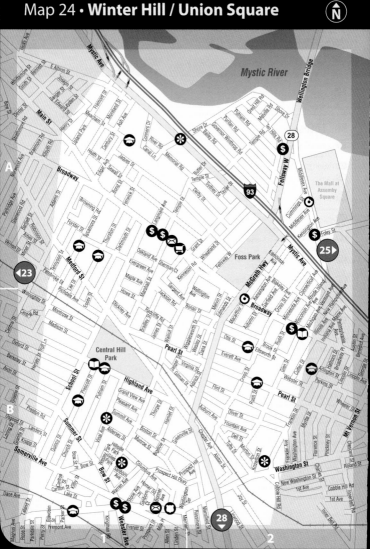

This area is home to Somerville City Hall, the city library, and plenty of streets that most outsiders find impossible to navigate. Union Square continues to be on its way up, attracting people who enjoy the vibe of Cambridge but can't afford to live there. Prospect Hill was where, on January 1, 1776, the first flag of the American colonies was raised.

Banks

- **Century Bank** • 102 Fellsway West
- **Citizens** • 328 Broadway
- **Citizens** • 40 Union Sq
- **Fleet** • 5 Middlesex Ave
- **Fleet** • 68 Union Sq
- **Sovereign Bank** • 125 Broadway
- **Winter Hill Bank** • 342 Broadway

Donuts

- **Dunkin' Donuts** • 220 Broadway
- **Dunkin' Donuts** • 76 Middlesex Ave

Libraries

- **Somerville East** • 115 Broadway
- **Somerville Main Library** • 79 Highland Ave

Police

- **Somerville Police Department** •
  220 Washington St

Post Offices

- 237 Washington St
- 320 Broadway

Schools

- **Arthur D Healey School** • 5 Meacham St
- **Cummings School** • 42 Prescott St
- **East Somerville Community School** • 115 Pearl St
- **Full Circle High School** • 11 Otis St
- **Lincoln Park Community School** •
  290 Washington St
- **Somerville High School** • 81 Highland Ave
- **St Ann's School** • 50 Thurston St
- **St Benedict's Little Flower School** • 17 Franklin St
- **Winter Hill Community School** • 115 Sycamore St

Supermarkets

- **Star Market** • 299 Broadway

Community Gardens

- **Edgerly Garden** • Hadley Ct
- **Mystic Community Garden** • 530 Mystic Ave
- **Somerville Community Growing Center** •
  22 Vinal Ave
- **Walnut Street Garden** • Giles Park at Walnut St

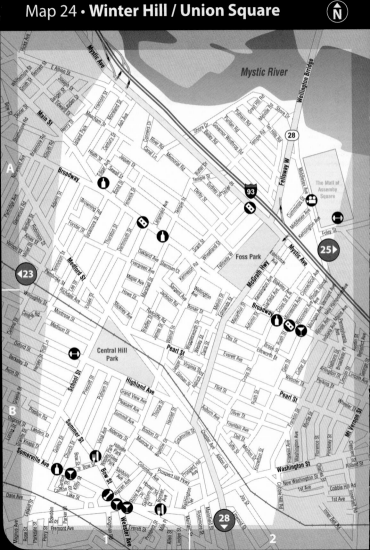

Map 24 • **Winter Hill / Union Square**

Map 24

The Neighborhood Restaurant and Bakery is a terrific spot for breakfast and lunch. Foodies in Union Square are mourning the passing of eat, a place that top chefs (including Mrs. Child herself) enjoyed. For a cheap, authentic Mexican lunch, check out Taqueria la Mexicana. Away from Union Square to the north, pickings are slim.

Bars

- **Khoury's State Spa** · 118 Broadway
- **The Independent** · 75 Union Sq
- **Tir Na Nog** · 366A Somerville Ave
- **Toast** · 70 Union Sq

Gyms

- **World Gym** · 16 Sturtevant St
- **YMCA** · 101 Highland Ave

Liquor Stores

- **Joe's Liquors** · 160 Broadway
- **Paul Revere Beverage** · 10 Main St
- **Pico's Liquor** · 329 Somerville Ave
- **Winter Hill Liquor Mart** · 313 Broadway

Movie Theaters

- **Loews Cineplex Assembly Square** ·
  35 Middlesex Ave

Pet Shops

- **Union Square Veterinary Clinic** · 37 Union Sq

Restaurants

- **Neighborhood Restaurant & Bakery** · 25 Bow St
- **Taqueria la Mexicana** · 247 Washington St

Video Rental

- **Broadway Video** · 137 Broadway
- **Cultural Brazil Video (Brazilian)** · 368 Mystic Ave
- **Palmer Video** · 345 Broadway

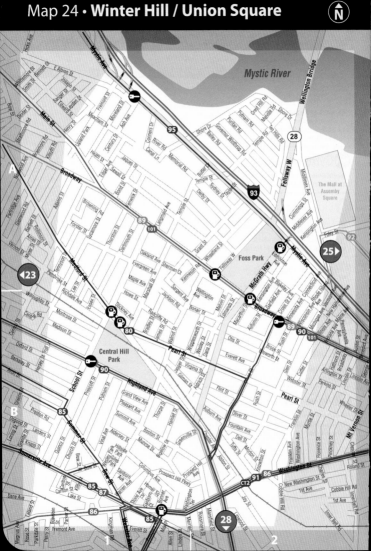

Map 24 • **Winter Hill / Union Square**

Mystic River

Wellington Bridge

The Mall at Assembly Square

Foss Park

Central Hill Park

Traffic around Union Square always stinks, largely because there's no T stop anywhere nearby. For years, residents have dreamed of a T extension to Union Square, but let's face it—this isn't happening any time soon. If you're approaching Union Square on Washington Street from the east, be sure to stay in the right lane to get onto Somerville Avenue and the left lane to get onto Webster Avenue.

Bus Lines

- **CT2** · Sullivan Station—Ruggles Station via Kendall/MIT
- **85** · Spring Hill—Kendall/MIT Station via Summer St & Union Sq
- **86** · Sullivan Sq Station—Cleveland Circle via Harvard/Johnson Gate
- **87** · Arlington Center or Clarendon Hill—Lechmere Station
- **89** · Clarendon Hill- Sullivan Sq Station via Broadway
- **90** · Davis Square—Wellington Station via Sullivan Square Station
- **91** · Sullivan Sq Station—Central Sq, Cambridge via Washington
- **92** · Assembly Sq Mall—Downtown via Sullivan Sq Station, Main St
- **95** · West Medford—Sullivan Sq Station via Mystic Ave
- **101** · Malden Center Station—Sullivan Square Station

Car Rental

- **Affordable Auto Rental** · 700 Mystic Ave
- **Americar Auto Rental** · 90 Highland Ave
- **Rent A Wreck** · 161 Broadway

Gas Stations

- **Gulf** · 212 Broadway
- **Gulf** · 231 Washington St
- **Merit** · 709 McGrath Hwy
- **Mobil** · 345 Medford St
- **Mobil** · 360 Medford St
- **Sunoco** · 258 Broadway

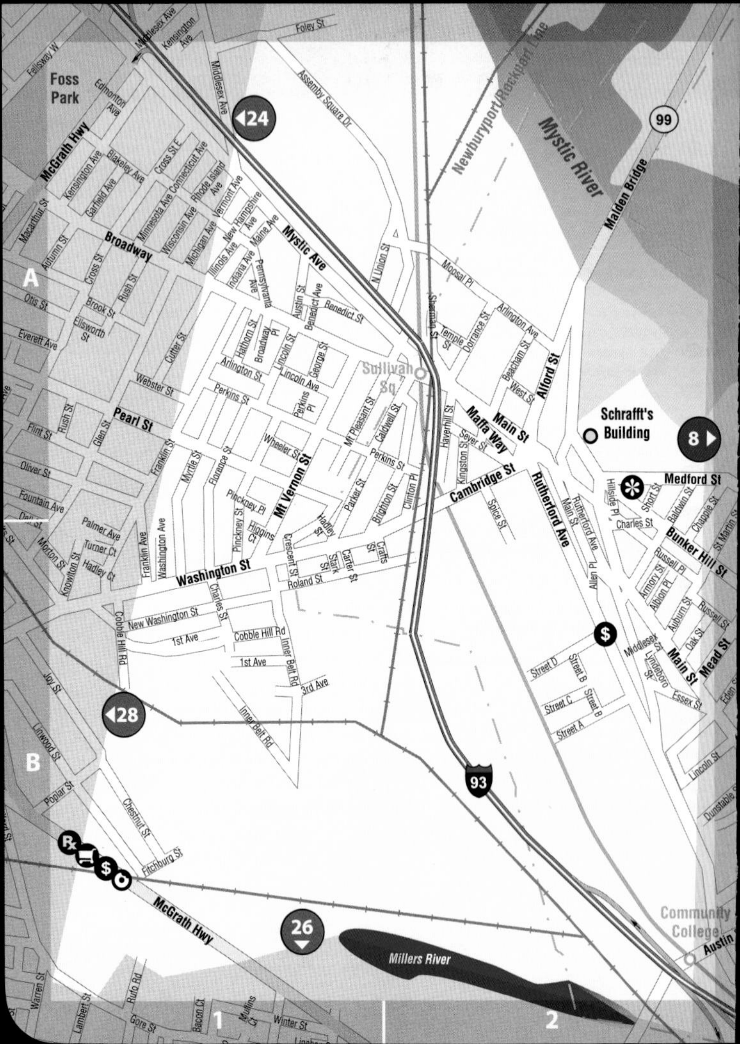

Map 25 · **East Somerville / Sullivan Square**

Foley St

Kensington Ave

Mystic River

Newburyport/Rockport Line

◀24

99

Foss Park

McGrath Hwy

Edmunton St

Assembly Square Dr

Maiden Bridge

Middlesex Ave

Broadway

Kensington Ave
Blakeley Ave
Cross St E

Minnesota Ave
Michigan Ave

Connecticut Ave

Rhode Island Ave
Vermont Ave
New Hampshire Ave

Mystic Ave

N Union St

Mount Pl

Arlington Ave
Beacham St
West St

Alford St

MacArthur St
Auburn St
Otis St

Brook St

Garfield Ave
Wisconsin Ave

New Jersey Ave

Main St

Temple St

Dorrance St

A

Everett Ave
Ellsworth Ave

Cutter St

Webster St

Rathburn St
Broadway
Arlington St

Austin St
Benedict St

Lincoln Ave

George St

Sullivan Sq

Schrafft's Building

8 ▶

Pearl St

Glen St

Myrtle St
Florence St

Perkins St

Caldwell St

Maffa Way

Medford St

Flint St

Franklin Ave

Wheeler St

Mt Pleasant St

Perkins St

Main St

Hillside

Charles St

Bunker Hill St

Oliver St

Washington Ave

Pinckney St

Tufts St

Clinton Pl

Cambridge St

Soley St

Rutherford Ave

Russell Pl

Mead St

Fountain Ave

Palmer Ave

Turner Ct

Pinckney St

Crescent St

Brighton St

Main St

Mishawum St

Bunker St
Lincoln St

Washington St

Hadley St
Morton St

Roland St

$

Essex St

Lincoln St

◀28

New Washington Rd

Cobble Hill Rd

1st Ave

Charlie St

1st Ave

Cobble Hill Rd

Inner Belt Rd

3rd Ave

Street D
Street C

Street B

Street A

93

B

Joy St

Linwood St

Chestnut St

Fitchburg St

Inner Belt Rd

Dunstable St

Poplar St

℞
🚲 $ ⊙

McGrath Hwy

Community College

Austin

Winter St

Gore St

Mount Vernon St

26 ▼

Millers River

1 | 2

In the early 20th century, Sullivan Square was New England's largest transportation hub, and the nearby Schrafft's building was the largest candy factory in the country. Today, most of this area (which includes the western edge of Charlestown) is an eyesore of overpasses and rail tracks, and Schrafft's has been converted into an office building.

Map 2

Banks

· **Fleet** · 22 McGrath Hwy
· **Key Credit Union** · 500 Rutherford Ave

Donuts

· **Dunkin' Donuts** · 14 McGrath Hwy

Landmarks

· **Schrafft's Building** · 529 Main St

Pharmacies

· **Brooks** · 14 McGrath Hwy

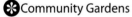Supermarkets

· **Star Market** · 14 McGrath Hwy

Community Gardens

· **Gardens for Charlestown** ·
  Medford St & Bunker Hill St

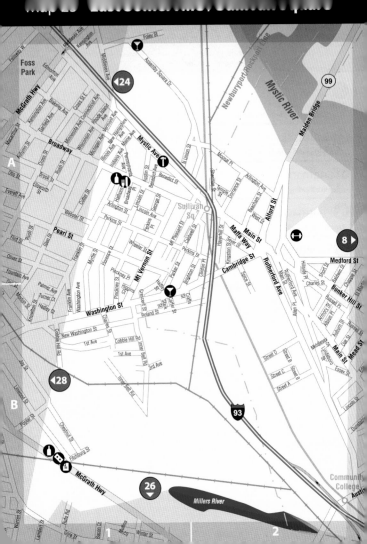

Vinny's at Night serves delicious home-style Southern Italian—it's an oasis in an area that doesn't offer much else. Youngsters and competitive men will probably enjoy the Good Time Emporium, a gargantuan game palace/sports bar. Otherwise, the best bet in the area is catching a Hollywood release at the Loews Assembly Square.

Bars

· **Good Time Emporium** · 30 Assembly Sq
· **Towne Lyne Café** · 108 Cambridge St

Copy Shops

· **Office Max** · 16 McGrath Hwy

Gyms

· **Fitcorp** · 529 Main St

 Hardware Stores

· **Home Depot** · 75 Mystic Ave

Liquor Stores

· **Bairos Liquors** · 78 Broadway
· **Sav-Mor Discount Liquors** · 13 McGrath Hwy

Restaurants

· **Vinny's at Night** · 76 Broadway

Video Rental

· **Hollywood Express** · 14 McGrath Hwy

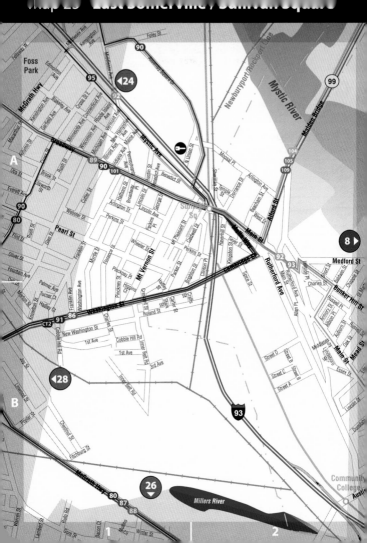

Sullivan Square is a major bus depot. The dozen buses that run through Sullivan Square, combined with bizarre traffic patterns around adjacent I-93, guarantee frequent bottlenecks. If you're driving around here, take deep breaths and try to be patient.

Subway
- **Community College**
- **Sullivan Sq**

Bus Lines

- **CT2** · Sullivan Station—Ruggles Station via Kendall/MIT
- **80** · Arlington Center—Lechmere Station via Medford Hills
- **86** · Sullivan Sq Station—Cleveland Circle via Harvard/Johnson Gate
- **87** · Arlington Center or Clarendon Hill—Lechmere Station
- **88** · Clarendon Hill- Lechmere Station via Highland Ave
- **89** · Clarendon Hill- Sullivan Sq Station via Broadway
- **90** · Davis Square—Wellington Station via Sullivan Square Station
- **91** · Sullivan Sq Station—Central Sq, Cambridge via Washington
- **92** · Assembly Sq Mall—Downtown via Sullivan Sq Station, Main St
- **93** · Sullivan Sq Station—Downtown via Bunker Hill St & Haymarket Station
- **95** · West Medford—Sullivan Sq Station via Mystic Ave
- **101** · Malden Center Station—Sullivan Square Station
- **104** · Malden Center Station—Sullivan Square Station
- **105** · Malden Center Station—Sullivan Square Station
- **109** · Linden Square—Sullivan Square Station via Glendale Square

Car Rental
- **Enterprise** · 37 Mystic Ave

Map 26 • East Cambridge/Kendall Square/MIT

East Cambridge is dominated by MIT and the buildings housing the tech companies that have set up shop nearby. Perennially confusing is the One Kendall Square complex not being located at Kendall Square—it's a few blocks up Broadway toward Cardinal Medeiros Avenue. (There's no telling how many people have been confused by this.) The Green Line between Science Park and Lechmere offers a fabulous view of the Zakim.

Banks

- **Boston Private Bank & Trust** · 1 Cambridge Ctr
- **Citizens** · 225 Cambridge St
- **East Cambridge Savings Bank** · 1 Canal Park
- **East Cambridge Savings Bank** · 292 Cambridge St
- **Fleet** · 100 Cambridgeside Pl
- **Fleet** · 2 Canal Park
- **Fleet** · 4 Cambridge Ctr
- **Fleet** · 226 Main St
- **Fleet** · 77 Massachusetts Ave
- **Fleet** · 84 Massachusetts Ave
- **Wainwright Bank & Trust** · 1 Broadway

Donuts

- **Dunkin' Donuts** · 1 Broadway
- **Dunkin' Donuts** · 100 Cambridgeside Pl
- **Dunkin' Donuts** · 5 Third St
- **Dunkin' Donuts** · 99 Cambridge St

o Landmarks

- **Harvard Bridge** · Massachusetts Ave

Libraries

- **O'Connell** · 48 Sixth St

Post Offices

- 303 Cambridge St
- 25 East St
- 250 Main St
- 84 Massachusetts Ave

Schools

- **Massachusetts Institute of Technology** · 77 Massachusetts Ave
- **Robert F Kennedy School** · 158 Spring St

Map 26 · **East Cambridge/Kendall Square/MIT**

Map 2

This area is home to three terrific and very different restaurants: The Blue Room (American), Helmand (Afghan) and Ajanta (Indian). Kendall Square Cinema offers a good combination of quality movies and decent theaters (the garage next door will validate parking). Quantum Books in Kendall Square (not One Kendall Square) is the best computer bookstore in the city.

🍸 Bars

- **Cambridge Brewing Company** · Onr Kendall Sq
- **Flattop Johnny's** · One Kendall Sq
- **Pugliese's** · 635 Cambridge St

💻 Coffee

- **Beantowne Coffee House** · One Kendall Sq
- **Seattle's Best** · 6 Cambridge Ctr
- **Starbucks** · 100 Cambridgeside Pl
- **Starbucks** · 2 Cambridge Ctr

📋 Copy Shops

- **Kinko's** · 600 Technology Sq
- **Quick Copy Printing** · 1 Broadway

🏋 Gyms

- **Boston Sports Club** · 6 Museum Way
- **Cambridge Racquet & Fitness Club** · 215 First St
- **Fitcorp** · 600 Technology Sq

🍾 Liquor Stores

- **660 Liquors** · 660 Cambridge St

🎭 Movie Theaters

- **Landmark Kendall Square Cinema** · One Kendall Sq
- **MIT Film Series** · 77 Massachusetts Ave

🐾 Pet Shops

- **Boston Tropical Fish & Reptiles** · 243 Monsignor O'Brien Hwy
- **Petco** · 119 First St

🍴 Restaurants

- **Ajanta** · 145 First St
- **Black Sheep Cafe** · 350 Main St
- **Blue Room** · One Kendall Sq
- **Cheesecake Factory** · 100 Cambridgeside Pl
- **Court House Seafood** · 498 Cambridge St
- **Davio's** · 5 Cambridge Pkwy
- **El Coqui** · 561 Cambridge St
- **Helmand** · 143 First St
- **Legal Sea Foods** · 5 Cambridge Ctr
- **Second Street Cafe** · 89 Second St

🛍 Shopping

- **Apple Store** · 100 Cambridgeside Pl
- **Best Buy** · 100 Cambridgeside Pl
- **Cambridge Antique Market** · 201 Monsignor O'Brien Hwy
- **Chocolate Truffle** · 2 Cambridge Ctr
- **Haviland Candy** · 134 Cambridge St
- **Mayflower Poultry** · 621 Cambridge St

📹 Video Rental

- **Video Oasis** · 625 Cambridge St

It's easier to get to the Cambridgeside Galleria using public transportation starting from Boston as opposed to starting from Cambridge. (Take the Green Line to Lechmere and head down First Street a few blocks.) The parking at the Galleria is reasonably priced and is handy if street parking is difficult to locate.

Subway

- ■ · **Lechmere**
- ■ · **Kendall/MIT**

Bus Lines

CT2 · Sullivan Station—Ruggles Station via Kendall/MIT

68 · Harvard/Holyoke Gate—Kendall/MIT via Broadway

69 · Harvard/Holyoke—Lechmere Station via Cambridge St

80 · Arlington Center—Lechmere Station via Medford Hills

85 · Spring Hill—Kendall/MIT Station via Summer St & Union Sq

87 · Arlington Center or Clarendon Hill—Lechmere Station

88 · Clarendon Hill- Lechmere Station via Highland Ave

Gas Stations

· **Shell** · 239 Monsignor O'Brien Hwy

Parking

Love it or hate it, Central Square is the genuine center of Cambridge. This area's showcase development is University Park, comprised of mostly aggressively modernist buildings. Check out what's emerged at 40 Landsdowne Street (with its trippy neon) and nearby Simmons Hall, an eyepopper built for MIT undergraduates. Cambridgeport looks like more old-school New England, but is in fact a very diverse part of already diverse Cambridge.

 Map 2

Banks

- **Cambridge Savings Bank** ·
  630 Massachusetts Ave
- **Citizens** · 20 Sidney St
- **Citizens** · 671 Massachusetts Ave
- **Citizens** · 689 Massachusetts Ave
- **Fleet** · 1000 Massachusetts Ave
- **Fleet** · 139 Massachusetts Ave
- **Fleet** · 622 Massachusetts Ave
- **Fleet** · 727 Massachusetts Ave
- **Sovereign Bank** · 515 Massachusetts Ave
- **Wainwright Bank & Trust** ·
  647 Massachusetts Ave

Libraries

- **Central Square** · 45 Pearl St

Police

- **Cambridge Police Department** · 5 Western Ave

Post Offices

- 770 Massachusetts Ave

Schools

- **Fletcher/Maynard Academy** · 225 Windsor St
- **Graham and Parks School** · 15 Upton St
- **Henry Buckner School** ·
  85 Bishop Richard Allen Dr
- **James F Farr Academy** · 71 Pearl St
- **Martin Luther King, Jr School** · 100 Putnam Ave
- **Morse School** · 40 Granite St

Supermarkets

- **Harvest Co-op Market** · 581 Massachusetts Ave
- **Star Market** · 20 Sidney St
- **Trader Joe's** · 748 Memorial Dr
- **Whole Foods Market** · 340 River St

Community Gardens

- **Field of Dreams Gardens** ·
  Hingham St at Putnam Ave
- **Green St Neighborhood Park** · Green St & Bay St
- **Simplex Community Garden** · 6 Emily St
- **Watson Street/Peggy Hayes Garden** ·
  Watson St at Brookline St

Map 27 • Central Square / Cambridgeport N

Central Square has a few nightspots that most Boston music fans are familiar with, including the Middle East and the Cantab Lounge. Check out Green Street Grill for zesty Caribbean cuisine. This area has an unusual concentration of supermarkets, including the only Trader Joe's in Cambridge. We tip our caps to the Miracle and its periodic-table menu, diverse music, tasty burgers, and killer roasted potatoes.

Bars

- **Asgard** · 350 Massachusetts Ave
- **Cambridgeport Saloon** · 300 Massachusetts Ave
- **Cantab Lounge** · 738 Massachusetts Ave
- **Enormous Room** · 567 Massachusetts Ave
- **Middle East** · 472 Massachusetts Ave
- **Miracle of Science** · 321 Massachusetts Ave
- **People's Republik** · 880 Massachusetts Ave
- **Phoenix Landing** · 512 Massachusetts Ave
- **Plough & Stars** · 912 Massachusetts Ave
- **River Gods** · 125 River St
- **The Cellar** · 991 Massachusetts Ave

Coffee

- **Carberry's Bakery & Coffee House** · 74 Prospect St
- **Cezanne Cafe & Bakery** · 424 Massachusetts Ave
- **Starbucks** · 655 Massachusetts Ave

Copy Shops

- **Classic Copy & Printing** · 26 Central Sq

Farmer's Markets

- **Cambridgeport** · Magazine St & Memorial Dr
- **Central Square** · Bishop Richard Allen Dr at Norfolk St

Gyms

- **Boston Sports Club** · 625 Massachusetts Ave
- **Cambridge Family YMCA** · 820 Massachusetts Ave

Hardware Stores

- **Economy Hardware** · 438 Massachusetts Ave
- **Pill Hardware** · 743 Massachusetts Ave

Liquor Stores

- **Dana Hill Liquors** · 910 Massachusetts Ave
- **Libby's Liquor Market** · 575 Massachusetts Ave

Restaurants

- **Asgard** · 350 Massachusetts Ave
- **Asmara** · 739 Massachusetts Ave
- **Brookline Lunch** · 9 Brookline St
- **Centro** · 720 Massachusetts Ave
- **Dolphin Seafood** · 1105 Massachusetts Ave
- **Green Street Grill** · 280 Green St
- **Hi-Fi Pizza & Subs** · 496 Massachusetts Ave
- **India Pavilion** · 17 Central Sq
- **Johnny's Luncheonette** · 1105 Massachusetts Ave
- **La Groceria** · 853 Main St
- **Mary Chung** · 464 Massachusetts Ave
- **Middle East** · 472 Massachusetts Ave
- **Miracle of Science** · 321 Massachusetts Ave
- **Moody's Falafel Palace** · 25 Central Sq
- **Picante Mexican Grill** · 735 Massachusetts Ave
- **Salts** · 798 Main St
- **Sunny's Diner** · 7 Landsdowne St
- **ZuZu!** · 474 Massachusetts Ave

Shopping

- **Cambridge Bicycle** · 259 Massachusetts Ave
- **Cheapo Records** · 645 Massachusetts Ave
- **Cremaldi's** · 31 Putnam Ave
- **Economy Hardware** · 438 Massachusetts Ave
- **Hubba Hubba** · 534 Massachusetts Ave
- **Looney Tunes** · 1001 Massachusetts Ave
- **Mass Army Navy Store** · 698 Massachusetts Ave
- **Micro Center** · 727 Memorial Dr
- **Mojo Music** · 904 Massachusetts Ave
- **Pearl Art & Craft Supplies** · 597 Massachusetts Ave
- **Sadye & Company** · 182 Massachusetts Ave
- **Second Coming Records** · 1105 Massachusetts Ave
- **Skippy White's** · 538 Massachusetts Ave
- **Toscanini's** · 899 Main St
- **University Stationery** · 311 Massachusetts Ave

Video Rental

- **Blockbuster** · 541 Massachusetts Ave
- **Hollywood Express** · 765 Massachusetts Ave

Transportation

Without a Cambridge city sticker, parking around Central Square is not easy. If you don't mind dropping a couple of bucks, the parking garages in University Park will get you pretty close. As for Mass Ave, 1) it's always busy with traffic, 2) it's almost always under construction, and 3) there's never any parking.

Subway
■ · Central

Bus Lines

CT1 · Central Square, Cambridge—BU Medical Center/BU Medical Campus

CT2 · Sullivan Station—Ruggles Station via Kendall/MIT

1 · Harvard/Holyoke Gate—Dudley Station via Mass Ave & BU Medical Center

47 · Central Sq, Cambridge—Broadway Station via South End Medical Area

64 · Oak Square—Central Sq, Cambridge or Kendall/MIT

68 · Harvard/Holyoke Gate—Kendall/MIT via Broadway

69 · Harvard/Holyoke—Lechmere Station via Cambridge St

70 · Cedarwood, N Waltham or Watertown Sq—University Park via Central Sq

70A · Cedarwood, N Waltham or Watertown Sq—University Park via Central Sq

83 · Rindge Ave—Central Sq, Cambridge via Porter Square Station

85 · Spring Hill—Kendall/MIT Station via Summer St & Union

91 · Sullivan Sq Station—Central Sq, Cambridge via Washington

Car Rental
· **Budget** · 220 Massachusetts Ave
· **Enterprise** · 25 River St
· **U-Haul** · 844 Main St

Gas Stations
· **Mobil** · 816 Memorial Dr
· **Shell** · 820 Memorial Dr
· **Sunoco** · 808 Memorial Dr

Parking

Map 28 · **Inman Square**

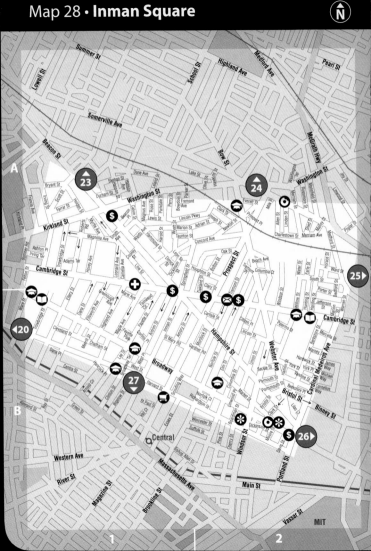

Map 2

The neighborhoods in and around Inman Square are a diverse, working-class group, but Inman Square proper and the area along the Cambridge-Somerville line have experienced renewal in the last handful of years. Always heavily residential, it's recently become busier because of the influx of restaurants and bars along Beacon Street, Hampshire Street and Cambridge Street.

$ Banks

- **Cambridge Savings Bank** · 1378 Cambridge St
- **Citizens** · 141 Portland St
- **East Cambridge Savings Bank** ·
  1310 Cambridge St
- **Fleet** · 120 Beacon St
- **Fleet** · 1400 Cambridge St

◎ Donuts

- **Dunkin' Donuts** · 222 Broadway
- **Dunkin' Donuts** · 282 Somerville Ave

✚ Hospitals

- **Cambridge Hospital** · 1493 Cambridge St

📖 Libraries

- **Cambridge Main Library** · 449 Broadway
- **Valente** · 826 Cambridge St

✉ Post Offices

- 1311 Cambridge St

🏫 Schools

- **Cambridge Rindge & Latin High School** ·
  459 Broadway
- **Cambridgeport School** · 89 Elm St
- **Castle School** · 298 Harvard St
- **Charles G Harrington School** · 850 Cambridge St
- **Longfellow School** · 359 Broadway
- **Somerville Charter School** · 15 Webster Ave

🛒 Supermarkets

- **Whole Foods Market** · 115 Prospect St

❀ Community Gardens

- **Broadway-Boardman Community Garden** ·
  Broadway & Boardman St
- **Moore Street Garden** · Moore St & Broadway

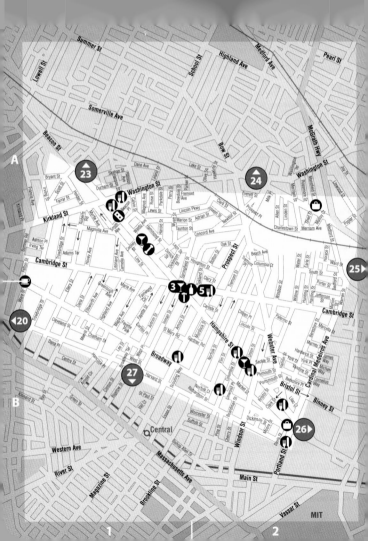

Sundries / Entertainment

Map 28

Inman Square has some great food and drink options. Try Magnolia's for southern or Cajun, try Oleanas for that special night out, or quaff a pint at Bukowski's before dining at the East Coast Grill & Raw Bar (where it's *all* good). Just up Beacon Street from Inman Square are EVOO, a great addition to the neighborhood, and Dali, the popular taparia.

Bars

- **Abbey Lounge** · 3 Beacon St
- **B-Side Lounge** · 92 Hampshire St
- **Bukowski's** · 1281 Cambridge St
- **The Druid** · 1357 Cambridge St
- **Thirsty Scholar Pub** · 70 Beacon St

Coffee

- **Starbucks** · 468 Broadway

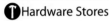Hardware Stores

- **Inman Square Ace Hardware** · 1337 Cambridge St

Liquor Stores

- **Charlie's Beer & Wine** · 1300 Cambridge St

Pet Shops

- **Fi-Dough** · 70 Beacon St

Restaurants

- **1369** · 1369 Cambridge St
- **Amelia's Trattoria** · 111 Harvard St
- **Argana** · 1287 Cambridge St
- **Atasca** · 279 Broadway
- **B-Side Lounge** · 92 Hampshire St
- **Dali** · 415 Washington St
- **East Coast Grill & Raw Bar** · 1271 Cambridge St
- **Emma's Pizzeria** · 40 Hampshire St
- **EVOO** · 118 Beacon St
- **Koreana** · 154 Prospect St
- **Magnolia's** · 1193 Cambridge St
- **Oleana** · 134 Hampshire St
- **S&S Restaurant** · 1334 Cambridge St

Shopping

- **Garment District** · 200 Broadway
- **Target** · 180 Somerville Ave

Video Rental

- **Knapp Video** · 116 Beacon St

Map 28 • **Inman Square**

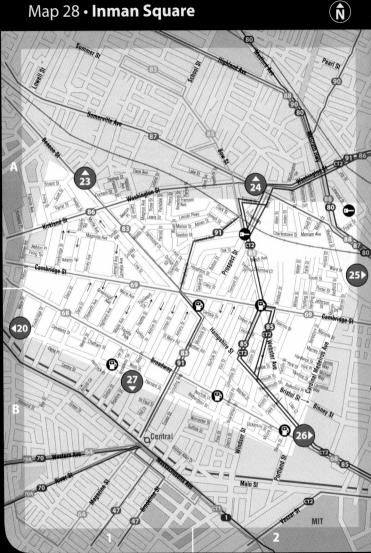

Map 2

The 69 bus is your best bet for getting to Inman Square from either Harvard Square or East Cambridge; on Sundays, though, you're probably better off flagging a cab. To go from Inman Square to Union Square, take the 91 bus. The Hess station at the intersection of Prospect Street and Hampshire Street has free air for your tires, a rarity in Boston these days.

Bus Lines

- **CT1** · Central Square, Cambridge—BU Medical Center/BU Medical Campus
- **CT2** · Sullivan Station—Ruggles Station via Kendall/MIT
- **1** · Harvard/Holyoke Gate—Dudley Station via Mass. Ave. & BU Medical Center
- **47** · Central Sq, Cambridge—Broadway Station via South End Medical Area
- **64** · Oak Square—Central Sq, Cambridge or Kendall/MIT
- **68** · Harvard/Holyoke Gate—Kendall/MIT via Broadway
- **69** · Harvard/Holyoke—Lechmere Station via Cambridge St
- **70** · Cedarwood, N Waltham or Watertown Sq—University Park via Central Sq
- **70A** · Cedarwood, N Waltham or Watertown Sq—University Park via Central Sq
- **80** · Arlington Center—Lechmere Station via Medford Hills
- **83** · Rindge Ave—Central Sq, Cambridge via Porter Square Station
- **85** · Spring Hill—Kendall/MIT Station via Summer St & Union Sq
- **86** · Sullivan Sq Station—Cleveland Circle via Harvard/Johnson Gate
- **87** · Arlington Center or Clarendon Hill—Lechmere Station
- **88** · Clarendon Hill- Lechmere Station via Highland Ave
- **90** · Davis Square—Wellington Station via Sullivan Square Station
- **91** · Sullivan Sq Station—Central Sq, Cambridge via Washington

Car Rental

- **Americar Auto Rental** · 251 Prospect St
- **U-Haul** · 151 Linwood St

Gas Stations

- **Citgo** · 277 Broadway
- **Exxon** · 209 Broadway
- **Hess** · 287 Prospect St
- **Mobil** · 320 Broadway
- **Shell** · 1001 Cambridge St

General Information

Location: 200 Mt. Vernon St, Columbia Point, Boston, MA 02125

Phone: 617-474-6534 (Bayside Expo)
                 617-474-6000 (Executive Conference Center)

Website: www.baysideexpo.com

Overview

Located three miles from downtown Boston, the Expo Center hails itself as "New England's largest conference center and hotel complex," with over 240,000 square feet of exhibit space and 40,000 square feet of meeting space. This distinction will change with the opening of the mammoth Boston Convention and Exhibition Center in Southie next year. Built on the site of a bankrupt mall and ringed by parking lots, the stark white, square Expo Center won't win any design awards, but the building is functional, allowing visitors to focus on the boat, auto, RV, trade, or flower show that attracted them there in the first place.

The center's single-level exhibit space includes 18 meeting rooms, a full-service restaurant, lounge, cafeteria, and concessions. While they are convenient, on-site vendors' price-to-quality ratios are not the best. It's more than $2 for a small cup of coffee, and that's for the standard stuff, not a chic, unpronounceable foreign blend. An alternative would be to tailgate in the Expo Center's immense parking lot, but that will cost you too. In recent years, parking rates have jumped from $8 per vehicle to $12, making the T the best choice for thrifty show-goers.

Adjacent to the exhibit space, the Executive Conference Center has everything an executive could wish for (well, almost everything), such as T-1 Internet access, wireless LAN, and wireless phone and video conferencing.

On nice days, be sure to take a drive around the back to the center's "bayside," where there are pleasant views of grassy Old Harbor, South Boston, and planes landing at Logan Airport.

Doubletree Club Boston Bayside
240 Mt. Vernon St; 617-822-3600

Adjacent to the Expo Center, this 197-room hotel's loftier rooms offer both city and ocean views. In addition to standard hotel amenities, such as a fitness room, lounge, and a tour/recreation desk, the Doubletree Club also offers free chocolate-chip cookies at check-in.

There's an Au Bon Pain coffee/pastry shop on the first floor and the hotel provides free shuttles to the airport (leaving every hour, 6 am to 10 pm) and downtown (every other hour, 9 am to 9 pm). Perhaps the biggest perk, though, is free parking.

How to Get There—Driving

From the south, use exit 15 off I-93. Turn right at the bottom of the ramp onto Columbia Road. Follow Columbia Road through the rotary and onto William J. Day Boulevard heading towards the beach. You'll drive past the State Police Station, which is on your right. Turn right at the blue sign for Bayside Expo Center.

From the north, take exit 15 off of I-93. Turn left at the bottom of the ramp onto Columbia Road and follow directions above.

Parking

Don't be fooled into off-site parking by the shifty folks at the Sovereign Bank parking lot across the street from the Expo Center. If you do, you'll have to lug your stuff across the street, only to walk by dozens of available spaces in the Expo Center lot. Make sure you follow the signs for On-site Parking at Bayside Expo Center. Parking is $12 on show days.

How to Get There—Mass Transit

Take the Red Line T or MBTA Commuter Rail to the JFK/UMass station. The Expo Center is directly across the street. The red "Beantown Trolley" runs from the T stop to the front entrance of the Expo Center, a distance of about a 1/2 mile.

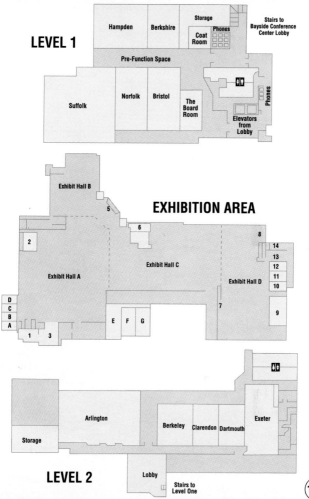

LEVEL 1

Hampden

Berkshire

Storage

Coat Room

Phones

Stairs to Bayside Conference Center Lobby

Pre-Function Space

Suffolk

Norfolk

Bristol

The Board Room

Phones

Elevators from Lobby

EXHIBITION AREA

Exhibit Hall B

5

6

8

2

14
13
12
11
10

Exhibit Hall A

Exhibit Hall C

Exhibit Hall D

D
C
B
A

7

9

E F G

1 3

LEVEL 2

Arlington

Berkeley

Clarendon

Dartmouth

Exeter

Storage

Lobby

Stairs to Level One

175

General Information

Mass Audubon: 781-259-9500; www.massaudubon.org
Wellfleet Bay Wildlife Sanctuary: 508-349-2615;
www.wellfleetbay.org

Overview

Jutting out from the mainland like a flexing arm, Cape Cod is home to 15 towns, with a permanent population of roughly 220,000 that swells to over 550,000 in the summer months. The entrance of the Cape is approximately 50 miles southeast of Boston, making the sandy beaches and picturesque shoreline a favorite summer getaway for Bostonians.

Grey days on the Cape are almost as good as the sunny variety, with the mist, fog, and calm seas conjuring images of sailors and fishermen past. On some summer days, bright blue skies give way to smogsets over distant Boston that are so pretty you'll wish everyone in the city drove an Escalade.

The Cape is not entirely serene—summer travelers from the mainland can expect lengthy traffic delays just past Plymouth, where the overburdened Bourne and Sagamore bridges offer passage over the Cape Cod Canal. Sixty-five miles east at the Cape's end sits bustling and bawdy Provincetown, home to the largest, loudest, and proudest gay community on the east coast. If Cape Cod isn't your bag, ferries can transport you south of the Cape to olde-timey Nantucket Island or old-moneyed Martha's Vineyard.

Lighthouses

Varying in shape, size, and level of function, lighthouses are a significant Cape Cod attraction. If you have time to visit a lighthouse or two, we recommend the Nobska Point Lighthouse at Woods Hole, an oft-photographed white tower at the southwestern tip of Cape Cod, the Cape Cod (Highland) Lighthouse in North Truro, or the Chatham Lighthouse on the southeastern corner of the Cape.

The Outdoors

After waiting all that time in traffic to get out to the Cape, you'll be eager to get outside and enjoy it. If the water calls, you can splash about at one of the Cape's many beaches, take a boat out to sea, dive or snorkel in the bay, canoe or kayak, parasail, or enjoy one of the whale- or seal-watching excursions that are on offer.

Flora and fauna enthusiasts come here to explore the lush plant and animal life at the Cape's many sanctuaries. The only sanctuary with a Visitor Center is the Audubon Society's Wellfleet Bay Wildlife Sanctuary, which boasts 1,000 acres of woodlands, wetlands, and grasslands that attract an exciting variety of wildlife, including songbirds and shorebirds. Five miles of scenic trails wind through the various habitats, while the Nature Center includes "green" elements such as solar heating and composting toilets. Inside the nature center, you'll find two 700-gallon aquariums that feature the underwater worlds of the salt marsh and tidal flats. Other sanctuaries on the Cape include Long Pasture near Barnstable, Skunknett River near Osterville, Sampson's Island (which is only accessible by private boat from local marinas and town landings), and Ashumet Holly near Falmouth.

Sports

Cape Cod is an ideal location for sport fishing. Charters and tours are available and, for those looking to have a little fun on the water, ships such as the Yankee offer party cruises, perfect for those who hate lugging around a heavy cooler. Be warned, drinking and waves are not always the best combo.

Landlubbers should know that golf is popular here. There are a dozen or so courses on the Cape, varying in price, size, and difficulty. One universal trait: they're all busy all the time in the summer. Biking is another favorite pastime in the area, with free trails including the epic RailTrail at Cape Cod National Park, which stretches for 26 miles. The trail runs along the bed of a defunct railroad (hence the name) from Dennis (get on at Route 134 just south of exit 9 from Route 6) to the South Wellfleet General Store.

The Towns

The Cape, about 70 miles in length, is often subdivided into three regions: Upper Cape, Mid Cape, and Outer Cape. For convenience, we'll tack "The Islands" on to this list, making this section "the Cape and the Islands," just as the TV weather people refer to it.

The Upper Cape—Includes the Falmouth, Mashpee, Sandwich, and Bourne areas. Close to the historical settlement of Plymouth and about 55 miles from downtown Boston, it is here that the Bourne and Sagamore bridges carry traffic over the Cape Cod Canal and onto the Cape. Here lies the beginning of the cranberry bog and seasonal tourist life. For the best views and smoothest journey, avoid the highways and take surface routes such as 28A that take you close to the water. If you're a film buff, you might consider a visit to Woods Hole, where part of the movie *Jaws* was filmed.

The Mid Cape—This region includes Dennis, Yarmouth, and Barnstable and its seven villages: Hyannis, Osterville, Centerville, Cotuit, West Barnstable, Barnstable Village, and Marstons Mills. Almost 70% of the Cape's population resides in the Hyannis area, resulting in the downtown remaining busy most of the year. Hyannis is home to the JFK Museum and the Ocean Street Docks, with ferries and tour boats leaving regularly in the summer for the islands of Nantucket and Martha's Vineyard. Much of the Mid Cape now lacks rustic charm, opting instead to reek of parking lot and chain store. Take the Old King's Highway (Route 6A) if you want to stay in the Cape mood.

The Outer Cape—Home of the peaceful Cape Cod National Seashore, Nickerson State Park, and the quiet towns of Brewster, Orleans, Eastham, Wellfleet, Chatham, Harwich, and Truro, it's difficult to imagine the awaiting spectacle at the very tip of the Outer Cape: Provincetown. At land's end sits one of the most "out" towns, where gay couples are as plentiful as seagulls and you're never sure whether that person strutting down the street is Cher, or some dude dressed as Cher. After a day in the sun, cruise into P-town for a night of revelry. Gay or straight, the town knows how to party. For full effect, visit during Carnival in August. www.provincetown.com

The Islands—Martha's Vineyard and Nantucket each have their own distinct feel. Nantucket, only three by nine miles, is a quaint New England destination where tourists roam the cobblestoned streets year round. In addition to shops and galleries, the downtown is also home to the Nantucket Whaling Museum. Martha's Vineyard, a preferred vacation spot of the Clintons, is well known for great beaches, ocean vistas, and the seaside villages of Oak Bluffs, Chilmark, Edgartown, and Tisbury. It's even better known for its well-heeled rich folk.

Want to start an instant argument on the Cape and Islands? Bring up the Cape Wind Project. Energy developers want to put over 100 windmills, each taller than the Statue of Liberty, in the shallow waters between the Cape, the Vineyard, and Nantucket. The windmills could generate enough electricity for the majority of the Cape and the Islands under normal conditions. The idea sounds like a winner, but wealthy landowners with waterfront property don't want their view ruined, so the fight goes on.

Ferries

If the idea of crawling along in weekend or holiday traffic doesn't appeal to you, there's another option for getting across the Cape. A number of ferry companies provide services between Boston and Cape Cod, from point to point on the Cape, and between the Islands.

Bay State Cruises Fast Ferry • 617-748-1428 • http://boston-ptown.com
Bay State offers two different services to Provincetown from the World Trade Center pier. Daily service in the summer (May 23–Sep 29) is provided by the Provincetown Express, with boats leaving Boston three times per day—8 am, 1 pm, and 5:30 pm—and returning at 10 am, 3 pm, and 7:30 pm. The journey takes only 1.5 hours and costs $35 one-way and $55 roundtrip. If you prefer traveling at a slower pace or you're on a budget, you might opt for the Provincetown II service—a 3-hour boat ride that leaves at 9:30 am Friday, Saturday, and Sunday (June 20–Sept 1) and costs a mere $18 one-way, $29 return. The boat leaves P-town at 3:30 pm.

Boston Harbor Cruises Provincetown Fast Ferry • 617-503-5539 • www.bostonharborcruises.com
The oldest ferry company in Boston offers a luxury high-speed catamaran ferry cruise with concierge service from Long Wharf in Boston to MacMillan Wharf in Provincetown. Travel time is 90 minutes and the fare is $37 one-way, $58 return. Ferry times vary depending on the day of the week and the season, but in peak times, the ferries leave at 9 am, 2 pm, and 6:30 pm from Thursday to Sunday (returning from P-town at 11 am, 4 pm, and 8:30 pm). On most other days between May 25 and October 1, ferries leave at 9 am and either 2 pm or 4 pm. Check the website for schedules.

Hy-Line Cruises • 508-778-2600 • www.hy-linecruises.com
Hy-Line provides ferry service among Hyannis, Nantucket, and Martha's Vineyard. The high-speed Grey Lady catamaran zips between Hyannis and Nantucket year-round, while the other services are seasonal. Ferries leave Hyannis for Nantucket daily at 6:30 am, 9:15 am, 12 pm, 3:15 pm, and 6 pm (and 8:45 pm in the summer). Return trips are at 7:50 am, 10:35 am, 1:20 pm, 4:35 pm, and 7:20 pm (and 10 pm in the summer). $33 one-way, $58 return, $5 each way for bikes.

Island Queen Ferry • 508-548-4800 • www.cape.com/~islqueen
The Island Queen travels between Falmouth Harbor (Falmouth Heights Road) and Martha's Vineyard from May to mid-October. The journey takes half an hour and costs $10 round-trip. The boat sails daily approximately once every hour and a half in the summer months beginning at 9 am and ending at 6 pm.

Steamship Authority • 508-693-9130 • http://web1.steamshipauthority.com
Steamship provides year-round service between Martha's Vineyard and Woods Hole, Nantucket and Hyannis, and between Martha's Vineyard and New Bedford. Check the website for schedule and fares.

Parks & Places • **Charlestown Navy Yard**

General Information

Address: Pier 1, Charlestown Navy Yard (near Bunker Hill)
Phone: 617-242-5601; groups: 617-241-7575
Hours: 10 am until 4 pm daily; free admission.
Website: www.nps.gov/bost/Visiting_Navy_Yard.htm

Practicalities

The Charlestown Navy Yard is a must-see for anyone who likes big ships or US naval history. The two main attractions are the USS Cassin Young and the USS Constitution, or "Old Ironsides" as she is sometimes called. The yard was established in 1800 as one of the first naval shipyards in the country and, when the Navy retired the yard in 1974, it became part of the Boston National Historic Park.

Attractions

Typical Fourth of July celebrations in Boston range from backyard barbecues to sunbathing on the beach, but the Navy Yard has its own unique tradition. With Independence Day comes the customary turning of the Constitution, an annual practice in which the great vessel is tugged out of the dock and rotated to ensure uniform weathering. The Cassin Young has the battle scars to show for its involvement in both the Second World War and the Korean War. The nearby Commandant's House, the oldest building in the yard, was formerly used as a living area and now serves as an elegant museum.

How to Get There—Driving

From the north via I-93, take exit 28 Sullivan Square/Charlestown, go under I-93 and follow signs to Sullivan Square. At the first traffic light bear left into the Sullivan Square rotary; take the second right onto Bunker Hill Street, turn right onto Chelsea Street and make an immediate left onto 5th Street. Go one block (5th Street dead-ends) and turn left onto 1st Avenue.

From the south, signage near the entrance of the new tunnel indicates "North Station, USS Constitution, Use Exit 26 Storrow Drive." Go left on Martha Road (which becomes Lomasney Way), left on Causeway Street, then left at N. Washington Street, and access the right lane as soon as possible. At the end of the bridge, turn right onto Chelsea Street.

From the west, take Massachusetts Turnpike (I-90) to I-93 N and follow "From the south" directions.

Parking

Though public transportation is strongly recommended for this area, discounted parking with Boston National Historical Park validation is available from the Nautica Parking Garage across from the park's Visitor Center on Constitution Road.

How to Get There—Mass Transit

Visitors can take a water shuttle to the Navy Yard from Long Wharf (every day of the week; $2.50 roundtrip) or Lovejoy Wharf (weekdays only; $2.50 roundtrip).

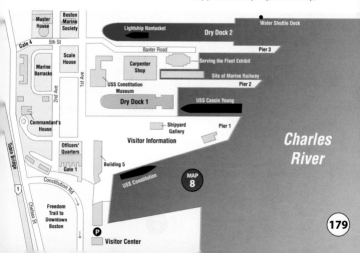

Overview

Copley Square is named after John Singleton Copley, whose claim to fame is being America's first great artist. Some of his portraits of America's Founding Fathers are on display at the Massachusetts Historical Society across the street from the square. The Boston Marathon, held each year on Patriot's Day (the third Monday in April), ends on Boylston Street. If you're interested in seeing a theater show, you'll find a BosTix outlet at the corner of Boylston Street and Dartmouth Street. The farmers' market takes place from June to October on Tuesdays and Fridays from 11 am to 6 pm. On the first Thursday after Thanksgiving, the Friends of Copley Square sponsors its annual Holiday Tree Lighting for the local community. In the warmer months of July and August, you can watch folk dancing performances on Tuesday evenings.

Architecture & Sculpture

The Boston Public Library is America's oldest public library. It has over seven million books, magnificent architecture, and busts of famous writers and prominent Bostonians. Big bonus: it now offers wireless Internet access. Across the street, Trinity Church, designed by notable architect H.H. Richardson, features neo-Romanesque design. Be sure to walk in; its stained glass windows are worth the trip inside.

John Hancock Tower

The John Hancock Mutual Life Insurance Company, which already inhabited buildings on Clarendon Street and Berkeley Street, needed more space to house its employees, so it opted to build a 60-story black glass tower. What better place to put it than next to the public library and an old church? Designed by architect I. M. Pei, and completed in 1976, the John Hancock Tower soon became famous for more than being the tallest building in New England.

Locals were upset when a foundation collapse in the early stages

of construction nearly sucked Trinity Church into the ground. They were a little more upset when, in January 1973, one of the building's 10,000-plus glass windows "popped off," shattering on the ground below, followed by dozens more 500-pound window panes. All told, 65 panes fell onto the roped-off area below the building before workers changed the solder used to mount the windows. In the meantime, locals had dubbed the Hancock "The Plywood Palace," in reference to the black plywood sheets put in place to substitute for the fallen panes. Not long after, engineers discovered the building was in danger of being sheared in half by the wind, resulting in another expensive fix. Today, all the construction drama is behind the Hancock Tower and locals have grown to love it.

The observation deck on the 60th floor, originally opened to the public in response to community feedback, was permanently closed for security reasons after the destruction of the World Trade Center.

How to Get There—Driving

From the south, follow I-95 N to I-93 N. Take exit 18 Massachusetts Avenue/Roxbury. Follow the signs to Massachusetts Avenue and turn right. Turn right on Huntington Avenue, then left onto Dartmouth Street. From the north, follow I-95 S to I-93 S. Take exit 26 North Station Storrow Drive. Follow Storrow Drive west to the Copley Square exit. Turn right onto Beacon Street and, after two blocks, turn left onto Clarendon Street. After five blocks, turn right onto St. James Avenue.

This is one of two examples in the city (the other being the Pru) where the "look up, locate the giant building, and drive towards it" method of navigation works well.

How to Get There—Mass Transit

Take the Green Line to the Copley stop. Alternatively, take the Orange Line to Back Bay station, exit, and walk up Dartmouth Street. Again, if you're not sure which way to go, look for the giant glass building.

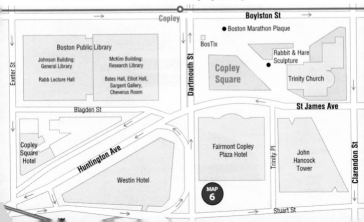

General Information

Address: Boston Common Visitor Center,
             147 Tremont St (between Temple Pl & West St)
Phone: 617-426-3115

Overview

The nation's oldest public park, Boston Common is the starting point of the Freedom Trail, the Black Heritage Trail, and the Emerald Necklace park system. The land was purchased by the Commonwealth of Massachusetts in 1634 to serve as livestock grazing ground. The city charged each household six shillings to pay for "The Commonage." (It was Tax-achusetts even back then!) But the Common wasn't just for livestock. People used it too—to watch other people being hanged at the gallows (like them cursèd Quakers), for public meetings, and for military drills. The gallows were removed in 1817 and cow grazing was officially banned in 1830, around the time that urban cow ownership began falling out of fashion. In 1910, the Olmsted brothers oversaw a massive landscape renovation, designating Boston Common as the anchor of the "Emerald Necklace," a system of connected parks that winds through many of Boston's neighborhoods.

Boston Common embodies the spirit of the city around it. Tourists, students, business people on lunch breaks, homeless Bostonians, and strolling older folks co-inhabit the park. On the lawn, squirrels and pigeons fight the latest chapter in their centuries-old gang war, while ducks enjoy the free bread on offer from park-goers.

Adjacent to the park is the Public Garden, former swampland that was filled in 1837. The nation's first botanical garden, its French style of ornamental beds and paths is in sharp contrast to the Common's informal, pastoral English layout.

Activities

The Freedom Trail (page 186) is a 2.5-mile path through downtown Boston that passes 16 of the city's historic landmarks. You'll find detailed route maps and information at the Visitor Center on Boston Common where the trail begins. Many of the sites along the red-painted line are free, others ask for a donation, others charge.

Frog Pond serves as a part-time ice-skating rink in winter and a splashing pool for children in summer. The long, smooth paths that traverse the Common make it ideal for cyclists, rollerbladers, scooters, joggers, and walkers. Throughout the year, the park plays host to concerts, plays, political rallies, and other formal and informal gatherings.

How to Get There

Tremont, Beacon, Charles, Park, and Boylston Streets bind Boston Common. Parking is available, believe it or not, under the Common on Charles Street. By car, take the Mass Pike (I-90) to the Copley Square exit. Go straight at the off ramp onto Stuart Street. Take a left onto Charles Street by the Radisson Hotel.

By mass transit, take the Green Line or the Silver Line bus to the Boylston T stop at the corner of Boylston Street and Tremont Street. This stop is heavily used by tourists and locals, so expect it to be extremely busy. Another equally busy option is to take the Red Line or Green Line to the Park Street T stop at the northeastern edge of the Common, by the State House.

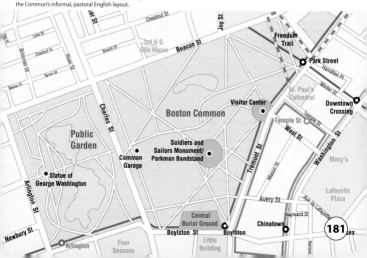

Overview

West Somerville's center for business, dining, and entertainment, Davis Square has become one of Boston's coolest places to be. Widely regarded as a north-of-the-river haven for hipsters, Somerville has been hailed as a model for urban renewal, although not all locals share that rosy view. Older residents to the east look down on Davis as a pierced, tattooed gentrifying monster perched on the edge of what has always been a working-class city.

If there's one thing Somerville doesn't want to be, it's Cambridge. It may in part be due to this attitude that Davis Square has evolved differently than other commercial areas with large student populations. Davis maintains a friendly, neighborhood feel and coffee shop personality through its focus on local business. There are chains in the area (a Starbucks, of course), but there is not the saturation seen in, say, Harvard Square.

Entry into the area's cultural art scene can be gained at any number of community events, including ArtBeat, an annual two-day arts festival sponsored by the Somerville Arts Council and usually held in late July (www.somervilleartscouncil.org). The Somerville Theater, a historic landmark in the square, offers Off-Broadway fare.

In addition to a variety of clubs and bars, Davis features record stores, retail outlets, galleries, a movie theater, and one of Boston's best bookstores, McIntyre & Moore (255 Elm Street). Its well-lit streets and centralized location between Harvard and Tufts make Davis Square a near-perfect spot for the night owl looking to have a good time. Good news: those things lurking in the shadows as you exit the T stop aren't muggers; they're statues (of people who just happen to look like muggers).

How to Get There—Driving

From Massachusetts Avenue, Central Square, and Harvard Square, take Mass Ave. west (toward Arlington) to Porter Square. Pass the Red Line T stop and KFC on left. Turn right onto Russell Street and at the end of Russell, take a left onto Highland Avenue. Davis Square is directly ahead.

From the north, take I-93 to exit 31/Rte 16. Stay in the right hand lane and turn right onto Harvard Street at the lights. Continue straight for two miles to the Powder House rotary. Take the fourth right around the rotary onto College Avenue. Go down the hill to Davis Square.

From the south, take I-93 to exit 29/Rte 28 S. Go through the light and straight under the elevated highway onto Mystic Avenue. Mystic runs alongside the expressway. Make a left onto Harvard Street (third light) and follow it for two miles to the Powder House rotary. Take the fourth right around the rotary onto College Avenue. Go down the hill to Davis Square.

From the west, take Rte 2 East and exit at 29. Stay in the left lane when the highway goes from four to two lanes (after the bowling alley). Bear left through lights onto Rte 16 E/Rte 3 N. At the second light make a right onto Broadway. Bear right at the next major intersection onto Holland Street. (Fire station on your right.) Follow Holland into Davis Square.

Parking

Davis Square experiences most of its parking congestion at night with the bustling nightlife in the area, but there is plenty of metered parking. There are also two public parking lots that are open after 6 pm and seven public parking lots that are metered before 6 pm and free at night. If you're visiting the Square, we advise you not to park in the local residents' spaces on side streets—parking tickets abound and residents have been known to leave nasty notes under wipers! Redbones (55 Chester Street) offers free bicycle valet parking for anyone visiting Davis Square.

How to Get There—Mass Transit

The Red Line stops at Davis Square at the intersection of College Avenue, Elm Street, and Holland Street, with easy access to all surrounding restaurants, stores, and venues.

Restaurants

- **Angelina's Pizza & Subs** (pizza & sub shop) • 230 Holland St • 617-776-1240
- **Anna's Taqueria** (Tex-Mex food) • 236 Elm St • 617-666-3900
- **Antonia's Italian Bistro** (Italian food) • 37 Davis Sq (College Ave) • 617-623-6700
- **Au Bon Pain** (fast French food) • 18 Holland St • 617-623-9601
- **Blue Shirt Café** (wraps & smoothies) • 424 Highland Ave • 617-629-7641
- **The Burren** (Irish pub food) • 247 Elm St • 617-776-6896
- **Café Rossini** (coffee shop) • 278-B Highland Ave • 617-625-5240
- **Carberry's Bakery Coffeehouse** (bakery & sandwiches) • 187 Elm St • 617-666-2233
- **Chieko Japanese & Korean** (Japanese & Korean) • 132 College Ave • 617-354-6888
- **China Sun** (Chinese food) • 7 Holland St • 617-625-6068
- **Cristo's Seven Star Pizza** (pizza) • 233 Elm St • 617-628-9090

- **Davis Square Pizza & Subs** (pizza & subs) · 351 Highland Ave · 617-625-2255
- **Denise's Homemade Ice Cream** (ice cream) · 4 College Ave · 617-628-2764
- **Diesel Café** (coffeehouse) · 257 Elm St · 617-629-8717
- **Diva Indian Bistro** (Indian food) · 246 Elm St · 617-629-4963
- **Dragon Garden Restaurant** (Chinese) · 261 Elm St · 617-623-4383
- **Fusion Express** (Asian food) · 195 Elm St · 617-623-3354
- **Gargoyles on the Square Bar & Grill** (American cuisine) · 219 Elm St · 617-776-5300
- **Golden Light Restaurant** (Chinese food) · 24 College Ave · 617-666-9822
- **Highland Avenue Cuisine** (seafood) · 2 Highland Ave · 617-625-8333
- **House of Tibet Kitchen** (Tibetan food) · 235 Holland Ave · 617-629-7567
- **Joshua Tree Bar & Grille** (bar & eclectic restaurant) · 256 Elm St · 617-623-9910
- **Mike's Restaurant** (Italian food, pizza) · 9 Davis Sq · 617-628-2379
- **Mr. Crepe** (French food, mostly crêpes) · 83 Holland Ave · 617-628-1500
- **Nick's Roast Beef** (sandwich shop) · 20 College Ave · 617-625-1497
- **Orleans** (new American cuisine) · 65 Holland Ave · 617-591-2100
- **Out of the Blue** (Italian & seafood) · 382 Highland Ave · 617-776-5020
- **Picante Mexican Grill** (healthy Mexican food) · 217 Elm St · 617-628-6394
- **Redbones** (BBQ, soul food) · 55 Chester St · 617-628-2200
- **Renee's Café** (café) · 198 Holland St · 617-623-2727
- **Rosebud Diner** (diner) · 381 Summer St · 617-666-6015
- **Rudy's Café** (Tex-Mex) · 248 Holland Street · 617-623-9201
- **Sabur Restaurant & Lounge** (seafood, Mediterranean) · 212 Holland Ave · 617-776-7890
- **Savannah Grill** (Mediterranean) · 233A Elm St · 617-666-4200
- **Sesa's Cold Cuts & Italian Specialties** (Italian) · 414 Highland Ave · 617-776-6687
- **Someday Café** (coffeehouse) · 51 Davis Sq · 617-623-3323
- **Spring Hill Variety & Deli** (deli) · 235 Highland Ave · 617-625-0603
- **Tacos Lupita Mexican Grill** (Mexican & Salvadoran food) · 13 Elm St · 617-666-0677
- **Virgies Rendezvous Café** (café) · 150 Highland Ave · 617-625-2330
- **Wing Works** (wings) · 201 Elm St · 617-666-9000
- **Yee Village Restaurant** (Chinese food) · 400A Highland Ave · 617-623-0330
- **Yummy Hut** (Chinese food) · 217 Highland Ave · 617-628-1128

Bars

- **The Burren** (Irish pub/restaurant) · 247 Elm St · 617-776-6896
- **Johnny D's Uptown Restaurant & Music Club** (club & restaurant) · 17 Holland St · 617-776-2004
- **The Joshua Tree** (bar & eclectic restaurant) · 256 Elm St · 617-623-9910
- **Sligo's** (bar) · 237 Elm St · 617-623-9651
- **PJ Ryan's** (bar) · 239 Holland Ave · 617-625-8200

Clothing Shops

- **Black & Blues** (unusual clothing) · 89 Holland St · 617-628-0046
- **Chinook Outdoor Adventure** (outdoor wear) · 93 Holland St · 617-776-8616
- **Goodwill** (thrift store) · 230 Elm St · 617-628-3618
- **Pluto** (clothes, housewares, gifts) · 215 Elm St · 617-666-2005

Entertainment

- **Somerville Theatre** (second-run movies in classic theater for discount prices and music acts) · 55 Davis Sq · 617-625-5700
- **Jimmy Tingle's Off Broadway Theater** (available for rent) · 255 Elm St · 617-591-1616

Other Goods & Services

- **Ace Wheelworks** (bike shop) · 145 Elm St · 617-776-2100
- **Alibrandi's Barber Shop** (barber shop) · 194 Holland St · 617-628-4282
- **Baker Travel** (travel agency) · 407 Highland Ave · 617-629-2660
- **Best Pest Control Services** (pest control) · 63A Elm St · 617-625-4850
- **Big Fish Little Fish** (pet store) · 55 Elm St · 617-666-2444
- **CD Spins** (record store) · 235 Elm St · 617-666-8080
- **Citizens Bank** (bank) · 212 Elm St · 617-629-3936
- **Davis Square Cleaners** (dry cleaners) · 237 Elm St · 617-628-3950
- **Davis Square Dental** (dentist) · 51 Holland St · 617-623-6767
- **Davis Square Martial Arts** (martial arts instruction) · 408 Highland Ave · 617-591-9656
- **Davis Square Shoe Repair** (shoe repair) · 260 Elm St · 617-776-8580
- **Downtown Wine & Spirits** (liquor store) · 225 Elm St · 617-625-7777
- **Disc Diggers** (used & discounted CDs) · 401 Highland Ave · 617-776-7560
- **Editorial Humor** (newspaper) · 240 Elm St · 617-666-2888
- **Errico Studio** (photographer) · 259 Elm St · 617-776-4611
- **Farmer's Bounty** (grocery store) · 234 Elm St · 617-625-5537
- **Fleet Bank** (bank) · 406 Highland Ave · 617-666-0288
- **Gulf** (gas station) · 371 Highland St · 617-776-9090
- **Lucky Market** (grocery store) · 54 Elm Pl · 617-776-0232
- **Mail Boxes Etc** (mailing services) · 411A Highland Ave · 617-776-4949
- **Massage Therapy Works of Davis Square** (massage therapy) · 255 Elm St · 617-684-4000
- **McIntyre & Moore** (used scholarly bookstore) · 255 Elm St · 617-629-4840
- **McKinnon's Choice Meat Market** (meat market) · 239A Elm St · 617-666-0888
- **Middlesex Federal Savings Bank** (bank) · 1 College Ave · 617-666-4700
- **Mission Church of Our Lord Jesus Christ** (Pentecostal church) · 130 Highland Ave · 617-628-5260
- **T.F. Murphy Florist** (florist) · 346 Highland Ave · 617-666-8050
- **Nellie's Wildflowers** (florist) · 72 Holland St · 617-625-9453
- **Somerville News** (newspaper) · 1 Davis Sq · 617-666-4010
- **Somerville Sewing Center** (sewing supplies) · 280 Elm St · 617-625-6668
- **Somerville YMCA** (YMCA) · 101 Highland Ave · 617-625-5050
- **Sovereign Bank** (bank) · 403 Highland Ave · 617-623-5875
- **Store 24** (convenience store) · 4 College Ave · 617-666-0650
- **Used Sound** (music gear) · 31 Holland St · 617-625-7707
- **Your Move Games** (gamer's den) · 400 Highland Ave · 617-666-5799
- **Farmer's Market** · May 21–Nov 26 · Wednesdays, 12–6 pm; at the corner of Day St & Herbert St

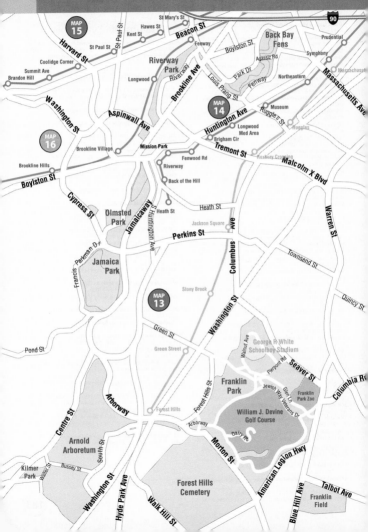

General Information

Address: Emerald Necklace Conservancy,
2 Brookline Place, Brookline, MA 02445
Phone: 617-232-5374
Website: www.emeraldnecklace.org

Overview

Although most known for Central Park, celebrated landscape architect Frederick Law Olmsted created a beautiful string of Boston parks when he moved to Brookline in 1883. Based on the idea that you'd be able to walk from Back Bay to Franklin Park barefoot and without worry, Olmsted's necklace has been broken over the years, both by the construction of the Casey Overpass near Franklin Park and by the conversion of the Riverway, Jamaicaway, and Arborway from pleasant carriage paths to major roads carrying highway-amounts of traffic. The city and conservation groups are putting together a "master plan" for the severed sections of the necklace and are trying to balance desire to restore the path with traffic concerns. The Boston Park Rangers offer walking and biking tours of the Necklace. If you're interested in a tour, call 617-635-7487.

Franklin Park

The largest park in the Emerald Necklace, Franklin Park is 500 acres in size. Within the park are the Zoo, an 18-hole golf course (617-265-4084), a 100-acre woodland, and a seven-acre pond. The Franklin Park Zoo (not part of Olmsted's original plan), which opened in 1911, is home to the "Butterfly Landing," a butterfly enclosure open seasonally from June through September. In the summer and fall of 2003, the zoo made headlines when adolescent gorilla "Little Joe" escaped from his enclosure—twice. The first time, he stayed on site. The second time, he ended up at a bus stop in Roxbury. Zoo Entry: adults $9.50, children $5, seniors $8; winter hours (Oct 1–Mar 31), 10 am–4 pm; summer hours, 10 am–5 pm weekdays and 6 pm weekends and holidays; www.zoonewengland.com; 617-541-LION.

Arnold Arboretum

The oldest arboretum in the country, Arnold Arboretum is named after James Arnold, who financed its construction. It displays world-renowned collections of shrubs and trees for education and research. People visit the park principally for the exotic greenery, which includes bonsai and lilac trees. Because Arnold left most of his estate to Harvard and the school uses the park as a nature museum, it seems only fair for the city government to allow the grand university to rent the land for a dollar a year. Winter hours (Nov–Feb), 9 am–4 pm weekdays, 10 am–2 pm weekends; summer hours (Mar–Oct), 9 am–4pm weekdays, 12 pm–4 pm weekends. Closed Sundays in January and February and also on holidays. Entry is free!

Jamaica Park

Affectionately called "the jewel in the Emerald Necklace," this park features Jamaica Pond, a 60-acre kettlehole formed by an ancient glacier. Natural springs make this pond, which is up to 90 feet deep, the largest and purest body of water within Boston. The pond is so clean that it serves as a back-up city reservoir. Although "Pinebank," the only original building in the Emerald Necklace, is now in a state of disrepair, the Boston Parks Department has plans to protect the site from further deterioration. Other buildings include a boathouse (617-522-6258) where canoes, sailboats, and rowboats can be rented, as well as an outdoor bandstand that sometimes hosts small orchestras. Fishing is one of the most popular activities and every year the City of Boston stocks the pond with trout, salmon, and the indigenous pickerel, bass, hornpout, and perch.

Olmsted Park

Built by the City of Boston in collaboration with the Town of Brookline, Olmsted Park showcases the landscape architect's unique design philosophy, with a series of dramatic vistas that help you understand why Olmsted is the Boston Brahmin equivalent of a rock star (the city boasts at least one Olmsted impersonator). A great feature of the park is the human-made Muddy River, currently the site of a major dredging project, where you can fish in the relative seclusion of Wards Pond. Substantial restoration is ongoing, with a new bike/pedestrian path system on the Brookline side from Jamaica Pond to Boylston Street (Route 9) currently completed.

Riverway Park

The narrowest park in the system, Riverway lies in the valley of the Muddy River, which is the boundary between Boston and Brookline. Wholly human-made, steep banks and edges wooded by majestic beech trees conceal the busy roadways beyond.

Back Bay Fens

Olmsted's engineering masterpiece, the Back Bay Fens was designed to solve the increasing problems caused by flushing out the stagnant Muddy River waterway at low tide. Transformed from salt- to fresh-water marsh after 1910 with the creation of the Charles River Dam, the Fens encompasses a variety of features including the elegant Rose Garden, War Memorials, and the Victory Garden. The Victory Garden was created during World War II to grow extra food for troops and is now tended to by local green thumbs who shell out $20 per year to maintain a plot. A former parking lot, the western end of the Fens was recently converted into more green space. Known primarily for its beauty, it is a notorious local fact that more than mere gardening takes place on the grounds—think George Michael.

Freedom Trail & Black Heritage Trail

PLACES OF INTEREST

Freedom Trail
1. State House
2. Park Street Church
3. Granary Burying Ground
4. King's Chapel
5. Ben Franklin Statue
6. Old Corner Bookstore
7. Old South Meeting House
8. Old State House
9. Boston Massacre Site
10. Faneuil Hall
11. Paul Revere House
12. Old North Church
13. Copp's Hill Burial Ground
14. Bunker Hill Monument
15. USS Constitution Museum

Black Heritage Trail
1. Shaw Memorial
2. Middleton House
3. Phillips School
4. Smith House
5. Charles Street Meeting House
6. Hayden House
7. Coburn Gaming House
8. Smith Court Residences
9. African Meeting House
10. Smith School

General Information

Address: Visitor Center, 147 Tremont Street
Freedom Website: www.thefreedomtrail.org
Black Heritage Website: www.afroammuseum.org/trail.htm
Walking Tours: Available during spring/summer/fall ($12 adults, $6 children)
Audio Tours: Audio players available at the Visitor Center. $12 rental; 617-227-8800
Trolley Tours: Available for groups of 20 or more; 617-227-8800

Freedom Trail Overview

An idea sparked by a journalist in 1958, Boston's Freedom Trail is a convenient linkage between Revolutionary War sites. Marked by a large red line either painted on the sidewalks or marked by red brick, the trail guides visitors from the Visitor Center on Boston Common to the Charlestown Navy Yard on the other side of the Charles River. The 2.5-mile trek passes by 16 different historical sites, including the Boston Massacre location, Paul Revere's house, a couple of old cemeteries, and Bunker Hill. Walking tours leave the Visitor Center every 30 minutes and a complete trail walk usually lasts approximately 90 minutes. Audio tours and trolley tours are also available.

Trail Head: The Boston Common—America's oldest public park, this 44-acre green is home to squirrels, pigeons, walkers, joggers, bikers, squirrels, pigeons, dogs, ducks, squirrels, and pigeons. See page 181.

1. **The State House**—The Massachusetts state government sits here, in the oldest building on Beacon Hill. Mon–Fri 10 am–4 pm; 617-727-3676.

2. **Park Street Church**—The Church was constructed in 1809 and has since stood as a testament to the Bostonian faith. 617-523-3383. Hours: Jun 17–Aug 31, Tue–Sat 9:30 am–3:30 pm. Summer worship services: Sundays 10:45 am and 5:30 pm. Winter worship services: Sundays 8:30 am, 11 am, 4 pm, and 6 pm.

3. **Granary Burying Ground**—An epitaph here reads "Revere's Tomb," near the resting places of both John Hancock and Samuel Adams, and a giant monolith paying tribute to the family of Boston-born Ben Franklin. Open daily 9 am–5 pm; 617-635-4505.

4. **King's Chapel**—The chapel was built with the objective that it "would be the equal of any in England." Summer hours: Mon, Thu, Fri, Sat 10 am–4 pm; winter hours: Sat 10 am–4 pm. Services are held Wednesdays 12:15 pm and Sundays 11 am; 617-227-2155.
King's Chapel Burying Ground—Older than the Granary and the final resting place of some of Boston's first settlers. Open daily, 9 am–5 pm; 617-635-4505.

5. **Benjamin Franklin's Statue/Site of the First Public School**—Boston Latin School, founded in 1635, is still open (but it's since moved to the Fenway). The old high school is considered the top public school in Boston. Sidewalks here are always packed with people going about their downtown routines, a reminder that Boston's past and present occupy the same small space.

6. **Old Corner Bookstore Building**—A steady bookseller since 1829. Mon–Fri, 9 am–5:30 pm. Sat 9:30 am–5 pm. Closed Sundays; 617-367-4004.

7. **Old South Meeting House**—"Voices of Protest," a permanent exhibit in the house, speaks of generations who made history under one roof. Nov–Mar, 10 am–4 pm. Apr–Oct, 9:30 am–5 pm. Adults $5, students and seniors $4, children (6-18) $1, children under 6 free; 617-482-6439.

8. **Old State House**—The building's lush exterior will draw you inside, where the Bostonian Society houses its museum of Boston's past and a library. Library: Tues–Thurs, 9:30 am–4:30 pm. Daily use fee: non-members $10, college students $5. Museum: Open daily 9 am–5 pm. Adults $5, older adults (62+) $4, students (over 18) $4, children (6-18) $1; 617-720-1713.

9. **Site of the Boston Massacre**—Cobblestones now mark this historic site.

10. **Faneuil Hall**—Shopping mixed with history, with some eateries to boot. If you like touristy knick-knacks, this is the place to shop. Open daily 9 am–5 pm. Historical talks every thirty minutes, 9:30 am–4:30 pm. See page 190.

11. **Paul Revere House**—See how Boston's patriot once lived. Keep in mind that when he lived there, the area wasn't filled with Italian restaurants. Apr 15–Oct 31, 9:30 am–5:15 pm. Nov 1–Apr 14, 9:30 am–4:15 pm. Closed Mondays, Jan–Mar. Adults $3, seniors and college students $2.50, children (aged 5-17) $1; 617-523-2338.

12. **Old North Church**—The oldest church building in Boston, this is where two lanterns were placed the night before the battles at Lexington and Concord. As you may recall, it was "one if by land, two if by sea." The British took boats across the Charles to make their way towards the now-famous western villages, so two lanterns were hung. Winter hours daily 9 am–5 pm. Summer hours daily 9 am–6 pm; 617-523-6676.

13. **Copp's Hill Burying Ground**—Many free African Americans now rest here. This spot was also used for public hangings. Open daily 9 am–5 pm; 617-635-4505.

14. **Bunker Hill Monument**—A 221-foot granite obelisk commemorates the Battle of Bunker Hill—the first major battle of the American Revolution. The monument sits atop Breed's Hill, where the misnamed battle actually took place. A visitor's center houses exhibits explaining how the battle came to be and how it was won. Open daily 9 am–4:30 pm; 617-242-5641.

15. **USS Constitution**—A.k.a. "Old Ironsides," America's oldest commissioned warship. Winter hours, Thurs–Sun 10 am–4 pm. Summer hours, daily 10 am–4 pm. Tours occur every half-hour; 617-242-5670. See Charlestown Navy Yard page 179.

Black Heritage Trail Overview

Running north from the State House, this trail recognizes the historical significance of Boston's African-American community. After the American Revolution, free black people congregated in the area now known as the North Slope of Beacon Hill. In 1790, when the first federal census was taken, Massachusetts was the only state in the country to record no slaves. The historic homes on the Black Heritage Trail are private residences and are not open to the public. The only two buildings you can enter are the African Meeting House and the Abiel Smith School.

1. **Robert Gould Shaw and the 54th Regiment Memorial**—Located on Boston Common, this monument was built in 1897 in honor of the first all-Black regiment who fought for the Union Army during the Civil War.

2. **George Middleton House**—(5-7 Pinckney St) George Middleton was the commander of an all-Black military company called the Bucks of America during the Revolutionary War. His house, erected in 1797, is the oldest standing wooden structure on Beacon Hill.

3. **The Phillips School**—(Anderson and Pinckney Streets) One of the first Boston public schools to be integrated in 1855 as a result of the historic court case, *Roberts v. Massachusetts*, which opposed the racial segregation of the city's schools.

4. **John J. Smith House**—(86 Pinckney St) John J. Smith was born free in Virginia in 1820 and eventually moved to Boston where he opened a successful barbershop that catered to many wealthy white customers from all over Boston. His shop served as a haven for anti-slavery debates and fugitive slaves.

5. **Charles Street Meeting House**—(Mt Vernon and Charles Streets) Built in 1807, the Charles Street Meeting House was originally the site of the segregated Third Baptist Church. After a failed attempt to desegregate the church, Timothy Gilbert and several other abolitionist sympathizers left the church to form the Free Baptist Church, the first integrated church in America.

6. **Lewis and Harriet Hayden House**—(66 Phillips St) Lewis and Harriet Hayden ran a boarding house out of their home, which was also a stop on the Underground Railroad. Lewis Hayden was an ardent African-American abolitionist and community leader who served as a delegate for the Republican Convention, fought for women's rights, and helped found the Museum of Fine Arts.

7. **John Coburn Gaming House**—(2 Phillips St) The site of one of the most lucrative Black-owned businesses in the city, the gaming house was built in 1843 and catered to Boston's white elite. John Coburn used the profits from the successful business to finance several abolitionist groups in the community, including the Massasoit Guards. Founded as an all-Black military company to support the state's troops in case of war, the Guards also patrolled Beacon Hill to protect African-Americans from slave catchers.

8. **Smith Court Residences** (3, 5, 7, 7A, & 10 Smith Ct) Five remaining wooden houses located on Beacon Hill's north slope were all purchased by middle-class African Americans from white landowners.

9. **The African Meeting House**—(8 Smith Ct) Founded as a response to racial discrimination in Boston's religious communities, the African Meeting House remains the oldest standing Black church building in the country. The structure was built using labor and donations from the African-American community. It was used for religious services, as a safe haven for political discussion, and as a makeshift school for Black children until the Abiel Smith School came into existence.

10. **Abiel Smith School**—(46 Joy St) Built in 1834 as the first schoolhouse in America to educate Black school children, the Abiel Smith School was under-funded, overcrowded, and under-staffed. Substandard conditions led to the historic *Roberts v. Massachusetts* court case and the desegregation of schools in 1855. Winter hours: 10 am–4 pm, Mon–Sat. Summer hours: 10 am–4 pm daily. Closed Thanksgiving, Christmas, and New's Year's Day. Admission is free.

Overview

Formerly a cattle grazing site four times its present size, Cambridge Common has been a hub of political and social activity for over 300 years. Even with the addition of tot lots and a softball field, this historical urban oasis remains an important place for ideas and protest. Just steps from Harvard University, in recent years activists have used the Common's corner on Massachusetts Avenue to protest everything from the occupation of Iraq, to Israelis in Palestine, to the existence of sport utility vehicles.

William Dawes, along with Paul Revere and Dr. Samuel Prescott, rode his horse across the Common on his way to warn those in Lexington and Concord that "the regulars are coming" (not that "the British are coming," which would have made no sense, since colonists still considered themselves British). Though Revere had a famous poem written about him and countless cities named after him, Dawes was commemorated with lousy bronze hoof prints in the pavement of the Common. On July 2, 1775, George Washington took control of the Continental Army camped on Cambridge Common. Three cannons that the colonists seized from the Lobsterbacks still sit by the flagpole. There's also a memorial to victims of the Irish Potato Famine.

Attractions

Relaxing and people watching are by far the best two activities to undertake on the Common. With its prime location next to Harvard Square, you can experience the feeling of being a Harvard student, without the excessive course fees and mandatory high IQ.

The park boasts a fenced-in playground, located on the corner of Garden and Waterhouse Streets, where you can release your kids for a while and let them roam safely. The playground was last renovated in 1990 (including the addition of a wooden climbing structure, swings, bridges, slides, and benches/ picnic tables) and is recommended for parents with children aged one to ten.

Sports

There's a softball field and areas for soccer and other light recreation, along with the typical bike paths for cyclists, skaters, joggers, and walkers. Despite its inextricable link with afternoon softball games, the rules say that the use of alcoholic beverages on the ball field is forbidden.

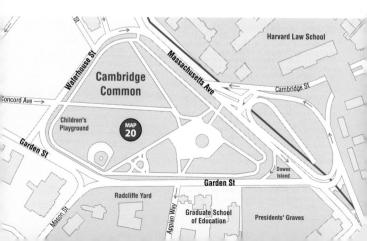

General Information

NFT map:	#2
Website:	www.faneuilhallmarketplace.com
Address:	4 South Market Bulding
Phone:	617-523-1300

Faneuil Hall

Faneuil Hall was built by Boston's wealthiest merchant, Peter Faneuil, in 1742. It's a historically poignant section of commercial property: the place where Samuel Adams rallied for independence (prior to his interest in brewing beer), where the doctrine of "no taxation without representation" was established, and where figures such as George Washington celebrated our country's freedom. It's still both a commercial spot and a meeting place, with shops on the first floor, the Great Hall on the second, and a museum on the third.

Since its inception, the Faneuil Hall Marketplace has been the shopping hub of the city, sporting over 70 shops and 14 restaurants. The marketplace alone attracts more than 12 million visitors a year and hosts numerous events and festivals. Local talent includes jugglers, mimes (yes, those too), magicians, and bands. If you're looking to be entertained while you shop, Faneuil Hall is your place.

Four buildings make up the marketplace: Faneuil Hall, Quincy Market, North Market, and South Market. Touristy and crowded at times, it's still one of the best places to buy souvenirs, shop in a mall-like environment, and try any number of different local dishes. We recommend picking up a lobster t-shirt while you're there. The Hall is open Monday through Saturday from 10 am to 9 pm, and from noon to 6 pm on Sundays. Shopping hours in the other marketplaces vary by vendor.

Quincy Market

Located directly behind Faneuil Hall, this is where you go to chow down. The center of the market has quite a few different places to eat, especially if you're looking to get a taste of the local seafood. Surrounding the food vendors is a semi-enclosed mall that includes unique places such as Cybersmith, an outlet for virtual reality gaming.

Like many places in Boston, Quincy Market is built on landfill in what used to be Boston Harbor. Unlike other sections, when you're in Quincy Market, you're standing on bones. The butchers who used to occupy the wharves behind Faneuil Hall would let their unusable animal parts pile up, creating a sanitation nightmare. Then, someone had the bright idea of throwing the bones in the water, which eventually helped fill the wharf area and allowed for the construction of Quincy Market.

Less crowded and with more shops and eateries, the North Market and South Markets stand on either side of Quincy Hall. The Markets offer a more relaxed restaurant eating experience, if you need to escape the clamor of the tourist scene.

Museum

Ancient and Honorable Artillery Company Museum; 617-227-1638; Mon–Fri 9 am-3:30 pm.
Located on Faneuil Hall's third floor, this museum and library showcases the history of the Ancient and Honorable Artillery Company. The oldest military organization in the US (and third-oldest in the world), this august body was established as the Military Company of Boston in 1637 and still holds military drills and participates in various ceremonial events. The museum proudly displays the company's artifacts. It is a unique collection that is well worth a visit for military and history buffs.

How to Get There—Driving

Faneuil Hall is adjacent to (now submerged) I-93. Drivers coming into Boston from the south on I-93 will have three options to exit from the new I-93 N: 1. Exit 20 (I-90/South Station) to South Station and then proceed northerly up Atlantic Avenue. 2. Exit 20 to I-90 E and follow signs to South Boston and then proceed back over the Moakley Bridge. 3. Exit 23 (Gov't Ctr.) and follow the signs towards "Aquarium".

Drivers coming into Boston from the west on the Mass Pike (I-90) will have two options: 1. Stay on I-90 E and take exit 25 (South Boston) and then proceed back over the Moakley Bridge; 2. Take exit 24A to South Station and then proceed northerly up Atlantic Avenue; 3. Take exit 24B to the new I-93 N tunnel, use exit 23 (Gov't Ctr.) and follow the signs towards "Aquarium".

Parking

There are over 10,724 places to safely leave your car within a two-mile radius of Faneuil Hall. If you want to opt for a parking garage, $8 parking is available after 5 pm on weekdays and all day Saturday, Sunday, and selected holidays with store validation. Discounted parking is available at 75 State Street with validation from any Faneuil Hall Marketplace merchant.

How to Get There—Mass Transit

Faneuil Hall Marketplace is conveniently located within a block of three T stops: the Green Line serves the Government Center & Haymarket stops. Catch the Blue Line for access to the Aquarium stop. And to get to the State stop, grab the Orange Line or the Blue Line.

Shopping

A Hat for Every Head (pushcart)
Abercrombie & Fitch
Accento
African Collections (pushcart)
ALFA Designs Building (pushcart)
Ann Taylor
April Cornell
Art For 'Em (pushcart)
Batik Adventure
Bill Rodgers Running Center
Boston All Stars
Boston Logos (pushcart)
Boston Sun Spot (pushcart)
Boxers To Go (pushcart)
Celtic Weavers
Coach
Conversations Building (pushcart)
The Crafty Rose
Cuoio
Custom Caps
Dalliance Incorporated
Designs by Sandra (pushcart)
The Dog House (pushcart)
Every Bead of My Heart (pushcart)
Express
Fantasy Island
Fresh Things
Harvest Fare (pushcart)
Head Games (pushcart)
Kristina's
La Cloche (pushcart)
Life is a Highway (pushcart)
Merry Trading Company (pushcart)
Nightshirts To Go (pushcart)
Nine West
Ocean Man (pushcart)
Orient Express (pushcart)
Orvis
Out of Left Field (pushcart)
Sea Boston USA (pushcart)
Sock It To Me
Victoria's Secret
Wilson's Leather

Goods & Gifts

Artists See Boston (pushcart)
Bath & Body Works
Boston Pewter Company
Bostonian Society Museum Shop
Cheers Gift Shop
Chesapeake Knife & Tool
The Christmas Dove
Crabtree & Evelyn
Crate & Barrel
Discovery Channel Store
Exotic Flowers
Faneuil Hall Heritage Shop

FYE (For Your Entertainment)
Gateway News
Geoclassics
Godiva Chocolatier
Happy Hangups (pushcart)
Henri's Glassworks
Illusions
Local Charm
Magic Rice (pushcart)
Magnetic Chef (pushcart)
The Massage Animals (pushcart)
The Monkey Bar (pushcart)
Museum of Fine Arts Store
Musically Yours (pushcart)
Origins
Picture You ½ Hour Photo
Plumage Jewelry (pushcart)
Sluggers Upper Deck Kiosk (pushcart)
Stuck on Stickpins (pushcart)
Sunglass Hut & Watch Station
Swatch
Teeny Billboards (pushcart)
Touch of Irish (pushcart)
Wit Crafts (pushcart)
Whippoorwill Crafts
Yankee Candle Company
Zoinks! A Wicked Cool Toy Store

Food

A La Carte
Al Mercantino
Ames Plow Tavern
Aris Barbeque
Baja Fresh Mexican Grill
Bangkok Express
Bistany International
Bombay Club
Boston & Maine Fish Co
Boston Chipyard
Boston Chowda
Boston Pretzel
Boston Pretzel & Lemonade (pushcart)
Boston Rocks
Brown Derby Deli
Carol Ann's Bake Shop
Cheers
Columbo Frozen Yogurt Shoppe
Colombo Yogurt (pushcart)
The Dog House
Durgin Park Restaurant
El Paso Enchiladas
Fisherman's Net
Il Panino
Joey's Gelateria
Kilvert and Forbes
KingFish Hall
La Pastaria
McCormick & Schmick's
Ming Tree

The Monkey Bar
The Monkey Bar (pushcart)
Naked Fish
North End Bakery
Philadelphia Steak & Hoagie
Piccolo Panini
Pinang
Pizzeria Regina
Plaza III, the Kansas City Steak House
The Prime Shoppe
Rustic Kitchen
Salty Dog Seafood Grill & Bar
Sarku Japan
Slugger's Dugout
Sluggers Ice Cream (pushcart)
Starbucks
Steve's Ice Cream & Fudge
Trattoria Il Panino
Walrus and the Carpenter
West End Strollers
Zuma's Tex Mex Café

Bars & Entertainment

Backstage Restaurant & Bar
The Black Horse Tavern
Cheers
Comedy Connection
J.J. Donovan's
Ned Devine's Irish Pub
TK's Jazz Café
Oar Bar & Grill
Parris
Seaside Restaurant & Bar

Services

BosTix Ticket Booth
Faneuil Hall Marketplace Information

Nearby Bars

The Atrium Lounge
Bell in Hand Tavern
Black Rose
Dockside Restaurant & Bar
The Exchange
Hennessey's
The Hong Kong at Faneuil Hall
Indulge Boston
Kitty O'Shea's
The Office
The Rack
The Place
Purple Shamrock
Q
Sissy K's
Union Oyster House
Vertigo

PLAZA LEVEL

SECOND LEVEL

THIRD LEVEL

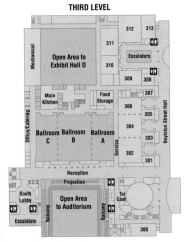

General Information

Address: 900 Boylston St, Boston, MA 02115
Phone: 617-954-2000
Websites: www.mccahome.com;
               www.advantageboston.com

Overview

The John B. Hynes Veterans Memorial Convention Center is a relatively small center, with just 193,000 square feet of exhibit space, a 25,000-square-foot ballroom, and 37 meeting rooms. The Hynes is ideally located in the Back Bay area, with many hotels, historical sites, and tourist attractions within close proximity. Public transportation takes you right to the front door via the Green Line's B, C, and D trains.

Every once in a while, someone proposes that they turn the Hynes into a casino. The idea gets a few days of press and then melts away. Such an interesting and dynamic move is unlikely. Democratic Senator Michael W. Morrissey has suggested that selling the Hynes and a casino license to the highest bidder would help ease the Commonwealth's current monetary woes. So far, House leaders have shown resistance to gambling proposals and Governor Mitt Romney has not yet stated publicly his position on casino gambling. If Morrissey has little support from his political colleagues, he has even less from Back Bay residents, who have vowed to vigorously oppose the proposal at every available opportunity. Any decision will likely be determined by a vote, which will have more chance of resulting in an affirmative outcome if the vote is citywide, rather than limited to Back Bay residents.

Once the only game in town for would-be conventioneers (aside from the Bayside Expo), the Hynes Convention Center will soon be playing second fiddle to the latest Boston semi-public venture. The Boston Convention and Exhibit Center will be located in Southie, far away from any subway line. The new convention center will offer over 500,000 square feet of exhibition space, 160,000 square feet of meeting space, 86 meeting rooms, and a 41,000 square foot ballroom with an adjacent 1,200-room hotel. In other words, it will be huge. Originally slated to open in the summer of 2004, the BCEC looks unlikely to open its doors to exhibitors until mid- to late-2005 at the earliest. Construction of the BCEC is running only slightly behind schedule, but it should be complete by June 2004. Back Bay residents have plenty of time to create placards and plan protest marches—the Hynes won't be hosting a casino any time soon.

Services

The Hynes is used for conferences, meetings, exhibitions, and most other events where groups of people gather together. To schedule an event and be assigned a personal coordinator, contact the sales department on 617-867-8236 or sales@bostonusa.com.

Catering services at the Hynes are provided by Aramark. If you are considering planning a catered event, contact Aramark on 617-954-2284.

How to Get There—Driving

Located in the Back Bay neighborhood, the Hynes is four miles from Logan Airport. Two major roadways, the I-93 and Mass Pike (I-90), will deliver you close to the venue. From I-93, take the Storrow Drive exit (26B). Follow Storrow Drive approximately two miles to the Fenway/Kenmore exit and head towards Fenway. Continue to the first set of lights and merge left onto Boylston Street.

From the Mass Pike, take exit 22 (Prudential/Copley Place), stay left as you exit and turn onto Huntington Avenue. At the next set of lights (Belvidere Street), take a right, follow the curve and bear right onto Dalton Street. At the lights turn right onto Boylston Street.

The main entrance to the Hynes is at 900 Boylston Street and is easily accessible to taxis and buses via an access lane, which is set apart from Boylston Street.

Parking

There are numerous parking garages within a three-block walk of the Hynes, totaling more than 4,500 spaces. There is metered parking available around the Hynes and adjacent streets, but these spots are hard to come by.

- Prudential Center Parking Garage, 800 Boylston St, $15 for an hour-and-a-half, with small increments up to 2.5 hours. Up to 10 hours runs $26, and the daily maximum is $32. 617-236-3060.
- Sheraton Boston Hotel Parking Garage, 39 Dalton St, $12 for 1 hour, $24 for 4–10 hours. 617-236-6172.
- Copley Place Parking Garage, 100 Huntington Ave (Corner of Huntington Avenue & Dartmouth Street), $6 for 1 hour, $22 for 3–10 hours. 617-369-5025.
- Boston Marriott Hotel Copley Place, 100 Huntington Ave, $10 for 1 hour, $32 for 7–24 hours. 617-236-5800.
- Westin Copley Place Parking Garage, 10 Huntington Ave, $10 for 1 hour, $28 for 3 hours. 617-262-9600.
- Colonnade Hotel Parking Garage, 120 Huntington Ave, $8 for 1 hour, $19 for 3–12 hours. 617-424-7000.
- Back Bay Hilton Hotel Parking Garage, 40 Dalton St, $8 for 1 hour, $20 for 3–12 hours. 617-236-1100.

How to Get There—Mass Transit

The subway stops just two blocks away from the Hynes. Take the Green Line (B, C, or D trains) to the Hynes Convention Center/ICA stop. The fare for the subway is $1.25 (D line—$1.50–$3). Once you get off the subway, exit at any entrance and follow the signs to the Hynes.

Long Wharf & Rowes Wharf

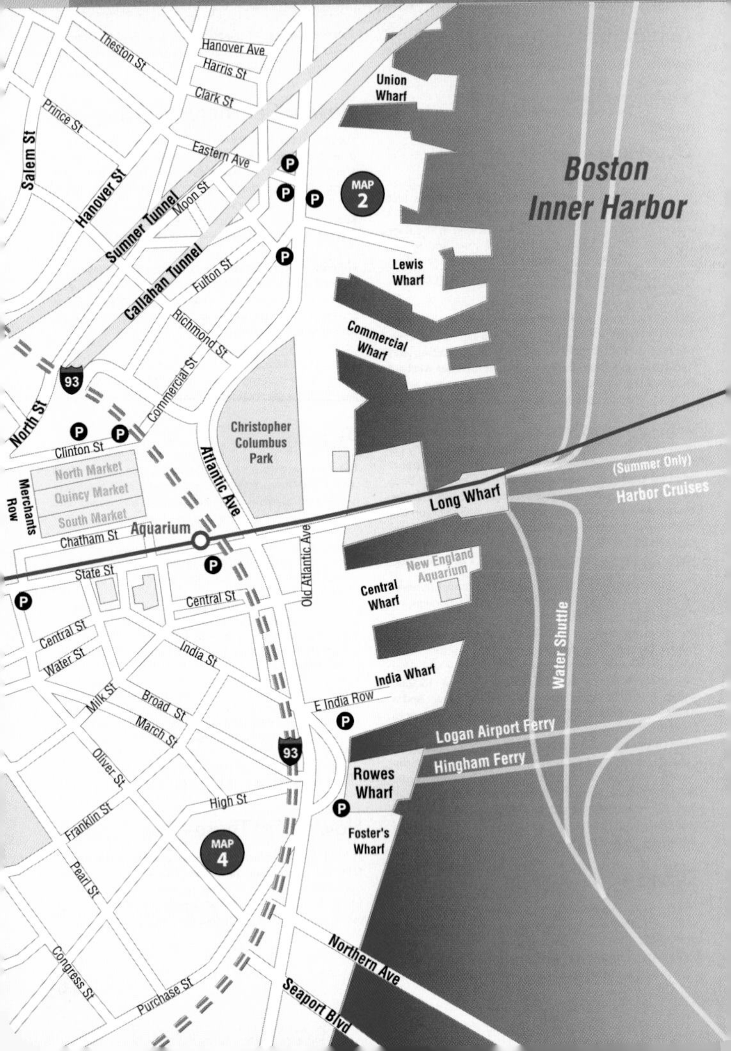

Boston Inner Harbor

Theston St
Hanover Ave
Harris St
Clark St
Prince St
Eastern Ave

Salem St
Hanover St
Sumner Tunnel
Callahan Tunnel

Moon St
Fulton St
Richmond St
Commercial St

Union Wharf

MAP 2

Lewis Wharf

Commercial Wharf

North St

93

Clinton St
North Market
Quincy Market
South Market

Merchants Row

Christopher Columbus Park

Atlantic Ave

Chatham St   Aquarium

State St

Old Atlantic Ave

Long Wharf

(Summer Only)
Harbor Cruises

Central St
Central St
Water St
India St
Milk St
Broad St
March St
Oliver St

E India Row

India Wharf

Central Wharf

New England Aquarium

Water Shuttle

93

Franklin St
High St

MAP 4

Rowes Wharf

Foster's Wharf

Logan Airport Ferry
Hingham Ferry

Pearl St
Congress St

Purchase St

Northern Ave
Seaport Blvd

Overview

Originally named Boston Pier, Long Wharf juts into Boston Harbor near State Street, while Rowes Wharf is further south, near Broad Street. In the 1700s, Long Wharf extended more than 1/3 of a mile into Boston Harbor, but the dumping of urban landfill has resulted in a significant portion of the pier being surrounded by land rather than water.

Attractions

During the warmer months, stop by The Landing Bar on Long Wharf for a drink in the sunshine. It's the perfect place for relaxing after work and before you board your ferry. If you're a Red Sox fan and you don't happen to have tickets, you can catch all of the action on the outdoor televisions!

The New England Aquarium is located at nearby Central Wharf and includes an IMAX Theatre. The Aquarium allows scientists and researchers to study marine and aquatic habitats and to educate the general public about pertinent conservation issues. One of the most exciting events to participate in is a "release party," when an animal is returned to its natural habitat. Recently, Cape Cod hosted the release of five sea turtles, marking the first time in over a decade that turtles were released in local waters rather than shipping them south. Weekdays 9 am–5 pm, weekends 9 am–6 pm, closed Thanksgiving Day. Adults $15.50, seniors $13.50, and children $8.50. www.neaq.org; 617-973-5200.

There are three separate whale-watching excursions that leave from the wharves.

- Liberty • 67 Long Wharf • 617-720-5738
- Boston Harbor Cruises • 1 Long Wharf • 617-227-4321
- Boston Harbor Whale Watch • 50 Rowes Wharf • 617-345-9866

If you're prone to seasickness or if watching whales isn't your bag, Christopher Columbus Park is just a few blocks west of Long Wharf. The playground for the little ones is top notch and its famous rose garden is dedicated to Rose Fitzgerald Kennedy (yes, a rose garden for Rose near Rowes Wharf).

Architecture

The Rowes Wharf Building at 30 Rowes Wharf looks similar in architecture to a Christian Orthodox church. The building relies heavily on polygonal symmetry and its ceiling dome resembles an onion. The secular building houses office space, a four-star hotel, and 100 luxury condominiums. There is a little-known observation area on the ninth floor named the Forester Rotunda, which offers views of both the city and harbor. Though not advertised, you can go through the Boston Harbor Hotel to gain access.

Ferries

Both Long Wharf and Rowes Wharf serve as ferry terminals for the MBTA. F1 transports people to and from Rowes Wharf and Hingham Shipyard. F2 and F2H stop at Long Wharf, Logan Airport, and the Fore River Shipyard. F2H also has limited service to Pemberton Point in Hull, the "H." The F4, which travels to the Charlestown Navy Yard, also uses the Long Wharf terminus. See Ferries page 239. For schedules and maps, go to www.mbta.com/traveling_t/schedules_boats.asp or call 617-222-5215.

How to Get There—Driving

To Long Wharf from the north, take I-93 and get off at exit 24–Callahan Tunnel. Follow the signs to Long Wharf Ferry Terminal. From the south, take exit 23–Government Center/Aquarium. Follow signs to the Aquarium. From the east, take the Sumner Tunnel to Boston, bearing right on Cross Street. Follow signs for I-93 S. Do not take the highway (to the left), but watch for the Dock Square sign (to the right). You'll see Haymarket and the Bostonian Hotel on the right. Follow the signs for Waterfront Surface Artery; Long Wharf is straight ahead on the left.

To Rowes Wharf, from the north, take I-93 (or Route 1 to I-93). Exit at High and Congress Streets. Turn left onto Congress and immediately left onto Atlantic Avenue. The wharf is on the right, two blocks past the Congress/Atlantic intersection.

Parking

There is *very* limited street parking in the area so, if you want to forego driving around to find a free spot, you should try one of the many parking garages that are all within walking distance of the various wharves. Parking fees can cost up $25 or more, depending on how long you stay. If you're willing to shell out the cash, here are a few nearby garages:

- The Rowes Wharf building features an underground discounted parking garage with an entrance on Atlantic Avenue.
- Harbor Garage at the Aquarium, 70 East India Row, 617-367-3847
- 75 State Street Garage, 75 State St, 617-742-7275
- Marketplace Center Garage, 200 State St, 617-367-4373
- Dock Square Garage, 20 Clinton St, 617-367-1885
- LaZ Parking, 290 Commercial St, 617-367-6412
- Sargent's Wharf Parking, 269 Commercial St, 617-367-1681
- 2 Atlantic Avenue Garage, 2 Atlantic Ave, 617-854-3365
- Lewis Wharf Parking, 28 Atlantic Ave, 617-227-3713

How to Get There—Mass Transit

Take the Blue Line to the Aquarium stop or Orange Line to the State stop. The 220 bus from the Quincy Center Red Line stop will also get you there.

Overview

Originally one of the least fashionable streets of Back Bay, Newbury Street has undergone quite a transformation, morphing into Boston's most popular shopping area and a good place to hang out and strut your stuff.

A beautiful stretch of real estate featuring late nineteenth and early twentieth-century architecture, Newbury Street runs eight blocks from the Public Garden west to Massachusetts Avenue. Stores pack the buildings, which were originally designed for residential use, making for a lot of oddly shaped, quirky boutiques. Featuring shops for all ages and tax brackets, from the upper-class Armani to the youthful Urban Outfitters, there are endless ways to spend money here.

In the summertime, the cafés spill out onto the sidewalk, providing a nice environment for those who want to sit and relax and increased difficulty for those who want to walk at regular speeds. For people watching, Newbury Street is the best spot in Boston. A veritable human car crash, you get to see the "hippest" elements of every age group, from 80-year-olds to eight-year-olds, interacting and fighting for space on the same small sidewalk.

History

The whole of Back Bay was swampland until about 1870, when workers completed a massive filling project. As a result, Back Bay is the only neighborhood in Boston to benefit from a modern concept called "urban planning." Streets actually cross each other at 90-degree angles, and at no point is there a traffic circle or an eight-way intersection. Unfortunately, fluctuations in the water table are rotting the wooden planks on which most of the area's structures sit. The result: Back Bay is sinking. It seems that Back Bay residents have more to worry about than the Hynes being converted to a casino.

The architecture on Newbury Street is fairly uniform due to most of the development occurring within the same half-century. Emmanuel Church, designed by Alexander Estey in 1862, was the first building completed on Newbury Street. The Church of the Covenant, built in 1865, houses some spectacular stained glass windows. Its Emmaus Window shines in the dimmest of lights.

How to Get There—Driving

Newbury Street is easy to get to. From I-93 take the Storrow Drive exit. Take the exit for Arlington Street, and proceed up Arlington until you hit Newbury. If you follow signs for either Boston Common or Copley Square you should be able to find Arlington fairly easily.

How to Get There—Mass Transit

From the Green Line you can get off at the Arlington stop, the Copley stop, or the Hynes/ICA stop.

All addresses are on Newbury St.

Clothing

A Pea in the Pod · #10 · maternity wear

Agnes b. · #172 · French clothing for men and women

Akris Shoe Salon · #16 · shoe store

Alan Bilzerian · #34 · designer clothes

Alan Rouleau Couturier · #91 · custom tailoring

Aldo · #180 · shoes and leather goods

Allen Edmonds · #36 · shoes and cedar products

Aliston Beat · #348 · urban clothes

The Altered Bride · #129 · bridal boutique

American Eagle Outfitters · #201 · youth clothes

Ana Hernandez Bridal · #165 · bridal boutique

Ann Taylor Inc. · #18 · women's clothes

Arche Shoes · #123 · shoes

Army Barracks Inc. · #328 · military duds

Banana Republic · #28 · men's and women's clothing

BCBG Max Azaria · #71 · women's designer clothing

Beaucage Salon · #71 · salon for men and women

Belle du Jour · #164 · lingerie

Best Fit Incorporated · #218 · custom-made clothing

Best of Scotland · #115 · sweaters at mill prices

Betsey Johnson · #201 · designer clothes

Betsy Jenney of Boston · #81 · women's unusual designer clothes

Bjoux · #141 · women's fashion

Boutique Giorgio Armani · #22 · clothes

Boutique Unique · #336 · clothes, jewelry, gifts, etc.

Brooks Brothers · #46 · classy clothing for men and women

Burberrys Limited · #2 · clothes for men and women

Calypso · #115 · women's clothing

Canyon Beach Wear · #229 · bathing suits

Cashmere Boston · #114 · cashmere products

Chanel · #5 · clothing and accessories

Classic Tuxedo · #249 · tuxedo shop

Closet Upstairs · #223 · consignment shop

The Closet · #175 · clothing

Cole Haan · #109 · men's and women's clothing

CP Shades · #139B · clothing

Cuoio · #115 · European shoes for women

Daniel Rene · #118 · couture clothing

Danielo Shoes · #224 · shoes

Diesel · #116 · clothing

DKNY · #37 · clothing

Dress Rehearsal · #252 · consignment shop

El Paso Inc. · #154 · western clothing, accessories, housewares

Emporio Armani · #210-212 · men and women's clothing

Ermenegildo Zegna · #39 · clothes

Estasi · #12 · clothing

Express · #401 · clothing

Eye of the Needle · #85 · preppie clothing

Fiandaca · #73 · couture clothing

Foil · #220 · women's clothing

Francesca Laurenzi · #170 · luxury sportswear

French Connection · #206 · men's and women's clothing

Frontier Clothing · #259 · clothing

Gap · #201 · clothing

GapKids · #201 · children's clothing

Guess · #80 · clothing

Hempest · #207 · hemp clothing

House of Culture · #286 · clothing

Industria Boutique · #222 · clothing

Intermix · #186 · women's clothing

Investments · #125 · shoes for women with larger feet

Jasmine Boutique · #333 · men's clothing

Jasmine Sola Shoes · #329 · shoes

Jessica McClintock · #201 · women's cocktail attire

John Fluevog Shoes · #302 · shoes

Kate Spade Shoes · #117 · shoes, purses, etc.

Kenneth Cole Productions · #128 · shoes

L'elite · #276 · clothing

La Boutique Reine · #134 · bridal boutique

Laura Ashley · #112 · clothing and home decor

Lilly Pulitzer Store · #133 · clothing

Lingerie Studio · #264 · lingerie

London Lace · #215 · Scottish lace

Longchamp Boston · #139A · French handbags

Lucky Brand · #229 · denim

Matsu · #259 · purses

Max Mara · #69 · women's clothing

Mudo · #205 · clothing

Nantucket Panache · #250 · women's clothing and home décor

Nine West · #201 · women's shoes

Oilily · #31 · Dutch clothing for women and children

Oilily Women's · #32 · women's clothes

Ozone · #338 · clothing

Parade of Shoes · #171 · shoes

Patagonia · #344 · clothing for the great outdoors

Players of Newbury Street · #251 · South Beach clothing

Quicksilver Boardriders Club · #326 · clothing and board gear

Ralph Lauren · #95 · clothing

Riccardi Boutique · #116 · clothing

Rockport · #83 · shoes

Rodier, Paris · #144 · clothing

Second Time Around Collections · #167 · new and consignment clothes

Serenella · #134 · European women's clothes

Skechers · #340 · shoes

Sola Men · #344 · men's clothing

Suzanne · #81 · special occasion clothing

Taste Boutique · #152 · clothing

Thom Brown of Boston · #331 · shoes

Timberland · #71 · clothing

Top Drawer Boston · #164 · lingerie

Toppers · #230 · hats

Urban Outfitters · #361 · clothing

All addresses are on Newbury St.

Restaurants

29 Newbury • #29 • new American food
Ben & Jerry's • #174 • ice cream
Bodhi Café • #335 • café food
The Capital Grille • #359 • steak house
Charley's Eating & Drinking Saloon • #284 • American food
Ciao Bella • #240 • Italian food
Daisy Buchanan's • #240 • bar
Espresso Royale Caffe • #286 • coffee house
Herrell's Ice Cream & Espresso Bar • #224 • café
J.P. Licks Ice Cream • #352 • local ice cream shop
Kashmir Restaurant • #279 • Indian food
La Famiglia Giorgio's • #250 • Italian food
Milano's Italian Kitchen • #45 • Italian food
Newbury Pizza & Subs • #225 • pizza & subs
Pho Pasteur • #119 • Vietnamese food
Piattini Wine Café • #226 • Italian food
Rebecca's Café & Catering • #112 • café and take-out
Saffron • #279A • Indian food
Scoozi • #237B • American food
Shino Express Sushi • #145 • Japanese food
Sonsie Restaurant • #327 • international cuisine
Steve's • #316 • Greek-American food
Tapeo Restaurant Tapas Bar • #266 • Spanish food
Tealuxe • #108 • tea bar
Thai Basil • #132 • Thai food
Thai Dish • #259 • Thai food
Torrefazione Italia • #45 • Italian coffeehouse
Travis Restaurant • #135 • breakfast, lunch, and dinner
The Wrap • #247 • wraps and smoothies

Services

119 Salon Group • #119 • hair salon
5 Star Travel Services • #164 • travel agency
Acote Hair Salon • #132 • men's and women's hairstyling
The Adams Center for Aesthetic Surgery • #2 • plastic surgeon
Alexanders Salon • #163 • beauty salon
Anastasia Design • #249 • graphic design
Aspect International Language School • #126 • language instruction
Astrid & Zofia European Skin • #20 • skin treatments
Austen's • #115 • beauty salon
Avanti Salon • #11 • hair and skin care
B.A. Perry, Hand Engraver • #115 • hand-engraving
Back Bay Framery and Photo • #303 • framing and photo finishing
Back Bay Hair Designs • #291 • hair salon
Back Bay Veterinary Clinic • #324 • veterinarian
Bang & Olufsen • #30 • home audio/video systems
Bella Sante • #38 • day spa
Bethany Union • #256 • Universalists haven for young women
Birmingham Associates • #115 • PR counselors
Black and White Inc. • #334 • full-service photo lab

Blades Board & Skate • #349A • boards, skates, and clothes
Boston Adventures • #211 • travel guide for Boston
Boston Architectural Center • #320 • architecture school
Boston Kung Fu Tai Chi Institute • #361 • martial arts school
Boston Photo Lab • #211 • photo processing
Boston Professional Teeth Whitening Spa • #75 • teeth whitening
Boston Rose Florist • #215 • florist
Bridgid Lee Salon • #176 • beauty salon
Bunnell Frame Shop • #166 • framing, oil and print restoration
Bush Cleaners • #219 • dry cleaners
Capelli International • #250 • day spa and salon
Carekey.com Inc. • #137 • portable health record
Cheryl Richards, Photographer • #247 • prints and portraits
Child Associates Inc. • #240 • landscape architects
Christie's Fine Art Auctioneers • #216 • appraisers and auctioneers
Christopher J. Hawes Color Design Group • #36 • hair colorists
Cititan • #91 • tanning
CITS Boston • #91 • travel agency
City Salon • #118 • hair salon
City Video • #240 • video store
Closet Solutions • #165 • closet organizing
Coco's Salon and Gallery • #35 • salon
Colortek • #251 • photo finishing
Concierge of Boston • #165 • concierge services
Condom World • #332 • sexual novelties
Copley Art Framing • #156 • framing
Council Travel • #273 • student travel agency
CVS • #240 • drugstore
Cybersound • #115 • MDI production facility
Dana Noble Associates • #11 • interior design
Daryl Christopher Limited • #37 • beauty salon
Dekwa Elements of Hair • #132 • feng shui-inspired hair salon
Dellaria Salons • #173 • hair salon
DeLuca's Market • #239 • grocery store
Dependable Cleaners • #110 • dry cleaning
Dependable Cleaners 316 • #316 • dry cleaning
Diego at the Loft • #11 • hair and nail services
Dutch Flower Garden • #164 • florist
E.S. Moon Makeup Artists • #218 • makeup artists
ECAP LLC • #137 • boutique investment banking firm
Eccentric Entertainment • #10 • entertainers and entertainment
Eclipse Salon Gallery • #167 • beauty salon
Ecocentrix • #30 • salon
Elaine Dalzell • #205 • advertising agency
Elizabeth Grady Skin Care Salon • #11 • skin care
E-Media Millworks • #222 • searchable audio/video database
Equinox Hair Design • #85 • salon and day spa
Eugene Lawrence—Interior Architecture • #115 • interior design

euroPResence USA • #181 • international PR network
Everbare Laser Hair Removal • #10 • laser hair removal
Exit 33 • #222 • graphic designers
Family Treasures Bookshop • #101 • ancestry research
For Eyes Optical Co. • #330 • eyeglass store
Fred Astaire Dance Studio • #361 • dance school
Fun in the Sun • #349 • group entertainment
Geoffrey Stein Studio • #348 • commercial photography
GHB Management Corporation • #242 • advertising agency
Giuliano, The Spa for Beauty & Wellness • #338 • spa
Great Cuts • #297 • salon
Grecco Ethridge Group • #323 • advertising agency
GunnDesign • #275 • design consultants
HDB Architects Inc • #38 • architecture firm
Healing Beauty Boutique • #115 • skin care salon
Highlights Hair Salon • #288 • hair salon
Hobbamock Design • #115 • graphic design
Hot Gossip • #207 • salon
Howie Green Design • #138 • all media design
I Soci Salon • #8 • beauty salon
Ibelle • #274 • hair salon
Incha's Nails & Skin Care • #215 • nails and skin care
Initiatives Inc. • #276 • management consultants
Jacquelyn International • #10 • hairwear options
James Joseph Salon • #168 • salon
James Patrick Salon • #121 • salon
Jean-Pierre Salon • #116 • salon
Jerel Roberts Salon • #138 • hair coloring and styling
JKW International Incorporated • #143 • foreign language services
John Lewis • #97 • gold and silver craftsmen
John Santini, The Studio for Hair • #330 • hair salon
John Stasio • #115 • spiritual mentoring
Johnson Paint and Art Supplies • #355 • art supplies
Jordan the Tailor • #133 • tailor
Katherine Gibbs Placement • #126 • job placement
Katherine Gibbs School • #126 • trade school
Konjo Salon of Elegance • #35 • beauty salon
Kortenhaus Communication • #137 • marketing and communications firm
Kosmetika European Skin Care • #77 • skin care
L'Elegance Art et Coiffure • #103 • salon
L'Atelier Salon • #174 • salon
La Tete Coiffure • #221 • salon
Lauren's Nails and Skin Salon • #164 • nails and skin salon
Les Amis • #91 • salon
Linen & Lace • #212 • window treatments
Loomis Group • #77 • marketing firm
Mail Boxes Etc. • #304 • mailing center
Mario Russo Salon at 9 Newbury • #45 • salon
Martucci Inc • #116 • advertising agency
Max's Instant Shoe Repair • #170 • shoe repair

Mechanique · #115 · salon
Media Networks · #18 · advertising services
Meeting Management Associates · #349 · meeting planners
Mia's Nail Studio · #168 · manicures
Michael P. Wasserman Inc · #349 · event planner
Michaud Cosmetics · #297 · eyebrow shaping and cosmetics
Mitchell Dell Architects Inc · #37 · architect firm
National Cell Phone Rentals · #36 · cell phone rentals
Newbury Acupuncture · #115 · acupuncture
Newbury Day Spa · #8 · day spa
Newbury Kitchens · #171 · kitchen and bath design
Newbury Natural Nails · #247 · nail salon
Newbury Visions · #215 · eyewear and exams
Niall Roberts Hair Studio · #253 · hair salon
Oasis Salon & Day Spa · #69 · salon and spa
Olin Center · #342 · test prep
One Eighty Visual Communication · #338 · communication consultants
Open Systems Advisors · #268 · business consultants
Peter & Yerem Hair · #20 · salon
Pierre Deux · #111 · French interior design
Pinckney Nail & Skin Salon · #224 · nail and skin salon
PLUM Computer Consulting · #304 · IT services
Pod Holding Inc. · #18 · private investors in stage companies
Pontes Buckley Advertising · #268 · advertising agency
Pour Moi Skin & Body Salon · #105 · day spa
Provident Financial Management · #268 · business management services
Q-Optical · #287 · eyeglass store
Quo Vadis · #288 · travel agency
Richard-Joseph Hair · #164 · salon
Roger E. Lussier Inc. · #168 · framing
Rosales Gottemoeller & Associates · #305 · architects
Royal Barry Wills Associates Inc · #8 · architects
S T A Travel · #297 · travel agency
Safar Coiffures · #235 · salon
Sal Sannizzaro Salon · #135 · salon
The Salon at 10 Newbury · #10 · salon
Salon Boccaccio · #161 · salon
Salon Luiz · #115 · salon
Salon Nordic Skin Care · #221 · skin care
Salon Persona · #331 · salon
Salon Pini and Company · #231 · salon
Salon Xenofon · #228 · salon
Sarni Cleaners of Boston · #170 · dry cleaners
School of Fashion Design · #136 · fashion school
Secret Garden · #338 · florist
See · #125 · eyeglass store
Smash Advertising · #69 · advertising agency
Society of Arts & Crafts · #175 · arts and craft organization
Solus at Acote · #132 · salon
Starr Hair Studio · #114 · salon
Swisse Natural Hair Salon · #174 · salon
Synergistics Personal Training Studio · #9 · massage
Tanorama of Boston Back Bay · #226 · tanning

Theatrix Events Inc. · #349 · special events coordinators
Trainor Associates Inc · #45 · advertising agency
Trinity Tours · #316 · travel agency
UMI · #75 · salon
Verite Music · #349 · music arrangers and composers
Vidal Sassoon · #14 · salon
Wallwork Curry · #181 · advertising agency
Wellesley Optical Co. Inc. · #216 · eyeglass shop
Whole Health Group · #45 · massage
Winston Flowers · #131 · florist
Yao Lis Kung Fu Academy Institute · #361 · martial arts
Young & Rubicam · #45 · PR firm

Gifts & Miscellaneous

4 Front Records · #279 · record store
A Needlepoint Store by Maryjo Cole · #11 · hand-painted needlepoint
Acme Fine Art · #38 · bought and sold modern American art
Alianza Contemporary Crafts · #154 · crafts in all mediums
Appleton's · #134 · over 150 artists showcased
Atelier Janiye · #165 · jewelry
Autrefois Antiques · #125 · antiques
Avenue Victor Hugo Bookshop · #353 · used bookstore
Back Bay Estate Jewelers · #129 · antique jewelry
Back Bay Harley-Davidson · #160 · motorcycles
Back Bay Oriental Rugs · #154 · rugs
Bauer Wines Spirits · #330 · liquor store
Bellezza Home and Garden · #129 · Italian ceramics
Boston Beat Imports · #279 · record store
Buddenbrooks Fine & Rare Books · #31 · bookstore
Cartier · #40 · jewelry
CD Spins · #324 · used CDs and tapes
Cellular Unlimited USA · #164 · cellphone accessories
Cigar Masters · #176 · retail and lounge
Décor International · #141 · home goods from around the world
Diptyque · #123 · French perfumerie
Domain Home Fashions · #7 · furniture
dona flor · #246 · home ceramics
Dorfman Jewelers · #24 · jewelry
Erwin Pearl · #4 · jewelry
European Watch Co. · #232 · watch repair and shop
Felicia's Cosmetics · #314 · cosmetics
Fine Time-Antique Timepieces · #279 · antique watches
Firestone and Parson · #8 · antique jewelry
Fresh · #121 · bath products
Gargoyles Grotesques & Chimeras · #262 · gothic architectural reproductions
Grovana of Switzerland · #217 · watch shop
Guido Frame Studio · #118 · ready-to-frame prints
Henry Solo · #35 · Italian pottery and gifts
Hold Everything · #349-351 · storage solutions
Hope · #302 · unique gift shop
In Touch · #192 · card and gift store

India Antiques Art & Music · #279 · Indian art, books, antiques
International Poster Gallery · #205 · poster store
International Rugs · #171 · home furnishings
James R. Bakker Antiques · #236 · antiques
Kakadu · #291 · homeware
Kitchen Arts · #161 · kitchen tools
L'Occitane · #179 · beauty products
La Ruche · #164 · home décor and stationary
Lords International Limited · #8 · cricket equipment
Mann Gallery–The Art of the Doll · #39 · unique dolls and gifts
Marcoz Antiques · #177 · antiques
Mars Records · #299 · rare records
Mayan Weavers · #268 · Native American crafts
Narutomi Grocer · #349 · grocery store
Needlepoint of Back Bay · #125 · needlepoint canvases
New England Historic Genealogical Society · #101 · library of genealogies
Newbury Comics · #232 · record and toy store
Newbury Street Jewelry and Antiques · #255 · jewelry and antiques
Niketown · #200 · everything Nike
Noras Convenience Store · #303 · convenience store
Oliviers & Company · #161 · olive oil store
Parks Paint & Hardware · #233 · hardware store
Placewares · #160 · organizing tools
Portico New York · #77 · furniture
Pottery Barn · #122 · home décor
Pratesi Linens · #110 · bed and bath linens
Selletto · #244 · garden-inspired home décor
Shambala Tibet · #270 · Tibetan artifacts
Silver Nation · #173 · silver accessories
Simon Pearce Glass · #115 · glasswares
Small Pleasures · #142 · jewelry
Spenser's Mystery Bookshop · #223 · mystery bookshop
Sterling Collection · #232 · silver jewelry
Sunglass Hut International · #182 · sunglass store
Swedenborg Book Store · #79 · books by Emanuel Swedenborg
Tea Merchant · #119 · tea shop
Teuscher Chocolates of Switzerland · #230 · chocolates
Time & Time Again · #172 · watch store
Tokai Pottery · #112 · Japanese pottery and textiles
Trident Booksellers and Café · #338 · bookstore and café
Video Express · #181 · video store
Virgin Megastore · #360 · record store
Wall · #232 · gallery
Watch Station · #184 · watch shop
Water Works · #103 · bathroom accessories
Wavetime Watch · #172 · watch store
Wedding List · #119 · wedding registry
Wrubel Gallery/The Nature Company · #201 · natural artifacts and art
Zoe · #279 · home décor

Parking Garages

Danker Donohue Garage · #341
Fitz Inn Auto Parks · #149

Parks & Places · **Prudential Center**

Stores

- 1 Caveau Wine Bistro
- 1 Marché Mövenpick
- 5 U. S. Post Office
- 11 Ann Taylor Loft
- 15 Au Bon Pain
- 17 Marchélino
- 19 Great Things from Boston
- 21 St. Francis Chapel
- 27 Ann Taylor
- 41 Olympia Sports
- 43 GameStop
- 46 Travel 2000
- 45 Eziba
- 47 Truffles Fine Confections
- 103 Legal Sea Foods
- 105 Danskin
- 107 Sephora
- 109 Hallmark
- 111 F Carreire
- 113 Talbots Collection
- 123 Elizabeth
- 125 Chico's
- 126 Walking Company
- 127 Body Shop
- 129 Alpha Omega
- 131 Landau Collection
- 133 Johnston & Murphy
- 135 Sunglass Hut
- 141 Speedo Authentic Fitness
- 143 Florsheim
- 145 Whippoorwill Crafts
- 147 Optica
- 149 Barami
- 151 Dapy
- 155 California Pizza Kitchen
- 157 Structure
- 159 Crane & Co.
- 161 Sweet Factory
- 163 Claire's
- 165 Yankee Candle
- 167 Swarovski
- 169 Arden B.
- 171 Papyrus
- 173 J. Jill
- 175 Levi's
- 177 Franklin Covey
- 179 Barnes & Noble
- 181 The Sharper Image
- 183 Sovereign Bank
- 189 The Cheesecake Factory
- 193 Berkshire Grill
- 197 FitCorp
- Prudential Tower- Top of the Hub

Food Court

- FC1 Everything Yogurt & Salad Café
- FC2 Panda Express
- FC3 Sbarro
- FC4 Poulet Rotisserie Chicken
- FC5 Boston Chowda
- FC6 Flamers
- FC7 Big Easy Cajun
- FC8 Sakkio Japan
- FC9 Ben & Jerry's
- FC10 Rebecca's Café
- FC11 Louis Barry Florist

General Information

Address:	800 Boylston Street, Boston, MA 02199
Phone:	1-800-SHOP-PRU or 617-236-3100
Website:	www.prudentialcenter.com

Overview

The Prudential Center opened in 1965 and, with its 52 stories, reigned as the city's tallest building until the 60-story Hancock tower was completed 11 years later. With the exception of the top two floors, which house an observation deck and a restaurant, the Prudential Tower is used mainly as office space. A street-level mall was opened in the 1990s and houses almost 50 shops, including Saks Fifth Avenue, and numerous restaurants and services. The "Pru" is also home to several apartment buildings and is connected to the Hynes Convention Center and the Sheraton Boston Hotel.

Sky Walk and Top of the Hub

Other than shopping, the Prudential Center's main attractions are its Sky Walk and Top of the Hub restaurant. The Sky Walk is open daily from 10 am until 10 pm, offering spectacular views of Boston and its suburbs, as well as the harbor, Blue Hill, and—way off in the distance—Cape Cod. The Sky Walk is $4 for adults and $3 for children and seniors. As you walk around the Sky Walk, focus on the huge windows, which are marked to help you locate some of Boston's more well-known features.

For a less informative, slightly more expensive, but extremely relaxing city view, go two floors up from the Sky Walk to the Top of the Hub restaurant and cocktail lounge. Though entrees there are pricey, juice and cocktails from the bar are fairly priced and served with a spectacular view. For about $5 apiece—a dollar more than the skywalk—you can peer down at the city or across at the top of the John Hancock Tower with beverage in hand. Note that the restaurant and lounge are very busy at night, especially when the jazz band is playing, and a casual, but "anti-slob" dress code is in effect.

How to Get There—Driving

From the north, take I-93 to exit 26 Leverett Connector/Storrow Drive, and follow it to the Copley Square exit on the left. Take a right onto Beacon Street and follow it to Exeter Street. Make a left onto Exeter Street and the Prudential Center Garage will be four blocks down on the right.

From the west, follow the Mass Pike (I-90) eastbound into Boston. Get off at exit 22, Copley Square/Prudential Center, and follow the signs for Prudential Center. This will take you directly to the Prudential Center Garage entrance on your right. The Mass Pike is accessible from Route 128/95.

From the south, take I-93 to exit 26, Leverett Connector/Storrow Drive, and follow to the Copley Square exit on the left. Take a right onto Beacon Street and follow it to Exeter Street. Take a left onto Exeter Street. The Prudential Center Garage will be four blocks down on the right.

If you get lost, try this: Look up. Notice the giant building that says "Prudential" on top. Drive towards it.

How to Get There—Mass Transit

The Green Line will take you to the Prudential T stop on Huntington Avenue (E train only), the Copley stop on Boylston Street at Dartmouth Street, and the Hynes/ICA stop on Newbury Street at Mass Ave. The Orange Line and the MBTA Commuter Rail both stop at Back Bay Station, just across the street from Copley Place.

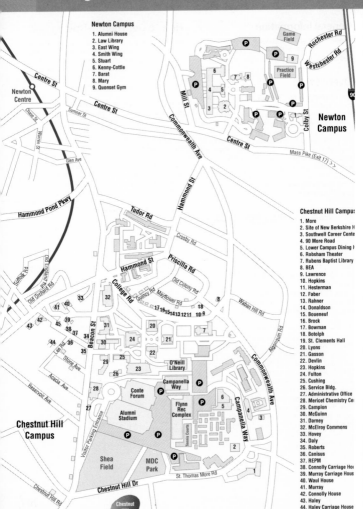

Newton Campus

1. Alumni House
2. Law Library
3. East Wing
4. Smith Wing
5. Stuart
6. Kenny-Cottle
7. Barat
8. Mary
9. Quonset Gym

Chestnut Hill Campus

1. More
2. Site of New Berkshire H
3. Southwell Career Center
4. 90 More Road
5. Lower Campus Dining H
6. Robsham Theater
7. Rubens Baptist Library
8. BEA
9. Lawrence
10. Hopkins
11. Hesterman
12. Faber
13. Rahner
14. Donaldson
15. Boueneuf
16. Brock
17. Bowman
18. Botolph
19. St. Clements Hall
20. Lyons
21. Gasson
22. Devlin
23. Hopkins
24. Fulton
25. Cushing
26. Service Bldg.
27. Administrative Office
28. Mericel Chemistry Cen
29. Campion
30. McGuinn
31. Darney
32. McElroy Commons
33. Hovey
34. Daly
35. Roberts
36. Canisus
37. REPM
38. Connolly Carriage Hou
39. Murray Carriage House
40. Waul House
41. Murray
42. Connolly House
43. Haley
44. Haley Carriage House

General Information

Main Campus:	140 Commonwealth Ave, Chestnut Hill, MA 02467
Phone:	617-552-8000
Website:	www.bc.edu
Newton Campus:	885 Centre Street, Newton Centre, MA 02459

Overview

It all began one day in Paris in 1534, when a group of students at the University of Paris got together and decided to combine their devotion to God with their commitment to the betterment of society. They called themselves the Society of Jesus, or the Jesuits. A few centuries later, in 1863, three Jesuits opened a college in the South End and cleverly named it Boston College. Beginning with just 22 students, the Jesuit profs envisioned an institution that would integrate intellectual development with religious and ethical growth.

Over the past century-and-a-half, the school has drifted a bit, both geographically and ethically. Once located in Boston proper, the school now sits six miles to the west, sprawling over 116 acres in Chestnut Hill and another 40 in Newton. And though still Jesuit through and through, today's BC students aren't exactly known for being pious or devout.

BC's 8,900 undergraduates and 4,600 graduate students have a bit of a bad reputation among locals and students at other area colleges—the stereotype pegs all BC guys as binge-drinking jock wannabees, clad in white hats, who are more likely on the quest for a fight than the quest for knowledge. It is widely rumored that the girls' appetite for Abercrombie & Fitch is matched only by their thirst for peach schnapps. Overlooked by naysayers is BC's excellent academic reputation. Its 11 colleges, schools, and institutes offer 14 degree programs in more than fifty fields of study, and *U.S. News and World Report* rated BC the 40th best college in the country. In 2003, BC took a big step in proving it's on par with higher-ranking schools downriver, such as Harvard and BU. For the first time, two BC students were selected as Rhodes Scholars and a school-record 14 Fullbright Grants were awarded.

Tuition

In the 2003-2004 academic year, undergraduate tuition amounted to $22,680, with room and board an additional $8,510. Add on books, lab fees, and personal expenses. Graduate student tuition, fees, and expenses vary by college. However, approximately 65% of students receive financial aid.

Sports

Boston College is hailed by *U.S. News and World Report* as having one of the top 20 overall college sports programs. Supporting 31 varsity and approximately 14 club and intramural sports, it has a diverse and strong athletic department. The varsity teams all compete on the NCAA Division I level. This past year the football team won the Motor City Bowl, making it BC's third consecutive bowl win. The biggest game every year is against Notre Dame. The soccer team also had great success by winning the 2002 Big East regular season and tournament titles and reaching the Elite Eight of the NCAA Tournament. The men's hockey team held the number one ranking for several weeks.

Culture on Campus

The Robsham Theater Arts Center is Boston College's creative center. Built in 1981, the theater seats 591 people. The building also includes a black box theater that seats 150-200 people. The three main departments housed in the facility are the Department of Theater Arts, the Robsham Dance and Theater Company, and the Boston Liturgical Dance Ensemble. Every year, the university presents four faculty-directed and two student-directed productions. Additionally there are about 20 musical and dance groups that perform throughout the year.

Another source of culture for Boston College is the McMullen Museum of Art. Located on the first floor of Devlin Hall, the museum is housed in one of the many neogothic buildings on the upper campus. It is free and open to the public. Aside from its notable permanent collection, the museum has frequent exhibitions of international and scholarly importance, from all periods and cultures. The hours of operation are Mon–Fri 11 am–4 pm and Sat–Sun 12 pm–5 pm.

Departments

Undergraduate Admissions	617-552-3100
A&S Graduate Admissions	617-552-3265
Carroll School of Management Graduate Admissions	617-552-3290
Connell School of Nursing Graduate Admissions	617-552-4928
Law School Admissions	617-552-4350
Lynch School of Education Graduate Admissions	617-552-4214
Graduate School of Social Work Admissions	617-552-4024
Student Services	617-552-3300
	800-294-0294
Athletic Departments and Tickets	617-552-3000
O'Neill Library	617-552-4470

Colleges & Universities • **Boston University**

General Information

Address:	One Sherborn Street, Boston, MA 02215
Phone:	617-353-2000
Website:	www.bu.edu

Overview

If you really want to go to school "in" Boston, BU might be your place. Consisting of a strip of buildings along Commonwealth Avenue, BU's campus doesn't win any points for style, beauty, or landscape architecture (since that would require having a clearly defined landscape). In fact, aside from several thousand red banners on the lamp-posts that say "Boston University" and a larger-than usual concentration of jaywalking young folk along Comm Ave., there's little indication you've entered BU's domain.

The fourth-largest private university in the country, the school's "campus" is the learning center for all students and the residence of many of its 30,000 undergraduates and grad students. The upshot of the ill-defined BU campus is that its students truly are living in the city. BU students make the best of the green space they have. "The Beach," a strip of greenery on the inbound side of Storrow Drive (which runs along the Charles), is a favorite springtime destination for socializing and sunbathing.

When the university was founded over 157 years ago, it was intended to be an institute solely for training ministers. However, as the years went by, it expanded in order to accommodate the needs and interests of its growing student population. Today Boston University students represent all 50 states, as well as 135 countries. There are 17 schools and colleges and, in terms of its courses, Boston University has a wide range of programs to choose from, including 60 different degree programs. BU also holds the distinction of having the most property owned by one non-government institution in the city of Boston.

Longtime president and infamous curmudgeon, John Silber, recently retired after more than a quarter-century of leading the school to wherever he pleased. His replace-ment, former NASA chief Daniel Goldin, was called off the job even before he began his first day due to conflicting ideas about how the university should be run. Goldin said he took the job on the condition that Silber would not occupy a seat on the board of trustees. The Executive Committee balked at this stipulation and, after a little mud was slung, Goldin's termination was signed, an embarrassing move for the university. An interim president will sit until the search for a new president is complete.

Tuition

Undergraduate tuition costs run at about $27,042 per year, with room and board an additional $8,978. Add on books, lab fees, and personal expenses. Graduate student tuition, fees, and expenses vary by college.

Sports

As students from other Boston-area schools wake up early to start drinking on Saturdays before the big football game, BU students sleep in. Though they have an otherwise solid sports program, the Terriers played their last football game in 1997. President Silber, in one of his many controversial and unpopular decisions, declared the football program too expensive and convinced the trustees to put an end to it.

Aside from the unfortunate demise of the football team, the Terriers have quite an impressive athletic department. With 23 NCAA Division I varsity sports, Boston University provides a rich environment for sports lovers. In recent years, Terrier teams have had much success, winning eight America East post-season tournament titles. In addition, they have had at least six teams advance to NCAA tournaments. The department prides itself on its equal emphasis on women's and men's varsity sports. The men's varsity ice hockey team is, by far, the most popular sports team at BU, with the most enthusiastic community support. There is fierce competition every year for the Beanpot—the "New England Invitational" tournament. In the past 51 years, BU has won the Beanpot 25 times, with Boston College being their biggest rival for the title.

Culture on Campus

The first university to have a music program, BU remains committed to the arts. The Boston University Art gallery is located at 855 Commonwealth Avenue. Although the gallery has no permanent collection, its architecture is like an exhibit unto itself. Alluding to both the Classical and the Medieval, the columns that adorn the façade are a rare beauty and have attracted many people on that basis alone. What makes the gallery even more unique is that the building that houses it is a converted Buick dealership. If this piques your interest, you'll be happy to learn that the gallery is open and free to the public, but only during the academic school year, Tues–Fri 10 am–5 pm and Sat–Sun 1 pm–5 pm.

Departments

Undergraduate Admissions 617-353-2300
Graduate Admissions 617-353-2696
Graduate School of Management 617-353-2670
School of Medicine 617-638-4630
School of Law 617-353-3100
School of Education 617-353-4237
School of Social Work 617-353-3765
Athletic Department and Ticket Office 617-353-3838
Mugar Memorial Library 617-353-3732

Building Legend

1. 1019 Commonwealth Ave (major residence)
2. Case Athletic Center
3. West Campus (major residence)
4. Office of Housing
5. Media Group
6. 10 Buick St (major residence)
7. Center for English Language and Orientation Programs
8. Comptroller; Financial Assistance; Registrar; Student Health Services
9. College of General Studies
10. College of Fine Arts; University Art Gallery
11. School of Hospitality Administration; Metropolitan College Academic departments and other programs
12. Boston University Academy
13. George Sherman Union; Dean of Students
14. Mugar Memorial Library; University Information Center
15. School of Law
16. Metropolitan College; Summer Term
17. School of Theology; University Professors Program
18. Marsh Chapel
19. Photonics Center
20. College of Arts and Sciences
21. School of Social Work
22. Graduate School of Arts and Sciences
23. The Tsai Performance Art Center
24. The Castle
25. Warren Towers (major residence)
26. Office of Information Technology
27. College of Engineering
28. Sargent College of Health and Rehabilitation Sciences
29. College of Communication
30. School of Education
31. Morse Auditorium
32. Biological and Physics Research Buildings
33. The Towers (major residence)
34. Chancellor's Office; President's Office; Provost's Office; Development and Alumni Relations
35. School of Management
36. 575 Commonwealth Ave (major residence)
37. Metcalf Science Center
38. Admissions Reception Center
39. Kenmore Classroom Building
40. Shelton Hall (major residence)
41. International Students and Scholars Office; Martin Luther King, Jr Center
42. University Computers
43. Barnes & Noble at BU
44. Hotel Commonwealth
45. Miles Standish Hall (major residence)
46. Danielson Hall (major residence) (off map)

1. Ansin Building
2. Cutler Majestic Theater
3. Little Building
4. Walker Building
5. Tufte Performance Production Cen
6. [Future] Campus Center
7. Student Reside
8. Student Union

General Information

Address: 120 Boylston Street, Boston, MA 02116
Phone: 617-824-8500
Website: www.emerson.edu

Overview

Emerson College is unique in that it is the only comprehensive college or university in the United States solely dedicated to communication and the arts in a liberal arts context. In close proximity to Boston's Theater District, Emerson is near all of the major media interests in the city. When it was founded in 1880, it was a small oratory school and over the years has expanded its curriculum to include other forms of communication. Today Emerson specializes in marketing, journalism, and performing, visual, and media arts. Emerson campuses also exist in Los Angeles and the Netherlands.

The enrollment is about 2,700 full-time undergraduates and 650 full-time graduate students, many of whom can be found sporting stylish haircuts and smoking outside Emerson buildings between classes. Most alumni go on to pursue careers in the communications and entertainment fields. Notable alumni include talk show host Jay Leno, actor Denis Leary, and entrepreneur and make-up artist Bobbi Brown.

Tuition

In the 2003-2004 academic year, undergraduate tuition fees were $22,144. Room and board was between $8,000-10,000. Add on books, service fees, activity fees, and personal expenses. Graduate student tuition, fees, and expenses vary by the number of credits taken.

Sports

Although Emerson does have an athletic department, it is not the top priority for the school. Since most of the students that attend Emerson College are interested primarily in the fields of communications and performing arts, sports are considered a lighthearted diversion. Still, Emerson College is a proud member of the NCAA Division III, the Eastern College Athletic Conference, and a charter member of the Great Northeast Athletic Conference.

Culture on Campus

Because Emerson considers itself more or less an art school, it prides itself on its theater. Called the Majestic Theater, and rightly so, it was built in 1903 as an opera house. In 2001, the college closed the theater temporarily for renovation. The theater reopened in the fall of 2003. Today, the historic venue seats 1,200 people and has become an integral part of the campus. Not only does it provide the venue for all types of productions by Emerson students, but also serves the greater New England community. It hosts more operas than any other theater in New England and is the top stop for most touring dance companies. To visit the theater or check out a performance, go to the theater box office, located at 219 Tremont Street in Boston, or call 617-824-8000.

Departments

Undergraduate Admissions Office......... 617-824-8609
Graduate Admissions Office............... 617-824-8610
Athletics Department..................... 617-824-8690
Library 617-824-8668

UMass-Boston

JFK Library

Massachusetts State Archives/ Commonwealth Museum

Columbia Pl

To Morrissey Blvd JFK/UMass T Stop

University Dr W

University Dr N

Clark Athletic Center

Quinn Admin

Healey Library

Science Center

Site of Student Center

McCormack

University Dr S

Wheatley (CCDE Office)

University Dr E

General Information

Address: 100 Morrissey Blvd, Boston, MA 02125-3393
Phone: 617-287-5000
Website: www.umb.edu

Overview

The University of Massachusetts Boston is one of the five campuses of the University of Massachusetts. The university is described as a sensibly priced, high-quality college that provides the best programs in the Boston area to people from all walks of life. The university prides itself on being a place that promotes diversity among the students and staff and in their commitment "to bring technical, intellectual, and human resources to the community." The PR line is a bit too eloquent to have been spoken by the school's most famous alum, Boston Mayor Thomas M. Menino. Not exactly renowned for his oratory skills, Menino graduated from UMass Boston at the age of 45 in 1988 with a degree in community planning. He is now well respected as a champion of the neighborhoods.

UMass Boston's campus, which has been described as a "concrete jungle," is only three miles from downtown Boston and is easy to reach by public transportation. Boston State College joined UMass to become the University of Massachusetts Boston in 1982.

Tuition

Undergraduate tuition costs run at about $16,887 per year and $6,227 if you're an in-state resident. Graduate tuition costs run at about $16,889 per year and $7,115 if you're an in-state resident.

Sports

The University of Massachusetts Boston offers 14 varsity sports, including basketball, soccer, lacrosse, and ice hockey, and is a member of the NCAA's Division III. The Beacon Fitness Center is open to all students and staff free of charge. The UMass teams are called the Beacons, carry the slogan "Follow The Light," and have been named All-Americans 93 times in seven sports.

UMass provides a community service program in which they offer free, or very low cost, use of all their athletic facilities and coaches to all private, school, charitable, and governmental organizations.

Culture on Campus

UMass Boston has a Performing Arts Department, which was formally known as the Theater Arts Department, the Dance Program, and the Music Department. The Music course provides grounding in music theory, history, and performance. Private music lessons are also available for one credit. There is a college Jazz Band, Chamber Orchestra, and Chamber Singers.

Departments

Undergraduate Admissions 617-287-6000
Graduate Admissions .617-287-6400
Performing Arts Department. 617-287-5640
Athletic Department. .617-287-7801
Healey Library 617-287-5903
Honors Program 617-287-5520
Jazz Band 617-287-6990

23. Quad Athletic Facility
24. Hilles Library
25. Harkness Commons/Child
26. Pound Hall/Administration Bldg
27. Maxwell-Dworkin/Pierce
28. Areeda/Langdell Hall/Library
29. Pierce
30. Austin
31. Jefferson Lab
32. Music Building
33. Gordon McKay Lab
34. Science Center/Cabot Science Library
35. Hoffman Lab/Mallinckroft Lab/
    Naito/Gibbs/Converse/Conant Lab
36. 38 Oxford/42 Oxford
37. Biological Labs
38. Fairchild Biochemistry Lab
39. Memorial Hall Sanders Theatre
40. Graduate School of Design/Gund Hall
41. Fogg Art Museum/Busch-Reisinger Museum
42. Carpenter Center
43. Barker Center
44. Loeb Library
45. Lamont Library
46. Widener Library
47. Adams House/Westmorely
48. American Repertory Theatre/
    Loeb Drama Center
49. Brattle Theatre
50. Taubman
51. One Eliot/Littauer/Belfer
52. Malkin Athletic Center

1. Beren Tennis Center
2. Dillon Field House
3. Briggs Cage
4. Blodgett Pool
5. Bright Hockey Center
6. Murr Center
7. Gordon Indoor Track
   & Tennis Facility
8. Cutting
9. Morgan Hall
10. Baker Library
11. Aldrich
12. Dean's House
13. Shad Hall
14. Chapel
15. Teele
16. Cumnock
17. Spangler Center
18. Burden
19. Baker Hall
20. McCollum
21. McArthur
22. Kresge

General Information

Address: University Hall, Cambridge, MA 02138
Phone: 617-495-1000
Website: www.harvard.edu

Overview

Chances are, you've heard a lot about Harvard. Chances are, you associate it with academic excellence, cutting-edge research, red brick, and students with at least two roman numerals after their names.

That stereotype hits the nail at least partly on the head. Founded in 1636, Harvard remains the richest and most revered university in the country (perhaps even the world). True to form, included in its pool of 18,000 undergrads and grad students are the children of royalty, famous actors and actresses, heirs, heiresses, and assorted other fortunate sons and daughters. The truth is that these folks are more the exception than the rule. Harvard's deep pockets have allowed it to offer generous scholarships and increase the cultural and financial diversity of its student population. The same loot helps them net world-class professors in each of its 12 schools and colleges.

With the goal of properly housing and educating "the best of the best" in all fields from arts and humanities to business and technology, Harvard is hungry for more than just talented minds. The university continues to gobble up land in Cambridge and across the river in Allston, disgruntling some locals.

Perhaps Harvard needs more space for its livestock. A phrase coined to mock the local dialect states that you cannot "park the car in Harvard Yard," since automobile traffic is prohibited there. However, an old contract clause allows each full professor to pasture one cow there. Assistant faculty members are allowed a sheep. Luckily for Harvard, no professor in recent memory has taken advantage of this opportunity.

Tuition

For the 2003-2004 academic year, undergraduate tuition, room, board, and college fees amount to $37,928. Graduate school tuition varies depending on the program.

Sports

Athletics at Harvard began around 1780, when a small group of students formed an early version of a fight club, challenging each other to wrestling matches. Since then, the spirit of athletic competition has been integral to the Harvard experience. Harvard introduced its crew team in 1844, which won its first championship just two years later. Since then, the men's heavyweight and lightweight crew teams have won 11 championships between them,

and the women's lightweight crew team has won five championships.

Years ago, Harvard was a football powerhouse, always ranked top ten in the nation. Harvard still consistently tops the Ivy League, and games against the likes of Yale still fill century-old Harvard Stadium on fall afternoons. The men's tennis team has also been a source of pride in the athletic department, consistently producing top-class players, many of whom have gone on to play professionally. In the fall of 2003, the team captured their second consecutive Eastern College Athletic Conference title.

Not all jocks are dumb: since 1920, Harvard athletes have netted 42 Rhodes Scholarships.

Not all nerds suck at sports: More than 100 Harvard athletes have participated in the Olympics.

Culture on Campus

Harvard boasts four art museums, each showcasing art from different parts of the world. It also has an extensive music and theater program. The music department performances are held in the prestigious Sanders Theater, renowned for its acoustics and design. Aside from hosting most of the orchestral and choral performances by Harvard groups, it is also a popular venue for professional groups such as the Boston Philharmonic, the Boston Chamber Music Society, and the Boston Baroque.

If you enjoy viewing dance, you can attend one of Harvard's various dance troupe performances at the Amelia Tataronis Rieman Center for the Performing Arts.

As the only not-for-profit theater company in the country that houses a resident acting company and an international training conservatory, the American Repertory Theater (A.R.T.) operates out of the Harvard University campus, making it a haven for theater enthusiasts.

A building shaped suspiciously like "Grammo: the Grammar Robot" of *Simpsons* fame houses the offices of the Harvard Lampoon on Mt. Auburn Street. Graduates of this famed humor publication have gone on to work for *Saturday Night Live*, *The Simpsons*, and *Late Night with Conan O'Brien* (O'Brien is a Harvard alum).

Departments

Undergraduate Admissions 617-495-1551
Graduate School of Arts and Sciences 617-495-1814
Kennedy School of Government 617-495-1100
Harvard Law School 617-495-4612
Harvard Medical School 617-432-1550
Harvard Business School 617-495-6000
Athletics Department and Ticket Office 617-495-2211

General Information

Address: 77 Massachusetts Avenue, Cambridge, MA 02139
Phone: 617-253-1000
Website: www.mit.edu

Overview

Just down the Chuck River from Harvard, MIT is one of the top tech schools in the world. The school's 900 faculty and 10,000 slide-rule-bearing graduate students and undergraduates inhabit a 153-acre "factory of learning" that features both neoclassical domes and some of the most modern-looking buildings in Boston.

MIT profs are infamous for assigning massive amounts of work, but a certain group of MIT students can't seem to get enough of engineering and spend their downtime planning and executing "hacks," which are technically elaborate pranks. A frequent target of hackers is MIT's Great Dome. In 1994, a replica of an MIT police cruiser appeared atop the dome. In 1996, it was donned with a gigantic beanie cap, complete with a fully functioning propeller. Just before the release of *Star Wars Episode One: The Phantom Menace*, students decorated the dome to look like the robot R2-D2. Another frequent target is Harvard. In 1990, during a Harvard-Yale football game, both players and spectators were surprised when an 8.5' x 3.5' rocket-propelled banner with the letters MIT sprang up from under the end zone as Yale lined up to kick a field goal.

Tuition

In the 2003-04 academic year, undergraduate tuition fees were $29,400. Room and board was approximately $7,850.

Sports

Whoever said science nerds can't play sports was totally right. Nevertheless, they keep trying, posting moderate success in both Division II and III. Believe it or not, MIT actually boasts the

1. Pierce Laboratory
2. Fluid Dynamics Laboratory/ Dept of Mathmatics
3. Maclaurin Buildings
4. Maclaurin Buildings
4A. 60 Vassar Street
5. Pratt School
6. Eastman Laboratories
6A. Spectroscopy Laboratory
6B. Solvent Storage
7. Rogers Building
7A. Rotch Library Extension
8. 21 Ames Street
8A. Basement Bldg 8
9. Center for Advanced Educational Services
10. Maclaurin Building
11. Homberg Building
12. 60 Vassar Street
12A. Waste Chemical Storage
13. Bush Building
14. Hayden Memorial Library
15. Dorrance Building
16. Wright Brothers Wind Tunnel
17. Dreyfus Building
18. Advanced Nuclear Systems/ Center for Experimental Study Dept of Nuclear Engineering
19. Compton Laboratories
20. Sloan Laboratories
21. Stata Center
22. Guggenheim Laboratory
23. EG & G Education Center
24. Sloan Laboratories
25. Fairchild Building

26. McNair Building
27. Fairchild Building
28. Brown Building
29. Lean Aerospace Initiative
30. Power Plant
31. Power Plant Annex
32. Cyclotron
33. Brain and Cognitive Sciences
34. Parsons Laboratory
35. Walker Memorial
36. Wood Sailing Pavilion
37. Green Building
38. Whitaker Building
39. MIT Alumni Pool
40. Alumni Houses: Munroe Hayden Wood

41. Alumni Houses: Walcott Bemis Goodale
42. Landau Building
43. Koch Biology Building
44. Gray House
45. Senior House
46. Wiesner Building
47. Mudd Building
48. Ford Building
49. Ford Building
50. Health Services

51. Whitaker College
52. Publications and References
53. 28 Carleton Street
54. Rinaldi Tile
55. Earth Resources Library
56. Suffolk Building
57. MIT Press
58. Muckley Building
59. Hayward St. Garage
60. Office of the Treasurer

largest number of NCAA-sponsored programs in the nation, and the coaches and students have received numerous awards for sports excellence. The heavyweight crew squads and the men's cross-country and track teams in particular have garnered accolades for the university.

Culture on Campus

In a time when arts and technology have pretty much merged, almost becoming indistinguishable at times, it is not hard to believe that MIT has an arts program. We highly recommend a visit to the MIT Museum. Holographic images, scientific photographs, and mechanical sculptures with names like "Untitled Fragile Machine" show just how beautiful math-type stuff can be.

The Weisner Building (designed by I.M. Pei) houses the Media Laboratory, which opened in 1985 and spent much of its first decade exploring digital video and multimedia. The Media Lab allows for interdisciplinary research, and the developing focus of study is on how electronic information impacts our daily lives—how we use it to think, express, and communicate ideas.

Many of the Media Lab's research projects are made possible through corporate sponsorship and the Lab fosters a positive relationship between academia and industry.

According to the MIT website, the Media Lab "houses a gigabit fiber-optic plant that connects a heterogeneous network of computers, ranging from fine-grained, embedded processors to supercomputers." Unfortunately, in its role as an academic research laboratory, the Media Lab is not able to accommodate visits from the general public.

Departments

Undergraduate Admissions 617-253-4791
Graduate Admissions 617-253-2917
School of Humanities Arts and Sciences 617-253-3450
School of Engineering 617-253-3291
School of Science 617-253-8900
Office of the Arts 617-253-4003
Athletic Department 617-253-4498

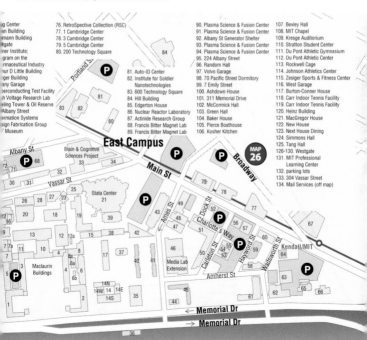

76. RetroSpective Collection (RSC)
77. 1 Cambridge Center
78. 3 Cambridge Center
79. 5 Cambridge Center
80. 200 Technology Square

81. Auto-ID Center
82. Institute for Soldier Nanotechnologies
83. 600 Technology Square
84. Hill Building
85. Edgerton House
86. Nuclear Reactor Laboratory
87. Actinide Research Group
88. Francis Bitter Magnet Lab
89. Francis Bitter Magnet Lab

90. Plasma Science & Fusion Center
91. Plasma Science & Fusion Center
92. Albany St Generator Shelter
93. Plasma Science & Fusion Center
94. Plasma Science & Fusion Center
95. 224 Albany Street
96. Random Hall
97. Volvo Garage
98. 70 Pacific Street Dormitory
99. 7 Emily Street
100. Ashdown House
101. 311 Memorial Drive
102. McCormick Hall
103. Green Hall
104. Baker House
105. Pierce Boathouse
106. Kosher Kitchen

107. Bexley Hall
108. MIT Chapel
109. Kresge Auditorium
110. Stratton Student Center
111. Du Pont Athletic Gymnasium
112. Du Pont Athletic Center
113. Rockwell Cage
114. Johnson Athletics Center
115. Zesiger Sports & Fitness Center
116. West Garage
117. Burton-Conner House
118. Carr Indoor Tennis Facility
119. Carr Indoor Tennis Facility
120. Heinz Building
121. MacGregor House
122. New House
123. Next House Dining
124. Simmons Hall
125. Tang Hall
126-130. Westgate
131. MIT Professional Learning Center
132. parking lots
133. 304 Vassar Street
134. Mail Services (off map)

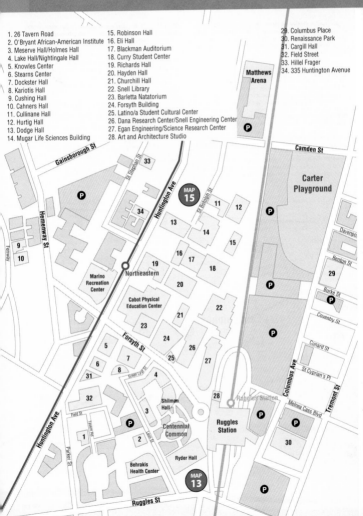

Northeastern University

1. 26 Tavern Road
2. O'Bryant African-American Institute
3. Meserve Hall/Holmes Hall
4. Lake Hall/Nightingale Hall
5. Knowles Center
6. Stearns Center
7. Dockster Hall
8. Kariotis Hall
9. Cushing Hall
10. Cahners Hall
11. Cullinane Hall
12. Hurtig Hall
13. Dodge Hall
14. Mugar Life Sciences Building

15. Robinson Hall
16. Eli Hall
17. Blackman Auditorium
18. Curry Student Center
19. Richards Hall
20. Hayden Hall
21. Churchill Hall
22. Snell Library
23. Barletta Natatorium
24. Forsyth Building
25. Latino/a Student Cultural Center
26. Dana Research Center/Snell Engineering Center
27. Egan Engineering/Science Research Center
28. Art and Architecture Studio

29. Columbus Place
30. Renaissance Park
31. Cargill Hall
32. Field Street
33. Hillel Frager
34. 335 Huntington Avenue

Matthews Arena

Carter Playground

Camden St

Gainsborough St

Hemenway St

Fenway

Huntington Ave

St Stephen St

St Botolph St

MAP 15

Davenpo...

Benton St

Marino Recreation Center

Northeastern

Cabot Physical Education Center

Forsyth St

Green Leaf St

Shilman Hall

Centennial Common

Behrakis Health Center

Ryder Hall

Ruggles St

Huntington Ave

Parker St

Field St

Tetlow Rd

Leon St

Ruggles Station

MAP 13

Burke St

Coventry St

Cunard St

St Cyprian's Pl

Melnea Cass Blvd

Columbus Ave

Tremont St

General Information

Main Campus: 360 Huntington Ave, Boston, MA 02115
Phone: 617-373-2000
Website: www.northeastern.edu

Overview

Northeastern University has come a long way since it began as a commuter school with a fairly unimpressive urban campus. In recent years the school has become an emerging national research university with sparkly new academic, athletic, and residential facilities. NU originally began as a five-year school with an academic model called "Practice Oriented Education," a program that combines education and internships (co-op). Recently the school has added more four- and five-year options, along with an internet-based correspondence school for a number of degrees.

Founded in 1898 as a part-time night school, Northeastern is located on more than 66 acres along Huntington Avenue, with three Green Line E train stops servicing the school. The current enrollment at NU is 13,757 full-time undergraduate students and 2,079 graduate students with a male-to-female ratio that is pretty evenly matched. However, cultural diversity isn't something that the university is known for. The most popular degree programs on offer are in Business, Health, and Engineering/Technology.

Tuition

Undergraduate tuition costs run at about $25,858 per year, with room and board being an additional $9,460. Books, lab fees, and personal expenses, as always, are extra. Graduate student tuition and fees vary by college, as do individual courses offered via the internet.

Sports

The Northeastern Huskies compete in Division I with varsity teams in nine men's and ten women's sports. The school's various teams had their finest collective performance ever in the 2002-03 season. The Huskies sent four teams to the NCAA playoffs and won a total of seven conference titles—Northeastern's most ever in both categories.

Culture on Campus

While Northeastern University doesn't have much in the way of the arts, it is located in a prime spot for cultural enrichment. Huntington Avenue, also known as "Avenue of the Arts," runs through the urban campus, providing a great opportunity to visit the various museums in the neighborhood. Among the most notable are the Isabella Stewart Gardner Museum and the Museum of Fine Arts. Massachusetts College of Art is also located just a few T stops away and Symphony Hall is next door.

Departments

Admissions............................. 617-373-2200
                                         617-373-3100 (TTY)
Bookstore 617-373-2286
Library 617-373-2354
Registrar 617-373-2300
Athletics Dept 617 373-2672
Ticket Office...........................617 373-4700

Undergraduate:
School of Arts & Sciences 617-373-3980
Bouve College of Health Sciences 617-373-3320
School of Business Administration ... 617-373-3270
School of Computer Science 617-373-2462
School of Criminal Justice............ 617-373-3327
School of Engineering 617-373-2155
School of Engineering Technology ... 617-373-2500
School of Nursing 617-373-3102
University College 617-373-2400

Graduate:
School of Arts & Sciences 617-373-3982
Bouve College of Health Sciences 617-373-2708
School of Business Administration ... 617-373-5992
School of Computer Science 617-373-2464
School of Criminal Justice............ 617-373-3327
School of Engineering 617-373-2711
School of Engineering Technology ... 617-373-2500
Law School............................ 617-373-2395
School of Professional Accounting ... 617-373-3244

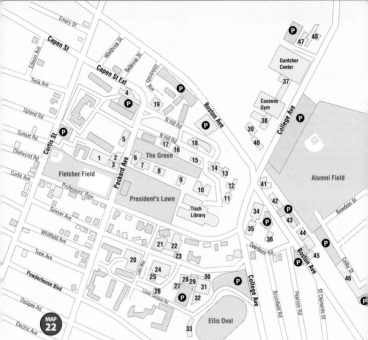

1. Cabot Center
2. Goddard Hall
3. Granhoff Family Hillel Center
4. Olin Center
5. Dana Lab
6. Barnum Hall
7. Ballou Hall
8. Goddard Chapel
9. Eaton Hall
10. Miner Hall
11. Paige Hall
12. Lincoln Filene Center
13. Braker Hall
14. East Hall
15. Packard Hall
16. Bendetson Hall
17. Central Heating Plant

18. Lane Hall
19. Dewick-MacPhie Hall
20. Bookstore
21. Elizabeth Van Huyson Mayer Campus Center
22. 55 Talbot Ave
23. Pearson Chemical Laboratory
24. Michael Lab
25. Academic Computing Bldg
26. Costume Shop
27. Jackson Gym
28. Batch Arena Theatre
29. Leir Hall
30. Cohen Auditorium
31. Aidekman Arts Center
32. Baronian Field House
33. Anderson Hall

34. Robinson Hall
35. Bromfield-Pearson
36. Bromfield House
37. Hamilton Pool
38. Halligan Hall
39. 177 College Ave
40. Office Services
41. Curtis Hall
42. Psychology Building
43. Bray Laboratory
44. Central Services
45. Bacon Hall
46. Science and Technology Center
47. Eliot-Pearson Child Development Center
48. Eliot-Pearson Children's School

General Information

Medford/ Somerville Campus: Medford, MA 02155
Boston Campus: 136 Harrison Ave,
Boston, MA 02111

Tufts General Phone: 617-627-5000
Website: www.tufts.edu
Tufts Administration Building: 169 Holland St,
Somerville, MA 02144

North Grafton Campus: 200 Westboro Rd,
North Grafton, MA 01536

Overview

There's a perception that Tufts is a school for kids who didn't make it into Harvard, which sits just two Red Line stops away. This is (mostly) not true. Tufts has academic prowess in its own right, especially in its engineering, veterinary, international relations, and science departments. The university has four campuses, with the Medford/Somerville campus being the main one.

There are about 5,500 students at the Medford/Somerville campus, the majority of whom are undergraduates enrolled in the College of Liberal Arts. The Medford/Somerville campus also houses the School of Engineering, the Graduate School of Arts and Sciences, and the School of Special Studies. Among other things, the school prides itself on diversity. They have a whole center devoted to lesbian, gay, bisexual, and transgender students, and on any given day the "viewpoints" section of The Tufts Daily—the school's surprisingly well done student newspaper—will have several pieces on the subject.

The Boston campus is centrally located and houses the School of Medicine, School of Dental Medicine, Sackler School of Graduate Biomedical Sciences, Jean Mayer USDA Human Nutrition Research Center on Aging, and The Gerald J. and Dorothy R. Friedman School of Nutrition Science and Policy.

Tuition

In the 2003-2004 academic year, undergraduate tuition fees were $28,896. Room and board cost an additional $8,640. Books, service fees, activity fees, and personal expenses are extra. Graduate student tuition, fees, and expenses vary by college.

Sports

If you ever find yourself at Tufts University and, more specifically, in the office of the Athletic Director, you might see a peanut butter jar with ashes in it. Don't be frightened, it's only Jumbo. Jumbo is the elephant mascot of Tufts University. The story is weird, but it is worth writing about. P.T. Barnum, of the Barnum and Bailey Circus, was one of the original trustees of Tufts. His prize act was an elephant named Jumbo. In 1885, Jumbo was hit by a train and killed. His stuffed body was donated to Tufts, where it was stored in a museum on campus that eventually became a student lounge. Sadly, however, the museum burned in 1975, along with Jumbo. The ashes in the jar are said to be those of Jumbo, though university officials say they have no evidence that that is the case. Luckily, they have his tail in a cardboard folder in their archives.

If that isn't enough to attract you to the sports, then maybe the recent successes of the golf and women's sailing teams will pique your interest.

There's also that old campus joke: "What's Brown and Blue and loses every weekend?" Answer: "The Tufts football team." It's not really funny, but often accurate.

Culture on Campus

Cultural activities are plentiful at Tufts if sports aren't your thing. In the Aidekman Arts Center on the Medford/Somerville campus, you'll find the Tufts University Art Gallery. Again the mantra seems to be diversity, diversity, and more diversity. The Gallery's mission is to explore art through all of its cultural complexities.

The Department of Drama and Dance is where all of the performing artists can be found. They regularly give performances at the Balch Arena Theater.

Departments

Undergraduate Admissions 617-627-3170
Graduate and Professional Studies 617-627-2295
The Fletcher School. 617-627-3700
School of Medicine 617-636-7000
School of Dental Medicine 617-636-6828
Sackler School of Graduate
  Biomedical Sciences 617-636-6767
School of Nutrition and Science Policy 617-636-3737
Athletics Department and Ticket Office. 617-627-3232
Balch Arena Theater 617-627-3493
Tisch Library. 617-627-3460

Overview

Bostonians don't just live by the water, they venture out onto it too. A testament to the popularity of H_2O-based activities in Boston Harbor and on the Charles River is the slew of yacht clubs and boating centers that hug the shores, with some boaters storing their crafts as far upriver as Watertown. Boston Harbor's reputation for being one of the country's dirtiest waterways has changed since the government spent $3.7 billion on a huge cleanup effort. In 1985, the Massachusetts Water Resources Authority (MWRA) was created to modernize water and sewer services in the Boston Metropolitan area and to manage the cleanup of the harbor, making it clean enough to swim in today without a chemical suit. Still, some boaters abuse the harbor by throwing cans, bottles, and bags of trash from their boats. If you see this happening, record the boat's number and report them to the Boston Police Harbor Patrol (617-343-4721). With any luck, the sizeable fine will force them to sell their boat and spend evenings stealing cans from neighbors' recycling bins to make ends meet.

Boston Harbor is home to 34 beautiful islands that have been designated as a National Recreation Area. If you find you need a break from sailing or motoring, you can dock your craft and explore these great little islands and their histories. On George's Island, you'll find the historic Fort Warren. The 62-acre Lovells Island has trails that pass by dunes, woods, picnic areas, the remains of Fort Standish, and a supervised swimming area. Deer Island has the Waste Water Treatment Plant, and most of the other islands have abundant wildlife, plant life, and

beautiful beaches.

If you want to go a bit farther out, consider Buzzards Bay to the south, which touches more than 280 miles of the Massachusetts coastline. Once past Rhode Island Sound to the Cape Cod Canal. Calmer waters inside the bay make it attractive to sailboats.

Back on the Charles (don't even think about pronouncing the "r"), crew rowing is a popular sport, particularly at the local colleges and universities. Laymen can utilize one of the many clubs and organizations that instruct non-rowers and hold races. The Head Of The Charles Regatta, held every fall, is the world's largest two-day rowing event. The race schedule includes single and team events and draws competitors from around the world. www.hocr.org.

If you're young, or have young ones, consider Community Boating, Inc. located between the Charles/MGH Red Line stop and the Hatch Shell. The non-profit group offers summer kayaking, windsurfing and sailing lessons for "juniors" between the ages of 10-17 for $1! All you need is parental permission and the ability to swim 75 yards. More information is available at www.community-boating.org.

Boston is also home to the CRASH—B World Indoor Rowing Championships, which is held annually in February at the Reggie Lewis Track & Athletic Center at Roxbury Community College. Racers row on the latest Concept 2 Model C ergometers, which are used by athletes at universities, clubs, schools and national teams around the globe. More information is available at www.crash-b.org.

Sailing/Boating Centers

Piers Park Sailing	95 Marginal St, Boston	617-561-6677	www.piersparksailing.org; hire/lessons/racing/sale
Boston Harbor Shipyard & Marina	256 Marginal St, Boston	617-561-1400	www.bhmarina.com; moorings/lessons
Community Boating	21 David Mugar Way, Boston	617-523-1038	www.community-boating.org; sailing lessons
Lincoln Sailing Center	PO Box 492, Hingham	781-741-5225	www.lincolnsailing.org; non-profit/lessons/sailing/rowing
Courageous Sailing Center	1 1st Ave, Charlestown	617-242-3821	www.courageoussailing.org; lessons/racing
Boston Sailing Center	The Riverboat at Lewis Wharf	617-227-4198	www.bostonsailingcenter.com; hire/courses/lessons/racing
MIT Sailing	3 Ames St, Cambridge	617-253-4884	www.mit.edu/activities/mit-sailing; lessons/racing
Boston Harbor Sailing Club	58 Batterymarch St, Boston	617-720-0049	www.bostonharborsailing.com; moorings/hire/lessons/clothing

Yacht Clubs

Bass Haven Yacht Club	10 McPherson Dr, Beverly	978-922-9712	
Boston Harbor Yacht Club	1805 Wm J Day Blvd, South Boston	617-267-9420	
Boston Yacht Club	1 Front St, Marblehead	781-631-3100	www.bostonyc.org
Braintree Yacht Club	9 Gordon Rd, Braintree	781-843-9730	
Corinthian Yacht Club	1 Nahant St, Marblehead	781-631-0005	www.corinthianyc.org
Danversport Yacht Club	161 Elliott St, Danvers	978-774-8620	www.danversport.com
Eastern Yacht Club	47 Foster St, Marblehead	781-631-1400	www.easternyc.org
Hull Yacht Club	Fitzpatrick Way, Hull	781-925-9739	www.hullyc.org
Jeffries Yacht Club	565 Sumner St, East Boston	617-567-9656	www.jeffriesyachtclub.com
Jubilee Yacht Club	126 Water St, Beverly	978-922-9611	www.jubileeyc.net
Metropolitan Yacht Club	39 Vinedale Rd, Braintree	781-843-9882	www.metyc.com
New Bedford Yacht Club	208 Elm St, South Dartmouth	508-997-0762	www.nbyc.com
Old Colony Yacht Club	235 Victory Rd, Dorchester	617-436-0512	
Peninsula Yacht Club	671 Sumner St, Boston	617-464-7901	www.pycboston.org
Plymouth Yacht Club	Union St, Plymouth 508-746-7207	781-436-9581	www.plymouthyachtclub.org
Port Norfolk Yacht Club	179 Walnut St, Dorchester	617-436-9581	
Sandy Bay Yacht Club	PO Box 37, Rockport	978-546-9433	www.sandybay.org
South Boston Yacht Club	1849 Columbia Rd, South Boston	617-268-6132	www.southbostonyc.com
Squantum Yacht Club	646 Quincy Shore Dr, Quincy	617-328-9759	www.squantumyc.org
Wianno Yacht Club	101 Bridge St, Osterville	508-428-2232	www.vsb.cape.com/~wianno/
Winthrop Yacht Club	649 Shirley St, Winthrop	617-846-9774	www.win-yc.org

Rowing Clubs

Community Rowing	PO Box 609, Newton	617-964-2455 (Apr–Oct)	www.communityrowing.org
		617-782-9091 (Nov–Mar)	
Whaling City Rowing Club	66 Spring St, New Bedford	508-997-4393	

General Information

A1 Trails: www.a1trails.com/biking/ma/boston.html
City of Boston Bicycling: www.ci.boston.ma.us/transportation/bike.asp
MassBike Bicycling in Boston: massbike.org/bikeways
MassBike Website: www.massbike.org
Ruebel BikeMaps: www.bikemaps.com
Friends of the Community Path: www.pathfriends.org
Boston Bicycle Show: www.nycbicycleshow.com/boston/index.php

Overview

Boston's streets are wide, pothole-free, and almost always have individual lanes set aside for bicycles. Oh no wait, that's Portland, Oregon. If you're biking the streets of Boston, you face the same perils as car and bus traffic on the city's narrow, congested, and craggy streets, without the side impact protection and air bags.

That said, Boston and the surrounding cities have made a real effort to increase the accessibility and safety of bike transportation. While most of the streets in the city of Boston are too narrow to accommodate bicycle lanes, the comparatively wide boulevards of Cambridge, Brookline, and Somerville offer a reserved strip for bikes. Bike-only or mixed use bike/pedestrian paths run through most of the city's parks, paralleling major roads such as the Riverway, Storrow Drive, and Memorial Drive. The amount of traffic in Boston means that bikers often reach their destination faster than those who drive the same route. Massbike.org offers tips on how to get your bike out to Logan Airport, a feat that's almost impossible by car from most approaches. If you're in Brighton, another amusing pastime is to race the Green Line B train down Commonwealth Ave.

It's not all fun and games. Danger lurks around every non-perpendicular corner. Be especially wary of:

- **Drivers**—Some would hit you just to spice up their commute.
- **Potholes**—They can sneak up on you, especially at night. Some are big enough to swallow you whole.
- **Trolley Tracks**—Green Line tracks will flip you over and buckle your wheel, especially in parts of Mission Hill, Jamaica Plain, and in Cleveland Circle, where the tracks run down the actual road and not in a protected lane. If you're going to cross the tracks, take them at a 90-degree angle.
- **Bridges**—All the bridges across the Charles are narrow and heavily trafficked. Some shoot steeply up and down over the river, reducing the ability of drivers to see you camped out on the shoulder.

If you plan on riding in Boston and you have a brain that you'd like to keep, invest in a helmet and a battery-powered red light to place below your seat or on your back.

If you cycle for recreation rather than to travel from A to B, you have many options in all parts of the city. A couple of the most popular bike trails are the Minuteman Bikeway, which is 11 miles long, and the Charles River Bikeway, which is 17 miles long. The Minuteman Bikeway is acclaimed as one of the best bike paths in the United States. Built by the Commonwealth of Massachusetts on an inactive rail bed, it passes through the historic area where the American Revolution began. It is managed and maintained by the four communities it passes through: Bedford, Lexington, Arlington, and Cambridge.

The Charles River Bikeway is longer than the Minuteman Bikeway, but it is an easier route, making it ideal for families. The path runs along both sides of the Charles River, between Galen Street Bridge in Watertown and the River Street Bridge in Boston, and from the Science Museum to Watertown Square.

For something a little longer and further away, the Bay Circuit Trail winds its way 150 miles from Newburyport on the North Shore to Duxbury on the South Shore, creating a "C" shape around Boston. Cycling enthusiasts refer to it as "Boston's outer Emerald Necklace."

Ruebel BikeMaps produces a map of riding paths and trails throughout the Greater Boston area and it is well worth the five-dollar price tag. It can be purchased at most area bookstores or through the Ruebel website. For real fanatics, Boston hosts the annual Boston Bicycle Show in early April at the Boston Center for the Arts. MassBike hosts many organized rides throughout the year, including the Fall Bike Rally in early October.

Bikes and Mass Transit

Bikes are allowed on the Red, Orange, and Blue Lines, MBTA Commuter Rail, and Crosstown (CT) bus routes during certain times and on the MBTA ferry boats at all times. Bikes are not permitted on the Green Line, the Mattapan Trolley, or other buses. On the subway and commuter rail, bikes are permitted during non-rush hour times (roughly 10 am–2 pm and after 7pm). Bikes are allowed at all subway stations except Park Street, Downtown Crossing (except to transfer), and Government Center. Crosstown buses are equipped with bike racks and can be used at any time. Other bus services do not provide racks and bikes are not permitted on board.

If you're traveling on commuter rail, wait for the conductor's instructions before entering or exiting the train. For subway commuters, head for the rear of the train. You're only allowed to enter the last carriage and, even then, there's a two-bikes-per-carriage limit. There is no extra fee for bikes on any public transportation.

Bike Shops

- **Ace Wheelworks** · 145 Elm St, Somerville · 617-776-2100
- **ATA Cycle** · 1773 Massachusetts Ave, Cambridge · 617-354-0907
- **Back Bay Bicycles** · 336 Newbury St, Boston · 617-247-2336
- **Bicycle Bill's** · 253 North Harvard St, Allston · 617-783-5636
- **Bicycle Exchange** · 2067 Massachusetts Ave, Cambridge · 617-864-1300
- **Bikes Not Bombs** · 59 Amory St, Roxbury · 617-442-0004
- **Broadway Bicycle School** · 351 Broadway, Cambridge · 617-868-3392
- **Cambridge Bicycle** · 259 Massachusetts Ave, Cambridge · 617-876-6555
- **Community Bike Supply** · 496 Tremont St, Boston · 617-542-8623
- **Cycle Sports** · 1771 Massachusetts Ave, Cambridge · 617-661-6880
- **Federico's Bike Shop** · 126 Emerson St, Boston · 617-269-1309
- **Ferris Wheels Bicycle Shop** · 64 South St, Jamaica Plain · 617-522-7082
- **International Bicycle Center** · 89 Brighton Ave, Brighton · 617-783-5804
- **Jamaica Cycle** · 667 Centre St, Jamaica Plain · 617-524-9610
- **Paramount Bicycle Repair** · 860 Broadway, Somerville · 617-666-6072
- **Park Sales & Service** · 510 Somerville Ave, Somerville · 617-666-3647
- **Ski Market** · 860 Commonwealth Ave, Boston · 617-731-6100

General Information

National Skate Patrol: www.nspboston.org
Skating Club of Boston: www.scboston.org

Overview

If you like the idea of lowering your center of gravity and darting around at high speeds on tiny little wheels or thin blades, then Boston is the perfect place for you. The city is jam packed with parks and rinks that accommodate inline skaters in the summer and ice-skaters in the winter.

Inline Skating

There are tons of places to skate in Boston, including paths that are in fairly good condition. Inliners enjoy a "not quite a vehicle, not quite a pedestrian" status that tends to confuse people into allowing them to skate almost anywhere.

Just as with cyclists, Boston drivers are not very sympathetic to skaters, so if you're navigating your way through Boston streets, stay alert. If you're skating for recreation, rather than transit, it is probably best to stick to the numerous parks and other public places designated for outdoor activities. If you are just visiting or don't have skates, one centrally located place that rents rollerblades, roller skates, and ice skates is Beacon Hill Skate Shop (135 Charles St, 617-482-7400). It is fairly inexpensive at $10/hour and $25 for the day. They only accept cash, so visit the ATM before you swing by and have your credit card ready to leave as a deposit. All rentals come with safety equipment.

Places to Inline Skate

A favorite haunt of Boston skaters is the Arnold Arboretum (125 Arborway, Jamaica Plain, 617-524-1718), which offers one of the most scenic (and hilly) skates in the area. The best thing about this place is that skaters are welcome seven days a week. It covers about a 2-3 mile distance and you don't have to worry about cars, though you might find yourself dodging quite a few people, particularly on sunny days.

Another great place to skate is Boston Common, but be forewarned that skating here is quite a challenge. The Common is usually crowded with tourists and business folk who don't take too kindly to being mowed down by skaters. The upside, though, is that you can take in Boston's history as you zip around this 1-2 mile area. The best way to get there is by taking the subway to Park Street. Note: Wearing skates on the subway is prohibited.

If you want to view the beautiful bridges that stretch over the Charles (like the abandoned railroad bridge by BU that reads "Yankees Suck" across half its length), and you want to do it without the hassle of a car or walking, the Charles River Bike Path is the route for you. Not only is it a popular trail for skaters, but bikers (hence the name) also relish this path. It runs along both sides of the river between the Galen Street Bridge in Watertown and River Street Bridge in Boston, and from the Science Museum to Watertown Square. The total length of the path back-and-forth is about 17 miles.

Ice Skating

On crisp winter days, when it almost seems unbearable to be outside, the thing that gets Bostonians out of bed is the thought of enjoying a leisurely skate on the famous Frog Pond at Boston Common. Either that or the thought of standing around the Frog Pond heckling skaters. Fees are $3 for those 14 and over, free for ages 13 and under. Skate rentals are $5 for children 13 and under, $7 for 14 and over, and lockers are available for one-dollar tokens. If you're a regular, you might consider buying an individual season pass for $100 or a family pass for $150. If you work close by, a lunchtime pass good Monday through Friday, 11 am to 3 pm (holidays excluded), is available for $60. For more information call 617-635-2120.

When Frog Pond gets too crowded, which it definitely does, try the skating rink in Larz Anderson Park in Brookline. The park is located on a former 64-acre estate and is the largest park in Brookline. In addition to the outdoor skate rink, the park has picnic areas, ball fields, and an incredible view of Boston. The only downside is that the skating rink is only open a few months every year, from December to February. Skating fees are $4 for adults and $3 for kids. Skate hire is $4. Season passes cost $85 and cover the entire family. Hours are Fri 7:30 pm–9:30 pm; Sat 12 pm–5 pm, 7:30 pm–9:30 pm; Sun 12 pm–5 pm. For more information call 617-739-7518.

Ice Skating Rinks

If you have your own skates, you might opt for one of the following rinks run by the Department of Conservation and Recreation, where skating is free in the winter:

Steriti Memorial Rink, 561 Commercial St, Boston, 617-523-9327
Daly Memorial Rink, 1 Nonantum Rd, Brighton, 617-527-1741
Reilly Memorial Rink, 355 Chestnut Hill Ave, Brighton,
   617-277-7822
The Skating Club of Boston, 1240 Soldiers Field Rd, Brighton,
   617-782-5900
Simoni Memorial Rink, 155 Gore St, Cambridge, 617-354-9523
Emmons Horrigan O'Neill Memorial Rink, 150 Rutherford Ave,
   Charlestown, 617-242-9728
Devine Memorial Rink, 995 William T Morrissey Blvd, Dorchester,
   617-436-4356
Porazzo Memorial Rink, 168 Coleridge St, East Boston,
   617-567-9571
Bajko Memorial Rink, 75 Turtle Pond Parkway, Hyde Park,
   617-364-9188
Flynn Memorial Rink, 2 Woodland Rd, Medford, 781-395-8492
LoConte Memorial Rink, 284 Locust St, Medford, 781-395-9594
Kelly Outdoor Skating Rink, 1 Marbury Tce, Jamaica Plain,
   617-635-PARK
Veterans Memorial Rink, 570 Somerville Ave, Somerville,
   617-623-3523
Murphy Memorial Rink, 1880 William J Day Blvd, South Boston,
   617-269-7060
Bryan Memorial Rink, 1275 VFW Pkwy, West Roxbury,
   617-323-9512

Gear

Beacon Hill Skate Shop, 135 Charles St S, Boston, 617-482-7400
Blades Board & Skate, 349A Newbury St, Boston,
   617-437-6300
Blades Board & Skate, 38 JFK, Cambridge, 617-491-4244
Coliseum Skateboard, 150 Huntington Ave, Boston,
   617-399-9900

General Information

Boston Parks and Recreation Office
Phone: 617-635-4505
Hotline: 617-635-PARK
Website: www.cityofboston.gov/parks

Brookline Recreation Department
Phone: 617-730-2084
Website: www.townofbrooklinemass.com/recreation/tennis.html

Cambridge Recreation Department
Phone: 617-349-6238
Website: www.cambridgema.gov

Department of Conservation and Recreation (Division of Urban Parks)
Phone: 617-722-5114
Website: www.state.ma.us/mdc/activ.htm#tennis

Outdoor Courts—Open to the Public

These public courts operate on a first-come, first-served basis. The majority of them are without lights, so get there early to get your game in. Although most courts are in good condition, some have pretty major divots a la the Boston Garden's parquet floor, making the ball spin in unexpected directions. Courts are managed either by the city or town recreation department or the Commonwealth's Department of Conservation and Recreation's Division of Urban Parks (DCR). Until last year, the DCR was the MDC (Metropolitan District Commission), so the courts might be labeled with the wrong acronym. Don't let it affect your game! Many locals also use the well-maintained school courts in the university-rich area. Each school has a different policy regarding outsiders depending on season, location, and the mood of the athletic director that particular day. Contact the schools or simply roll the dice.

Park		Map	Park		Map
Boston Common	Boylston St & Charles St	3	Library Park	Broadway	
Bromley-Heath Deck (DCR)	Southwest Corridor Park	14	Longwood Playground	Newall Rd	16
Carter Playground	Columbus Ave	13	LoPresti Park	Summer St & Jeffries St	9
Cassidy Playground	Beacon St & Acacia Ave	18	Malcolm X Park	Dale St & Bainbridge St	13
Charlesbank Park (DCR)	Charles St	1	Marine Park (DCR)	Day Blvd	11
Charlestown High	Medford St	8	Mission Hill Deck (DCR)	Southwest Corridor Park	14
Clifford Playground	Norfolk Ave & Proctor St	12	North End Park (DCR)	Commercial St	2
Columbus Park	Columbus Rd	10	Pagoda Park	Kneeland St & Lincoln St	4
Constitution Beach (DCR)	Orient Heights		Porzio Park	Maverick Sq	9
Cook Street Playground	Hill St & Cook St	8	Ramsey Park	Shawmut Ave	7
Coolidge Playground	Kenwood St	19	Rindge Field	Haskell St	22
Devotion Playground	Stedman St	19	Ringer Playground	Allston St & Griggs Pl	19
Driscoll School	Washington St	19	Riverside Press Park	River St	27
Edwards Park	Main St		Rogers Park	Lake St & Foster St	18
Franklin Park	Forest Hills St		Savin Hill Park	Grampian Wy	
George Dilboy Field (DCR)	Alewife Brook Pkwy	22	Saxton J Foss Park (DCR)	McGrath Hwy & Broadway	24
Glacken Field	Huron Ave		South Street Mall	South St & Carolina Ave	14
Harambee Park	Blue Hill Ave & Talbot Ave		Stony Brook Deck (DCR)	Southwest Corridor Park	14
Harvard Street Playground	Harvard St	28	Trotter School Playground	Humboldt Ave & Waumbeck St	13
Hoyt Field	Western Ave	27	Waldstein Playground	Dean Rd	18
Hunt Playground	Almont St & Blue Hill Ave		Walker Playground	Norfolk St	
Jeep Jones Park	King St	13	Warren Playground	Eliot St	

Private Courts

Belmont Tennis Club	30 Kilburn Rd, Belmont	617-484-9833
Boston Tennis Club	653 Summer St, Boston	617-269-4300
Hatherly Country Club	663 Hatherly Rd, Scituate	781-545-9891
Mount Auburn Athletic Club	57 Coolidge Ave, Watertown	617-923-2255
South Shore YMCA	75 Mill St, Hanover	781-829-8585
Sportsmen's Tennis Club	930 Blue Hill Ave, Boston	617-288-9092
Waltham Athletic Club	249 Lexington St, Waltham	781-899-5000
Weston Racquet Club	132 West St, Waltham	781-890-4285
Winchester Indoor Lawn Tennis	41 East St, Winchester	781-729-4040
Woburn Racquet Club	9 Webster St, Woburn	781-933-8850

Hiking in Boston

Though it's not the greatest place to drive, Boston is a great place to walk. Whether it's some light exercise or a serious trek that you are looking for, the city has a surprisingly wide array of hikes and walks to choose from. The trails that are closest to the city tend to be more scenic walks than hikes—appropriate for strolling students or families who want to get out and about in the city. If you are eager to get some real hiking done, you'll need to be prepared for a drive. On the outskirts of Boston, you'll find quite a few reservations that provide rigorous hiking trails as well as breathtaking views of the city and a taste of Massachusetts nature. If none of that is hardcore enough for you, the White Mountains of New Hampshire are just a Zipcar away.

A great source of information about various trails is the book *Exploring in and Around Boston on Bike and Foot* by Lee Sinai (Appalachian Mountain Club Books).

Beacon Hill-Back Bay

It's a "scenic walk" if you're visiting the area and a "commute" if you live in Back Bay and work at the State House. It's an easy walk and one well suited for both children and adults. There are many fun landmarks to stop and explore along the way, including the Public Garden, which is home to the famous Swan Boats. The walk also passes through the Boston Common—the oldest park in the United States and an integral part of Boston. Begin the walk at the corner of Trinity Place and St. James Avenue at the John Hancock Tower. The Back Bay-Beacon Hill walk is only two miles and takes about an hour at strolling pace.

Arnold Arboretum

Harvard's Arnold Arboretum, located in Jamaica Plain, occupies 265 acres and boasts a dizzying array of woody plants. You can take a free guided tour of the grounds (call 617-524-1718 x100 for schedules) or amble the three-mile trail at your own pace. There are plenty of amazing trees and flowers to keep your eyes occupied along the way. This botanical haven can be accessed by taking the Orange Line to Forest Hills. The entrance is two blocks from the T stop. Restrooms are available in the Hunnwell Visitor Center, located next to the entrance gate.

Fresh Pond Reservation

This is a favorite of local residents, Harvard students, and other folk north of the river. Located only one mile from the university and six miles from downtown Boston, it offers a rather easy 2.5-mile trail around comely Fresh Pond Reservoir. The relative ease of the trail makes this an ideal spot for joggers, cyclists, and skaters. If you bring your dog, be sure to check out the pooper-scooper dispensers! To reach the reservation by train, take the Red Line to Alewife (last stop). By car, follow Route 2 east or west to Fresh Pond Parkway. The reservation lies on the corner of Huron Avenue and Fresh Pond Parkway. The best entrance to the reservation is located directly across from Wheeler Street.

Mount Auburn Cemetery

Hailed as America's first garden cemetery, Mount Auburn provides two miles of leisurely walking, alternating between paved walkways and unpaved footpaths. Aside from the 86,000 graves, the cemetery is home to over 4,000 native and foreign trees. Located just 1.5 miles west of Harvard Square, the cemetery can be reached via Route 2 or 3 to Route 16 at the Mount Auburn/ Brattle Street intersection on Fresh Pond Parkway. If you follow Mount Auburn Street (Rte. 16) west for two blocks, you will reach the entrance. Contact the Friends of Mount Auburn Cemetery (617-547-7105) for information about guided tours and lectures. No dogs allowed.

Forest Hills Cemetery

Overshadowed in popularity for no good reason by Mount Auburn Cemetery, Jamaica Plain's Forest Hills Cemetery features 275 acres of beautifully sculpted landscape. One of its most impressive features is Lake Hibiscus, which is home to a Buddhist-inspired lantern lighting festival every summer. The best thing about Forest Hills Cemetery is its close proximity to the Forest Hills T stop. To get there by car, take the Arborway east over the Casey Overpass. After the overpass, take the exit for the cemetery, located on your right on Shea Circle.

Hammond Pond Reservation

Hammond Pond is an odd place for a reservation, located behind a suburban mall in Chestnut Hill. You can see the department stores as you hike through the 200 acres of woodlands. It's also one of the few places to rock climb in Boston that's not an indoor wall. The best place to start is at the entrance to the reservation, which is located on the left of Hammond Pond at the north side of the parking lot. Walk through the metal gate and remain on the wide main path that will take you through the woods. If you are interested in rock climbing, you'll see rocks to your left a little way along the path. If climbing rocks is not your thing, continue on for two miles of easy walking.

Breakheart Reservation

Hidden amidst strip malls and fast-food joints along Route 1, this 675-acre reservation is a treasure for hikers lucky enough to stumble across it. There are miles and miles of scenic views and plenty of strenuous trails if you're looking for a good workout. To get there, take Route 1 to the Lynn Fells Parkway exit towards Melrose and Stoneham. Turn right onto Forest Street and follow the signs to Breakheart Reservation. A good place to begin your hike is on the paved Pine Tops Road, which is located next to the parking lot adjacent to the headquarters building.

Skyline Trail

This nearly 10-mile trail is located in Blue Hills Reservation (near Milton), the largest open space within 35 miles of Boston. To get there, take Route 138 to exit 3 towards Houghton's Pond. After taking the exit, turn right at the stop sign onto Hillside Street and travel for approximately one mile until you reach Houghton's Pond. The trail winds through rocky hills and provides great scenic views of the city. It also has an elevation gain of 2,500 feet, making it somewhat strenuous. If that's not your bag, there are tons of less challenging trails in the park. To find out about them, buy a color-coded trail map for $1 at the park headquarters building.

Middlesex Fells Reservation Eastern Section

Located seven miles north of Boston, Middlesex Fells is a 2,000-acre reservation with some of the area's most challenging hikes. Middlesex Fells is off I-93, past the Stone Zoo. Parking is available on Pond Street. The beginning of the trail is located on the south side of Pond Street and begins behind a Virginia Wood sign near Gate #42. The trail is approximately five miles long. It is fairly strenuous and involves climbing and descending rocky slopes.

Moose Hill Wildlife Sanctuary

This is the oldest and second–largest Massachusetts Audubon Society (MAS) sanctuary. Moose Hill covers 1,800 acres and offers more than 15 miles of well-marked trails. One trail in particular, the Warner Trail, provides an exceptional view from 491 feet. To get this view, you have to climb Bluff Head. The best way to get to Moose Hill is off of Route 128/I-95 south. Take exit 10. At the end of the ramp, make a left towards Sharon Street; then travel a quarter-mile and turn right onto Route 27 towards Walpole. After half a mile, turn left onto Moose Hill Street. Follow the MAS signs to the parking lot on the left. Find your way to the Visitor Center. All of the trails stem from there.

Golf Courses

	Address	Phone	Par	Fees (WD/WE)	*
Amesbury Golf & Country Club	50 Monroe St, Amesbury	978-388-5153	36	$24/$26	S
Amherst Golf Club	365 S Pleasant St, Amherst	413-253-3520	36	$25/$25	S
Hickory Ridge Golf Club	191 W Pomeroy Ln, Amherst	413-253-9320	74	$40/$50	S
Rolling Green Golf Course	311 Lowell St, Andover	978-475-4066	27	$18/$18	P
Beverly Golf & Tennis Club	134 McKay St, Beverly	978-922-9072	73	$31/$37	P
Country Club of Billerica	51 Baldwin Rd, Billerica	978-667-9121	66	$24/$26	P
Franklin Park Golf Course	1 Circuit Dr, Boston	617-265-4084	70	$25/$32	P
Putterham Meadows Golf Club	1281 W Roxbury Pkwy, Boston	617-739-5822	71	$27/$38	P
White Pines Golf Course	549 Copeland St, Brockton	508-587-2916	36	$18/$18	P
Fresh Pond Golf Course	691 Huron Ave, Cambridge	617-349-6268	35	$28/$35	P
Cape Ann Golf Course	99 John Wise Ave, Essex	978-768-7544	35	$25/$27	P
Foxborough Country Club	33 Walnut St, Foxborough	508-543-3972	72	$50/$50	S
Millwood Farms Golf Course	175 Millwood St, Framingham	508-877-1221	53	$19/$22	P
Groton Country Club	94 Lovers Ln, Groton	978-448-3996	36	$20/$26	P
Shaker Hills Golf Club	146 Shaker Rd, Harvard	978-772-2227	71	$70/$75	P
Crystal Springs Golf Club	940 N Broadway, Haverhill	978-372-8021	72	$18/$25	S
South Shore Country Club	274 South St, Hingham	781-749-1747	72	$29/$33	P
Pinecrest Golf Club	212 Prentice St, Holliston	508-429-9871	66	$20/$26	P
Hopedale Country Club	90 Mill St, Hopedale	508-473-9876	35	$27/$32	S
Candlewood Golf Club	75 Essex Rd, Ipswich	978-356-5377	32	$16/$16	P
Pine Meadows Golf Course	255 Cedar St, Lexington	781-862-5516	35	$32/$36	P
Maplewood Golf Course	994 N Field Rd, Lunenburg	978-582-6694	35	$17/$22	P
Sagamore Spring Golf Club	1287 Main St, Lynnfield	781-334-3151	70	$31/$38	P
Willowdale Golf Course	54 Willow St, Mansfield	508-339-3197	30	$13/$15	P
Green Harbor Golf Club	624 Webster St, Marshfield	781-834-7303	71	$29/$34	P
Maynard Country Club	50 Brown St, Maynard	978-897-8465	34	$35/$35	S
Mount Hood Golf Course	100 Slayton Rd, Melrose	781-665-8139	69	$33/$40	P
Hickory Hills Golf Course	200 N Lowell St, Methuen	978-686-0822	71	$34/$38	P
Merrimack Golf Course	210 Howe St, Methuen	978-685-9717	72	$22/$28	S
Cherry Hill Golf Course	323 Montague Rd, N Amherst	413-256-4071	35	$15/$17	P
Chemawa Golf Course	350 Cushman Rd, N Attleboro	508-399-7330	69	$20/$25	P
Ballymeade Country Club	125 Falmouth Woods Rd, N Falmouth	508-540-4005	72	$75/$90	S
Presidents Golf Course	357 W Squantum St, N Quincy	617-328-0277	70	$25/$30	P
Kelly Greens Golf Course	1 Willow Rd, Nahant	781-587-0840	30	$20/$31	P
Lost Brook Golf Club	750 University Ave, Norwood	781-769-2550	54	$19/$23	P
Norwood Country Club	400 Providence Hwy, Norwood	781-769-5880	71	$24/$29	P
Bay Pointe Country Club	Onset Ave, Onset	508-759-8800	72	$35/$38	S
Pembroke Country Club	W Elm St, Pembroke	781-826-5191	75	$40/$53	S
Waverly Oaks Golf Club	444 Long Pond Rd, Plymouth	508-224-6700	72	$75/$85	P
Atlantic Country Club	450 Little Sandy Pond Rd, Plymouth	508-759-5533	72	$60/$70	P
Squirrel Run Country Club	Carver Rd, Plymouth	508-746-5001	57	$25/$25	P
Rockland Golf Course	276 Plain St, Rockland	781-878-5836	54	$23/$24	P
Rockport Golf Club	Country Club Rd, Rockport	978-546-3340	36	$30/$30	S
Rowley Country Club	235 Dodge Rd, Rowley	978-948-8190	36	$28/$32	S
Bass River Golf Course	62 High Bank Rd, S Yarmouth	508-398-4112	72	$45/$45	P
Blue Rock Golf Course	48 Todd Rd, S Yarmouth	508-398-9295	55	$45/$45	P
Cedar Glen Golf Club	60 Water St, Saugus	781-233-0161	35	$23/$26	P
Scituate Country Club	91 Old Driftway Rd, Scituate	781-545-7666	35	$27/$27	S
Widows Walk Golf Course	250 The Driftway, Scituate	781-544-7777	72	$32/$42	P
Stoneham Oaks Golf Course	101 Montvale Ave, Stoneham	781-438-7888	27	$17/$19	P
Unicorn Golf Course	460 William St, Stoneham	781-438-9732	35	$26/$30	P
Cedar Hill Golf Club	1137 Park St, Stoughton	781-344-8913	33	$15/$20	P
Butternut Farm Golf Club	115 Wheeler Rd, Stow	978-897-3400	70	$45/$45	P
Wedgewood Pines Country Club	215 Harvard Rd, Stow	978-461-2810	71	$35/$45	S
Touisset Country Club	221 Pearse St, Swansea	508-678-7991	35	$16/$19	P
Tewksbury Country Club	65 Livingston St, Tewksbury	978-640-0033	33	$28/$32	P
Trull Brook Golf Course	170 River Rd, Tewksbury	978-851-6731	72	$35/$38.50	P
New Meadows Golf Club	30 Wildes Rd, Topsfield	978-887-9307	35	$28/$32	P
Tyngsboro Country Club	Pawtucket Blvd, Tyngsboro	978-649-7334	35	$21/$25	P
Mink Meadows Golf Club	Golf Club Way, Vineyard Haven	508-693-0600	35	$55/$55	S
Little Harbor Country Club	Little Harbor Rd, Wareham	508-295-2617	56	$21/$21	P
Chequessett Yacht & Country Club	Chequessett Neck Rd, Wellfleet	508-349-3492	37	$40/$40	S
Lakeview Golf Club	Route 1A, Wenham	978-468-9584	31	$20/$22	P
Wenham Country Club	94 Main St, Wenham	978-4684714	67	$30/$35	S
Indian Meadows Golf Club	275 Turnpike Rd, Westborough	508-836-5460	36	$25/$28	S
Nabnasset Lake Country Club	47 Oak Hill Rd, Westford	978-692-2560	35	$28/$28	S
Woburn Country Club	1 Country Club Rd, Woburn	781-933-9880	34	$24/$27	P

* S=Semi-Private, P=Public

Swimming

Swimming	Address	Phone	Rates	Map
Pools				
Blackstone Community Center	50 W Brookline St	617-635-5162	$25 per year	7
Boston Chinatown Neighborhood Center	885 Washington St	617-635-5129	$3 for adults, $1 for kids	3
Brighton/Allston Pool	380 N Beacon St	617-254-0106	Free	5
Brookline Swimming Pool	60 Tappan St	617-730-2778	Residents pay $4 (adult) or $2 (under 18) per visit, non-resident rates are $6 (adult) and $3 (under 18)	17
Cambridge Family YMCA	820 Massachusetts Ave	617-661-9622	Have to be a member!	27
Central Branch YMCA	316 Huntington Ave	617-536-6950	Have to be a member!	5
Charlestown Community Center	255 Medford St	617-635-5169	$25 per year	8
Clougherty Pool	5 Austin St	617-635-5173	Free	16
Condon Community Center	200 D St	617-635-5100	$7 per year	10
Conners Memorial Pool	River St	781-899-0106	Free	1
Dealtry Memorial Pool	114 Pleasant St	617-923-0073	Free	16
Harborside Community Center	312 Border St	617-635-5114	$20 for adults, $4 for kids	9
Latta Brothers Memorial Pool	325 Rindge Ave	617-666-9236	Free	22
Mason Pool	159 Norfolk Ave	617-635-5241	$10 per year (adult), $5 (under 18)	28
McCrehan Memorial Pool	356 Rindge Ave	617-354-9154	Free	22
Mirabella Pool	Commercial St	617-635-5235	Indoor $10 for adults, kids under 5 free	2
Oak Square YMCA	615 Washington Ave	617-782-3535	Have to be a member!	18
Paris Street Community Center	112 Paris St	617-635-5125	$15 per year	9
Paris Street Pool	133 Paris St	617-635-5125	$15 per year (E. Boston residents), $25 per year (Boston residents), $60 per year (outside city)	9
Veteran's Memorial Pool	719 Memorial Dr	617-354-9381	Free	27
Walden Pond State Reservation	915 Walden St	978-369-3254	Free, $5 parking	14
Wellbridge Atlantic	695 Atlantic Ave	617-439-9600	Have to be a member! Membership starts at $77 per month.	4
Beaches				
Boston Harbor Island National Park	Boston	617-223-8666	Free	
Constitution Beach	Orient Heights, E Boston	617-727-5114	Free	
Crane Beach	Argilla Road, Ipswich	978-356-4354	$2.50 parking for members, plenty more for non-members	
Nantasket Beach	Nantasket Ave	617-727-8856	Free	
Peddock's Island	Boston Harbor	617-727-7676	Free	
Revere Beach	Revere Beach Blvd	617-727-8856	Free	
Winthrop Beach	Winthrop Shore Dr	617-482-1722	Free	
World's End	Martins Lane, Hingham	978-482-1722	$4.30 adults, under 12 free	

Bowling Lanes

Bowling Lanes	Address	Phone	Fees
Big League Bowling	1834 Centre St	617-323-7291	$3–$3.25, $2 for shoes, kids 7 under free
Boston Bowl	820 Morrissey Blvd	617-889-1552	$2.70–$4.25 per person/per game. $3.55 for adult shoes. $2.55 for kids shoes (under 12)
Central Park Lanes	10 Saratoga St	617-567-7073	$1.50–$2 per person/per game. $.75 for shoes
Kings	10 Scotia St	617-266-2695	$6.50 per person/ per game. $4 for shoes
Lanes & Games	195 Concord Turnpike	617-876-1533	$3 per person/per game. $1.50–$2 for shoes.
Lucky Strike Lanes	289 Adams St	617-436-2660	$3 per person/per game. $1.50–$2 for shoes.
Sacco's Bowl Haven	45 Day St	617-776-0552	$2.50 per person/per game $1 shoes
South Boston Candlepin	543 E Broadway	617-464-4858	$3.50 per person/per game $1.50 shoes
Milky Way Lounge & Lanes	403-405 Centre St	617-524-3740	$25 per lane, shoes included

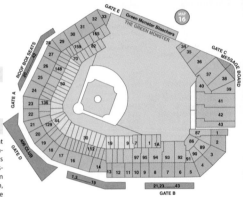

General Information

4 Yawkey Way, Boston, MA 02215
Red Sox Website: www.redsox.com
Phone: 877-REDSOX9

Overview

Crouched beneath the giant Citgo sign just outside Kenmore Square, Fenway Park is the crooked little heart of Boston—a place where locals from all walks of life sit arm-to-arm, enjoying $5 beers, a deep love of the Sox, and an even deeper hatred of the Yankees.

Fenway's old. The first game at Fenway Park on April 20, 1912 got bumped off the front page of the Boston newspapers by the breaking news of the Titanic sinking a few days earlier. It is hands-down the best major league stadium in which to watch a baseball game. The smallest big-league park, seating just 33,871, the new owners have been squeezing every last dime out of the place (ads and seats on the Green Monster, Bruce Springsteen concerts, etc.) so the "lyric little bandbox" looks to be around for a few more years.

Eighty-plus years of near misses and finishing behind the Yankees has led to an intense, belligerent, and sometimes manic fan base, creating an enjoyable game atmosphere. Due to its size, there are few bad seats at Fenway. Even the bleacher seats offer decent views of the game. Just try not to sit in the right field grandstand, where the seats don't face home plate for some ridiculous reason and you have to crane your neck left to see anything other than the Monster or Manny Ramirez daydreaming in left field.

How to Get There—Driving

Driving isn't the best idea; parking is tight and traffic can be pretty bad on game days. If you must drive, take I-93 to Storrow Drive west. Take the Fenway exit off Storrow Drive and turn right onto Boylston Street for parking.

Parking

Fenway does not provide parking. There are garages around, charging from $5 to $20, but they tend to fill up quickly, as does the limited street parking.

How to Get There—Mass Transit

Take the Green Line to Kenmore and follow the crowd to the ballpark. If you're on the D train of the Green Line, use the Fenway stop. The MBTA Commuter Rail's Worcester/Framingham line also goes to Yawkey, a short walk from Fenway Park. Subway tokens cost $1.25. Commuter Rail fares range from $1.25 to $6. If you want to get tricky, you can catch a free shuttle that leaves from Northeastern University before and after every game.

How to Get Tickets

For individual game and season ticket information, call the Red Sox box office at 877-REDSOX9, or visit the team's website. Ticket prices range from $10 to $70. Standing room only seats are available at the Red Sox box office at 9 am the day of every game. Scalpers are also everywhere in Kenmore Square. Ebay.com and the "tickets" section of boston.craigslist.org are also good places to look, but beware of scams. Scalpers' rates are highest for Yankees games and during playoff runs. Expect to pay at least double face value for tickets to these games.

General Information

Address: One Patriot Place, Foxborough, MA 02035

Phone: 508-543-8200

Websites: GilletteStadium.com
NewEnglandPatriots.com
RevolutionSoccer.net

$49- Upper Level, Corner/End Zone

$65- Upper Level, Sideline

$75- Mezzanine Level, Corner/End Zone

$75- Lower Level, Corner/End Zone

$99- Lower Level, Sideline

Overview

As far as NFL franchises go, the New England Patriots were a joke until Bill Parcells took over as head coach in 1993 and Robert Kraft bought the team in 1994. They continued to play in a mediocre stadium until 2002. Old Schaefer/Sullivan/Foxboro Stadium was an unsightly, obsolete, charmless concrete slab, but at least the Pats sent it packing in style. The last game at Foxboro Stadium was the hotly debated Snow Bowl vs. the Oakland Raiders. Depending on your hometown, QB Tom Brady either fumbled or "tucked" the football during a key late-game possession (it was a tuck). The Pats won, propelling them to their 2002 Super Bowl Championship.

The 2002 season brought the opening of Gillette Stadium, which was supposed to be called CMGI Field until CMGI, an internet company, found itself without the dough for the lucrative naming rights deal. Local shaving giant Gillette stepped in at the last minute and, while the name is still weirdly corporate, at least it's local. The Pats did it right, building a state-of-the-art facility with little niceties like a New England lighthouse and a replica of the Longfellow Bridge at one end of the field. With a seating capacity of 68,000, Gillette Stadium is also the home of Major League Soccer's New England Revolution, as well as a venue for major concerts.

How to Get There—Driving

From Boston, take I-93 S to I-95 S; take I-95 S to exit 9 (Wrentham) onto Route 1 S. Follow Route 1 S approximately 3 miles to Gillette Stadium (on the left).

Parking

The lots open four hours before Pats games and three hours before concerts and other events, leaving plenty of time for tailgating. General Seating ticket holders should enter P2 or P5 from Route 1. Follow signs for "General Stadium Parking." Disabled parkers and limos should head for P2, while buses and RVs need P6. For Patriots games, cars cost $30 to park, RVs are $75, limos are $100, and buses are $150. The prices vary for other Gillette events.

How to Get There—Mass Transit

MBTA Commuter Rail trains leave South Station for Foxboro Station, and it will cost you $10 for a round-trip ticket. The train leaves the stadium 30 minutes after the game.

How to Get Tickets

With fans trying desperately to block the memory of the horrific end to the 2003 Red Sox season, the Pats are once again the top dogs of the Boston sports world. To get on the season ticket waiting list, visit the Patriots' website and have 50 bucks a seat on hand for a deposit. For regular tickets, call Ticketmaster at 617-931-2222. Tickets range from $49 to $99. As with everywhere else, scalpers can be found roaming the parking lots and approaches to the stadium. Ebay.com and similar websites also accommodate folks who are selling and buying tickets.

225

General Information

Address: One Fleetcenter Pl,
Boston, MA 02114
Phone: FleetCenter: 617-624-1050
Celtics: 617-854-8000
Bruins: 617-624-1900
Websites: www.fleetcenter.com
www.bostonceltics.com
www.bostonbruins.com

Overview

The Celtics and the Bruins used to play in the greatest of indoor professional sports venues, the Boston Garden. The old-fashioned barn had obstructed views, rats, a dank odor, a lack of ale, and a crusty old guy playing the organ. As with most truly awful buildings, Bostonians loved it. If you watch footage of the Celts' 1984 NBA Finals victory over the Lakers you'll see fans crowding the sidelines and rushing the court with time left on the clock. Bruins games could be even less civil and more fun.

In 1995, both the Celtics and the Bruins said goodbye to the Garden and moved next door to the FleetCenter. The recent acquisition of Fleet by the Bank of America means that the name of the stadium will probably be changed to Bank of America Center once the merger is complete. The 19,600-seat FleetCenter has all that you would expect from a modern stadium: rocket-launched t-shirts, luxury box TVs, and airline and casino promotions during timeouts. It's clean and you can get better food than at the Garden—but, even with the Celts and B's doing fairly well in past years, it just doesn't have the presence and personality of the Garden. Perhaps that's why Big Dig engineers made the costly blunder of 'forgetting' the FleetCenter existed when they created the project's blue prints.

In addition to sporting events, the FleetCenter hosts concerts and the circus and will be home to the 2004 Democratic National Convention. It has also recently become a postcard staple with the recent completion of the gorgeous Leonard P. Zakim Bunker Hill Bridge nearby.

How to Get There—Driving

If at all possible, don't. If you have to, try these routes. From the north, take I-93 to exit 26A/Leverett Circle, Cambridge. Follow the signs towards North Station/FleetCenter. Take a right at the end of the ramp, and the stadium is on your left. From the south, take the new tunnel on I-93 to exit 26 Storrow Drive. After the exit, stay left and follow the signs for North Station. Watch out, it's a left-hand exit. The FleetCenter will be on your left.

Parking

Reason #2 not to drive. The FleetCenter doesn't have its own parking facilities, but there are several nearby garages ready and willing to gouge you, though some are as low as $5.

How to Get There—Mass Transit

The FleetCenter sits atop the North Station Commuter Rail station, which services the northern suburbs. Directly outside are the North Station Green Line and Orange Line subway stops. The Charles/MGH Red Line stop and the Bowdoin Blue Line stop are less than a 10-minute walk away. The MBTA commuter boat stops at Lovejoy Wharf, a short walk from North Station. Subway tokens are a $1.25, commuter rail fares range from $1.25 to $6, and commuter boat prices range from 60¢ to $1.20.

How to Get Tickets

To get Celtics season tickets, call 617-523-3030 or visit the Celtics' website. They offer full-season, half-season, or 12-game packages. Individual ticket prices range from $10 nosebleed seats to $150, with the most expensive seats being $700 courtside (season tickets only).

To get Bruins season tickets, call 617-624-BEAR or visit the Bruins' website. The B's offer full-season, half-season, and 10-game packages, with individual ticket prices ranging from $19 to $99, topping-out with the mysteriously un-priced Premium Club (if you have to ask, you can't afford them).

If you don't have tickets but have cash to burn, scalpers can be found on Causeway Street on game days.

History

It all started right after World War II. When the good people at the Massachusetts Department of Public Works noticed that cars were gaining in popularity and that people were flocking to the suburbs, they decided that some major highways needed to be built. The first to be completed was I-93, the Central Artery, which was hailed at the time as "a futuristic highway in the sky."

It soon became apparent that the highway sucked. I-93 was ugly, disrupted neighborhoods, and had a high accident rate due to the excessive number of on- and off-ramps in its 1.5-mile route through Boston. Recognizing the disaster that was the Central Artery, community groups fought successfully to stop other major highway projects. Two plans that never came to fruition were the Inner Belt (unbuilt I-695), which would have taken traffic around I-93 via a new, ten-lane BU bridge, and the Southwest Corridor Highway (unbuilt I-95), which would have run from the 93/128 split and up through Hyde Park and JP to downtown.

Although averting construction of two new highways was somewhat of a victory, I-93 was still operating at triple its capacity, resulting in traffic jams at most hours of the day. The suggested solution to the congestion problem was to dig a highway under the city—a hugely challenging engineering proposition. Planning the project took the entirety of the 1980s and construction began in September 1991. More than 12 years and $14.6 billion later, the project is finally starting to wind down.

What is the Big Dig?

"The Central Artery/Tunnel Project is the largest, most complex and technologically challenging highway project ever," says the BigDig.com website. They left out "most corrupt, over-budget, and behind schedule." Boston is dismantling the elevated expressway that cut through downtown and relocating it underground. The project includes a series of tunnels, a new bridge, and, if there's money left over, a new ring of green space to be known as the Rose Kennedy Greenway.

At present, all traffic in the city is running underground and crews are demolishing the old, elevated I-93 viaduct to make way for the parks. Below ground, everything is not complete, however. The Mass Pike and Ted Williams Tunnel are both operating smoothly, as is I-93 northbound, but the southbound side will face construction delays for a while to come. Southbound traffic is being sent through the old, three-lane Dewey Square (South Station) tunnel, which was a part of the old I-93 system. When it is complete, a maximum of five lanes will run southbound.

The Ted Williams Tunnel has proven to be an easy and reliable way to get to the airport, and the Zakim Bridge is a gorgeous addition to the skyline. When you can see the North End and the waterfront from downtown, view the sky from Causeway Street, and when the ramps and exits downtown stay in the same places for more than a week, it'll be easier to appreciate the impact of the Big Dig. Right now it's just a pain in the ass.

Go to www.bigdig.com for updates.

Transit · **Logan Airport**

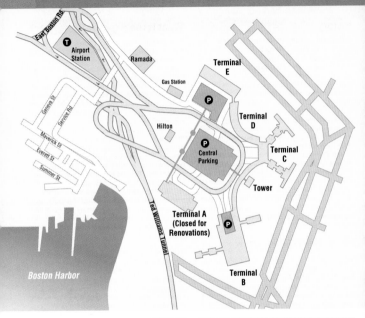

Airline	Terminal	Phone Number
Aer Lingus	E	800-474-7424
AeroMexico	E	800-237-6639
Air Canada/Air Canada Jazz	C	888-247-2262
Air Canada Jazz	E	888-247-2262
Air France	E	800-237-2747
Air Jamaica	E	800-523-5585
AirTran	D	800-247-8726
Alaska Airlines	B	800-223-5730
Alitalia	E	800-223-5730
America West	B	800-235-9292
American (except int'l arrivals)	B	800-433-7300
American (int'l arrivals only)	E	800-433-7300
American Eagle	B	800-433-7300
ATA	B	800-435-9282
British Airways	E	800-AIRWAYS
Cape Air	C	800-352-0714
Charters	D	
Continental	C	800-523-3273

Airline	Terminal	Phone Number
Delta Air Lines	C	800-221-1212
Delta Connection	C	800-221-1212
Delta Shuttle	B	800-933-5935
Icelandair	E	800-223-5500
JetBlue	E	800-538-2583
KLM	E	800-225-2525
Lufthansa	E	800-399-5838
Midwest	C	800-452-2022
Northwest	E	800-225-2525
SATA	E	800-762-9995
Song	C	800-359-7664
Swiss	E	877-359-7947
TACA	E	800-535-8780
United	C	800-864-8331
United Express	C	800-864-8331
US Airways	B	800-428-4322
US Airways Express	B	800-428-4322
US Airways Shuttle	B	800-864-8331
Virgin Atlantic	E	800-862-8621

General Information

Website: www.massport.com/logan
Phone: 617-561-1800

Overview

In general, airports are not the most comfortable or pleasant places to spend time and, in this sense, Logan's like all the rest—delays, awful food, the 300-pound sweaty guy snoring and drooling by the gate who you just know will end up sitting next to you in coach… The eighth-busiest airport in the United States, Logan International features all the lines, security checkpoints, and two-mile cab runs of most major airports. It has the added bonus of being located in an area of the country where weather can ground planes at any time of the year. But why dwell on the negatives? Thanks to the completion of a good portion of the Big Dig, getting to Logan is now much less of a chore (well, except from the north). Completion of the Ted Williams Tunnel and the controversially unnamed I-93 tunnel (Republican Governor Romney doesn't want it named after former Democratic Speaker of the House Tip O'Neill) means reaching the airport is now a whole lot easier.

Jutting into the harbor from East Boston, Logan opened in 1923 as the "temporary occupant" on a filled piece of land originally intended to be a port. By 1939, flying contraptions had proven their worth and the site was made permanent. The airport is named after Lt. General Edward Lawrence Logan, a local who went to Harvard, served in the Spanish-American War, and served in the Massachusetts House of Representatives and Senate. He also chaired the Metropolitan District Commission, a now-defunct organization that managed everything from swimming pools to the upkeep of major roadways such as Storrow Drive and the Riverway.

The neighborhood of East Boston and Logan Airport recently concluded a lengthy legal battle over the addition of a new runway, with victory going to Logan and Massport. Logan plans to build the runway to make more dough and alleviate delays. Eastie doesn't want it because of the added noise and pollution. The rest of the city skipped those articles in the paper.

How to Get There—Driving

Getting to the airport from the west or south is now easier with the completion of the I-93 northbound and I-90 portions of the Big Dig. If you're coming from the north, you'll have to deal with some delays since the Dig is not yet complete (expect constant rerouting as they work towards their early '05 completion date). To get to Logan, take I-93 to the Callahan Tunnel or the Ted Williams Tunnel. The Pike dead ends into the airport, so it's easy to find from the west. Once you're downtown, there are signs for the airport everywhere, making it kind of hard to miss. Check out www.massport.com for Big Dig updates.

Parking

Hourly and daily parking is available at each terminal. Rates range from $2 to $22 during the day, and $11 to $22 a day for overnight parking. Also offered is an $80 weekly parking rate in the Economy lot.

How to Get There—Mass Transit

Taking the T might be the easiest, cheapest, and most hassle-free way to get to Logan. No parking, no traffic, no Big Dig, and a token costs $1.25. Logan is a quick ride up the Blue Line from downtown at the oh-so conveniently named Airport stop. Once off the subway, your travels have not ended. A free shuttle takes you to your terminal, with buses running from 6:30 am until 1 am. If you're coming in from the 'burbs, check out the Logan Express buses, which service Braintree, Framingham, Peabody, and Woburn. A Park-and-Ride system is in place and, although the prices for parking and buses vary, they will always be cheaper than taking a cab. If you're near the water, the MBTA's Harbor Express water taxi can get you from Long Wharf to the airport in less than ten minutes.

How to Get There—Taxi

Depending on where you're coming from, a cab could be as much as $20-30. Don't worry about shopping around for better prices; cabbies' rates are regulated by the city and always the same. Boston Cab: 617-536-5010; Checker Cab: 617-536-7000; City Cab: 617-536-5100; Green Cab (Somerville) 617-623-6000; Cambridge Cab: 617-776-5000.

Rental Cars (on-airport)

Alamo	800-327-9633
Avis	800-831-2847
Budget	800-527-0700
Dollar	800-800-4000
Hertz	800-654-3131
National	800-227-7368
Enterprise	800-325-8007 (off-airport)
Thrifty Car Rental	800-367-2277 (off-airport)

Hotels

Hilton Logan International Airport, 617-568-6700 (on-airport)
Embassy Suites Boston Logan Airport, 207 Porter St, 800-872-4683 (on-airport)
Hampton Inn Logan Airport, 230 Lee Burbank Hwy, 781-286-5665
Holiday Inn Boston, 225 McClellan Hwy, 617-569-5250
LanghamBoston, 250 Franklin St, 617-451-1900
Omni Parker House, 60 School St, 617-227-8600
Harborside Hyatt Hotel, 101 Harborside Dr, 617-568-1234
Wyndham Boston Tremont, 275 Tremont St, 617-426-1400
Wyndham Boston Downtown, 89 Broad St, 617-556-0006
Marriott Long Wharf, 296 State St, 617-227-0800
Harborside Inn, 185 State St, 617-723-7500
Millennium Bostonian Hotel, Faneuil Hall Marketplace, 617-523-3600
Boston Harbor Hotel, Rowes Wharf on Atlantic Ave, 800-752-7077
Ritz Carlton Boston Common, 10 Avery St, 617-574-7100

General Information

Websites: www.massport.com; www.bigdig.com

Overview

Boston has the Charles and Mystic Rivers cutting through it and Boston Harbor to the east, so there are quite a few bridges spanning a lot of dirty water. The Charles separates Boston from Cambridge, necessitating the Boston University Bridge, the Harvard Bridge (a.k.a the Mass Ave Bridge), the Longfellow Bridge, and bridges at Eliot Street, JFK Street, Western Avenue, and River Street. The Harvard Bridge and the Longfellow Bridge, which looks like a series of salt and pepper shakers, offer the best views of the skyline. An abandoned railroad bridge by Boston University has become the target of neighborhood groups. The bridge declares "Yankees Suck" in eight-foot high graffiti. The neighborhood wants the graffiti removed, but no one has actually done anything about it yet.

A few years ago, then-Celtics coach Rick Pitino promised to hang himself from the BU Bridge if the Celts missed the playoffs, which they then proceeded to do. He did snap and skip town, but he is still alive and kicking, coaching at Louisville. The new Leonard P. Zakim Bunker Hill Bridge connects downtown with Charlestown and has become everybody's favorite new landmark, making an appearance in every local news opening skyline shot. Further along is the Charlestown Bridge, which connects the North End and Charlestown and was long ago the scene of many Irish/Italian gang fights.

To the northeast is the Tobin Bridge, which connects Charlestown with Chelsea. This is the bridge from which Charles Stuart leapt to his death after the cops figured out it was actually him—and not "some black guy"—who shot and killed his wife and unborn child before shooting himself in the leg to suggest robbery. The Tobin has a toll for some reason and will run you anywhere from 30¢ to $7 depending on the size of your vehicle and whether you have a resident commuter permit. The Evelyn Moakley Bridge, the Seaport Boulevard Bridge, and a decrepit old footbridge span the Fort Point Channel from downtown to the developing Fort Point neighborhood.

Bridge	Engineer	Length	Opened
Anderson Bridge	Wheelright, Haven and Hoyt		1913
Arthur Fiedler Foot Bridge	Shepley, Bulfinch, Richardson & Abbot		1954
Boston University Bridge	Desmond and Lord		1928
Charlestown Bridge			
Congress Street Bridge			
Eliot Bridge	Maurice Witner		1951
Evelyn Moakley Bridge	Ammann & Whitney	800'	
Harvard Bridge	William Jackson	2,165'	1891/1990
John W. Weeks Foot Bridge	McKim, Mead and White		1927
Lagoon Foot Bridge	William Preston		1869
Longfellow Bridge	Edmund Wheelright	1,768'	1904
Lovejoy Wharf Foot Bridge			
Malden Bridge			
Mystic River Bridge			
River Street Bridge	Bellows, Aldrich & Gray	330'	1926
Storrow Dr Connector Bridge	HNTB Corporation	830'	1999
Tobin Memorial Bridge	J.E. Grenier Co.	1,525'	2/27/1950
(vehicles only; toll: 30¢ residents, $2 other)			
Western Avenue Bridge	John Rablin	328'	1924
Zakim Bunker Hill Bridge (vehicles only)	Christian Menn	1,432'	10/4/2002

General Information

Boston Website:
www.cityofboston.gov/transportation/driveandpark.asp
Brookline Website:
www.town.brookline.ma.us/transportation
Cambridge Website: www.cambridgema.gov
Somerville Website:
www.ci.somerville.ma.us/departments/trafficparking
Massachusetts RMV:
www.state.ma.us/rmv
Boston Phone: 617-635-4680
Brookline Phone: 617-730-2177
Cambridge Phone: 617-349-4300
Somerville Phone: 617-625-6600

Overview

Planning a city's traffic flow is a significant thing. In Washington DC, Benjamin Banneker designed beautiful, broad boulevards that are still in use today. In the 1950s, autocratic New York transportation chief Robert Moses designed an amazingly efficient system of highways and parkways. In Boston, witch-fearing farmers built paths wherever it was easiest and where their cows preferred. The result is the dysfunctional chaos of present day. As small farming villages such as Brighton, Dorchester, and Roxbury fused, so did their under-planned streets.

Whenever a large number of streets meet together at strange angles, it's called one of two things. If there are businesses involved, it's called a square (e.g. Harvard Square). Squares are not square. They usually have six or seven feeder streets. In high-speed situations, roads intersect in "traffic circles," a.k.a. "rotaries." The ability to properly navigate these dangerous, but efficient, interchanges is a source of pride for Boston drivers.

And proud they should be. Boston drivers are the best in the country, which is something you will realize once you understand the rules of the road—a system based on the idea that everyone who learned to drive anywhere else sucks. The rules:

Be aggressive: Drive the streets of Boston. Don't let the streets drive you. You will often find yourself needing to make four-lane changes in 100 feet, weave in and out of crowded rotaries, or drive at 60 mph on narrow roads within inches of the oncoming lane.

"The whites of their eyes": Driving in Boston, especially in more traditional neighborhoods such as East Boston, East Somerville, Southie, and Charlestown, involves quite a bit of communication with your fellow drivers. Eye contact and gestures will let you know if they will let you into their lane, are upset that you cut them off, or if they applaud your recent ballsy driving maneuver. This will also be a good opportunity to see if they hate you. Drivers in other cities may inadvertently cut off others in their race to "get there first," but in Boston, driving is often spite-based. If you are disliked for any reason (for instance, if you drive a yuppie car in Southie) people will cut you off just for fun.

Check your directions, check them again: Another thing about those yokel farmers who planned the roads is that they weren't terribly creative when it came to names. As a result, there are no less than six different Washington Streets, five Walnut Streets, and five Tremont Streets within in this book's coverage area. If you include surrounding communities, the numbers jump even higher. Know which city's and neighborhood's version of a street you are aiming for. Also, be wary about directions like "that bridge with the construction on it" or "that Dunkin' Donuts on the corner," since that could be any block in the city. If someone tells you to take a right or a left, ask how much of a right or a left. Knowing if you need a turnaround right, hard right, soft right, or straight right makes all the difference.

Get lost anyway: There's really no good way of preparing for what's in store. Just do it. Leave yourself some extra time and space to enjoy being lost. After a while, all the lost driving experiences will connect. One day, you will find yourself giving an absurdly long, complicated, and landmark-based set of directions to a confused out-of-towner. It will be official. You will be a Mass-hole.

Highlights & Hints

- The Jamaicaway: A beautiful road, running through and over Frederick Law Olmsted's Emerald Necklace. Unfortunately, it was designed for horse carriages. Today, it is a reluctant highway, accommodating huge numbers of cars traveling at high speeds around steeply banking turns and over hills. Head-on collisions and fatalities are an unfortunate fact of life here. Be careful.
- Commonwealth Avenue street plan (from left to right while facing west): A sidewalk, parking, single inbound lane, parking, a sidewalk, two lanes of inbound, sidewalk, inbound Green Line B, outbound Green Line B, sidewalk, two lanes outbound, sidewalk, parking, single outbound lane, parking, sidewalk again. Commonwealth Ave packs all of this in an area that Texans wouldn't deem wide enough for a two-lane road. On your way from Kenmore Square west to the suburbs, you'll encounter hills, masses of bikers and BU students, legal left turns through three lanes of traffic and two trolley lanes, illegal right turns that everyone takes anyway, green lights that require stopping, and red lights you're expected to know to ignore. Enjoy.
- The JFK/UMass exit off I-93: **Everyone** has a blinking yellow light. **No one** knows what that means. Close your eyes and go.
- On paper, the rule is that you yield to traffic that is already in the rotary.
- There is only one Boston neighborhood where the streets meet at right angles—Back Bay. Maybe that's why it's sinking into the Charles River right now.
- No self-respecting Driving in Boston page would be complete without information on the Big Dig. Except for this one. The Big Dig gets its own section (see page 227).

Zipcar General Information

www.zipcar.com · 617-491-9900

History

Zipcar rents cars out by the hour. You can tell that the people who started it are from Cambridge by reading their website: "People would achieve transportation nirvana by having a transit pass and a Zipcard in their pockets. The result would be reduced congestion, fewer auto emissions, more green space, and a revolution in urban planning." That's Cantabridgian for "Give us $8.50/hr, we'll give you a Jetta." Once you get your "Zipcard," you visit www.zipcar.com, reserve a nearby car, get in, and go. This seems like the smartest idea on wheels if you live in congested areas like the North End, Allston, or Harvard Square and you need to get somewhere the T can't take you. The $300 deposit, refundable or not, seems to kind of defeat the whole purpose but, any way you shake it, it's cheaper and probably less of a hassle than owning a car.

How It Works

The idea is that you go online and reserve one of the hundreds of cars available at zipcar.com. A quick phone call will get you the same result. Once you reserve an available car, you pop along to the location where it has been parked and use your Zipcard to unlock the car. When you are done you return it to the same spot where you picked it up.

Your Zipcard will only open your car for the time that you have reserved it. During this period, no one else can open the car you have reserved. The car unlocks when the valid card is held to the windshield.

Costs

The cost of Zipcar varies depending on the location, but generally they run between $8.50-$10.50 an hour. There is a Night Owl Special between the hours of midnight and 6 am, when the cost is only $2 an hour. A 24-hour reservation, which is the maximum amount of time that a car can be reserved, costs about $75-95, with an additional 18 cents per mile after 125 free miles. Membership costs are additional.

Car Rental

If traditional car rental is more your style, or you'll need a car for more than 24 hours at a time, try one of the many old-fashioned car rental places in Boston.

Map 1
- Avis · 3 Center Plaza · 617-534-1400
- Dollar · 209 Cambridge St · 617-723-2065

Map 3
- Budget · 24 Park Plaza · 617-451-3201
- Dollar · 26 Park Plaza · 617-634-0006
- Hertz · 30 Park Plaza · 617-338-1500

Map 4
- Enterprise · 1 International Pl · 617-261-7447

Map 5
- Avis · 41 Westland Ave · 617-534-1400
- Enterprise · 800 Boylston St · 617-262-8222

Map 6
- Dollar · 110 Huntington Ave · 617-578-0025
- Hertz · 120 Huntington Ave · 617-338-1506

Map 9
- Airways Rent A Car · 161 Orleans St · 617-542-4197
- National · 6 Tomahawk Dr · 617-569-6700

Map 10
- Hertz · 164 Seaport Blvd · 617-204-1165

Map 12
- Enterprise · 230 Dorchester Ave · 617-268-1411
- U-Haul · 985 Massachusetts Ave · 617-442-5600

Map 13
- Enterprise · 839 Albany St · 617-442-7500

Map 14
- Enterprise · 3430 Washington St · 617-522-4160

Map 18
- Merchants Rent A Car · 12 Wirt St · 617-254-9995
- Rent-A-Wreck · 2022 Commonwealth Ave · 617-254-9540
- U-Haul · 240 N Beacon St · 617-782-0355

Map 19
- Adventure Rent-A-Car · 139 Brighton Ave · 617-783-2825
- Budget · 95 Brighton Ave · 617-254-3340
- Enterprise · 292 Western Ave · 617-783-2240
- Enterprise · 996 Commonwealth Ave · 617-738-6003
- Ferris Service Station · 455 Harvard St · 617-232-2111
- U-Save Auto & Truck Rental · 25 Harvard Ave · 617-254-1000

Map 20
- Alamo · 1663 Massachusetts Ave · 617-661-8747
- Avis · 1 Bennett St · 617-534-1400
- Thrifty · 110 Mt Auburn St · 617-876-2758

Map 22
- U-Haul · 2480 Massachusetts Ave · 617-354-3058

Map 23
- Aardvark Auto Rental · 378 Highland Ave · 617-776-4648
- Enterprise · 377 Summer St · 617-628-2266

Map 24
- Affordable Auto Rental · 700 Mystic Ave · 617-776-6800
- American Auto Rental · 90 Highland Ave · 617-623-9223
- Rent-A-Wreck · 161 Broadway · 617-776-8500

Map 25
- Enterprise · 37 Mystic Ave · 617-625-1770

Map 27
- Budget · 220 Massachusetts Ave · 617-497-1801
- Enterprise · 25 River St · 617-547-7400
- U-Haul · 844 Main St · 617-354-0500

Map 28
- Americar Auto Rental · 251 Prospect St · 617-576-0202
- U-Haul · 151 Linwood St · 617-625-2789

General Information

Websites:

Boston: *www.cityofboston.gov/transportation/parking.asp*

Brookline: *www.town.brookline.ma.us/transportation/parking/parking.html*

Cambridge: *www.cambridgema.gov/~Traffic/rpp/sticker_visitor.html*

Somerville: *www.ci.somerville.ma.us/cityservices/permit_parking.asp*

Phones:

Boston: 617-635-4410
Brookline: 617-730-2000
Cambridge: 617-349-4700
Somerville: 617-625-6600

Overview

You will get at least one ticket a month. It doesn't matter what you do and how careful you are, they will get you. Maybe there was street cleaning the night before. Maybe there was a parking ban because of snow (when there's snow, the only way to avoid a ticket is to drive around until the snow melts). Or maybe you got towed because there's a construction project and you missed the half-hidden "Tow Zone" sign that workers positioned conveniently on the sidewalk under a discarded pizza box.

Seriously though, parking in Boston can be a pain. Depending on where you live, you might want to reconsider even owning a car. The North End and Allston are crowded neighborhoods with narrow streets, and they're filled with cars. Somerville, Cambridge, and Brookline aren't quite as bad for parking, but the options are still limited. Parking can be difficult because of the abundance of resident-only parking areas. If you're a resident, all you have to do is get a permit, and you're all set. If not, you get a ticket or towed. Boston residents get more belligerent about the parking the colder and snowier it gets. Chairs start showing up in people's spaces and God help you if you move them (learn to love the key marks on your car). Narrow streets with parking on both sides, combined with poor driving by some means that the sidewswiping of parked cars is not uncommon. Tuck in your mirrors. Some T stops offer parking, most don't. There are a few reasonable parking facilities downtown, but most of them are out of town. There are parking garages underneath Post Office Square Park and, believe it or not, Boston Common.

How to Get Permits

In Somerville, take a lease or a current bill with your address and your registration to 133 Holland Street. In Boston, take your registration and a current bill with your address to City Hall, Room 224, at Government Center. All Brookline wants is 15 bucks, and apparently they don't care where you live. Brookline Town Hall is at 333 Washington Street. In the People's Republic of Cambridge, you need your registration, saying that either you or your car, they're not clear which, weighs less than 2.5 tons, and proof of residency. You can visit the website and download the form and send copies of the above with a check for $8 (bargain!) to Cambridge Traffic, Parking & Transportation, Resident Parking, 238 Broadway, Cambridge, MA 02139.

Towing

Cars get towed for snow emergency, street cleaning, and other emergency violations, so keep an eye out for nor'easters, third Thursdays, and massive construction. If your car gets towed, you're looking at about $100 to get it back.

The Boston BTD Tow Lot is located at 200 Frontage Road, near the Andrew T stop in Dorchester/Southie. The City of Boston website says that "walking is not encouraged" due, obviously, to the Big Dig. Cabs can be hailed at the Andrew T stop.

Brookline, Somerville, and Cambridge use private, commercial lots to store your newly towed car. Call one of the numbers above, and they'll be able to tell you where your car is. Hopefully.

The Somerville tow lot is, for reasons unknown, Pat's Auto Body on the McGrath Highway near Union Square.

Cambridge either has a top-secret tow lot or it rotates. If your car gets towed, they ask you to call the police (617-349-3300), who will presumably then tell you where your car is.

Brookline has a similarly clandestine car imprisonment system. A call to their transportation/parking office should unearth your car.

Tickets

Because it allows them to take your money immediately, all four places offer online ticket payment. Tickets are dispensed for offenses such as double-parking, expired meters, non-resident parking on a resident-only street, street cleaning violations, and the city/town needing money. Regardless of the city, you're looking at about 50 bucks per infringement.

General Information

MBTA Website: www.mbta.com
Phone: 617-222-5000

Overview

The T is broken up by color into four separate lines (Red, Orange, Blue, and Green) and one new, half-assed, pre-tend-to-be-a-subway-when-I'm-not line (the Silver Line). The T is great for cutting through the city, with all lines, except the Green Line B, moving you from one side of the city to the other at a decent clip. But if you need to get a ride from, say, Davis Square (Somerville) to Cleveland Circle (Brighton), well... you can't. Despite the relative proximity of the two places, you have to go downtown on one line (Red) and back out on another (Green)—an 11-mile trip to connect destinations that are 6.5 miles apart. The T is supposedly working on an "Urban Ring" line to fix this, but don't hold your breath. It will be a matter of decades, not years, before a solution is up and running. Another perplexing phenomenon is that the last call at bars in Boston is 1 or 2 am, but the last train leaves the station at 12:30 am—not all of the Redcoat traditions have been overcome. Recently the T has started running buses along the subway routes until 2:30 am, but other than that, you're stuck with cabs.

The Green Line: It is actually the oldest operational subway in the country, and you can tell. Not a grown-up subway like the Red, Orange, and Blue Lines, the Green Line features light-rail "trolleys"—130-foot-long green Twinkies that shoot you beneath the city of Boston before emerging onto streets and getting stuck in traffic. On the bright side, the new Italian-made "Breda" trolley cars seem to be derailing less often lately, though still running rather slowly.

The Green Line runs from Lechmere in Cambridge as far as Kenmore in Boston. Along the way are the Museum of Science, FleetCenter (North Station), Faneuil Hall, Boston Common, Back Bay, and Fenway Park. At Kenmore, the B (Boston College), C (Cleveland Circle), and D (Riverside) trains diverge and emerge from the ground as trolleys. The E train parts ways two stops back at Copley. The B is the slowest train, because god forbid the Boston University kids walk anywhere. Lots of stops + lots of red lights = long rides. The B takes you through BU, Allston, Brighton, and as far as Boston College. The C runs along Beacon Street in Brookline, through Coolidge Corner to Cleveland Circle, in the Brighton neighborhood of Boston. Once off the train at Cleveland Circle, note the trolley making a wide circle-turn through four-way traffic, which, for some reason, leads to a lot of accidents at that spot. The D runs through Fenway and Brookline Village to Chestnut Hill before hitting several Newton neighborhoods. The E (Heath Street) train splits before Kenmore at Copley and services Symphony Hall, Mission Hill, Northeastern University, the Museum of Fine Arts, and several hospitals. Don't believe the maps that will tell you E trains terminate at Forest Hills. This service was "temporarily" suspended in 1986 and debate over its possible restoration is causing much debate south of Heath Street in Jamaica Plain. Meanwhile, the 39 bus will take you from Heath Street to Forest Hills.

The Orange Line: The Orange Line was an elevated trolley running above Washington Street until the 1980s. Now, it's a legitimate train that runs below the Southwest Corridor Park. The park and the new Orange Line follow a path originally designed for the extension of I-95 through Boston. Community groups defeated the proposal in 1979, convincing officials to put a subway and park on the land instead. This lack of a I-95 led, indirectly, to the $14.6 billion Big Dig. Power to the people. The Orange Line runs from Oak Grove in Malden to Forest Hills in Jamaica Plain. Along

the way you hit Sullivan Square, Bunker Hill Community College (or USC, the University of Southern Charlestown), FleetCenter (North Station), Faneuil Hall, Downtown Crossing, Chinatown, New England Medical Center, and a few stops in Roxbury and Jamaica Plain.

The Blue Line: Who takes the Blue Line? Comparatively few commuters. MBTA ridership figures show only about 55,000 daily boardings on the Blue Line, compared to 160,000 on the Orange, 214,000 on the Red, and 225,000 on the Green. Running from Bowdoin Street downtown to Wonderland in Revere, this is the line you want to be on for fishing or flying, or to bet on horses and dogs. On your way east, you'll pass the Aquarium, Logan Airport, Suffolk Downs, Revere Beach, and Wonderland Dog Track.

The Red Line: The T's flagship line, the Red Line runs from Alewife in Cambridge through Davis Square in Somerville, Harvard Square, MIT, the Esplanade, the Common, Southie, and Dorchester. At the JFK/UMass stop—where, coincidentally, you'll find both the JFK Library and the University of Massachusetts at Boston—the line splits into the Ashmont train to Dorchester (with a connecting trolley to Mattapan) and the Braintree train, which runs through Quincy. A fun game to play on the Red Line: try to predict which student riders and professor-looking people will get off at which university stops. Bet with your friends.

The Silver Line: This is actually a high-speed bus line. It was supposed to be a new trolley, but officials reneged on a deal to build tracks on the line, which runs through some of Boston's poorer neighborhoods. Despite its identity crisis, the Silver Line runs pretty well from Dudley Square in Roxbury to Downtown Crossing. The MBTA plans to extend Silver Line service all the way to Logan Airport later this year.

Parking

Your chances of finding parking increase as you move further away from downtown, but generally only end cap stations and suburban stations have day parking. Even if you find a garage or lot, they fill up quickly on weekdays. Prices vary. Parking in resident spots will result in a ticket ($35-$50) and, in some areas, a keying.

Fares and Passes

A subway token is $1.25, but if you get on the outbound Green Line west of Kenmore (or Symphony on the E train), it's free. Monthly subway passes are $44, and combo passes, which can also be used on buses, are $71. Passes are sold at certain T stops and in some stores. To find out where to buy a pass, or to buy one online, visit www.mbta.com.

General Information

MBTA Website: www.mbta.com
Phone: 617-222-5000

Overview

The Commuter Rail is a series of lines servicing the outer limits of Greater Boston, the suburbs, and as far out as Worcester and Providence, Rhode Island.

The Commuter Rail is split between the northern routes that leave from North Station and the southern routes that leave from, believe it or not, South Station. It's an actual train, with comfy seats, tickets, and ticket-takers walking the aisles. All things considered, riding the Commuter Rail is a pleasant experience. The state is working to update all of the stations, outfitting them with new platforms, electronic signaling, and new ramps and elevators to make them handicapped accessible. As with any major transit network, there are occasional (read: daily) delays on the Commuter Rail. Still, a ride on the rail is 1000 percent less stressful than driving in and out of the city everyday, and a great option for day-trippers who want to enjoy Boston, rather than just get lost in it.

Debate still rages over whether to reinstate long-suspended commuter rail service to the South Shore on what is known as the "Greenbush Line." The project is expected to cost over $400 million, and that's not even counting the 50-90 percent incompetence tax that goes with all public projects in Mass. Some want the line restored to offer a car-free alternative for folks in Braintree, Weymouth, Hingham, and Cohasset. Others hate the plan. Mention it on any Commuter Rail trip and you're likely to get an earful from someone on one side or the other.

Parking

Parking is available in every Commuter Rail stop except Ayer, Belmont, Endicott, Foxboro, Greenwood, Hastings, Mishawum, Morton Street, Natick, Newtonville, Plimptonville, Prides Crossing, Porter, Silver Hill, Uphams Corner, Waverley, West Newton, Wilmington, Windsor Gardens, and Yawkey. Rates vary, with some as low as $2 per day.

Fares and Passes

The Commuter Rail ranges in price from $1.25 to $6. You can buy a ticket on the train but, depending on how busy the train is and the ticket-taker's mood, they can add a surcharge for not buying a ticket in advance. Monthly passes range from $71 (Zone 1A and 2A only) to $198, with varying perks like subway, bus, and ferry use. Passes are sold at certain T stops and other locations, as well as online at MBTA.com.

MBTA Ferries

General Information

MBTA Website: www.mbta.com
Phone: 617-222-5000

Overview

The MBTA Commuter Ferry connects Boston to the airport and is one of the best routes in and out of Charlestown and other shore side communities. One thing that makes the T boat better than any other form of Boston transportation is the fun factor. On a nice day, it seems well worth it to pay $1.25 for a quick jaunt across the harbor. The views of the city are gorgeous and, since the routes run in the Inner Harbor, the ride is fairly smooth, even in bad weather. There is something deliciously Olde Timey about ferrying across the harbor.

All ferry stops are accessible to wheelchair users. If you plan on taking your bike with you, bicycles board free with a paying customer.

Parking

Parking is available at every commuter ferry stop, although some stops only offer street parking. Rates vary, with some as low as $2 per day.

Fares and Passes

Inner Harbor ferries (serving Charlestown, Long Wharf, Lovejoy Wharf, World Trade Center, and Courthouse) are $1.50, and commuter boats to Hull, Quincy, and Hingham cost $6, payable by a crewmember when boarding the boat.

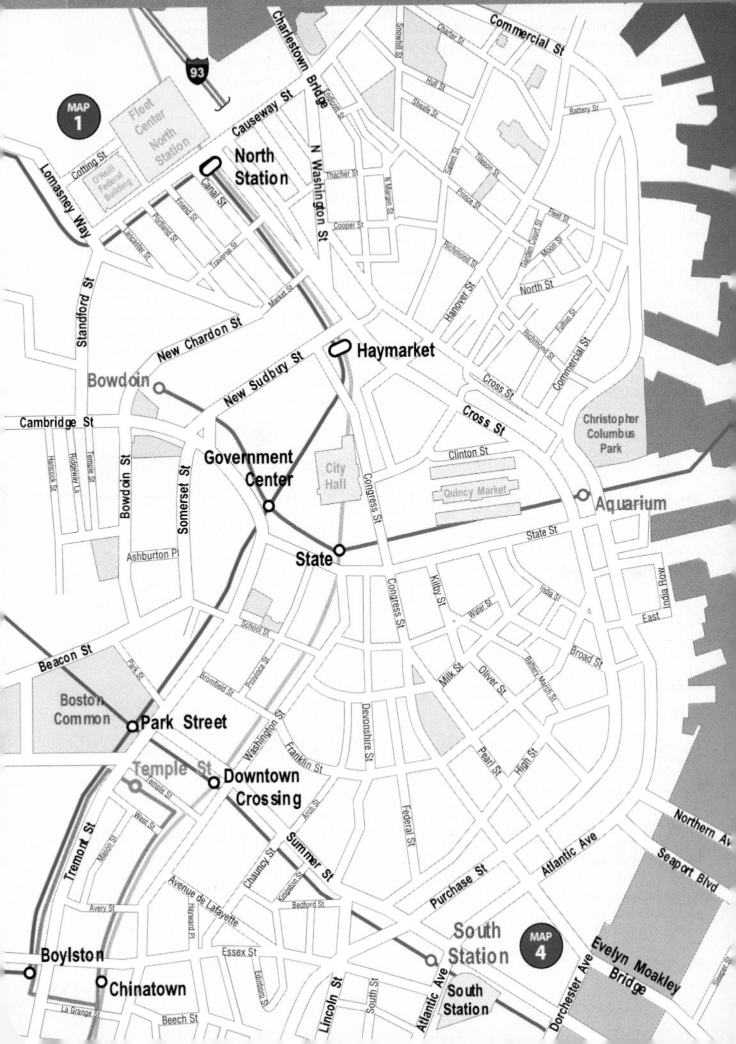
MAP 1
Fleet Center North Station
O'Neill Federal Building
93
Charlestown Bridge
Causeway St
Commercial St
Charter St
Snowhill St
Hull St
Sheafe St
Battery St
Endicott St
Cotting St
Lomasney Way
North Station
Canal St
Friend St
Portland St
Lancaster St
Traverse St
N Washington St
Thacher St
Cooper St
N Margin St
Salem St
Tileston St
Prince St
Fleet St
Garden Court St
Moon St
Richmond St
Hanover St
North St
Fulton St
Richmond St
Commercial St
Market St
Standford St
New Chardon St
Haymarket
New Sudbury St
Bowdoin
Cross St
Cross St
Christopher Columbus Park
Cambridge St
Hancock St
Ridgeway La
Temple St
Bowdoin St
Somerset St
Government Center
City Hall
Congress St
Clinton St
Quincy Market
Aquarium
State St
State
Ashburton Pl
Congress St
Kilby St
India St
India Row
East
Water St
School St
Beacon St
Park St
Bromfield St
Province St
Milk St
Oliver St
Battery March St
Broad St
Boston Common
Park Street
Washington St
Devonshire St
Franklin St
Pearl St
High St
Temple St
Downtown Crossing
Temple St
West St
Arch St
Federal St
Northern Av
Seaport Blvd
Tremont St
Mason St
Summer St
Chauncy St
Kingston St
Atlantic Ave
Purchase St
Avenue de Lafayette
Avery St
Hayward Pl
Bedford St
South Station
MAP 4
Boylston
Essex St
Evelyn Moakley Bridge
Chinatown
Edinboro St
Lincoln St
South St
Atlantic Ave
South Station
Dorchester Ave
La Grange St
Beech St
Sleeper St

General Information

Websites: *www.amtrak.com/stations/bon.html (North)*
www.amtrak.com/stations/bos.html (South)
www.amtrak.com (Amtrak)
www.MBTA.com (MBTA)
www.greyhound.com (Greyhound)
Amtrak Phone: 800-872-7425 (800-USA-RAIL)
MBTA Phone: 617-222-5000
Greyhound Bus Phone: 800-752-4841

Overview

North Station and South Station are the main Amtrak and MBTA Commuter Rail depots in Boston. North Station, near the North End and underneath the FleetCenter, houses the Commuter Rail, Amtrak, and the North Station subway stop, which is actually the last elevated station in Boston. South Station, on Atlantic Avenue and Summer Street at the gateway to South Boston, provides the same services, along with a bus terminal and a large domed area with a food court, a bar, a newsstand, and a bookstore.

Traveling between Stations

There is a one-mile gap between the two stations and there has been talk of creating a "North-South Rail Link" between them. The North Station stop is on the Orange and Green Lines of the MBTA subway, while the South Station stop is on the Red Line. Yes, it *is* crazy that the stations aren't on the same line and don't directly connect to each other. No, they're not going to do anything to correct the problem in the near future. Yes, they could have rolled it into the Big Dig project, since they were digging under the city anyway. No, we don't know why they didn't. Yes, it does seem odd that they spent billions to improve automobile transportation while ignoring public transportation.

After a decade of Big Dig, few Bostonians are psyched for another subterranean construction project, especially one that would cost $7 billion (and that's without overruns). As it is, someone from New York going to Maine has to get off the train at South Station and either take a cab, take two subway trains, or walk to get to North Station to take the train to Maine.

How to Get There—Driving

Both are located off of I-93 in downtown Boston. North Station is exit 26 (Storrow Drive), and South Station is exit 20.

Parking

The MBTA says there's no parking at either station, but "street or private parking may exist." It doesn't. You might find an outrageously expensive garage, but that's about it.

How to Get There—Mass Transit

North Station is on the Green Line and Orange Line. South Station is on the Red Line. Tokens are $1.25.

Amtrak

Amtrak trains leave out of North Station and South Station going north to Portland, Maine and south to NYC and beyond. When you go north, they call it the Downeaster (that's Maine-ese for "near Canada"). When you go south, they call it a bunch of things, including "the Federal," "the Acela," and the mundanely titled "Regional." The Acela is Amtrak's flagship route, offering "high-speed" service from South Station to NYC, Philly, and DC, with stops along the way. On a good day, the Acela chugs from Boston to New York in 3.5 hours, which is still only slightly faster than a bus and, at $90 a ticket, nine times as expensive as a Chinatown-to-Chinatown bus (see Greyhound and China-town Buses, page 240). Luckily, a well-known local is working to update Amtrak. Former Massachusetts governor, Democratic presidential hopeful, and tank-driver Michael Dukakis is Vice President of the Amtrak Reform Board. He's a big fan of public transportation, walking, and picking up litter. The tank only comes out on special occasions.

Baggage Check

Three items of baggage, weighing up to 50 lbs, may be checked up to 30 minutes prior to departure. Three additional pieces may be added for a fee. (Two carry-on items allowed.) No dangerous, fragile, valuable items, animals, or household goods can be checked.

How to Get Tickets

To get train tickets, call Amtrak or visit their website. Fares vary depending on your destination and how far in advance you book. Check the website to see if they have a Rail Sale for the route you want to take.

Going to New York

The one-way fare is $64-76 and the journey takes about 4.5 hours from South Station. You could cut your journey time to around 3.5 hours by going express on the Acela, but you will have to fork out $92 for the convenience (and comfort).

Going to Philadelphia

Amtrak offers 10 trains daily to Philadelphia. A one-way ticket will cost you $74-92, and it will take you about 5.5 hours. The speedier Acela Express will set you back $130-152, but the journey takes just over five hours.

Going to Washington D.C.

A trip to Washington on the regular Amtrak train will cost you $81-106 and will take you 8–9 hours. The Acela Express train costs $141-165 and takes 6.5 hours.

Greyhound & Chinatown Buses

Greyhound Website: www.greyhound.com
Fung Wah Bus Website: www.fungwahbus.com
Sunshine Bus Website: www.sunshineboston.com
Lucky Star Bus Website: www.luckystarbus.com

Greyhound Phone: 800-752-4841
Fung Wah Bus Phone: 617-338-1163
Sunshine Travel Phone: 617-695-1989
Lucky Star Bus Phone: 888-881-0887

Overview

Greyhound buses leave out of the South Station bus terminal, and they'll take you *anywhere*. It ain't the Concorde, but it'll get you there eventually. Round-trip fares range from $98 to $238. There are 3,700 stations in North America.

If you want to get to New York City for *really* cheap, take one of the Chinatown buses. Round trip on each will only cost you $20, as long as the "promotional fares" don't go up, but they've been "promotional" for more than a year in most cases and give no sign of budging. The fleet ranges from small coaches (especially on the Fung Wah) to full-blown buses with bathrooms and TVs. If you take a later Chinatown bus out of NYC, you will get into Boston after the T closes, meaning you'll have to pay for a cab. The cab ride around Boston costs more than the 200-plus mile journey from New York. Also check out the Chinatown bus websites for transport to destinations such as the Mohegan Sun Casino, Niagara Falls, and Acadia National Park.

How to Get There—Driving

South Station is at Atlantic Avenue and Summer Street at exit 20 off I-93. The Greyhound bus terminal is in the taller building behind the South Station dome building. The C-Town buses' departure point is the corner of Beach Street and Harrison Avenue. Take exit 24 off I-93, follow signs for Beach Street.

Parking

More than likely not going to happen.

How to Get There—Mass Transit

The Greyhound Bus Terminal is part of South Station, which is on the MBTA Red Line as well as being the end point for the southern routes of the commuter rail. Subway tokens cost $1.25.

All Chinatown buses depart from the same area near the corner of Beach Street and Harrison Avenue in Chinatown. To get there from the Chinatown, stop off the Orange Line, turn left out of the Medical Center side of the station. The next intersecting street will be Beach Street, where you'll find folks handing out pamphlets and asking if you're going to New York. It's also less than a half-mile walk from South Station. From there, take a left out of the station and walk a quarter of a mile to Kneeland Street. Take a right and then another right on Harrison Avenue. Beach Street is one block up.

MBTA Buses

MBTA Website: www.mbta.com
Phone: 617-222-5000

Overview

Every day, intrepid T bus drivers pilot their behemoth vehicles down too-narrow streets filled with angry drivers, errant pedestrians, unfortunate bikers, and, in the winter, ice and snow (a simple "thank you" to the driver as you get off the bus isn't too much to ask). MBTA buses run everywhere the subway doesn't, and even some places it does. Usually, at least one of any bus route's end points is a subway station. The T also runs several popular express buses from the outlying neighborhoods to downtown via the Mass Pike or other highways.

Bostonians who are reliant on MBTA buses, and those stuck behind them in traffic, are getting a better deal these days. The T is in the process of replacing the bulk of its aging diesel fleet with new Compressed Natural Gas (CNG) buses. Identifiable by their blue strip and the low roar of their engines, the new buses reduce emissions by up to 90 percent and, so far, are cleaner on the inside as well (give it a few years). Some buses on busy routes feature low floors and articulated midsections, such as those used along the two-year-old "Silver Line"—Washington Street's wannabe subway—and JP's 39 bus.

After the bars close on Fridays and Saturdays, buses pick up the slack for the subway with the Night Owl service, running along the subway routes until 2:30 am. The MBTA always seems to be threatening to discontinue the popular, though unprofitable, Night Owl service, citing budget concerns. So, before you bank on a late-night bus ride home, ask and make sure the service still exists.

Fares and Passes

Most buses are 90¢ a ride, some random zones cost $1.55, and the express buses range from $2.20 to $3.75. Monthly bus passes are $31, and subway/bus combos are $71. Bus passes can be bought at several T stations or online at MBTA.com. The Night Owl costs $1.50 a ride and accepts subway passes.

All area codes are 617 unless otherwise noted.

Name	Address	Phone	Map

Gas Stations

Name	Address	Phone	Map
Exxon	239 Cambridge St	523-3394	1
Exxon	1420 Boylston St	236-4596	15
Exxon	198 Western Ave	782-1224	19
Mobil	273 E Berkeley St	542-5155	7
Mobil	470 Meridian St	567-6021	9
Mobil	85 Southampton St	442-9600	12
Mobil	1301 Boylston St	247-1789	15
Mobil	816 Memorial Dr	354-8243	27
Mobil	345 Boylston St	738-4706	17
Mobil	343 Fresh Pond Pkwy	354-2114	21
Shell	1 Rutherford Ave	242-9655	8
Shell	52 Meridian St	567-8100	9
Shell	1001 Boylston St	354-8925	28
Shell	1241 Boylston St	247-7905	15
Shell	525 Huntington Ave	427-2247	15
Shell	207 Magazine St	354-5565	12
Shell	820 Memorial Dr	497-6585	27

Convenience Stores

Name	Address	Phone	Map
Store 24	157 Brighton Ave	782-6065	19
Store 24	363 Tremont St	350-0046	3
Store 24	405 West Broadway	269-1652	10
Store 24	555 East Broadway	269-1669	10
Store 24	1219 Commonwealth Ave	782-5135	19
Store 24	542 Commonwealth Ave	424-8856	16
Store 24	140 Main St	241-7865	8
Store 24	281 Huntington Ave	267-5668	5
Store 24	177 State St	367-0034	2
Store 24	1912 Beacon St	738-4874	18
Store 24	141 Massachusetts Ave	353-1897	5
Store 24	1750 Washington St	247-4841	7
Store 24	241 Market St	783-9193	18
Store 24	509 Cambridge St	782-3900	19
Store 24	957 Commonwealth Ave	783-5466	19
Store 24	1441 Beacon St	731-3757	17
Store 24	321 Broadway	497-6275	28
Store 24	1 Neptune Rd	569-7028	9
Store 24	14 Maverick St	567-6025	9
Store 24	684 Centre St	524-9893	14
Store 24	4 College Ave	666-0650	23
White Hen Pantry	120 Byron St	567-7978	9
White Hen Pantry	250 Cambridge St	367-8238	1
White Hen Pantry	342 Hanover St	723-5569	2
White Hen Pantry	1864 Massachusetts Ave	547-7255	23
White Hen Pantry	204 Maverick St	569-7069	9

Copy Shops

Name	Address	Phone	Map
Copy Cop	815 Boylston St	267-9267	5
Ikon Document Services	3 Center Plaza	371-1300	1
Kinko's	2 Center Plaza	973-9000	1
Kinko's	10 Post Office Sq	482-4400	4
Kinko's	187 Dartmouth St	262-6188	6
Printing Plus	151 Pearl St	426-0808	8

Pharmacies

Name	Address	Phone	Map
CVS	35 White St	876-4037	23
CVS	210 Border St	567-3236	9
Walgreens	1 Central Sq	569-5278	9

Bowling (yes, bowling)

Name	Address	Phone	Map
Boston Bowl	820 Morrissey Blvd	889-1552	

Restaurants

Name	Address	Phone	Map
IHOP	1850 Soldiers Field Rd	787-0533	18
News	150 Kneeland St	426-6397	4
South Street Diner	178 Kneeland St	350-0028	4

Shipping

Name	Address	Phone	Map
Ground Ex (HQ)	PO Box 130349	1-888-9PARCEL	

Plumbers

Name	Address	Phone	Map
Drain King	N/A	439-3929	
Geo Robbins & Co	46 Brooks St	484-0464	9

Veterinary

Name	Address	Phone	Map
Angell Memorial Animal Hospital	350 S Huntington Ave	522-7282	14

Locksmiths

Name	Address	Phone	Map
Greater Boston 24 Hour Lock Smith		254-8674	
Champion Locks		723-7000	
Mass Ave Lock	125 St Botolph St	247-9779	6
Securitech Lock	Mead St	254-8866	
24-7 Locksmith			
ABC Lock & Keys Services		522-2646	
Boston Lock & Safe	30 Lincoln St	787-3400	4
Safemasters	678 Salem St	781-321-8803	

Louis Prang St

Fenway St

Louis Prang St

Riverway

Brookline Ave

Short St

Plymouth St

Pilgrim Rd

Tetlow St

Beth Israel
Deaconess
Medical Center
(BID)

Palace Rd

BID

BID

Judge Baker
Children's
Center

BID

Harvard
Institute of
Medicine

CH

CH

Blackfan Circle

Louis Pasteur Ave

Channing Lab/BWH

CH

CH

MAP
15

Longwood Ave

Joslin
Diabetes
Center

Joslin Pl

Autumn St

Deaconess Rd

Beth Israel
Deaconess
West Campus
(BID)

Binney St

Dana-Farber
Cancer Institute
(DFCI)

Jimmy Fund Way

Children's
Hospital (CH)

Harvard
School of
Dental
Medicine

HMS

Harvard Medical
School (HMS)

Longwood
Medical Are

Conant St

Huntington Ave

CH

DFCI

CH

CH

CH

Harvard School
of Public Health

Peabody St

Shattuck St

HMS

Wigglesworth St

Worthington St

Conway
Library

Riverway

BID

Brigham and
Women's
Hospital (BWH)

Francis St

Brigham
Circle

Netherlands Rd

Fenwood Rd

Vining St

Fenwood Road

Tremont St

Torpie St

S Whitney St

S Alphonsus St

Parker Rd

Brookline Ave

New Whitney St

Mission Park Dr

Kempton St

S Huntington Ave

St Alphonsus Rd

Alleghany St

Mission Park

Shepherd Ave

Mission Hill

Traveler St

Pequot St

Darling St

Calumet St

Smith St

Pearl St

Riverway

Riverway

Colum

Copenger St

Parker Hill Ter

Eldora St

Sunset St

S Huntington Ave

Iroquois St

Sachem St

Hillside St

Fisher St

Hospitals

The medical facilities of Boston are considered to be among the best in the world, and have been the location of many medical firsts, including:

1938: Surgical procedure to correct a congenital cardiovascular defect, performed by Dr. Robert Gross.

1944: Human ovum successfully fertilized in test tube by researchers at Peter Bent Brigham Hospital.

1947: Successful pediatric remission of acute leukemia achieved by Dr. Sidney Farber.

1948: Polio virus isolated at Children's Hospital.

1954: Successful kidney transplant took place at the Peter Bent Brigham Hospital.

1959: Oral contraceptive shown to be effective by Dr. John C. Rock.

A few of the major hospitals:

The Longwood Medical Area features 21 medical and academic institutions within a couple of blocks, including globally renowned institutions such as Brigham and Women's Hospital, Beth Israel Deaconess Medical Center, Children's Hospital, Dana-Farber Cancer Institute, Joslin Diabetes Center, and the Center for Blood Research. Four of the nation's top five recipients of National Institute of Health (NIH) research funding are Longwood institutions. Longwood is also the home to the Harvard Medical, Dental, and Public Health Schools. It is arguably the world's leading center for health care and medicine.

Massachusetts General Hospital is the oldest and largest hospital in New England. MGH first opened its doors in 1811 and now hosts over 42,000 inpatients a year.

Hospital	Address	Phone	Map
Arbour-HRI Hospital	227 Babcock St	617-731-3200	19
Beth Israel Deaconess Medical Center	330 Brookline Ave	617-667-7000	16
Boston University Medical Center	715 Albany St	617-638-8000	7
Brigham and Women's Hospital	75 Francis St	617-732-5500	15
Cambridge Hospital	1493 Cambridge St	617-665-1000	28
Children's Hospital	300 Longwood Ave	617-355-6000	15
Dana-Farber Cancer Institute	44 Binney St	617-632-3000	15
Franciscan Children's Hospital	30 Warren St	617-254-3800	17
Massachusetts Eye and Ear Infirmary	243 Charles St	617-523-7900	1
Massachusetts General Hospital	55 Fruit St	617-726-2000	1
Mount Auburn Hospital	330 Mt Auburn St	617-492-3500	20
Somerville Hospital	230 Highland Ave	617-591-4600	23
St Elizabeth's Medical Center	736 Cambridge St	617-789-3000	18
Tufts-New England Medical Center	750 Washington St	617-636-5000	3
VA Boston-Jamaica Plain Campus	150 S Huntington Ave	617-232-9500	14

Police

Important Phone Numbers:
All Emergencies: 911
Crime Stoppers: 800-494-TIPS
Boston Area Rape Crisis Center (BARCC): 617-492-RAPE
Mayor's 24-Hour Service: 617-635-4500
State Police: 617-523-1212
Website: www.ci.boston.ma.us/police

Statistics	2003	2002	2001	2000
Murder	21	32	31	26
Rape	140	216	202	202
Robbery	1556	1369	1372	1431
Aggravated Assault	2394	2393	2492	2683
Burglary	2449	2202	2164	2269
Grand Larceny	9075	10305	9657	10010
Grand Larceny (auto)	4036	4098	4408	4138

Police Station	Address	Phone	Map
Brookline Police Department	350 Washington St	617-730-2222	17
Cambridge Police Department	5 Western Ave	617-349-3300	27
Boston District A-1	40 New Sudbury St	617-343-4240	2
Boston District A-7	69 Paris St	617-343-4220	9
Boston District B-2	135 Dudley St	617-343-4270	13
Boston District C-6	101 W Broadway	617-343-4730	10
Boston District D-14	301 Washington St	617-343-4260	18
Boston District D-4	650 Harrison Ave	617-343-4250	7
Boston District E-13	3345 Washington St	617-343-5630	14
Somerville Police Department	220 Washington St	617-625-1600	24

General Information · FedEx Locations

* Last pick-up, pm.

Map 1 {.*}

Drop box	7 Bulfinch Pl	7:45
Drop box	170 Canal St	7:30
Drop box	25 New Chardon St	7:30
Kinko's	2 Center Plaza	7:30
Drop box	1 Beacon St	6:30
Drop box	101 Merrimac St	6:30
Drop box	100 Charles River Plaza	6:30
Drop box	50 Stanford St	6:00
Drop box	60 Garden St	6:00
Drop box	131 Beverly St	5:00
Drop box	1 Bowdoin Sq	4:30

Map 2 {.*}

Service Center	60 State St	9:00
Drop box	240 Commercial St	8:00
Drop box	343 Commercial St	8:00
Drop box	200 State St	7:45
Drop box	1 Congress St	7:45
Drop box	28 State St	7:30
Drop box	77 N Washington St	7:30
Drop box	98 N Washington St	7:30
Drop box	1 Boston Pl	7:00
Drop box	66 Long Wharf	7:00
Drop box	141 Tremont St	6:00
Drop box	10 St James Ave	6:00
Drop box	260 Tremont St	5:00
Mail Boxes Etc	198 Tremont St	5:00
Mail Boxes Etc	44 School St	4:00

Map 3 {.*}

Service Center	333 Washington St	8:00
Service Center	16 Tremont St	8:30
Drop box	75 Arlington St	7:45
Drop box	821 Washington St	7:30
Drop box	265 Franklin St	7:15
Drop box	45 School St	7:00
Drop box	750 Washington St	7:00
Drop box	73 Tremont St	7:00
Drop box	260 Franklin St	7:00
Drop box	470 Atlantic Ave	7:00
Drop box	99 High St	7:00
Drop box	136 Harrison Ave	7:00
Drop box	80 Boylston St	6:30
Drop box	50 Milk St	6:30
Drop box	31 Milk St	6:30
Drop box	99 Summer St	6:30
Drop box	270 Congress St	6:30
Drop box	10 Park Plaza	6:00
Drop box	35 Kneeland St	5:30
Kinko's	21 Congress St	5:00
Drop box	200 Lincoln St	4:00
Drop box	7 Ave de Lafayette	4:00

Map 4 {.*}

Service Center	160 Federal St	9:00
Drop box	85 Franklin St	8:00
Drop box	75 Federal St	8:00
Drop box	1 International Pl	8:00
Drop box	125 Summer St	8:00
Drop box	101 Arch St	8:00
Drop box	1 Financial Ctr	8:00
Drop box	150 Federal St	8:00
Drop box	225 Franklin St	8:00
Drop box	100 Federal St	8:00
Drop box	21 Custom House St	7:45
Drop box	155 Federal St	7:30
Drop box	100 Summer St	7:30
Drop box	745 Atlantic Ave	7:30
Drop box	45 Batterymarch St	7:30
Drop box	88 Broad St	7:30
Drop box	1 Federal St	7:15

Map 5 {.*}

Drop box	815 Boylston St	8:00
Drop box	800 Boylston St	8:00
Drop box	116 Huntington Ave	7:00
Drop box	200 Clarendon St	7:00
Mail Boxes Etc	110 Huntington Ave	6:00
Mail Boxes Etc	398 Columbus Ave	6:00
Penfield's	10 Huntington Ave	6:00
Drop box	95 Berkeley St	5:00
Mail Boxes Etc	304 Newbury St	5:30
Drop box	380 Stuart St	4:30
Drop box	207 Massachusetts Ave	4:00
Drop box	800 Boylston St	4:00

Map 6 {.*}

Service Center	575 Boylston St	8:30
Drop box	200 Berkeley St	8:00
Drop box	197 Clarendon St	8:00
Drop box	200 Clarendon St	8:00
Drop box	500 Boylston St	8:00
Drop box	162 Columbus Ave	7:15
Drop box	142 Berkeley St	7:30
Drop box	399 Boylston St	7:30
Drop box	699 Boylston St	7:30
Drop box	31 St James Ave	7:30
Kinko's	187 Dartmouth St	7:30
Drop box	101 Huntington Ave	7:00

Map 7 {.*}

Drop box	88 E Newton St	8:15
Drop box	700 Albany St	8:00
Drop box	80 E Concord St	8:00
Drop box	818 Harrison Ave	7:45

Map 8 {.*}

Drop box	149 13th St	7:00
Drop box	1 Constitution Plaza	7:00
Drop box	101 Main St	7:00
Drop box	1 Main St	6:45
Drop box	20 City Sq	6:30
Drop box	1 Thompson Sq	6:30
Drop box	23 Austin St	6:00

Map 9 {.*}

Drop box	50 Meridian St	7:00
Drop box	256 Marginal St	7:00
Drop box	280 Summer St	7:00
Drop box	430 W Broadway	7:00
Drop box	2 Central Sq	6:00

Map 10 {.*}

Drop box	68 Fargo St	8:00
Drop box	313 Congress St	7:30
Drop box	2 Seaport Ln	7:30
Drop box	25 Thomson St	7:30
Drop box	1 Gillette Park	7:00
Drop box	88 Black Falcon Ave	7:00

Map 11 {.*}

Drop box	1 Design Center Pl	7:00
Drop box	212 Northern Ave	7:30
Drop box	775 Summer St	9:00
Service Center	775 Summer St	9:00
Drop box	100 Newmarket Sq	5:00
Drop box	1010 Massachusetts Ave	5:00

Map 12 {.*}

Drop box	1 Widett Circle	6:00
OfficeMax	8 Allstate Rd	6:00
Drop box	55 Roxbury St	4:00

Map 13 {.*}

Drop box	716 Columbus Ave	7:45
Drop box	1135 Tremont St	7:30
Drop box	677 Huntington Ave	6:30
Drop box	550 Huntington Ave	6:00
Drop box	20 Shattuck St	5:30
Mass Mental Health Ctr	74 Fenwood Rd	5:30
Drop box	221 Longwood Ave	5:00
Partners Health Care	1620 Tremont St	5:00
Mail Boxes Etc	360 Huntington Ave	2:30

General Information · FedEx Locations

* Last pick-up, pm.

Map 15 *

Drop box	300 Longwood Ave	8:00
Drop box	44 Binney St	8:00
Drop box	300 The Fenway	7:45
Drop box	4 Blackfan Circle	7:30
Drop box	360 Huntington Ave	7:30
Drop box	43 Leon St	7:30
Drop box	180 Longwood Ave	7:00
Drop box	75 Francis St	7:00
Drop box	200 Longwood Ave	7:00
Drop box	188 Longwood Ave	7:00
Service Center	44 Binney St	7:00
Drop box	150 S Huntington Ave	6:30
Drop box	1 Joslin Pl	6:15
Hearthstone Place	10 Brookline Pl	6:00
Staples	401 Park Dr	6:00
Drop box	15 Deerfield St	5:00
Kinko's	534 Commonwealth Ave	5:00

Map 16 *

Drop box	375 Longwood Ave	7:30
Drop box	771 Commonwealth Ave	7:30
Drop box	80 Brookline Ave	7:00
Drop box	605 Commonwealth Ave	7:00
Drop box	675 Commonwealth Ave	7:00
Drop box	890 Commonwealth Ave	7:00
Drop box	330 Brookline Ave	7:00
Drop box	364 Brookline Ave	6:45
Beth Israel Hospital	1 Deaconess Rd	6:30
Beth Israel Hospital	1 Overland St	6:30
Drop box	1 Autumn St	6:30
Drop box	44 Cummington St	6:30
Drop box	590 Commonwealth Ave	6:30
Drop box	110 Francis St	6:30
Drop box	1 Brookline Pl	6:30
Drop box	1309 Beacon St	5:00

Map 17 *

Copy Cop	1295 Beacon St	6:30
Kinko's	1370 Beacon St	6:30
Children's Hospital Trust	138 Harvard St	6:00
Cypress	235 Cypress St	6:00
Mail Boxes Etc	258 Harvard St	6:00
Drop box	207 Washington St	6:00

Map 18 *

Service Center	276 Washington St	8:30
Drop box	736 Cambridge St	7:00
Drop box	20 Guest St	7:00
Drop box	424 Washington St	7:00
Cambridgeport Bank	1380 Soldiers Field Rd	6:45
Drop box	119 Braintree St	6:45
OfficeMax	400 Western Ave	6:45
Drop box	1170 Commonwealth Ave	6:30
Drop box	12 Oxford St	6:30
Mail Boxes Etc	1085 Commonwealth Ave	5:30

Map 19 *

Drop box	214 Lincoln St	7:45
Drop box	1065 Commonwealth Ave	7:00
Drop box	1505 Commonwealth Ave	7:00
Drop box	881 Commonwealth Ave	7:00
Drop box	501 Cambridge St	7:00

Map 20 *

Kinko's	1 Mifflin Pl	8:00
Drop box	33 Kirkland St	7:30
Drop box	60 Harvard Way	7:15
Drop box	48 Quincy St	7:15
Drop box	35 Oxford St	7:00
Drop box	124 Mt Auburn St	7:00
Drop box	1563 Massachusetts Ave	7:00
Drop box	20 University Rd	7:00
Drop box	50 Church St	7:00
Ikon Express	117 Western Ave	7:00
Kennedy School of Govt.	79 JFK St	7:00
Drop box	1 Brattle Sq	6:00
Harvard Univ.	230 Western Ave	6:00
Holyoke Ctr	1350 Massachusetts Ave	6:00
Drop box	147 Sherman St	5:30

Map 22 *

Drop box	199 Alewife Brook Pkwy	7:00
Drop box	150 Cambridge Park Dr	7:00
Drop box	2067 Massachusetts Ave	7:00
Drop box	48 Grove St	7:00
Rounder Records	5 Cameron Ave	7:00
Drop box	90 Sherman St	6:00
Staples	186 Alewife Brook Pkwy	6:00
Drop box	1 Davis Sq	5:30

Map 23 *

Drop box	1972 Massachusetts Ave	7:00
Porter Exchange-Lesley College	1815 Massachusetts Ave	7:00
Drop box	500 Rutherford Ave	7:00
Mail Boxes Etc	1770 Massachusetts Ave	6:30
Drop box	66 Union Sq	6:30
Drop box	237 Washington St	6:30
Dlm / Clear Channel	36 Bay State Rd	6:00
OfficeMax	16 McGrath Hwy	6:00
Pinnacle Properties	52 Roland St	5:30

Map 24 *

Drop box	100 Fellsway W	7:00
Drop box	5 Middlesex Ave	7:00

Map 25 *

Drop box	529 Main St	7:45

Map 26 *

Drop box	400 Technology Sq	7:30
Drop box	1 Kendall Sq	7:00
Drop box	43 Thorndike St	7:00
Drop box	1 Memorial Dr	7:00
Kinko's	600 Technology Sq	7:00
Drop box	25 First St	7:00
Drop box	5 Cambridge Ctr	7:00
Drop box	245 1st St	7:00
Cambridgeside Galleria	100 Cambridgeside Pl	6:30
Drop box	215 First St	6:30
Drop box	1 Broadway	6:00
Drop box	4 Cambridge Ctr	6:00
Drop box	55 Cambridge Pkwy	6:00
Drop box	31 Ames St	6:00
Drop box	222 3rd St	5:00

Map 27 *

Drop box	350 Massachusetts Ave	7:15
Drop box	359 Green St	7:00
Drop box	26 Landsdowne St	7:00
Drop box	575 Memorial Dr	7:00
Drop box	21 Erie St	7:00
Drop box	38 Sidney St	7:00
Drop box	675 Massachusetts Ave	7:00
Drop box	1000 Massachusetts Ave	7:00
Drop box	1033 Massachusetts Ave	7:00
Drop box	64 Sidney St	7:00
Drop box	950 Cambridge St	6:30
Drop box	432 Columbia St	6:30
Drop box	201 Broadway	6:00
US Trust	141 Portland St	6:00
Drop box	790 Memorial Dr	6:00
Drop box	875 Massachusetts Ave	6:00
Drop box	840 Memorial Dr	6:00

Map 28 *

Drop box	120 Beacon St	6:30

Post Offices & Zip Codes

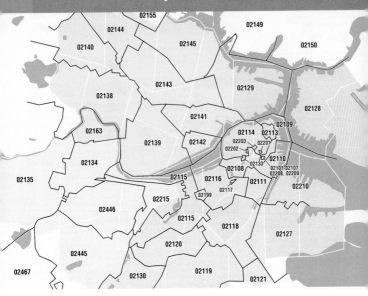

Post Office	Address	Phone	Zip	Map
Allston	47 Harvard Ave	789-3769	02134	19
Astor	207 Massachusetts Ave	247-2429	02115	5
Back Bay Annex	390 Stuart St	236-7800	02116	6
Boston University	775 Commonwealth Ave	266-0665	02215	16
Brighton	409 Washington St	254-5026	02135	18
Brookline	1295 Beacon St	738-1649	02446	17
Brookline Village	207 Washington St	566-1557	02445	17
Cambridge Main Office	770 Massachusetts Ave	575-8700	02139	27
Cathedral	59 W Dedham St	266-0989	02118	7
Charles Street	136 Charles St	723-7434	02114	1
East Boston	50 Meridian St	561-3900	02128	9
East Cambridge	303 Cambridge St	876-8558	02141	26
East Street Annex	25 East St	494-9898	02141	26
Fort Point	25 Dorchester Ave	654-5302	02205	4
Hanover Street	217 Hanover St	723-6397	02113	2
Harvard Square	125 Mt Auburn St	876-3883	02138	20
Inman Square	1311 Cambridge St	864-4344	02139	28
Jamaica Plain	655 Centre St	524-3620	02130	14

Post Office	Address	Phone	Zip	Map
John F Kennedy	25 New Chardon St	523-6566	02114	1
John W McCormack	90 Devonshire St	720-3800	02109	4
Kendall Square	250 Main St	876-5155	02142	26
Kenmore	11 Deerfield St	437-1113	02215	16
Lafayette	7 Ave de Lafayette	423-7822	02111	4
Melvin Pharmacy	1558 Commonwealth Ave	556-2281	02135	18
Mission Hill	1575 Tremont St	566-2040	02120	15
MIT	84 Massachusetts Ave	494-5511	02139	25
Porter Square	1953 Massachusetts Ave	876-5599	02140	23
Prudential Center	800 Boylston St	267-4164	02199	5
Roxbury	55 Roxbury St	427-4898	02119	13
Soldiers Field	117 Western Ave	547-4250	02163	19
Somerville	237 Washington St	666-2332	02143	24
South Boston Station	444 E 3rd St	269-9948	02127	10
State House	24 Beacon St	742-0012	02133	1
West Somerville	58 Day St	666-2255	02144	22
Winter Hill Branch	320 Broadway	666-5225	02145	24

Though Boston is chiefly known for its college-town feel, there is plenty for the younger set to enjoy. You're bound to find something to hold the attention of your little ones among the many, MANY museums and parks.

The Best of the Best

- **Best Kid-Friendly Restaurant:** Full Moon (344 Huron Ave, Cambridge, 617-354-6699). Full Moon is the brainchild of two restaurateurs who also happen to be moms. The result is a restaurant that features a sophisticated menu with an extensive wine list for adults and a tasty assortment of kids' tried-and-true favorites. With sippy cups, toy buckets at every table, and a play area with any toy imaginable, Full Moon gives you "grown-up dining with a kid-friendly twist."

- **Quaintest Activity:** Swan Boats in the Public Garden (Public Garden, 617-522-1966). Owned and operated by the same family for over 120 years, the swan boats are a quaint fixture of the Public Garden. The people-paddled boats can hold up to 20 passengers during the 15-minute cruise around the lagoon and under the world's smallest suspension bridge. An inexpensive treat for all.

- **Funnest Park:** Rafferty Park (799 Concord Ave, Cambridge). One of the area's best-hidden playgrounds, this wooded park provides tons of fun stuff for older children, including a new metal climbing structure with a twisty slide, wobbly bridge, boat-shaped sand box, and a mini schoolhouse with a chalkboard roof. Basketball hoops, tennis courts, and a baseball field reside next door.

- **Coolest Bookstore:** Curious George Goes to Wordsworth (1 JFK St, Harvard Square, Cambridge, 617-498-0062). With floor-to-ceiling shelves jam packed with books for children of all ages, there's something for everyone in this charming jungle-themed bookstore. And if you're tired of reading, they've got TOYS.

- **Best Rainy Day Activity:** Children's Museum (300 Congress St, Boston, 617-426-8855). This world-renowned museum has designed early learning experiences for children of all ages with its inventive hands-on exhibits. Permanent exhibits include the Japanese House where children get to experience the culture of Kyoto, Japan through a replica of a silk merchant's house, as well as a Hall of Toys where children can look at toys of the past, but not touch.

- **Cutest Event:** The Annual Ducklings Day Parade (Boston Common). Held every year on Mother's Day, the parade commemorates Robert McCloskey's children's book *Make Way for Ducklings* set on Boston Common. Children come dressed as their favorite duckling character ready to parade.

- **Neatest Store:** Irving's Toy and Card Shop (371 Harvard St, Brookline, 617-566-9327). Since 1939, Irving's has been a favorite neighborhood source for ice cream, candy, and little nostalgic toys galore. This small store is packed with everything you never knew you needed from kazoos, to jacks, to tiny plastic farm animals.

Shopping Essentials

- **9 Months Maternity and Infant Wear** (mom & baby clothes) 318 Harvard St, Coolidge Corner Arcade, Brookline, 617-566-2233
- **Barefoot Books Store** (kids' books) 1771 Massachusetts Ave, Cambridge, 617-349-1610
- **Barnes & Noble:**
  395 Washington St, Downtown, 617-426-5184
  325 Harvard St, Brookline, 617-232-0594
  800 Boylston St, Prudential Center, 617-247-6959
- **Black Ink** (stamps) 101 Charles St, Boston, 617-723-3883
- **Borders Books & Music:**
  10-24 School St, 617-557-7188
  100 Cambridgeside Pl, Cambridgeside Galleria, Cambridge, 617-679-0887
- **Buck A Book:**
  42 Court St, 617-367-9419
  45 Franklin St, 617-357-6505
  236 Hanover St, 617-523-3905
  276 Elm St, Somerville, 617-776-1919
- **Calliope** (toys & kids' clothes) 33 Brattle St, Cambridge, 617-876-4149
- **The Children's Book Shop** (kids' books) 237 Washington St, Brookline, 617-734-7323
- **Coop for Kids at the Harvard Coop** (kids' books) 1400 Massachusetts Ave, Harvard Square, Cambridge, 617-499-2000
- **Curious George Goes to Wordsworth** (kids' books & toys) 1 JFK St, Harvard Square, Cambridge, 617-498-0062
- **Discovery Channel Store** (educational gifts) 40 South Market Building, Faneuil Hall, 617-227-5005
- **Fish Kids** (kids' clothes) 1378 Beacon St, Coolidge Corner, Brookline, 617-738-1006
- **Henry Bear's Park** (kids' books & toys) 361 Huron Ave, Cambridge, 617-547-8424
- **KB Toys** (toys) 100 Cambridgeside Pl, Cambridgeside Galleria, Cambridge, 617-494-8519
  300 Harvard St, Brookline, 617-975-3953
- **The Magic Hat** (magic store) 200 State St, Faneuil Hall Marketplace, 617-439-8840
- **No Kidding** (toys) 19 Harvard St, Brookline, 617-739-2477
- **Oilily** (kids' clothes) 32 Newbury St, 617-247-9299
- **Red Wagon** (kids' toys & clothes) 69 Charles St, 617-523-9402
- **Saturday's Child** (kids' clothes) 1762 Massachusetts Ave, Cambridge, 617-661-6402
- **Sloane's** (kids' shoes) 1349 Beacon St, Coolidge Corner, Brookline, 617-739-0582
- **Stellabella Toys** (toys) 1360 Cambridge St, Inman Square, Cambridge, 617-491-6290
- **Toys R Us** (toys) 200 Alewife Brook Pkwy, Fresh Pond Shopping Center, Cambridge, 617-576-8697
- **Varese Shoes** (European kids shoes) 285 Hanover St, 617-523-6530
- **Zoiks!** (toys) Faneuil Hall Marketplace, 617-227-6266

Parks for Playing

Kids need fresh air. And singing into the rotating fan doesn't count. Take them out for a swing. In addition to the roomy Boston Common and Cambridge Common, Boston boasts many smaller neighborhood parks:

- **Charlesbank/Esplanade Playground** (Charles Street at Longfellow Bridge). Recently renovated, this large play area features several climbing structures, slides and swings for all ages with a nearby snack bar, which is open in the summer months.
- **Christopher Columbus Park** (Atlantic Ave & Commercial Wharf, Boston). One large climbing structure dominates this playground that is mostly geared towards the six-and-under set.
- **Clarendon Street Playground** (Clarendon Street & Commonwealth Avenue). This fenced and gated area provides ample scope for the imagination of all aged children. The park features several climbing structures, slides, swings, and a sand area along with a larger open area for games of tag and soccer.
- **Constitution Beach** (Orient Heights, East Boston). The beach features lifeguarded swimming areas, a bathhouse with a snack bar, tennis courts, and a playground with lots of climbing and sliding prospects.
- **Emerson Park** (Davis Avenue & Emerson Street, Brookline). The Park boasts one of the town's oldest spray pools with lots of trees for shade and a casual open space for tag.
- **Huron Avenue Playground** (Huron Avenue, Cambridge). This newly renovated play area provides two climbing structures for children of all ages as well as a play train and spray fountain for the summer months. The lack of tree shade may bother some parents.
- **Langone Park** (Commercial Street). The park features a brand-new playground with multi-age, multi-level climbing structures and a swing set looking out on the edge of the harbor, great for that flying-across-water feeling. There are also three bocce courts and a baseball field.
- **Larz Anderson Park** (Newton, Avon, & Goddard Streets, Brookline). The largest park in Brookline holds an enclosed playground, picnic areas, ball fields, and an outdoor skating rink open December though February.
- **Millennium Park** (VFW Highway & Gardner Street, West Roxbury). This park is larger than the Boston Common and FleetCenter combined and located on the site of the former Gardner Street landfill. The park provides picnic areas, play structures, and hiking and walking trails, as well as access to the river for boating and fishing.
- **Myrtle Street Playground** (Myrtle & Irving Streets). Situated at the top of Beacon Hill, this playground features several climbing structures, a glider, a fire pole, swings, and a crazy daisy.
- **Public Garden** (Between Arlington & Charles Streets). The first public botanical garden in the US, the Public Garden is 24 acres of flowers and green in the bustling city. Among the park's winding pathways and tranquil lagoon are the prized bronze statues of a mama duck and her brood commemorating the famous children's book *Make Way for Ducklings.*
- **Rafferty Park** (799 Concord Avenue, Cambridge). One of the area's best-hidden playgrounds, this wooded park provides tons of fun stuff for older children, including a new metal climbing structure with a twisty slide, wobbly bridge, boat-shaped sand box, and a mini-schoolhouse with a chalkboard roof. Basketball hoops, tennis courts, and a baseball field reside next door.
- **Raymond Street Park** (Walden & Raymond Streets, Cambridge). Located on the shady side of the field, this playground

is split up into two sections: one sandy, sunken area for the younger toddlers and one area for older children, equipped with a large climbing structure. Play gear ranges from a bridge to swing sets, including one handicapped swing seat.
- **Stoneman Playground** (Fairfield & Massachusetts Avenues, Cambridge). This playground is divided into a toddler area and an older children's space, with entertaining activities for both groups. Supervised model sailboat racing and fishing takes place on Sundays in the summer months.

Rainy Day Activities

It rains in Boston. A lot. It's also one of the windiest cities in the country. Foul weather can drench even the highest aspirations for outdoor fun. Here are some dry alternatives:

Museums with Kid Appeal

- **Abiel Smith School/Afro-American Museum** (46 Joy St, 617-725-0022). The first publicly funded grammar school built for African Americans with interactive exhibits for kids.
- **Children's Museum** (300 Congress St, 617-426-8855). This world-renowned museum has designed early learning experiences for children of all ages with its inventive hands-on exhibits. Permanent exhibits include the Japanese House where children get to experience the culture of Kyoto, Japan through a replica of a silk merchant's house, as well as a Hall of Toys where children can look at toys of the past, but not touch.
- **New England Aquarium** (Central Wharf, 617-973-5200). You'll see fish and other aquatic life of all shapes and sizes at this entertaining destination. Among the many exhibits you'll find here are the sea lion show and a supervised hands-on demonstration that allows children to touch sea stars, snails, and mussels. There are also whale-watching trips and summer classes available.
- **Museum of Science** (Science Park, 617-723-2500). This award-winning interactive science museum features myriad permanent and changing exhibits that include a Virtual Fish Tank where children see life through the eyes of a fish. The museum also houses the Charles Hayden Planetarium featuring sky and laser shows and the five-story IMAX Mugar Omni Theater. Various science classes are also available.
- **Museum of Transportation** (Larz Anderson Park, 15 Newton St, Brookline, 617-522-6547). Located in the grand Carriage House, this museum features an extensive exhibit on the history of the automobile, as well as America's oldest car collection.

Other Indoor Distractions

- **The Clayroom** (1408 Beacon St, Brookline, 617-566-7575). Paint your own pottery place. Great for parties.
- **Lanes and Games** (195 Concord Turnpike, Rte 2, Cambridge, 617-876-5533). Candlepin bowling and ten-pin lanes for the whole family.
- **Ryan Family Amusements** (82 Lansdowne St, Boston, 617-267-8495). Candlepin and bumper bowling, a game room, plus the always-popular Mystic Bowling—funky black lights, music, and a creepy, lane-hugging haze create a truly cosmic bowling experience.
- **Puppet Showplace Theater** (32 Station St, Brookline, 617-731-6400). This 100-seat theater has been putting on shows for Boston's young brood for over 30 years. The company stages classic puppet shows, as well as many original productions. Shows are recommended for children five and older. Great for parties.

Outdoor *and* Educational

For when you've come to realize your children are a little too pale from sitting inside and playing video games all day.

- **Franklin Park Zoo** (1 Franklin Park Rd, Boston, 617-541-LION). A zoo that holds all the standard zoo fare, plus the Butterfly Landing exhibit, a tented outdoor area where you walk among over 1,000 butterflies in free flight. Adults: $9.50, children (2-15): $5, under 2: free.

- **Duck Tours** (departure points: Prudential Center and Museum of Science, information: 617-267-DUCK). Tickets are sold inside the Prudential Center and Museum of Science beginning at 8:30 am with an additional ticketing location at Faneuil Hall. A Boston Duck is an original WWII amphibious landing vehicle taking guests on an 80-minute tour (rain or shine), around the city by land and by sea. Kids are encouraged to quack at passersby.

Classes

Boston kids can participate in any number of structured activities that could help to mold and shape them like the blobs of clay that they are.

- **Boston Ballet School** (19 Clarendon St, Boston, 617-456-6264). Ballet classes beginning at age three.

- **Boston Casting** (129 Braintree St, Suite 107, Allston, 617-254-1001). Acting classes for kids five and up.

- **Boston Children's Theatre** (321 Columbus Ave (Studio/Office), Boston, 617-424-6634). "Theatre for children by children," this theatre group has children involved in all phases of production. Acting classes and a summer creative arts program where kids can learn stage combat, clowning, and juggling are also offered.

- **Brookline Arts Center** (86 Monmouth St, Brookline, 617-566-5715). A non-degree school for the visual arts. Classes are designed for children ages two to teen in subjects ranging from jewelry-making to sculpture.

- **Cambridge Multicultural Arts Center** (41 Second St, Cambridge, 617-577-1400). A program designed for Cambridge residents to promote cross-cultural interchange using dance, music, writing, theater, and the visual arts.

- **Community Music Center of Boston** (34 Warren St, Boston, 617-482-7494). A music program designed to promote musical development through experimental learning for ages five months to 14 years. The center also offers visual arts classes, summer programs, and individual instruction.

- **French Cultural and Cultural Center** (53 Marlborough St, Boston, 617-912-0400). French classes for children three to ten.

- **Full Moon** (344 Huron Ave, Cambridge, 617-354-6699). This kid-friendly restaurant offers cooking classes for parents and children ages three and up.

- **Grace Arts Project** (Grace United Methodist Church, 56 Magazine St, Cambridge, 617-864-1123). The program offers non-sectarian classes in art, music, and tutoring.

- **Grub Street Writers, Inc.** (265 Willow Ave, Somerville, 617-623-8100). Boston's only private writing school offering workshops and summer courses for young adults.

- **Happily Ever After** (799 Concord Ave, Cambridge, 617-492-0090). The classes use fitness with creative stories and games for children aged three to six. Great for birthday parties.

- **Hill House** (127 Mt. Vernon St, Boston, 617-227-5838). A non-profit community center offering downtown residents activities such as inline skating, karate, and youth soccer teams.

- **IceStars Skating Program** (Boston Common, Frog Pond, Boston, 617-635-2121). Group and private ice skating lessons are provided for kids three and up. Skates are provided, helmets are required.

- **Jeanette Neill Children's Dance Program** (261 Friend St, Boston, 617-523-1355). Since 1979, the program has offered children aged three to 12 an "intelligent dance alternative" with its focus on education, not production.

- **Jose Mateo's Ballet Theatre** (Old Cambridge Baptist Church, 400 Harvard St, Cambridge, 617-354-7467). A professional performance company providing children ages three through 18 with ballet instruction.

- **Larz Anderson Skating Rink** (25 Newton St, Brookline, 617-739-5183). Skating lessons are available at this rink, open from December to February, with an adjacent children's and beginner's area. Hockey boards and backstops recently added.

- **Longy School of Music** (1 Follen St, Cambridge, 617-876-0956). Music instruction for children 12 months to 18 years.

- **Made By Me in Harvard Square** (1154 Massachusetts Ave, Cambridge, 617-354-8111). A paint-your-own-pottery studio. Great for birthday parties.

- **Make Art Studio** (44 N Bennett St, Boston, 617-227-0775). Children ages four to 13 are encouraged to "choose their own medium" with guidance and instruction in small, age-appropriate classes.

- **Mudflat Studio** (149 Broadway, Somerville, 617-628-0589). For the past 30 years, the studio has offered hand-building, pot throwing, and individual workshops for children starting at age four.

- **Museum of Fine Arts** (465 Huntington Ave, Avenue of the Arts, Boston, 617-267-9300). The museum offers weekday and Saturday instruction that combines gallery study and creative expression for children ages five to 18.

- **New School of Music** (25 Lowell St, Cambridge, 617-492-8105). Newborns and up are provided with musical instruction for all levels of interest and skill, as well as musical theater classes for the older kids.

- **North Cambridge Family Opera** (23 North St, Cambridge, 617-492-4095). Adults and children aged seven to 14 get the opportunity to participate in a real, theatrical and operatic production.

- **North End Music and Performing Arts Center** (Paul Revere Mall, between Hanover and Unity Streets, Boston, 617-227-2270). The center offers classes in music, language and the performing arts to North End residents.

- **New England Conservatory** (290 Huntington Ave, Boston, 617-585-1100). Music lessons for kids starting at age four at the oldest independent school of music in the US.

- **Oak Square YMCA** (615 Washington St, Brighton, 617-782-3535). The center provides children of all ages with instruction in swimming, gymnastics, basketball, and art as well as after school programs.

- **The Skating School of Boston** (1240 Soldiers Field Rd, Boston, 617-782-5900). Classes for skaters and hockey players of all levels.

- **Topf Center for Dance Education** (551 Tremont St, Boston, 617-482-0351). The center focuses on providing underserved youth access to classes in jazz, tap, ballet, hip hop, and African dancing.

- **Upon a Star** (441 Stuart St, Studio 4, Boston, 617-859-7700). Music and movement classes for children aged 14 months to three years.

- **Wang YMCA of Chinatown** (8 Oak St W, Theater District/Chinatown, Boston, 617-426-2237). Activities ranging from swimming instruction to music and art classes for children of all ages.

- **Wheelock Family Theatre** (180 The Riverway, Boston, 617-879-2147). The Theatre offers classes for kids ages four to 17.

For more information visit www.gocitykids.com

Recently, the Massachusetts Supreme Judicial Court ruled that same-sex partners could marry, a move that's fairly indicative of the opinion of most Bostonians—that gays and lesbians should enjoy the same rights as their straight counterparts. While not as open about its gay-friendliness as cities like San Francisco or Provincetown, Boston has a thriving gay community and a fairly accepting populace.

Websites

GayNewEngland.net: www.gaynewengland.net
A guide to accommodations, bars, clubs, resources and news.

PinkWeb: www.pinkweb.com
"The GLBT yellow pages for New England and beyond."

PrideSports Boston:
www.geocities.com/pridesportsboston
A network of 20+ sports teams and organizations in the Boston area. 617-937-5858.

Roommate Connection:
www.dwellings.com/roommateco/gtrc.html
Boston's only gay owned and operated roommate referral agency. 617-262-5712.

Out In Boston: www.outinboston.com
Information about local news and events; also has personal ads, business ads, and chat.

HERE Boston: www.hereboston.com
Presents news and information "in a fair, entertaining, non-conglomerate format."

Gay & Lesbian Advocates & Defenders (GLAD):
www.glad.org
New England's leading legal rights organization dedicated to ending discrimination based on sexual orientation.

Greater Boston Business Council: www.gbbc.org
Seeks to foster and promote the vitality and pro-ductivity of Boston's GLBT business and professional community.

Craig's List: boston.craigslist.org
General community site (for straights, gays and everyone else) that offers heavily trafficked "men seeking men" and "women seeking women" sec-tions, as well as other community-related listings and information.

Boston Gay Men's Chorus: www.bgmc.org
Now in its twenty-first year, the BGMC, through its collaboration with The Boston Pops, was the first gay chorus in the world to be recorded with a major orchestra on a major label.

Provincetown Business Guild: www.ptown.org
A gay and lesbian guide to P'town.

Publications

Bay Windows—New England's largest gay and lesbian newspaper is a weekly publication that has local, national and international news as well as community events and guides. Also online at www.baywindows.com.

in newsweekly—News and entertainment weekly, including a calendar of events and a club guide. Also online at www.innewsweekly.com.

Bookshops

We Think The World of You—540 Tremont St, Boston. 617-574-5000. www.wethinktheworldofyou.com

Calamus Bookstore—92B South St, Boston 617-338-1931. www.calamusbooks.com

Sports

PrideSports Boston—A network of 20+ sports teams and organizations in the Boston area. www.geocities.com/pridesportsboston

Boston Gay Basketball League—The country's largest GLBT basketball league. www.bgbl.com

Beantown Softball League—GLBT softball since 1978. www.beantownsoftball.com

Boston Bay Blades—For rowers and scullers. www.bayblades.org/boston

FrontRunners Boston—Welcomes joggers, walkers and runners of all experience levels. www.mindspring.com/~frontrunners/index.htm

Health Centers and Support Organizations

Fenway Community Health—Provides high-quality medical and mental health care to Boston's gay and lesbian community; also a leader in HIV care. 7 Haviland St, Boston, 617-267-0900. www.fenwayhealth.org.

Greater Boston PFLAG—For parents and friends of lesbians and gays. 866-GBP-FLAG. www.gbplflag.org.

Boston Alliance of Gay Lesbian Bisexual and Transgender Youth—For young people 22 and under. www.bagly.org.

Gay Men's Domestic Violence Project—Offers shelter, guidance and resources to allow gay, bisexual, and transgender men in crisis to remove themselves from violent situations and relationships; also operates a 24-hour free-of-charge crisis center. 800-832-1901. www.gmdvp.org.

The Network—Provides information and resources for battered lesbian, bisexual and transgender women. 617-423-SAFE. www.thenetworklared.org.

Dignity Boston—An inclusive community of GLBT Catholics. 617-421-1915. www.dignityboston.com.

Annual Events

Boston Pride Week—Begins on a Friday in June with a flag raising at City Hall; the parade and festival usually take place on the Saturday of the following weekend. 617-262-9405. www.bostonpride.org.

Boston Gay/Lesbian and Transgender Film Festival—Usually held in May at the MFA. 617-368-3305. www.mfa.org.

Boston-New York AIDS Ride—3,000 riders bike 325 miles to raise money for AIDS-related organizations. Usually takes place in July. 866-648-0747. www.aidsride.org/new.

Venues – Lesbian

- **Club Hollywood Boston** • 41 Essex St, Boston; 617-417-0186
- **Kristin Porter Dyke Night** at Midway Cafe (Thursdays) • 3496 Washington St, Jamaica Plain; 617-524-9038
- **Tiger Lily** (Saturdays) • 8 Westland Ave, Boston; 617-267-8881

Venues – Gay

- **The Alley** • 14 Pi Alley, Boston; 617-263-1449
- **Avalon** (Sundays) • 15 Lansdowne St, Boston; 617-262-2424
- **Axis** (Mondays) • 13 Lansdowne St, Boston; 617-262-2437
- **Buzz** (Saturdays) • 51 Stuart St, Boston; 617-482-3939
- **Club Cafe** • 209 Columbus Ave, Boston; 617-536-0966
- **Dedo** • 69 Church St, Boston; 617-338-9999
- **Eagle** • 520 Tremont St, Boston; 617-542-4494
- **Fritz** • 26 Chandler St, Boston; 617-482-4428
- **HERE** (Tuesdays) • 711 Boylston St, Boston; 617-437-0002
- **Jacque's** • 79 Broadway St, Boston; 617-426-8902
- **Machine** • 1254 Boylston St, Boston; 617-536-1950
- **Man-Ray/Campus** (Thursdays) • 21 Brookline St, Cambridge; 617-864-0400
- **Paradise** • 180 Massachusetts Abe, Cambridge; 617-494-0700
- **Ramrod** (only leather on Fridays and Saturdays) • 1254 Boylston St; 617-266-2986
- **Vapor** • 100 Warrenton St, Boston; 617-695-9500

General Information · **Hotels**

Boston is notorious for being short on hotel rooms and most places downtown will set you back more than $200 a night per room. This is apparently no deterrent for the Democratic National Committee, who chose Boston to host their convention in 2004.

Close to downtown you'll find the historic old hotels: The Park Plaza and the Ritz-Carlton are on Arlington Street. The Westin Copley Place, the Fairmont Copley Plaza, and the Lenox are near Copley Square. Fun fact: at the OmniParker House on Tremont Street, Malcolm X worked as a waiter and Ho Chi Minh worked as a bus boy.

Along the waterfront sits the Marriott, which ia adjacent to Tia's, an outdoor bar in the summer. Further along is the Boston Harbor Hotel, a gigantic hotel with a hole in the middle..

Lately a lot of ultra-fancy boutique hotels have been opening, such as Nine Zero on Tremont Street and the Charlesmark Hotel in Copley Square. The ultra-modern Ritz-Carlton at Millennium Place recently opened at Tremont Street above a movie theater, a restaurant, and a Sports Club LA.

The Marriott's Custom House is located in one of Boston's most prominent historic landmarks, the Custom House Tower. Completed in 1847, the structure was described by Walt Whitman as being "the noblest form of architecture in the world." Before the Custom House was built, the site was home to Federal Hall (demolished in 1812), where George Washington was sworn in as the country's first President on April 30, 1789.

Across the river in Cambridge, you have a wide range of choices. The Charles Hotel and the Sheraton Commander are more upscale places in Harvard Square. There's a Radisson in Kendall Square, and near Porter Square you'll find the Mary Prentiss Inn, a nice bed and breakfast.

Somerville has a Holiday Inn and a Tage Inn, and that's about all.

If you're in town this summer and you pick one of the nicer places, especially one with a good bar, the odds of running into some well-known political folks are pretty good. The odds of not being able to book a room anytime close to the Democratic National Convention are also very strong.

Map 1 · Beacon Hill / West End

Holiday Inn	5 Blossom St	617-742-7630	$229	
John Jeffries House (B&B)	14 David G Mugar Way	617-367-1866	$95-165	
Onyx Hotel	155 Portland St	617-557-9955	$149	★★★★
Shawmut Inn	280 Friend St	617-720-5544	$129-169	★★★
XV Beacon Hotel	15 Beacon St	617-670-1500	$445	

Map 2 · North End / Faneuil Hall

Boston Marriott Long Wharf	296 State St	617-227-0800	$339-449	★★★★★
Golden Slipper (floating B&B)	Lewis Wharf	781-545-2845	$175	
Harborside Inn	185 State St	617-723-7500	$159	
Marriott's Custom House	3 McKinley Sq	617-310-6300	$230-300	
Millennium Bostonian Hotel	26 North St	617-523-3600	$139-309	★★★
Regal Bostonian Hotel	24 North St	617-523-3600	$139-309	★★★

Map 3 · Downtown Crossing / Park Square / Bay Village

Boston Park Plaza Hotel	64 Arlington St	617-426-2000	$179-309	★★★
Doubletree Boston	821 Washington St	617-956-7900	$179	★★★
Four Seasons Hotel	200 Boylston St	617-338-4400	$500	★★★★★
Hyatt Regency Boston	1 Ave de Lafayette	617-912-1234	$225	
Milner Hotel	78 Charles St S	617-426-6220	$99	
Nine Zero Hotel	90 Tremont St	617-772-5800	$339	★★★★★
Omni Parker House	60 School St	617-227-8600	$169-219	
Radisson Hotel Boston	200 Stuart St	617-482-1800	$209	★★★
Ritz-Carlton Boston	15 Arlington St	617-536-5700	$350	★★★★★
Ritz-Carlton Boston Common	10 Avery St	617-574-7100	$325	★★★★★
Wyndham Tremont Boston Hotel	275 Tremont St	617-426-1400	$209	

Map 4 · Financial District / Chinatown

Boston Harbor Hotel	70 Rowes Warf	617-439-7000	$195	★★★★
Langham Hotel	250 Franklin St	617-451-1900	$275-895	★★★★
Wyndham Boston	89 Broad St	617-556-0006	$169	★★★★

Map 5 · Back Bay (West) / Fenway (East)

436 Beacon Street Guest House	436 Beacon St	617-536-1302	$89-139
Commonwealth Court Guest House	284 Commonwealth Ave	617-424-1230	$105-150
Eliot Hotel	370 Commonwealth Ave	617-267-1607	$315 ★★★★
Hilton Boston Back Bay	40 Dalton St	617-236-1100	$100-400 ★★★★
Midtown Hotel	220 Huntington Ave	617-262-1000	$119-239 ★★1/2
Newbury Guest House (B&B)	261 Newbury St	617-437-7666	$155-190 ★★★
Oasis Guest House	22 Edgerly Rd	617-267-2262	$119-140
Sheraton Boston Hotel	39 Dalton St	617-236-2000	$299-339

Map 6 · Back Bay (East) / South End (Upper)

Boston Marriott Copley Place	110 Huntington Ave	617-236-5800	$279 ★★★★★
Charlesmark Hotel	655 Boylston St	617-247-1212	$149-249 ★★★
Colonnade Hotel	120 Huntington Ave	617-424-7000	$149-285 ★★★★
Copley House	239 W Newton St	617-236-8300	$675 weekly
Copley Inn	19 Garrison St	617-236-0300	$125
Copley Square Hotel	47 Huntington Ave	617-536-9000	$275 ★★★
Fairmont Copley Plaza Hotel	138 St James Ave	617-267-5300	$279 ★★★★
John Hancock Hotel & Conference Center	40 Trinity Pl	617-933-7700	$149
Lenox Hotel	710 Boylston St	617-536-5300	$308-695 ★★★★
The College Club	44 Commonwealth Ave	617-536-9510	$140
Westin Copley Place	10 Huntington Ave	617-262-9600	$319 ★★★★

Map 7 · South End (Lower)

Chandler Inn	26 Chandler St	617-482-3450	$169 ★★
Clarendon Square Inn (B&B)	198 W Brookline St	617-536-2229	$168
Encore Bed & Breakfast	116 W Newton St	617-247-3425	$130-190
Shawmut Guest House (B&B)	332 Shawmut Ave	617-266-7035	$125

Map 8 · Charlestown

Residence Inn Tudor Wharf	34 Charles River Ave	617-242-9000	$239

Map 9 · East Boston

Embassy Suites Boston at Logan	207 Porter St	617-567-5000	$199 ★★★★

Map 11 · South Boston (East)

Seaport Hotel	1 Seaport Ln	617-385-4000	$199-279

Map 12 · Newmarket / Andrew Square

Best Western Inn Roundhouse Suites	891 Massachusetts Ave	617-989-1000	$159-169
Holiday Inn Express	69 Boston St	617-288-3030	$199 ★★★★

Map 15 · Fenway (West) / Mission Hill

Best Western Longwood Medical	342 Longwood Ave	617-731-4700	$179-349 ★★
Howard Johnson	1271 Boylston St	617-267-8300	$135

Map 16 · Kenmore Square / Brookline (East)

American Experience (B&B)	72 Bay State Rd	617-267-4388	$130
Beacon Inn	1087 Beacon St	617-566-0088	$119-129
Beacon Townhouse Inn	1047 Beacon St	617-232-0292	$145
Beacon Townhouse Inn II	1023 Beacon St	617-232-2422	$145
Gryphon House (B&B)	9 Bay State Rd	617-375-9003	$169-215
Holiday Inn Boston at Brookline	1200 Beacon St	617-277-1200	$209
Hotel Buckminster	645 Beacon St	617-236-7050	$99 ★★1/2
Hotel Commonwealth	500 Commonwealth Ave	617-933-5000	$219-349 ★★★★
Longwood Inn (B&B)	123 Longwood Ave	617-566-8615	$89-109

General Information · **Hotels**

Map 17 · Coolidge Corner / Brookline Hills

Bertram Inn (B&B)	92 Sewall Ave	617-566-2234	$159	
Coolidge Corner Guest House	17 Littell Rd	617-734-4041	$79-139	
Courtyard by Marriott Brookline	40 Webster St	617-734-1393	$189	
Samuel Sewall Inn (B&B)	143 St Paul St	617-713-0123	$145-185	

Map 18 · Brighton

Best Western Terrace Inn	1650 Commonwealth Ave	617-566-6260	$129	
Days Inn	1800 Soldiers Field Rd	617-254-0200	$99-159	

Map 19 · Allston (South) / Brookline (North)

Abercrombie's Farrington Inn	23 Farrington Ave	617-787-1860	$85	
Brookline Manor Inn	32 Centre St	617-232-0003	$145	
Days Inn	1234 Soldiers Field Rd	617-254-1234	$109-159	★★★★
Doubletree Guest Suites	400 Soldiers Field Rd	617-783-0090	$149-179	★★★

Map 20 · Harvard Square / Allston (North)

Charles Hotel	1 Bennett St	617-864-1200	$229-350	★★★★
Harvard Square Hotel	110 Mt Auburn St	617-864-5200	$259	★★★★
Mary Prentiss Inn (B&B)	6 Prentiss St	617-661-2929	$169-249	
Sheraton Commander Hotel	16 Garden St	617-547-4800	$155-175	
The Inn at Harvard	1201 Massachusetts Ave	617-491-2222	$119-475	★★★★

Map 21 · West Cambridge

Best Western Hotel Tria	220 Alewife Brook Pkwy	617-491-8000	$129-169	★★★

Map 22 · North Cambridge / West Somerville

A Cambridge House B&B Inn	2218 Massachusetts Ave	617-491-6300	$99-189	★★★

Map 24 · Winter Hill / Union Square

Holiday Inn Boston/Somerville	30 Washington St	617-628-1000	$161	★★★★
Tage Inn Boston-Somerville	23 Cummings St	617-625-5300	$109-139	★★★

Map 26 · East Cambridge / Kendall Square / MIT

Hampton Inn Boston/Cambridge	191 Monsignor O'Brien Hwy	617-494-5300	$149	★★★
Hotel Marlowe	25 Edwin H Land Blvd	617-868-8000		
Kendall Hotel	350 Main St	617-577-1300	$189	
Marriott Cambridge	2 Cambridge Ctr	617-494-6600	$159-179	★★★
Residence Inn by Marriott–Cambridge	6 Cambridge Ctr	617-349-0700	$319	★★★1/2
Royal Sonesta Hotel Boston	5 Cambridge Pkwy	617-806-4200	$209-279	★★★★
University Park Hotel at MIT	20 Sidney St	617-577-0200	$179-229	

Map 28 · Inman Square

A Bed & Breakfast in Cambridge	1657 Cambridge St	617-868-7082	$125	
A Friendly Inn at Harvard (B&B)	1673 Cambridge St	617-547-7851	$117	
An Urban Homestead (B&B)	283 Windsor St	617-354-3116	$75-95	
Harding House (B&B)	288 Harvard St	617-876-2888	$135	
Hyatt Regency Cambridge	575 Memorial Dr	617-492-1234	$235-280	★★★★
Irving House at Harvard (B&B)	24 Irving St	617-547-4600	$100-130	
Prospect Place (B&B)	112 Prospect St	617-864-7500	$125	
Radisson Hotel Cambridge	777 Memorial Dr	617-492-7777	$129-199	★★★1/2

General Information

Websites:
Boston: www.bpl.org
Brookline: www.town.brookline.ma.us/library
Cambridge: www.ci.cambridge.ma.us/~cpl
Somerville: www.somervillepubliclibrary.org

Phones:
Boston: 617-536-5400
Brookline: 617-730-2370
Cambridge: 617-349-4040
Somerville: 617-623-5000

Overview

The Boston Public Library, founded in 1848, was the first publicly supported municipal library in the United States. Interestingly, it was also the first public library to lend a book and the first to conceive of a children's room.

The library is comprised of two buildings. Facing Copley Square is the McKim Building (the "old wing"), which was designed by noted 19th-century architect Charles Follen McKim and opened in 1895. The old wing houses the departments of the "Research Library". Facing Boylston Street is the Johnson Building (the "new wing"), which was designed by noted 20th-century architect Philip Johnson and opened in 1972. The new wing is home to the departments of the "General Library".

There's a lot more in these august edifices than just books. The old wing features a delightful "sculpture courtyard" that offers readers a most un-library-like

place to relax. Inside the old wing is an enormous set of murals painted by John Singer Sargent. Better known as a portrait painter, Sargent intended for these murals to be his masterpiece. Also in the old wing is a set of allegorical murals by Pierre Puvis de Chavannes and the architecturally significant Bates Hall. The new wing has less knock-out art, but it does have "The Goose Girl." The BPL offers guided tours to help you get a grip on all that the library has to offer.

Beyond being the nation's first publicly supported municipal library, the BPL was the first to open a branch library. From that beginning the BPL now operates 27 branch libraries, each of which apparently holds "special treasures" and offers free wireless internet access. Check out the details on the BPL's good website.

Of course, each of Brookline, Cambridge and Somerville has its own public library. Check their websites for details and opening hours.

Library	Address	Phone	Map
Boston Public Library	700 Boylston St	617-536-5400	6
Boudreau	245 Concord Ave	617-349-4017	21
Brighton	40 Academy Hill Rd	617-782-6032	18
Brookline Main Library	361 Washington St	617-730-2370	17
Cambridge Main Library	449 Broadway	617-349-4040	28
Central Square	45 Pearl St	617-349-4010	27
Charlestown	179 Main St	617-242-1248	8
Connolly	433 Centre St	617-522-1960	14
Coolidge Corner	31 Pleasant St	617-730-2380	19
Dudley	65 Warren St	617-442-6186	13
East Boston	276 Meridian St	617-569-0271	9
Faneuil	419 Faneuil St	617-782-6705	18
Honan-Allston	300 N Harvard St	617-787-6313	19
Jamaica Plain	12 Sedgwick St	617-524-2053	14
Kirstein Business	20 City Hall Ave	617-523-0860	3
North End	25 Parmenter St	617-227-8135	2
O'Connell	48 Sixth St	617-349-4019	26
O'Neill	70 Rindge Ave	617-349-4023	22
Parker Hill	1497 Tremont St	617-427-3820	15
Somerville East	115 Broadway	617-623-5000 x2970	24
Somerville Main Library	79 Highland Ave	617-623-5000	24
Somerville West	40 College Ave	617-623-5000 x2975	23
South Boston	646 E Broadway	617-268-0180	12
South End	685 Tremont St	617-536-8241	7
Valente	826 Cambridge St	617-349-4015	28
Washington Village	1226 Columbia Rd	617-269-7239	10
West End	151 Cambridge St	617-523-3957	1

If you've just moved to Boston and need a crash course on the "sights", you must check out the **Freedom Trail** (see page 186). Yes, it's touristy, but it's the best self-guided tour of Revolution-era Boston and gives you the skinny on aspects of Boston colonial history that every resident should know. To gain a better appreciation of just where it is you've moved to, hit the top of the **Prudential Tower** for a bird's eye view, which will show you that Boston has a lot more hills and water than you might have suspected. For a more human perspective, get familiar with the Charles River with a stroll along the **Esplanade** or, for a walk with an impressive view of Beacon Hill and Back Bay, cross the **Harvard Bridge** and take a stroll along Memorial Drive in Cambridge. For a nice rest, grab a snack in Harvard Square and a find a tree in **Harvard Yard** to chill under.

If it's wet out, fret not—there's plenty to see indoors. The Museum of Fine Arts (see page 273) is world-class. The **Isabella Stewart Gardner Museum** may not have the singles action encouraged by the MFA, but the collection is first-rate and the setting (inspired by a fifteenth-century Venetian palace) is stunning. The ornate interior of **Trinity Church** and the classical courtyard of **Boston Public Library** (directly across Copley Square) are also impressive.

If you've already checked out Boston's big hits, you should experience some of Boston's lesser-known, but rather intriguing, landmarks. The **Dreams of Freedom** museum explores the immigrant experience in Boston. The **Mapparium** at the Christian Science Center is a treat for geography freaks. And just as some very rich people collect art, very rich universities collect museums. Among Harvard's museums are the **Fogg Art Museum** (focusing on Western art) and the **Arthur M. Sackler Gallery** (more for Eastern art and featuring an outstanding collection of jade).

Also, be sure to visit the fauna at the **New England Aquarium**, the flora at the **Arnold Arboretum**, the interior of the **Wang Center for the Performing Arts**, and one of Boston's lesser-known artistic gems, the **Mission Church Basilica**.

All area codes are 617 unless otherwise noted.

Map 1 · Beacon Hill / West End

Boston Athenaeum	10 1/2 Beacon St	227-0270	Featuring books from George Washington's library.
FleetCenter	150 Causeway St	624-1050	Sterile replacement for Boston Garden.
Leonard P Zakim Bunker Hill Bridge	Causeway St & I-93		World's widest cable-stayed bridge. Boston's newest landmark.
Longfellow Bridge	Cambridge St & Charles St		The "salt and pepper shaker bridge."
Make Way for Ducklings	Charles St & Beacon St		Inspired by the Robert McCloskey children's book.
Massachusetts General Hospital	55 Fruit St	726-2000	Well-regarded downtown hospital.

Map 2 · North End / Faneuil Hall

Christopher Columbus Park	Atlantic Ave		Not to be confused with Columbus Park in Southie.
Faneuil Hall	Congress St at North St	523-1779	Faneuil Hall (that is, the building) dates from 1742.
Holocaust Memorial	Congress St at Union St	457-8755	Six glass towers, with victims' numbers, representing six camps.
New England Aquarium	Central Wharf	973-5200	Check out penguin snack-time.
Old North Church	193 Salem St	523-6676	"One if by land, two if by sea."
Old State House	206 Washington St	720-1713	Oldest surviving public building in Boston.
Paul Revere House	19 North Sq	523-2338	Where Paul was born and raised.

Map 3 · Downtown Crossing / Park Square / Bay Village

Arlington Street Church	351 Boylston St	536-7050	Congregation dates from 1729, building from 1861.
Boston Irish Famine Memorial	School St & Washington St		Statue commemorating the Great Hunger of the 1840s.
City Hall	1 City Hall Plaza	635-4000	A.k.a. the box Faneuil Hall came in.
Colonial Theater	106 Boylston St	426-9366	Boston's oldest continuously operating theater, since 1900.
Four Seasons Hotel	200 Boylston St	338-4400	The preferred local home of the Rolling Stones.
Granary Burying Ground	Tremont St & Park St	635-4505	Featuring John Hancock, Mother Goose, many others.

Omni Parker House	60 School St	227-8600	One-time employees include Ho Chi Minh and Malcolm X.
State House	Beacon St at Park St	727-3679	Finished in 1797. Gold dome added later.
Swan Boats	Arlington St & Boylston St	522-1966	Since 1877. Ideal for wee ones.
Wang Center	270 Tremont St	482-9393	Eye-popping, opulent interior. A must see.

Map 4 · Financial District / Chinatown

Boston Harbor Hotel	70 Rowes Wharf	439-7000	The "building with a hole in the middle."
Children's Museum	300 Congress St	426-8855	Featuring the giant Hood milk bottle.
Chinatown Gate	Beach St & Hudson St		"Everything under the sky is for the people."
Custom House Tower	3 McKinley Sq		Boston's first "skyscraper," completed in 1915.
Dreams of Freedom	1 Milk St	338-6022	Boston's immigration museum. Worth checking out.
Federal Reserve	600 Atlantic Ave	973-3463	Easy-to-spot, built in 1983.
Filene's Basement	426 Washington St	348-7848	Discount apparel since 1908.
Old South Meeting House	310 Washington St	482-6439	Where Sam Adams gave the order for the Boston Tea Party.
South Station	Atlantic Ave & Summer St		Coolest morning announcer in the business.

Map 5 · Back Bay (West) / Fenway (East)

Hynes Convention Center	900 Boylston St	954-2000	New convention center will steal plenty of business.
Institute of Contemporary Art	955 Boylston St	266-5152	Back Bay museum with rotating exhibits, film.
Prudential Tower	800 Boylston St	236-3100	The other tall building. Equally loved and reviled.
Symphony Hall	301 Massachusetts Ave	266-1492	Home of the Boston Symphony Orchestra.

Map 6 · Back Bay (East) / South End (Upper)

Boston Public Library	700 Boylston St	536-5400	An underrated place to relax.
Christian Science Center	175 Huntington Ave	450-3790	Mother Church, Mapparium, reflecting pool. Quite nice.
Hatch Shell	Esplanade		Where the Pops play each July 4.
John Hancock Tower	200 Clarendon St		New England's tallest building, designed by I.M. Pei.
Trinity Church	206 Clarendon St	536-0944	Episcopal church. Completed in 1877.

Map 7 · South End (Lower)

| Cathedral of the Holy Cross | 1400 Washington St | 542-5682 | Mother church of the Archdiocese of Boston. |

Map 8 · Charlestown

Bunker Hill Monument	Monument Ave	242-5641	Actually on Breed's Hill, zanily enough. Long story.
Charlestown Navy Yard	Constitution Rd & Warren St	242-5601	Home of the USS Constitution ("Old Ironsides").
Tobin Memorial Bridge	US-1		Lovingly photographed in *Mystic River*.
Warren Tavern	2 Pleasant St	241-8142	One of Paul Revere's favorite watering holes.

Map 10 · South Boston (West)/Fort Point

| Boston Tea Party Ship & Museum | Congress St Bridge | 338-1773 | Site of Revolutionary tomfoolery. |

General Information · **Landmarks**

Map 11 · South Boston (East)

Black Falcon Terminal	1 Black Falcon Ave	330-1500	Heavily trafficked cruise boat terminal.
Fleet Boston Pavilion	290 Northern Ave	728-1690	Music venue.
World Trade Center Boston	200 Seaport Blvd	385-5090	Event space that's part of "The Seaport Experience."

Map 14 · Jamaica Plain

Arnold Arboretum	125 Arborway	524-1718	Operated by Harvard. Quite pleasant.
Doyle's Cafe	3484 Washington St	524-2345	Reliable landmark. Serves decent pubgrub.
The Round House	36 Atherton St		Round since 1856. Not open to the public.

Map 15 · Fenway (West) / Mission Hill

Isabella Stewart Gardner Museum	280 The Fenway	278-5180	Housed in a beautiful building. Relax in the atrium.
Mission Church Basilica	1545 Tremont St	445-2600	Mission Hill landmark. Recently renovated.
Museum of Fine Arts	465 Huntington Ave	267-9300	Boston's largest museum. See movies here too.
Reggie Lewis Track & Athletic Center	1350 Tremont St	541-3535	Named after the Celtics player/local hero.

Map 16 · Kenmore Square / Brookline (East)

BU Bridge	Essex St & Mountfort St		Arguably Boston's best river/skyline view.
Citgo Sign	Commonwealth Ave & Beacon St		Beloved Kenmore Square landmark.
Fenway Park	4 Yawkey Way	267-9440	Home to the Red Sox since 1912.

Map 19 · Allston (South) / Brookline (North)

John F Kennedy Birthplace	83 Beals St	566-7937	Small, open to the public.
The Publick Theater	1400 Soldiers Field Rd	332-0546	Outdoor Shakespeare in Brighton.

Map 20 · Harvard Square / Allston (North)

Fogg Art Museum	32 Quincy St	495-9400	Harvard's oldest art museum.
Harvard Stadium	Soldiers Field Rd		The nation's oldest stadium.
John Harvard Statue	Harvard Yard		The "statue of the three lies."
Out of Town News	0 Harvard Sq	354-7777	The sensible Harvard Square rendezvous spot.

Map 22 · North Cambridge / West Somerville

Cambridge School of Culinary Arts	2020 Massachusetts Ave	354-2020	Chef factory.
Somerville Theater	55 Davis Sq	625-4088	Late-run movies and live music.

Map 23 · Central Somerville / Porter Square

Powderhouse	College Ave & Broadway	Revolutionary War-era gunpowder store, park centerpiece.

Map 25 · East Somerville / Sullivan Square

Schrafft's Building	529 Main St	Once the country's largest candy factory.

Map 26 · East Cambridge / Kendall Square / MIT

Harvard Bridge	Massachusetts Ave	Known to most as the "Mass Ave Bridge."

Overview

There's always something to do in Boston. From long-standing traditions to made-up events designed to allow merchants to lighten your wallet, it's easy to keep busy. And while most of these events involve drinking in some form or other, there's plenty to do for everyone. Speaking of drinking, the Democratic National Convention descends on Boston in late July.

- **First Night** · Dec. 31/Jan. 1 · www.firstnight.org · Celebrate the new year with music, art, and bitter, freezing cold.
- **Martin Luther King, Jr. Prayer Breakfast** · Jan. 20 · www.bchigh.edu · Prayer and eggs.
- **Black History Month Music Celebration** · Early February · www.berklee.edu · A week of Coltrane, Marley, Gaye, D, etc. at Berklee.
- **Chinese New Year** · Mid-February · www.bcnc.net · Fireworks in Chinatown.
- **St. Patrick's Day Parade** · Sunday after March 17 · 617-635-3911 · Irish pride, binge drinking on display in Southie.
- **St. Patrick's Day/Evacuation Day** · March 17 · www.cityofboston.gov · Irish politicians made up a holiday supposedly commemorating the day the British left Boston so they could booze all day March 17.
- **An Ras Mor** · Around March 17 · www.srr.org · Run around Somerville; enjoy post-race craic at the Burren.
- **Ras na hEireann** · Around March 17 · www.clydesdale.org · Run around Cambridge; enjoy post-race craic at The Asgard.
- **Charbo's Run** · March 23 · www.coolrunning.com · Road race in Dorchester to commemorate slain state trooper Mark Charbonnier.
- **Red Sox Opening Day** · Early April · www.redsox.com · Unofficial holiday, official renewal of local psychosis cycle; stage 1: optimism.
- **Boston Marathon/Patriots Day** · Third Monday in April · www.baa.org · Another local pseudo-holiday for watching ultimate athletic achievement, and drinking. Plus, 11:30 am Red Sox game.
- **Walk for Hunger** · 1st Sunday in May · www.projectbread.org · 20-mile walk to benefit soup kitchens and shelters.
- **Wake Up the Earth Festival** · Early May · spontaneouscelebrations.org/events · Hippies and children alike enjoy stilt walking, puppets…
- **Festival of the Madonna di Anzano** · June 3 · www.northendweb.com · Italian culture in historic neighborhood.
- **Chowderfest** · June 6 · www.bostonharborfest.com/chowderfest · Clam chowder cook-off to the death on City Hall Plaza.
- **Scooper Bowl** · June 8-10 · www.jimmyfund.org · Gorge yourself on ice cream for charity.
- **Boston Gay Pride Parade** · June 14 · www.bostonpride.com · Food, music, art, and parade.
- **Bunker Hill Day** · June 15 · http://charlestown.ma.us/bunkerhillday.html · Townie pride.
- **Bloomsday** · June 16 · www.southofboston.net · Readings from James Joyce's *Ulysses* on Boston Common.

- **Boston Globe Blues and Jazz Festival** · Mid-June · www.bostonglobe.com/jazzfest · Jazz and blues on the waterfront.
- **July 4th** · Guess · www.july4th.org · Ridiculously crowded Boston Pops concert and fireworks on the Esplanade.
- **Democratic National Convention** · July 28-31 · www.boston04.com · Dem delegates from all 50 state and beyond get drunk and try to get laid. Also, they pick someone to run for president.
- **Khoury's State Spa Big Man Run** · Late July · www.clydesdale.org · The nausea-enthusiast's holiday, a 4.8-mile race in Somerville, in which you stop 3 times to consume a hot dog and a beer.
- **Festival of St Agrippina** · Aug. 3-5 · www.northendweb.com · Italian guys carry giant statue around North End, yuppies wonder what the hell is going on.
- **Festival of the Madonna del Soccorso** · Aug. 16-19 · www.northendweb.com · Italian culture in now-largely-yuppified neighborhood.
- **Restaurant Week** · Mid-August · www.boston.com · A week of good deals at hoity-toity downtown restaurants for the great unwashed.
- **Boston Film Festival** · Early September · www.bostonfilmfestival.org · More than likely showing the same movies as every other film festival.
- **Boston Freedom Rally** · Sept. 12 · www.masscann.org · That ain't freedom they're smoking.
- **Harpoon Brewery Oktoberfest** · 1st weekend in October · www.harpoon.com · Sausage, polka, and wicked strong beer.
- **Somerville 5K** · 1st weekend in October · www.srr.org · Run around Somerville for the Somerville Homeless Coalition. Also, cool t-shirts.
- **Opening Night at the Symphony** · Early October · www.bso.org · Bring your black tie.
- **Harvard Square Oktoberfest** · Mid-October · www.harvardsquare.com · Barneys and beer.
- **Head of the Charles** · Third weekend in October · www.hocr.org · College kids, apparently unaware of the existence of motors, row boats down the Charles.
- **Boston Turkish Festival** · Oct. 29–Nov. 31 · www.cityofboston.gov · Turkish culture in Downtown Crossing.
- **Halloween** · Oct. 31 · www.salemweb.com · People flock to Salem, America's scariest town.
- **Gobble Gobble Gobble Run** · Thanksgiving Day · www.srr.org · Run around Somerville and drink Guinness at The Burren, all before Turkey Day dinner.
- **Holiday Pops** · December · www.bso.org · Keith Lockhart gets even more cheery.
- **Boston Common Menorah Lighting** · December · www.cityofboston.gov · Jewish ceremony presided over by Italian mayor.
- **Enchanted Village** · Nov. 23 through Holiday season · www.cityofboston.gov · Turn-of-the-century holiday scene populated by creepy robots.
- **Prudential Center Christmas Tree Lighting** · 1st Saturday in December · 617-236-2366 · Humongous tree from Nova Scotia, given as thanks for this one time we helped them out.

And this is good old Boston.
The home of the bean and the cod.
Where the Lowells talk to the Cabots,
And the Cabots talk only to God.
    —John Collins Bossidy (a toast given
        at a Harvard dinner in 1910)

Useful Phone Numbers

Emergencies	911
Boston Board of Elections	617-635-4635
Somerville Board of Elections	617-625-6600
Cambridge Board of Elections	617-349-4361
Brookline Town Clerk	617-730-2010
Keyspan	617-469-2300
NStar	800-592-2000
RCN Cable	800-746-4726
Comcast	888-633-4266
Verizon	800-870-9999
Boston City Hall	617-635-4000
Somerville City Hall	617-625-6600
Brookline Town Hall	617-730-2000
Cambridge City Hall	617-349-4000
Boston Police Headquarters	617-343-4200
General Info	411

Websites

www.notfortourists.com/web-bos.html—
    The ultimate city web directory.
www.boston.citysearch.com—
    Provides excellent overview to almost every business,
    landmark and attraction in the city.
*www.harvardsquare.com—*Goings-on in Cambridge.
www.boston-online.com—
    Forums and fun facts; guide to Boston English.
*www.boston.com—*Website of the *Boston Globe*.
boston.craigslist.com—
    Classifieds in almost every area, including personals,
    apartments for rent, musicians, and more.
*www.cityofboston.gov—*Boston government resources.
www.cambridgema.gov—
    Cambridge government resources.
www.somervillema.gov—
    Somerville government resources.
www.town.brookline.ma.us—
    Brookline government resources.

We're the First!!!

- America's first subway: MBTA
- America's first public library
- America's first public park: Boston Common
- First Thanksgiving
- America's first regularly issued newspaper: *Boston News-Letter*
- America's first public school: Boston Latin
- First First Night New Year's celebration
- America's first college: Harvard
- First telephone demonstrated by Alexander Graham Bell
- First person-to-person e-mail
- First flag of the American colonies raised on Prospect Hill (January 1, 1776)

Boston Timeline

A timeline of significant Boston events (by no means complete)

1620 Mayflower arrives in Plymouth.
1621 First Thanksgiving in Plymouth.
1630 Dorchester, first part of Boston, founded by Gov. John Winthrop.
1634 Boston Common, first public park in America, opens.
1635 Boston Latin School, first public secondary school in America, opens.
1636 Harvard College opens.
1692 Witchcraft Trials begin in Salem.
1693 Society of Negroes founded.
1704 First regularly issued American newspaper, the *Boston News-Letter*.
1716 First American lighthouse built in Boston Harbor.
1770 Boston Massacre.
1773 Boston Tea Party.
1775 Revolutionary War begins at Lexington and Concord.
1775 Battle of Bunker Hill.
1776 First American flag raised on Prospect Hill in Somerville.
1776 British evacuate Boston.
1780 John Hancock becomes first elected Governor of Massachusetts.
1788 Massachusetts ratifies Constitution.
1795 The "new" State House built.
1796 John Adams, of Quincy, elected second president.
1806 African Meeting House, first church built by free blacks, opens.
1820 Maine separates from Massachusetts.
1824 John Quincy Adams elected sixth president.
1831 William Lloyd Garrison publishes first abolitionist newspaper, the *Liberator*.
1837 Samuel Morse invents electric telegraph machine.
1845 Sewing machine invented by Elias Howe.
1846 Boston dentist William T.G. Morton publically demonstrates the value of anesthesia in surgery.
1846 From 1846 to 1849, 37,000 Irish people flee the Potato Famine for Boston.
1860 From 1860 to 1870, the Back Bay is filled in, greatly increasing the landmass of Boston.
1860 From 1860 to 1880, Boston annexes Charlestown, Brighton, Roxbury, West Roxbury, and Dorchester, greatly expanding Irish power.
1863 University of Massachusetts at Amherst chartered.
1872 *Boston Globe* prints its first newspaper.
1872 Great Fire of 1872.
1876 First telephone demonstrated by Alexander Graham Bell.
1877 Helen Magill becomes first woman PhD in US (at BU).
1882 John L. Sullivan becomes bare-knuckle boxing champ.
1886 *Irish Echo* newspaper founded.
1888 Construction begins on Boston Public Library.
1892 JFK grandfather John F. "Honey Fitz" Fitzgerald elected to state senate.
1894 Honey Fitz elected to US Congress.
1896 First US public beach opens in Revere.
1897 First American subway opens.
1900 Symphony Hall opens.
1901 Boston Red Sox play first game against New York Yankees.
1903 Red Sox (then the Americans) win first World Series.
1906 Honey Fitz becomes first Boston-born Irish-American mayor.
1912 Fenway Park opens.
1914 James Michael Curley elected mayor for the first time.
1915 Custom House Tower completed, tallest building in Boston at time.
1918 Red Sox win their last World Series.

1920 Red Sox owner Harry Frazee sells Babe Ruth to Yankees for $100,000, incurring supposed "Curse of the Bambino."
1920 Irish-Italian gang fights begin.
1924 Boston Bruins play first game.
1924 World's first mutual fund.
1927 Sacco and Vanzetti wrongly executed for robbery shootings.
1928 Boston Garden opens.
1928 First computer invented at MIT.
1929 Bruins win their first Stanley Cup trophy.
1934 JFK father "Old Joe" Kennedy named SEC chairman.
1939 Ted Williams plays first game for Red Sox.
1941 Ted Williams hits .406, last player to hit over .400.
1946 JFK elected to Congress.
1946 Boston Celtics play first game.
1946 Red Sox lose World Series after tragic player error.
1947 Microwave oven invented at Raytheon.
1947 First Polaroid camera invented.
1947 Dr. Sidney Farber introduces chemotherapy.
1950 Red Auerbach becomes Celtics coach.
1952 Boston Braves play final game in Boston, move to Milwaukee.
1956 Celtics draft Bill Russell.
1957 Massachusetts Turnpike opens.
1958 Celtics win first of 16 championships.
1959 Central Artery opens.
1960 West End neighborhood of Boston demolished.
1960 Boston Patriots play first game.
1960 John F. Kennedy elected 35th president.
1960 Ted Williams homers in last at-bat for Red Sox.
1962 From 1962 to 1964, Boston Strangler kills 13 women. Albert DeSalvo is convicted and killed in prison.
1963 JFK assassinated in Dallas.
1964 Prudential Tower built.
1965 Havlicek steals the ball! Celtics win championship.
1966 Bobby Orr plays first game as a Bruin.
1966 Edward W. Brooke becomes first black elected to US Senate since Reconstruction.
1967 Red Sox' "Impossible Dream" season ends in defeat.
1971 First e-mail sent by Bolt, Beranek and Newman.
1972 John Hancock building, tallest in Boston, nears completion, giant windows start falling out.
1974 Federal court declares "de facto segregation" of Boston public schools; orders desegregation. Demonstrations and violence ensue.
1975 Carlton Fisk hits 12th inning game 6 homer, does baseline foul pole dance, Sox go on to lose game 7.
1975 Gangster Whitey Bulger begins relationship with FBI agents, reign as Boston's biggest crimelord.
1976 First First Night New Year's celebration.
1978 Bucky Dent! Sox lose to Yanks.
1978 Celtics draft Larry Bird.
1986 Patriots lose Super Bowl XX to Chicago Bears.
1986 Celtics win 16th and last championship.
1986 Celtics draft pick Len Bias dies of a drug overdose.
1986 Red Sox lose World Series Game 6 to Mets after excruciating 10th inning error, go on to lose game 7.
1987 Big Dig construction begins in Charlestown.
1987 Cleanup of Boston Harbor begins.
1988 Governor Michael Dukakis runs for president; rides tank; loses to Bush the First.
1989 Charles Stuart kills wife and unborn child, shoots self to suggest robbery, later jumps to death from Tobin Bridge.
1993 Celtics captain Reggie Lewis dies.
1993 Former Mayor Ray Flynn named ambassador to Vatican, holds Pope's umbrella.

1993 Thomas M. "Mumbles" Menino elected Boston's 1st Italian-American Mayor.
1995 Boston Garden closes; FleetCenter opens.
1995 Whitey Bulger goes on the lam after his FBI handlers are indicted.
1997 Patriots lose their second Super Bowl (to Green Bay).
1998 *Boston Globe* columnists Patricia Smith and Mike Barnicle fired over fabrications and plagiarism, respectively.
2000 Celtic Paul Pierce nearly stabbed to death at Boston nightclub.
2001 Jane Swift becomes first female governor of Massachusetts.
2001 Planes that destroy NYC World Trade Center leave Logan Airport.
2002 After a 0-2 start, New England Patriots win their first Super Bowl.
2002 Ted Williams dies, cryogenically frozen in two pieces.
2002 Catholic clergy sexual abuse scandal explodes; Cardinal Bernard Law resigns amid controversy.
2003 Billy Bulger forced to resign as UMass president due to controversy about his gangster brother, Whitey.
2003 New scar layer: Red Sox lose heartbreaking ALCS to Yankees.

Essential Boston Movies

The Boston Strangler (1968)	*Monument Ave* (1998)
The Thomas Crown Affair (1968)	*Next Stop Wonderland* (1998)
Between the Lines (1977)	*A Civil Action* (1998)
The Verdict (1982)	*Heist* (2001)
Glory (1989)	*Legally Blonde* (2001)
School Ties (1992)	*Mystic River* (2003)
Good Will Hunting (1997)	

Essential Boston Songs

"Dirty Water" — The Standells
"Charlie on the MTA" — The Kingston Trio
"Please Come to Boston" — Dave Loggins
"They Came to Boston" — The Mighty Mighty Bosstones
"The Boston Burglar" — traditional
"The Ballad of Sacco & Vanzetti" — Joan Baez
"Massachusetts" — The Bee Gees
"Sweet Baby James" — James Taylor
"Highlands" — Bob Dylan
"Down at the Cantab" — Little Joe Cook & the Thrillers
"Twilight in Boston" — Jonathan Richman
"Government Center" — Jonathan Richman

12 Essential Boston Books

All Souls, Michael Patrick McDonald
Black Mass, David Lehrer and Gerard O'Neill
The Bostonians, Henry James
The Curse of the Bambino, Dan Shaughnessy
The House of the Seven Gables, Nathaniel Hawthorne
John Adams, David McCullough
Johnny Tremain, Esther Forbes
Love Story, Erich Segal
Little Women, Louisa May Alcott
Make Way for Ducklings, Robert McCloskey
Mystic River, Dennis Lehane
Walden, Henry David Thoreau

General Information • Media

Television

2	WGBH	(PBS)	www.wgbh.org
4	WHDH	(CBS)	www.whdh.com
5	WCVB	(ABC)	www.thebostonchannel.com
7	WBZ	(NBC)	www.wbz.com
17	WUNI	(Univision)	www.wunitv.com
25	WFXT	(FOX)	www.wfxt.com
38	WSBK	(UPN)	www.upn38.com
44	GBH2	(PBS)	www.wgbh.org
56	WLVI	(WB)	www.wlvi.com
66	WUTF	(TeleFutura)	www.univision.com
68	WBPX	(PAX)	www.pax.tv

AM Radio

590	WEZE	Religious
680	WRKO	Talk
740	WJIB	Instrumental Pop and Light Oldies
850	WEEI	Sports
950	WROL	Religious
1030	WBZ	News/Talk/Sports
1090	WILD	Urban
1150	WJTK	Religious
1260	WMKI	Radio Disney
1510	WWZN	Sports
1600	WUNR	Ethnic
1670	none	Allston-Brighton Free Radio

FM Radio

88.1	WMBR	MIT
88.9	WERS	Emerson College
89.7	WGBH	NPR
90.3	WZBC	Boston College
90.9	WBUR	NPR
91.9	WUMB	Folk, Jazz, Public
92.9	WBOS	Modern Adult Contemporary
94.5	WJMN	Hip-Hop, R&B
95.3	WHRB	Harvard University
96.3	W242AA	Public
96.9	WTKK	Talk
98.5	WBMX	Modern Adult Contemporary
100.7	WZLX	Classic Rock
101.3	WFNX	Alternative
101.7	WFNX	Alternative
102.5	WCRB	Classical
103.3	WODS	Oldies
104.1	WBCN	Modern Rock
104.9	WRBB	Northeastern University
105.7	WROR	Oldies/Classic Rock
106.7	WMJX	Soft Rock
107.3	WAAF	Hard Rock
107.9	WXKS	Pop

Print Media

Boston Globe	135 Morrissey Blvd	617-929-2000	Daily broadsheet
Boston Herald	One Herald Sq	617-426-3000	Daily tabloid
Boston Phoenix	126 Brookline Ave	617-536-5390	Weekly alternative
Boston Metro	320 Congress St	617-338-7917	Free, tiny M-F paper
Boston Magazine	300 Massachusetts Ave	617-262-9700	Glossy magazine
The Improper Bostonian	142 Berkeley St, 3rd Floor	617-859-1400	Free entertainment and lifestyle magazine
The Weekly Dig	242 E Berkeley St	617-426-8942	Weekly alternative
Somerville Journal	240A Elm St	617-625-6300	Weekly Somerville news
Cambridge Chronicle	240A Elm St	617-577-7149	Weekly Cambridge news
Brookline TAB	254 Second Ave	617-566-3585	Weekly Brookline news
Boston Business Journal	200 High St, Suite 4b	617-330-1000	Boston bidness
The Pilot	2121 Commonwealth Ave	617-746-5889	Catholic weekly
Boston Review	E53-407 MIT	617-258-0805	Intellectual political and literary magazine
Boston Irish Reoprter	150 Mt Vernon St	617-436-1222	Weekly free Irish-American news
Jewish Advocate	15 School St	617-367-9100	Weekly Jewish-American news
Mass High Tech	529 Main St, Suite 602	617-242-1224	Weekly technology magazine

All right, let's get this out of the way: we have outdated, puritanical blue laws, and there isn't a bar or club open past 2 am. The nightlife scene is more or less dominated by the pub/bar, so there aren't that many clubs to choose from, though they are increasing in number. They still close at 2 am. You're on your own figuring out any illegal after-hours tomfoolery.

Clubs are always in flux. Places close, themes change, and cover charges double, so it always makes sense to check a resource like *The Phoenix* before rounding up your crew and hitting the town.

Most of the bigger, well-known clubs in Boston are on Lansdowne Street, behind Fenway Park. They draw large student crowds and get particularly busy when the Sox are in town. **The Modern** and **Tequila Rain** offer lots of techno and lots of tight, shiny clothes, while a good number of mainstream music events are held at **Axis** and **Avalon**. Not far from Fenway, **Sophia's** focuses on salsa and jazz. For a night out in the Theater District, consider the enormous **Roxy** (big on Latin and house), **Venu** (big on Brazilian and European) or **Pravda 116** (big on vodka).

SW1 in Downtown Crossing used to be a members-only type deal but now allows general access. **The Place**, on Broad Street, touts itself as a sports bar/nightclub hybrid, but it's basically just a nightclub. One of the Oakland Athletics pitchers got into a fight at **Q**, a new club near Faneuil Hall. The Alley complex is made up of **The Big Easy, The Sugar Shack, La Boom,** and way, way too many seriously drunk college kids.

For rock, check who's playing at **Paradise Rock Club** on Comm Ave or **Midway Cafe** in JP. Two of Boston's best-known rock venues, **The Middle East** and **T.T. The Bear's Place,** sit next to each other in Central Square. Central Square is also home to **Phoenix Landing** (which morphs from an Irish pub into a dance club on most nights) and **Man-Ray**, which has two large rooms spinning goth, alternative boypop, trance, house, or industrial depending on the night. For local band performances you should also check out **Skybar, the Abbey Lounge, Tir Na Nog, The Burren,** and **The Cantab Lounge.**

Machine, Ramrod and **Vapor** are primarily gay. For years, Avalon has hosted a huge gay night on Sundays (still very popular, and quite a capital-C Club experience). Jacque's is Boston's primary drag club, with shows on most nights.

All area codes are 617 unless otherwise noted.

Club / Cabaret	Address	Phone	Map
711 Boylston	711 Boylston St	437-0002	6
Abbey Lounge	3 Beacon St	441-9631	28
An Tain	31 India St	426-1870	4
Aqua	120 Water St	720-4900	4
Aria	246 Tremont St	338-7080	3
Avalon	15 Lansdowne St	262-2424	16
Axis	13 Lansdowne St	262-2437	16
The Big Easy	1 Boylston Pl	351-2510	3
Bill's Bar & Lounge	5 1/2 Lansdowne St	241-9678	16
Boston Rocks	245 Quincy Market	726-1110	2
The Burren	247 Elm St	776-6896	22
The Cantab Lounge	738 Massachusetts Ave	354-2685	27
Club Martin	137 Pearl St	423-4792	4
Dad's Beantown Diner	911 Boylston St	296-3237	5
Embassy	30 Lansdowne St	536-2100	16
Estelle's	888 Tremont St	427-0200	13
Europa Nightclub	51 Stuart St	482-3939	3
Exchange	148 State St	726-7601	2
Felt	533 Washington St	350-5555	3
Great Scott	1222 Commonwealth Ave	566-9014	19
Green Briar	304 Washington St	789-4100	18
Hannah's	499 Broadway	629-5322	23
Jacque's	79 Broadway St	426-8902	3
The Kells	161 Brighton Ave	782-9082	19
La Boom	25 Boylston Pl	357-6800	3
Level	295 Franklin St	338-1000	4
Linwood Grill	69 Kilmarnock St	267-8644	15
Machine	1256 Boylston St	536-1950	15
Man-Ray	21 Brookline St	864-0400	26
Matrix	279 Tremont St	542-4077	3
Middle East	472 Massachusetts Ave	864-3278	27

Club / Cabaret	Address	Phone	Map
Midway Cafe	3496 Washington St	524-9038	14
The Modern	36 Lansdowne St	536-2100	16
NYC Jukebox	275 Tremont St	542-1123	3
Paradise Rock Club & Lounge	969 Commonwealth Ave	562-8800	19
Parris	Fanueil Hall Marketplace	248-8800	2
Phoenix Landing	512 Massachusetts Ave	576-6260	26
The Place	2 Broad St	523-2081	2
Pravda 116	116 Boylston St	482-7799	3
Purple Shamrock	1 Union St	227-2060	2
Q	25 Union St	742-2121	2
The Rack	24 Clinton St	725-1051	2
Ramrod	1254 Boylston St	266-2986	15
Roxy	279 Tremont St	678-3231	3
Ryles Jazz Club	212 Hampshire St	876-9330	28
Scullers Jazz Club	400 Soldiers Field Rd	562-4131	19
Sissy K's	6 Commercial St	248-6511	2
Soho	386 Market St	562-6000	18
Skybar	518 Somerville Ave	623-5223	23
Sophia's	1270 Boylston St	351-7001	15
Sugar Shack	1 Boylston Pl	351-2510	3
SW1	48-50 Winter St	423-6767	3
Tequila Rain	3 Lansdowne St	859-0030	16
Tir Na Nog	366 Somerville Ave	628-4300	24
Toast	70 Union Sq	623-9211	24
TT the Bear's Place	10 Brookline St	492-2327	27
Vapor	100 Warrenton St	695-9500	3
Vertigo	126 State St	723-7277	2
Western Front	343 Western Ave	492-7772	26

263

Together with its food renaissance, Boston's bar scene has developed nicely over the past several years (not too much of a surprise in what comic Jon Stewart once called the "drinkingest" town anywhere). No longer just about Irish pubs and beer joints catering to the barely legal, Boston's bar scene, like its restaurant scene, provides a little something for everyone.

Beer

Fortunately, most Boston bars offer more than just Guinness and Bud Light. Brewing their own recipes are **Boston Beer Works**, **Cambridge Brewing Company**, **John Harvard's Brew House**, and **Rock Bottom Brewery** (where the IPA and the stouts are better than the lagers). Large beer selections can be found at **Sunset Grill & Tap**, **Bukowski's**, and **Anam Cara**. **Redbones**, best known for its barbecue, also has a good slate of suds.

Sports

In a town where practically every bar has at least two TVs, it's easy to find a place showing the Sox or the Patriots.

For a sports-friendly atmosphere (i.e., game sound not muted), try almost any spot along Causeway Street or Canal Street. If you're desperate to see your (non-Boston) team, try **Coolidge Corner Clubhouse** or **Lir**.

Swank

Straddling the line between bar and "club" are those bars that sell more cocktails than beer but don't prevent the fashion-unconscious (or average-looking) from coming in for drinks. Places to order a bastardized martini include **Vox Populi**, **Saint**, and **Blue Cat Cafe**.

Dive

What is a dive bar? To paraphrase Potter Stewart, we know one when we see one. To wit: **Sullivan's Tap**, **Cambridge-port Saloon**, **Mary Ann's**, and **Crossroads**. The **Cantab Lounge** isn't a real dive—it does serve dinner, after all. If you want to drink in a real dive, pull up a stool at Charlie Flynn's on Tremont Street. *This* is a dive.

All areas codes are 617 unless otherwise noted.

Map 1 • Beacon Hill / West End

21st Amendment	150 Bowdoin St	227-7100	Favorite of the State House crowd.
Beacon Hill Pub	149 Charles St		Dive popular with young Hill residents.
Boston Beer Works	112 Canal St	896-2337	Cavernous suds shop near Fleet Center.
Cheers	84 Beacon St	227-9605	If you must.
Grand Canal	57 Canal St	523-1112	Pub across from Fleet Center. 22 taps.
Hill Tavern	228 Cambridge St	742-6192	Middling Beacon Hill hangout.
Hurricane O'Reilly's	150 Canal St	722-0161	Crowded New Orleans/Irish sports bar.
Sullivan's Tap	168 Canal St		Dive. Proper before Celtics and Bruins games.
The Four's	166 Canal St	720-4455	Large tavern near the Fleet Center.

Map 2 • North End / Faneuil Hall

Bell in Hand Tavern	45 Union St	227-2098	Welcoming thirsty travelers since the 18th century.
Black Rose	160 State St	742-2286	Tourist-crowded, unremarkable.
			Try somewhere else first.
Green Dragon Tavern	11 Marshall St	367-0055	Pretend you're Sam Adams while having the same.
Ned Devine's	Quincy Market	248-8800	Sizeable "Irish" bar. Best avoided.
The Office	5 Broad St	367-5806	An almost-dive, popular mostly with men.
Tia's on the Waterfront	200 Atlantic Ave	277-0828	Warm-weather party house.

Map 3 • Downtown Crossing / Park Square / Bay Village

Felt	533 Washington St	350-5555	Upscale pool hall. DJ most nights.
MJ O'Connor's	27 Columbus Ave	482-2255	Large Irish pub. Outdoor seating when warm.
Parker's Bar	60 School St	227-8600	Elegant. Try the Boston Creme martini.
Pravda 116	116 Boylston St	482-7799	Home of "two international vodka bars."
The Littlest Bar	47 Province St	523-9667	Certified by Guinness as the record-holder. Irish.
The Tam	222 Tremont St		That rare thing, a well-lit dive bar.
Whiskey Park	64 Arlington St	542-1483	Swank, inexplicably popular. Dress up.

Map 4 • Financial District / Chinatown

Black Rhino	21 Broad St	263-0101	Nothing too special, but has a roof deck.
Elephant & Castle	161 Devonshire St	350-9977	Large pub handy for groups. Skip the food.
JJ Foley's	21 Kingston St	338-7713	Attracts a big after-work crowd.
Jose McIntyre's	160 Milk St	451-9460	Casual DJ and dance spot. Popular and simple.
Les Zygomates	129 South St	542-5108	French bistro. Comprehensive wine list, pleasant bar.

Mr Dooley's Boston Tavern	77 Broad St	338-5656	Irish. Popular after-work drinking spot.
News	150 Kneeland St	426-6397	Terrific Leather District late-night spot.
Times Restaurant and Bar	112 Broad St	357-8463	Irish. Live music and DJs.
Trio	174 Lincoln St	357-8746	Riding the lounge wave. Good food, though.

Map 5 · Back Bay (West) / Fenway (East)

Blue Cat Cafe	94 Massachusetts Ave	247-9922	More for cocktails than food. Stylish, DJ.
Bukowski's	50 Dalton St	437-9999	100+ beers served with loud, eclectic music.
Crossroads	495 Beacon St	262-7371	Dive popular for its late last call.
Dillon's	955 Boylston St	421-1818	Revisiting the Roaring '20s.
Kings	10 Scotia St	266-2695	Bowling, pool, TV sports. Goofy but fun.
Lir	903 Boylston St	778-0089	"Upscale Irish." Large, handy for sports watchers.
Our House East	52 Gainsborough St	236-1890	Branch of Allston college-kid hangout.
Sonsie	327 Newbury St	351-2500	People-watching mainstay. Nice French-doors street exposure.
The Last Drop	421 Marlborough St	262-5555	Supposed latest last call in Boston.
Top of the Hub	800 Boylston St	536-1775	Great view from the top of the Pru.
Wally's Café	427 Massachusetts Ave	424-1408	Cramped jazz landmark. For everyone at least once.

Map 6 · Back Bay (East) / South End (Upper)

Anchovies	433 Columbus Ave	266-5088	Easy-going neighborhood joint.
Clery's	113 Dartmouth St	262-9874	Bar with food. Location is its best attribute.
Saint	90 Exeter St	236-1134	"Nightery" for aspiring high-rollers, scenesters.
The Rattlesnake	384 Boylston St	859-8555	Hit the roof deck in the summer.
Vox Populi	755 Boylston St	424-8300	Large and competent, but strangely soulless.

Map 7 · South End (Lower)

Delux Cafe	100 Chandler St	338-5258	Small, hip spot with good eats, music.
Donovan's Tavern	1505 Washington St	247-9538	Neighborhood local.
Waltham Tavern	298 Shawmut Ave	338-8542	Ladies welcome, apparently.

Map 8 · Charlestown

Ninety Nine	29 Austin St	242-8999	... bottles of beer on the wall ...
Sullivan's Pub	85 Main St	242-9515	Relaxed pub off of Thompson Square.
Tavern on the Water	1 Pier 6 at E 8th St	242-8040	Good on a warm afternoon. Skyline view.
Warren Tavern	2 Pleasant St	241-8142	One of Paul Revere's favorite watering holes.

Map 9 · East Boston

Lobby Bar	267 Frankfort St	439-4165	The lobby of what, precisely, is unclear.
Pony Lounge	411 Chelsea St	567-9775	Karaoke on weekend nights.
Trainor's Cafe	129 Maverick St	567-6995	Neighborhood local.

Map 10 · South Boston (West) / Fort Point

Baggot Inn	110 Dorchester St	268-4323	Irish sports broadcasts and brunch on Sunday.
Blackthorn Pub	471 W Broadway	269-1159	Real Irish. Pours a mean Guinness.
The Cornerstone	16 W Broadway	269-9553	Broadway Square, erm, cornerstone. Parking in rear.
Lucky's	355 Congress St	357-5825	Well-liked retro cocktail lounge. Music most nights.
The Quiet Man	11 W Broadway	269-9878	Pub. Try the steak tips.
Shenanigans	332 W Broadway	269-9509	Plenty of Guinness pints pulled in here.

Map 11 · South Boston (East)

Boston Beer Garden	734 E Broadway	269-0990	Had a makeover recently. Long wine list too.
Corner Tavern	645 E 2nd St	269-9891	Locals only.
L Street Tavern	658 E 8th St	268-4335	No-nonsense local. Appears in *Good Will Hunting*.
Playwright	658 E Broadway	269-2537	For socializing and television watching.

Arts & Entertainment • **Bars**

All areas codes are 617 unless otherwise noted.

Map 12 • Newmarket / Andrew Square

Aces High	551 Dorchester Ave	269-7637	Check out their "new drinks and decor."
Dot Tavern	840 Dorchester Ave	288-6288	Neighborhood local.
Killarney Tavern	1295 Massachusetts Ave	436-9037	Irish pub.
Sports Connection Bar	560 Dorchester Ave	268-4119	Featuring "a big screen TV."

Map 13 • Roxbury

Biarritz Lounge	177 Dudley St	445-6769	DJs on weekend nights, live music on Sundays.
C & S Tavern	380 Warren St	442-7023	Neighborhood local.
Slades Bar & Grill	958 Tremont St	442-4600	Dancing, live jazz on weekend nights.

Map 14 • Jamaica Plain

Brendan Behan Pub	378 Centre St	522-5386	Well-liked Irish local. Relaxed atmosphere.
Costello's Tavern	723 Centre St	522-9263	Now with live music on some nights.
Doyle's Cafe	3484 Washington St	524-2345	Reliable landmark. Serves decent pubgrub.
Midway Café	3496 Washington St	524-9038	Cozy local featuring a variety of live bands.
Milky Way Lounge and Lanes	405 Centre St	524-3740	Perennial JP fave. Choc-a-block events calendar.
Triple D's	437 Huntington Ave	522-4966	Favorite of bikers and young folk alike.

Map 15 • Fenway (West) / Mission Hill

Flann O'Brien's	1619 Tremont St	566-7744	Spirited Brigham Circle local.
Sophia's	1270 Boylston St	351-7001	Latin dancing most nights.
The Baseball Tavern	1306 Boylston St	437-1644	Decent choice for no-frills pre-game beer.

Map 16 • Kenmore Square / Brookline (East)

An Tua Nua	835 Beacon St	262-2121	Pub and dance club popular with twentysomethings.
Atlas Bar & Grill	3 Lansdowne St	437-0300	Sports-focused spot. Some pre-Sox outdoor seating.
Audubon Circle	838 Beacon St	421-1910	Chill out with tasty bar food.
Boston Billiard Club	126 Brookline Ave	536-7665	Capacious, down the street from Fenway Park.
Cask'n Flagon	62 Brookline Ave	536-4840	Just behind the Green Monster. Nothing special.
Jillian's	145 Ipswich St	437-0300	Pool, arcade games, bar food, etc. Dress code.
PJ Kilroy's	822 Beacon St	266-3986	Liked by Sox fans and students.
Who's on First?	19 Yawkey Way	247-3353	Fun Fenway dive.

Map 17 • Coolidge Corner / Brookline Hills

Anam Cara	1648 Beacon St	277-2880	Focus here is on the beers.
Matt Murphy's Pub	14 Harvard St	232-0188	Well-liked Irish pub. Good food.
The Last Drop	596 Washington St	787-1111	Sibling of Marlborough Street bar.

Map 18 • Brighton

Boyne	458 Western Ave	782-2418	Irish pub.
CitySide	1960 Beacon St	566-1002	Hit the patio if it's nice outside.
Green Briar	304 Washington St	789-4100	Pub with frequent live rock.
Joey's	416 Market St	254-9381	Don't ask for Joey.
Mary Ann's	1937 Beacon St		BC student dump.
Soho	386 Market St	562-6000	Sleek, large dining spot-cum-nightclub.

Map 19 • Allston (South) / Brookline (North)

Avenue Bar & Grille	1249 Commonwealth Ave	782-9508	Popular Allston crowd-pleaser.
Harper's Ferry	156 Brighton Ave	254-9743	Good place for live, unthreatening rock and blues.
Kinvara Pub	34 Harvard Ave	784-9300	Attracts actual Irish people. Features "beer garden."
Model Cafe	7 N Beacon St	254-9365	Fun place frequented by few deadheads.
Our House	1277 Commonwealth Ave	782-3228	College bar with board games, plenty of couches.
Paradise Rock Club & Lounge	969 Commonwealth Ave	562-8800	New kitchen serves tasty food in the Lounge.
Sunset Grill & Tap	130 Brighton Ave	254-1331	100+ taps pour fun for beer connoisseurs.
Tonic	1316 Commonwealth Ave	566-6699	Pretty mod for Allston. Met Lounge is downstairs.
Wonder Bar	186 Harvard Ave	351-2665	Decent two-level bar featuring jazz.

Arts & Entertainment • **Bars**

Map 20 • Harvard Square / Allston (North)

Cambridge Common	1667 Massachusetts Ave	547-1228	Lizard Lounge performance space is downstairs.
John Harvard's Brew House	33 Dunster St	868-3585	Large and loud, good for crowds.
Noir	1 Bennett St	861-8010	More pretentious than sophisticated.
Redline	59 JFK St	491-9851	A decent spot, but too often cramped.
Shay's Lounge	58 JFK St	864-9161	Wine bar with outdoor seating. Wear your blazer.
Temple Bar	1688 Massachusetts Ave	547-5055	Popular and impressed with itself.
West Side Lounge	1680 Massachusetts Ave	441-5566	For those who find Temple Bar too pretentious.

Map 22 • North Cambridge / West Somerville

Johnny D's Uptown	17 Holland St	776-2004	Music nightly, wide variety.
PJ Ryan's	239 Holland St	625-8200	Brick and beer bar.
Redbones	55 Chester St	628-2200	Don't dig on swine? Then come for the beers.

Map 23 • Central Somerville / Porter Square

Christopher's	1920 Massachusetts Ave	876-9180	Good for relaxing on a wet day.
Joshua Tree	256 Elm St	623-9910	Sleek Davis Square spot. Plenty of taps.
Sligo Pub	237A Elm St	623-9651	A landmark of sorts.
The Burren	247 Elm St	776-6896	Well-known pub with nightly Irish session.

Map 24 • Winter Hill / Union Square

Khoury's State Spa	118 Broadway	776-0571	Large, easy-going joint. Pool, darts.
The Independent	75 Union Sq	440-6021	Up-and-coming Irish pub. Decent food.
Tir Na Nog	366A Somerville Ave	628-4300	Irish. Music every night.
Toast	70 Union Sq	623-9211	"A new concept in lounges," apparently. DJs.

Map 25 • East Somerville / Sullivan Square

Good Time Emporium	30 Assembly Sq	628-5559	Enormous. TVs, arcade games, batting cage, etc.
Towne Lyne Café	108 Cambridge St	242-9348	Chaucerian spelling contributes needed cachet.

Map 26 • East Cambridge / Kendall Square/MIT

Cambridge Brewing Company	1 Kendall Sq	494-1994	Decent microbrews. Some outdoor seating.
Flattop Johnny's	1 Kendall Sq	494-9565	Cambridge's best large pool hall.
Pugliese's	635 Cambridge St	491-9616	Cambridge's oldest family-owned bar.

Map 27 • Central Square / Cambridgeport

Asgard	350 Massachusetts Ave	577-9100	Enormous "Celtic" gastropub.
Cambridgeport Saloon	300 Massachusetts Ave		Smoking ban spells trouble for this dive.
Cantab Lounge	738 Massachusetts Ave	354-2685	Legendary quasi-dive. Little Joe Cook still plays.
Enormous Room	567 Massachusetts Ave	491-5550	Trendy couch lounge with tasty bar food.
Middle East	472 Massachusetts Ave	864-3278	Venerable venue that gets high-profile music bookings.
Miracle of Science	321 Massachusetts Ave	868-2866	Energetic neighborhood mainstay. Owners: new draft beers please!
People's Republik	880 Massachusetts Ave	492-8632	Toast 'til 2:00.
Phoenix Landing	512 Massachusetts Ave	576-6260	Irish pub with club music every night.
Plough & Stars	912 Massachusetts Ave	441-3455	Well-loved local. Frequent live music.
River Gods	125 River St	576-1881	Hipster house. DJs spin frequently.
The Cellar	991 Massachusetts Ave	876-2580	Stuck between Central and Harvard? Here you go.

Map 28 • Inman Square

Abbey Lounge	3 Beacon St	441-6931	Boston's "best dive bar"? You decide. Music nightly.
B-Side Lounge	92 Hampshire St	354-0766	Hip spot that deserves its reputation.
Bukowski's	1281 Cambridge St	497-7077	100+ beers. More chill than its Boston brother.
The Druid	1357 Cambridge St	497-0965	Well-liked pub.
Thirsty Scholar Pub	70 Beacon St	497-2294	Laid-back neighborhood local. Good food, too.

Up until a few years ago, there weren't many choices for movie theaters, especially downtown. After the Cheri in Back Bay closed, if you wanted to see a big, new blockbuster movie, you had to go to the 'burbs, or at least the outer edges of Somerville and Cambridge.

That's changed recently, most notably with the openings of the **Loews Boston Common** and the **AMC Theatres Fenway 13**. A few years ago, the Millennium Place (a name that becomes more dated with every day that goes by) skyscrapers went up at the southeast corner of the Boston Common, and Loews opened a megaplex on the first floor. Around the same time, the Fenway 13 opened up just outside of Kenmore Square in the old Sears Roebuck building. A little further out is the **National Amusements Circle Cinema** near BC in Brighton, where you can indulge both your interests in popular cinema and late-seventies design.

Loews has also positioned itself on the outer edges of Boston. In Somerville's Assembly Square, you'll find the **Loews Assembly Square** and the **Loews Fresh Pond** is located in Cambridge's Fresh Pond. They clearly didn't spend a hell of a lot of time naming the places.

Two things Boston has never been short on are late-run theaters and art-house theaters (and combinations thereof). We're pretentious and cheap, apparently. This phenomenon is never more apparent than in the People's Republic of Cambridge, where you'll find the **Brattle Theater**, the **Harvard Film Archive**, and the **Loews Harvard Square** in Harvard Square and the **Landmark Kendall Square Cinema** in Kendall Square. Over in Davis Square, there's the newly spiffed up **Somerville Theatre**. Back across the river, you can check out cheap and quirky movies at the **Loews Copley Place** or the **Coolidge Corner Theater**, a Brookline landmark.

If you've never been to the Classic Film Series at the **Wang Center**, you should. All the films are indeed classics, and there's that sumptuous interior... Better still, admission is free.

On a sad note, the Bombay Cinema 2 (itself located in the old Allston Cinema) has closed. For a short time Boston's premier venue for Bollywood releases, the building will be demolished to make room for a Staples.

Huge-screen freaks should hit the **Mugar Omni Theater** at the Museum of Science and the **Simons IMAX Theatre** at the New England Aquarium. If you just have to shop for furniture before seeing a movie, you owe yourself a trip to Jordan's Furniture out in Natick where, for reasons we're still struggling to determine, there's an on-site 3-D IMAX theater. (Coming soon: Bernie & Phyl retaliate by building a drive-in behind their Saugus showroom...)

Movie Theater	Address	Phone	Map
AMC Theatres Fenway 13	201 Brookline Ave	617-424-6266	16
Brattle Theatre	40 Brattle St	617-876-6837	20
Coolidge Corner Theatre	290 Harvard St	617-734-2500	17
Harvard Film Archive	24 Quincy St	617-495-4700	20
Institute for Contemporary Art	955 Boylston St	617-266-5152	5
Landmark Kendall Square Cinema	1 Kendall Sq	617-494-9800	26
Loews Boston Common	175 Tremont St	617-423-3499	3
Loews Cineplex Assembly Square	35 Middlesex Ave	617-628-7000	24
Loews Cineplex Copley Place	100 Huntington Ave	617-266-1300	6
Loews Cineplex Fresh Pond	168 Alewife Brook Pkwy	617-661-2900	22
Loews Cineplex Harvard Square	10 Church St	617-864-4580	20
MIT Film Series	77 Massachusetts Ave	617-258-8881	26
Museum of Fine Arts	465 Huntington Ave	617-369-3300	15
Museum of Science Omni Theater	Science Park	617-723-2500	1
National Amusements Circle Cinema	399 Chestnut Hill Ave	617-566-4040	18
Simons IMAX Theatre	Central Wharf	866-815-4629	4
Somerville Theatre	55 Davis Sq	617-625-5700	22
Wang Center	270 Tremont St	617-482-9393	3

If you're familiar with every painting at the **Gardner**, every print at the **MFA**, every fish in the **Aquarium**, and every cobblestone on the **Freedom Trail**, perhaps you should check out…

Beer! The **Boston Beer Museum**, run by the good people at the Boston Beer Company (brewers of Samuel Adams), has exhibits on brewing and beer memorabilia. Or, how about …

Robots! The **MIT Museum** has an on-going exhibit focusing on advancements in robotics. Or, …

Bugs! Check out the **Museum of Comparative Zoology**, one of the components of the **Harvard Museum of Natural History**. Or …

Sports! The **Sports Museum of New England** has a really cool giant woodcarving of Larry Bird. Or, …

History! Check out the **Boston Tea Party Ship and Museum**, the **USS Constitution Museum** (and actual ship), and the **Bunker Hill Museum**. For more local history, you can visit the **Old State House Museum** in Downtown Crossing. Not far from that on Joy Street is the **Museum of Afro-American History**. Or, …

Dirt! Fans of dirt, particularly celebrity dirt, should check out the **Museum of Dirt**. The museum, which is less a museum and more like a small gallery inside the offices of a marketing company in the Marine Industrial Park, showcases dirt from around the world. Like the finest art galleries, the Museum of Dirt operates on an irregular schedule, so call ahead. Unlike the finest art galleries, the museum apparently accepts contributions, so if you have some particularly interesting dirt to proffer you might want to give them a call.

If you want to take in some art during a drive out of town, check out the **DeCordova Museum and Sculpture Park** in Lincoln (not far from Route 2 and Route 128). The DeCordova hosts the only permanent public sculpture park in New England. The modern art museum on the site charges admission, but the sculpture park is free. More information is available at www.decordova.org.

Museum	Address	Phone	Map
Ancient and Honorable Artillery Company	Faneuil Hall	617-227-1638	2
Arthur M Sackler Museum	485 Broadway	617-495-9400	20
Boston Athenaeum	10 1/2 Beacon St	617-227-0270	1
Boston Beer Museum	30 Germania St	617-522-9080	14
Boston Children's Museum	300 Congress St	617-426-8855	4
Boston Tea Party Ship and Museum	Congress St Bridge	617-338-1773	10
Bunker Hill Museum	43 Monument Sq	617-242-1843	8
Busch-Reisinger Museum	32 Quincy St	617-495-9400	20
Fogg Art Museum	32 Quincy St	617-495-9400	20
Gibson House Museum	137 Beacon St	617-267-6338	6
Harrison Gray Otis House	141 Cambridge St	617-227-3956	1
Harvard Mineralogical & Geological Museum	24 Oxford St	617-495-3045	20
Harvard Museum of Comparative Zoology	26 Oxford St	617-495-3045	20
Harvard Museum of Natural History	26 Oxford St	617-495-3045	20
Harvard Semitic Museum	6 Divinity Ave	617-495-4631	20
Institute of Contemporary Art	955 Boylston St	617-266-5152	5
Isabella Stewart Gardner Museum	280 The Fenway	617-566-1401	15
Laser Fantasy International	Science Park	617-589-0175	1
Longyear Museum	1125 Boylston St	800-278-9000	5
Loring-Greenough House	12 South St	617-524-3158	13
Mapparium/Christian Science Museum	200 Massachusetts Ave	617-450-7000	5
MIT List Visual Arts Center	20 Ames St	617-253-4400	26
MIT Museum	265 Massachusetts Ave	617-253-4444	26
Museum of Afro-American History	46 Joy St	617-742-1854	1
Museum of Dirt	36 Drydock Ave	617-585-7000	10
Museum of Fine Arts	465 Huntington Ave	617-267-9300	15
Museum of Science	Science Park	617-723-2500	1
Museum of Useful Things	370 Broadway	617-576-3322	28
National Center for Afro-American Artists	300 Walnut Ave	617-442-8614	13
New England Aquarium	Central Wharf	617-973-5200	2
Nichols House Museum	55 Mount Vernon St	617-227-6993	1
Old South Meeting House	310 Washington St	617-482-6439	1
Old State House	206 Washington St	617-720-3290	2
Paul Revere House	19 North Sq	617-523-2338	2
Peabody Museum of Archaeology and Ethnology	11 Divinity Ave	617-496-1027	20
Revolving Museum	288-300 A St	617-439-8617	10
Somerville Museum	1 Westwood Rd	617-666-9810	23
Sports Museum of New England	One FleetCenter Pl	617-624-1234	1
USS Constitution Museum	Charlestown Navy Yard	617-426-1812	8

MAP
15

1. Japanese Art
2. Islamic Art
3. Brown Gallery
4. Indian Art
5. Egyptian Mummies
6. Graphics
7. Musical Instruments
8. Nubian Art
9. Etruscan Art
10. Greek Art
11. Near-Eastern Art
12. 18th Century American Furniture
13. 18th Century French Art
14. 18th Century Boston
15. English-Silver
16. 19th Century American
17. American Federal
18. Copley & Contemporary
19. American Neoclassical & Romantic
20. American Folk Painting
21. 19th Century Landscape
22. American Modern
23. American Masters
24. Early 20th Century American & European
25. Chinese Art
26. Egyptian Art
27. Roman Art
28. Medieval Art
29. Euro Decorative Arts
30. Impresses
31. 19th Century French & English
32. Post-Impressionism
33. Coolidge Collection
34. 18th Century Italian
35. Dutch & Flemish Art
36. Renaissance
37. Spanish Chapel
38. Baroque Art
39. Himalayan Art
40. Tapestries
41. Special Exhibitions

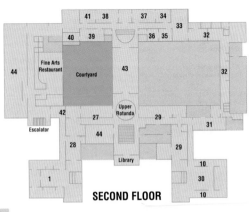

SECOND FLOOR

Closed to the Public

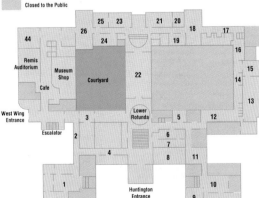

FIRST FLOOR

General Information

Address:	465 Huntington Avenue
	Boston, MA 02115
Website:	www.mfa.org
Phone:	617-267-9300

Overview

The Museum of Fine Arts, Boston's largest and most famous art institution, is always an ideal destination for anyone seeking a little cultural enrichment. The vast and extensive permanent collection of paintings and sculpture and the various lectures, films, concerts, and special traveling exhibitions offer something for everyone. And while you're there soaking up a little sophistication, enjoy a meal at one of the museum's three restaurants and buy an artifact from the gift shop, or some of them there little postcards with the pretty paintings on them. The museum needs the money. Though it's one of the largest art museums in the country, it receives little public funding. This, in part, accounts for the high admission fee. But don't worry: you get what you pay for.

Opening Hours

Mon, Tues, Sat & Sun; 10 am–4:45 pm
Wed, Thurs & Fri; 10 am–9:45 pm
Special exhibitions close 15 minutes before the museum closes. The gift shop is open until 5:45 pm on Saturdays.

Admission & Prices

Adults—$15 (30-day, 2-visit ticket)
Senior citizens & college students—$13 (30-day, 2-visit ticket)…though college students can usually get in for free with a flash of a student ID card.
Youth 7-17—$6.50 or FREE ($6.50 on school days until 3 pm, free at all other times)
School groups—$5 per student (after 3 pm admission is free for school groups)
Wednesday evenings 4 pm–9:45 pm general admission is by voluntary contribution.

Tickets for entry can be purchased at the museum. Tickets for concerts, films, lectures, or special exhibitions can be bought online at www.mfa.com.

Amenities

ATM	Gallery Stool (FREE)
Baby Changing Area	Nursing Room
Change Machine	Pay Phones
Coat Rooms (FREE)	Rest Rooms
Elevators	Wheelchairs (FREE on a first-come, first-served basis)

How to Get There—Driving

From Storrow Drive, take the Fenway/Kenmore exit. From the exit, take a left at the first traffic light towards Boylston Street inbound. At the second traffic light, turn right. Drive past a third traffic light. At the fourth traffic light, take a right onto Hemenway Street and proceed to the end of the street. Take a left onto Forsyth Street and proceed one short block. At the traffic light, take a right onto Huntington Avenue. The museum is located a few lights down and on your right.

From the north (Route 1 and I-95), cross the Mystic River/Tobin Bridge and follow signs to Storrow Drive. From there, follow the directions "From Storrow Drive" above.

From the south, Route 3 merges with I-93. Follow the Expressway to Downtown Boston and take the Storrow Drive exit. From there, follow the directions "From Storrow Drive."

From the west, take the Massachusetts Turnpike I-90 E. Upon approaching the Boston city limits, look for the Prudential Center/Copley Square exit (exit 22). It will be the first exit after the Cambridge/Brighton toll plaza. You will enter a tunnel and exit 22 will be on your right. Upon entering the exit ramp, get into the left lane (Prudential Center) and follow the exit to Huntington Avenue. Follow Huntington Avenue past the Christian Science Center (take underpass), and Northeastern University. The museum is located a few lights down and on the right.

Parking

There is limited parking available at the museum, including two parking lots on Museum Road. The cost for members is $2.50 each half-hour, $12 maximum. Non-members can expect to pay $3.50 for each half-hour with a $22 maximum for the day. A far cheaper option is public transportation.

How to Get There—Mass Transit

The museum is close to the Green Line Museum stop (E train only) or the Orange Line Ruggles stop. Or, take the 39 bus to the Museum stop or the 8, 47, or CT2 buses to the Ruggles stop.

Boston is a good city for art galleries. Lots of colleges = lots of art galleries.

Although Boston is an "old" city, it has embraced new art throughout its history. One manifestation of Boston's interest in contemporary art is the sheer number of art galleries along Newbury Street, home to most of Boston's higher-profile salons. The **Chase Gallery** specializes in showing mid-career artists, while the **Pepper Gallery** exhibits art with a humorous edge. Newbury Street is also home to one of the **Martin Lawrence Galleries**, which is dedicated to increasing the understanding and appreciation of fine art. If you're looking to buy at any of these galleries, you'd better have a healthy bank balance.

Across the river in Inman Square is the **Zeitgeist Gallery**. This venerable institution tends to be a bit more off the wall and hosts fantastic performances and events. Up the road in Davis Square is **Gallery Bershad**, which showcases up-and-coming local artists.

With the gentrification of Davis Square complete, most of the artists up and moved to Fort Point. The **Fort Point Arts Community Gallery** displays the works of many of these loft-dwellers. Look for more galleries to open up around Washington Street in the South End (oh, sorry – SoWa …) in the next couple of years. Many galleries have websites that offer details about their focus and their current exhibitions. A collection of links to the websites of some of these galleries can be found on the website of the Boston Art Dealers Association (www.bostonart.com).

That's just the tip of the artistic iceberg in the city. Every college has a few art galleries, and many bars, restaurants, and coffee shops shill paintings for the starving, as-yet-unrecognized artiste crowd.

All areas codes are 617 unless otherwise noted.

Map 1

Soprafina	99 Beacon St	498-0999
Victoria Munroe Fine Art	59 Beacon St	523-0661

Map 3

Alpha Gallery	14 Newbury St	536-4465
Barbara Krakow Gallery	10 Newbury St	262-4490
Beth Urdang Gallery	14 Newbury St	424-8468
Chappell Gallery	14 Newbury St	236-2255
Harcus Gallery	6 Melrose St	451-3221
Howard Yezerski Gallery	14 Newbury St	262-0550
Miller Block Gallery	14 Newbury St	536-4650
Oni Gallery	684 Washington St	542-6983
Scollay Square Gallery	1 City Hall Plaza, 3rd floor	635-3245
St George Gallery	245 Newbury St	450-0321

Map 4

Artemis Gallery	92 South St	338-4122

Map 5

Fenway Art Center	50 Gloucester St	536-0127
Gargoyles, Grotesques & Chimeras	262 Newbury St	536-2362
Kaji Aso Gallery	40 St Stephen St	247-1719
New Art on Newbury	285 Newbury St	267-7727

Map 6

Acme Fine Art	38 Newbury St	585-9551
Alianza Gallery	154 Newbury St	262-2385
Arden Gallery	129 Newbury St	247-0610
Artful Hand Gallery	100 Huntington Ave	262-9601
Camelot Gallery	221 Newbury St	424-1884
Chase Gallery	129 Newbury St	859-7222
Childs Gallery	169 Newbury St	266-1108
Copley Society	158 Newbury St	536-5049
Creiger-Dane Gallery	36 Newbury St	536-8088
Exoticar Model Gallery	114 Newbury St	267-8368
French Library and Cultural Center	53 Marlborough St	266-4351
Gallery NAGA	67 Newbury St	267-9060
International Poster Gallery	205 Newbury St	375-0076
Judi Rotenburg & Gallery	130 Newbury St	437-1518
Just Africa Gallery	201 Newbury St	536-1648
Kelly Barrette Fine Art	129 Newbury St	266-2475
Kidder Smith Gallery	131 Newbury St	424-6900
L'Attitude Gallery	218 Newbury St	927-4400
Martin Lawrence Galleries	77 Newbury St	369-4800
Nielsen Gallery	179 Newbury St	266-4835
Pepper Gallery	38 Newbury St	236-4497
Pucker Gallery	171 Newbury St	267-9473
Robert Klein Gallery	38 Newbury St	267-7997
Rolly-Michaux Gallery	290 Dartmouth St	536-9898
Wentworth Gallery	73 Newbury St	262-8770

Map 7

Ars Libri	500 Harrison Ave	357-5212
Berenberg Gallery	4 Clarendon St	536-0800
Bromfield Art Gallery	27 Thayer St	451-3605
Gallery AA/B	535 Albany St	574-0022
Genovese / Sullivan Gallery	23 Thayer St	426-9738
Kingston Gallery	450 Harrison Ave	423-4113
Mario Diacono Gallery	500 Harrison Ave	560-1608
MPG	450 Harrison Ave	437-1596
NAO Project Gallery	535 Albany St	451-2977

Map 10

Fort Point Arts Community Gallery	300 Summer St	423-4299
Studio Soto	63 Melcher St	426-7686

Map 11

Artists Foundation	516 E 2nd St	464-3561
Diana Levine Art Gallery	1 Design Center Pl	338-9060

Map 14

Arts & More	31 Germania St	522-0089

Map 17

Gateway Gallery	62 Harvard St	734-1577

Map 19

Brookline Community Center for the Arts	14 Green St	738-2800
Elias Fine Art	120 Braintree St	783-1888

Map 20

Cambridge Artists' Cooperative	59A Church St	868-4434

Map 22

Gallery Bershad	99 Dover St	629-9400

Map 21

Kathryn Schultz Gallery	25 Lowell St	876-0246

Map 23

Lux	257 Highland Ave	625-9257

Map 24

Brickbottom Gallery	1 Fitchburg St	776-3410

Map 26

Art Interactive	130 Bishop Richard Allen Dr	498-0100
Cambridge Mulitcultural Art Center	41 Second St	577-1400

Map 28

Out of the Blue Gallery	106 Prospect St	354-5287
Zeitgeist Gallery	1353 Cambridge St	876-6060

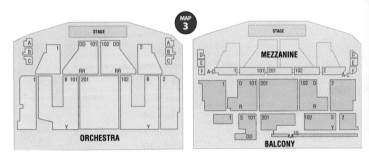

General Information

Address: Hamilton Place,
              Boston, MA 02108
Website: http://boston.cc.com/orpheum.asp
Phone: 617-679-0810
Ticketmaster: www.ticketmaster.com

Overview

Residing in a dead-end alleyway, the Orpheum is the place in Boston to catch the latest and greatest musical acts. Opened in 1852, the theater has been renovated several times but still exudes the same dilapidated charm it has always possessed. Tchaikovsky's First Piano Concerto and the Boston Symphony Orchestra's inaugural concert were both held at the Orpheum looooong ago. The theater has also hosted the Opera Company of Boston, seats 2,800, and doesn't have a bad seat in the house.

How to Get Tickets

Tickets can be purchased from the Orpheum Theatre Box Office Monday–Saturday 10 am–5 pm, at all Ticketmaster outlets, on the web at www.ticketmaster.com, or by phone at 617-679-0810.

How to Get There—Driving

From the north, take I-93 S to the Haymarket Square exit. Take a left at the second set of lights onto Tremont Street. Go six blocks down Tremont and the theater is located on the left.
From the south, take I-93 N to the Chinatown/South Station exit. At the lights take a left onto Kneeland Street, take a right onto Charles Street, a right onto Beacon Street and a right onto Tremont Street. Go about 100 yards and it's on your left at Hamilton Place.
From the west, take the Mass Pike east to the downtown Boston South Street Station exit. At the lights make a left onto Kneeland Street, turn right onto Charles Street, right onto Beacon Street and right onto Tremont Street. Go about 100 yards and it's on your left at Hamilton Place.

Parking

There is very limited street parking along with the nearest paid parking lot on Tremont Street.

How to Get There—Mass Transit

Take the Red or Green Line to the Park Street stop, or the Orange Line to Downtown Crossing. The theater is within a short walking distance from both stops.

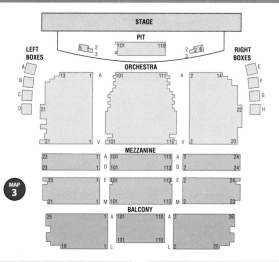

General Information

Address: 265 Tremont Street, Boston, MA 02116
Website: www.wangcenter.org
Phone: 617-482-9393
Tele-charge: www.telecharge.com; 800-447-7400

Overview

As part of the Wang Center for the Performing Arts theatrical complex, the Shubert Theatre is considered the "Little Princess" to the Wang Theatre's "Grand Dame." The small venue opened in 1910 with 1,600 seats and has undergone two major renovations since. In 1925, the widening of Tremont Street brought about the loss of the theater's elaborate entranceway, and in 1996, $6 million went into restoring and improving the theater's original, ornate French Renaissance architecture. The intimacy of the Shubert remained intact, and the theatre is now home to many Boston arts organizations, as well as several touring companies. Broadway shows, including such classics as *The King and I* and *South Pacific* debuted at the Shubert before moving onto Broadway.

How to Get Tickets

You can purchase tickets for the Shubert Theatre online at www.telecharge.com or by calling Tele-charge at 800-447-7400.

How to Get There—Driving

From the north, take the Chinatown exit off I-93. Turn right at Kneeland Street. Go straight for several blocks and then turn left onto Tremont Street. The Theatre is on your right.

From the south, take I-93 to exit 20/South Station. Follow the ramp toward South Station. Turn left on Kneeland Street and left again on Tremont Street. The theater is on your right.

From the west, take the South Station exit from the Mass. Turnpike. Turn left onto Kneeland Street and left again on Tremont Street. The theater is on your right.

Parking

There are a number of parking lots around the area. Try the parking lot on the corner of Tremont and Stuart Streets, the Radisson Hotel on Stuart Street, the Kinney Motor Mart on Stuart Street, or the Fitz-Inn lot on Kneeland Street.

How to Get There—Mass Transit

The following two subway stops are only one block from the theater: the Orange Line's New England Medical Center stop and the Green Line's Boylston Street stop. The Red Line's Park Street stop on Tremont Street is three or so blocks from the theater.

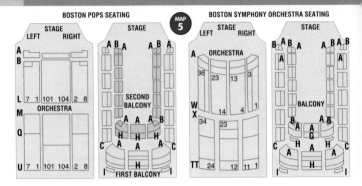

General Information

Address:	301 Massachusetts Avenue, Boston, MA 02115
Website:	www.bostonsymphonyhall.org
Phone:	617-266-1492
Tickets:	617-266-1200; www.bso.org

Overview

Symphony Hall is regarded as one of the finest concert halls in the world. It was the first hall designed to take into account scientifically derived acoustic principles that make for a near-perfect technical sound experience. It took about 17 months to build in 1900 and cost around $771,000. The hall seats 2,625 people in the Boston Symphony Orchestra (BSO) season and 2,371 in the Boston Pops Orchestra season. One feature worth noting is the Aeolian-Skinner organ with 67 stops and 5,130 pipes. The building also contains conference rooms, restrooms, coat checks, and the Symphony Shop. In the past, the Hall has hosted auto shows, mayoral inaugurations, meetings of the Communist Party, and a performance by Harry Houdini. The tradition of hosting non-traditional events looks set to continue. In 2003, the US Open Squash Tournament was held at Symphony Hall using portable glass courts placed just below the stage.

Function rooms and hall spaces are available for rental to the general public, and free tours offer an insight into the history and features of Symphony Hall.

How to Get Tickets

You can get tickets to any of the Symphony Hall Performances by phoning 617-266-1200 or 617-638-9283 (TDD/TTY), online at www.bso.org, or in person at the Symphony Hall box office.

How to Get There—Driving

From the north, take I-93 to the Storrow Drive exit. Once you're on Storrow Dr, bear left towards Copley Sq/Back Bay. Turn right onto Beacon Street. Turn left onto Clarendon St. Turn left onto St James Ave. Bear left onto Huntington Avenue, and Symphony Hall is on the corner of Huntington and Massachusetts Avenues.

From the south, take I-93 to exit 18 towards Mass. Ave/Roxbury. Go straight onto Frontage Rd North. Take a left onto the Mass Ave. Connector. Turn right onto Massachusetts Avenue. Symphony Hall is on the corner of Huntington and Massachusetts Avenues.

From the west, take I-90, to the Prudential Center/Copley Square exit and merge onto Huntington Avenue. Symphony Hall is on the corner of Huntington and Massachusetts Avenues.

Parking

There are two paid parking garages on Westland Avenue and limited street parking. If you have a ticket stub for a performance, then the Prudential Center Garage offers discount parking on the same day.

How to Get There—Mass Transit

The Green Line's E train will take you to the Symphony stop, while the other Green Line trains will get you close at the Hynes Convention Center stop. An alternative is to take the Orange Line to the Massachusetts Avenue stop.

The 1 bus, which runs down Massachusetts Avenue from Harvard Square to Dudley Square, will take you directly to Symphony Hall.

General Information

Address:	270 Tremont Street, Boston, MA 02116
Website:	www.wangcenter.org
Phone:	617-482-9393
Tele-charge:	www.telecharge.com
	800-447-7400

Overview

Though it has undergone several name changes and heavy renovation over the years, the Wang Theatre remains a prominent feature of the Boston theater scene. Located in the Wang Center for the Performing Arts and with more than 3,600 seats, it plays big brother to the Shubert Theatre across the street.

Opened in the "Roaring Twenties" (1925) as the Metropolitan Theatre, the venue was considered to be a "magnificent movie cathedral" with its ornate interior resembling something from Louis XIV's palace. Renamed the Music Hall in 1962, the theater became home to the then-fledgling Boston Ballet. As the years passed, the shiny gem began to lose some of its luster and, in 1980, control of the property was transferred to a non-profit organization known as The Metropolitan Center. Some minor renovations were made but it wasn't until 1983, when Dr. An Wang stepped in to resuscitate the theater, that things took a turn for the better. Since the restoration, the theater has been host to such classics as *Les Miserables* and *The Phantom of the Opera* and still houses one of New England's largest movie screens, which is used for the annual Classic Film Series. Near the holidays, one can't help but chuckle when posters advertise *Nutcracker at the Wang.*

How to Get Tickets

You can purchase tickets for the Wang Theatre online at www.telecharge.com or by calling Tele-charge at 800-447-7400. The Wang Theatre Box Office, which is open Monday through Saturday from 10 am until 6 pm, also sells tickets and you'll avoid some of those nasty service charges levied by external vendors.

How to Get There—Driving

From the north, take the Chinatown exit off I-93. Follow the signs toward Chinatown. Turn right at Kneeland Street. Go straight for several blocks and then turn left onto Tremont Street. The theater is on your left.

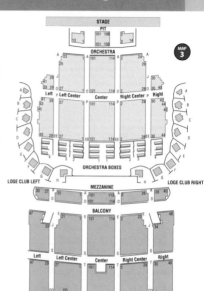

From the south, take I-93 to exit 20/South Station. Follow the ramp toward South Station. Turn left on Kneeland Street and left again on Tremont Street. The theater is on your left.

From the west, take the South Station exit from the Mass Pike. Turn left onto Kneeland Street and left again on Tremont Street. The theater is on your left.

Parking

There are a number of parking lots around the area. Try the parking lot on the corner of Tremont and Stuart Streets, the Radisson Hotel on Stuart Street, the Kinney Motor Mart on Stuart Street, or the Fitz-Inn lot on Kneeland Street.

How to Get There—Mass Transit

The following two subway stops are only one block from the theater: the Orange Line's New England Medical Center stop and the Green Line's Boylston Street stop. The Red Line's Park Street stop on Tremont Street is three or so blocks from the theater.

Hungry?

Seafood

Legal Sea Foods has the highest profile among local fishmongers and deserves its good reputation. **McCormick and Schmick's** sells quality fish in a chophouse atmosphere. Worth the trip to Inman Square is **East Coast Grill & Raw Bar**, which also excels at barbecue. For something cheaper in Cambridge, try **Dolphin Seafood** and **Court House Seafood**. Of course, in this home of the cod, any restaurant with a good chef should be able to be figure out how to buy and cook fresh fish.

Italian

Boston is blessed by numerous outstanding Italian restaurants. In the North End, **Mamma Maria** and **Bricco** are two among many standouts. On the other side of the river, **La Groceria** is less fancy but sturdy, **Vinny's at Night** dishes out Southern Italian to a loyal following, and **Centro** combines high quality with low-key elegance.

East Asian

As with the North End and its Italian food, a short list of places to get good Chinese food in Chinatown will necessarily omit some good spots. If you want somewhat sedate surroundings in Chinatown, try **New Shanghai**. Want Thai? Try **Brown Sugar**. Korean? Try **Koreana**. Sushi? Try **Blue Fin**. Cambodian? **Elephant Walk**. Cheap Vietnamese? Try **V Majestic** in Allston or one of the pho joints in Chinatown.

South Asian

Central Square (home to reliable standby **India Pavilion**) is no longer the only place to get good Indian food. Consider trying

Bukhara in Jamaica Plain, **Ajanta** near Kendall Square, or **Indian Quality** in Kenmore Square. For something different (and pleasant), try the Afghan cuisine at **Helmand**. We await the opening of Boston's first Iraqi restaurant.

Pizza

Few foods inspire as much passion (and contentiousness) as pizza; as such, identifying Boston's best pizza is a thankless task. That said, if you need a new pie to try, check out traditionalists **Antico Forno**, **Pizzeria Regina**, **Santarpio's**, or **Upper Crust**, upscale **Figs**, **Emma's**, or **Cambridge, 1**, or cheap-and-tasty **Hi-Fi**.

Bars

Better known as drinking and meeting spots, but also serving damn good pub grub, are **The Asgard**, **Audubon Circle**, **B-Side Lounge**, **Grendel's Den**, **James's Gate**, **Matt Murphy's Pub**, **Miracle of Science**, **The Paradise**, and **Silvertone Bar & Grill**.

Grease

Diner enthusiasts should try **Mike's City Diner**, **South Street Diner**, **Johnny's Luncheonette**, or **Rosebud Diner**. For a big breakfast, consider **Sound Bites**, **Brookline Lunch**, or the slightly more civilized **Trident Bookstore and Cafe**. Now if only The Tasty would magically de-appear...

Top-End

Want to celebrate a special occasion? Have your concierge reserve a table downtown at **Aujourd'hui**, **The Federalist**, **Mantra**, **No. 9 Park**, or **Radius**, in the South End at **Hamersley's Bistro** or **Union Bar and Grille**, around Back Bay at **Mistral**, **L'Espalier**, **Grill 23**, **Great Bay**, or **Clio**, or over the river at **Harvest**, **Rialto**, **EVOO**, **Oleana**, or **The Blue Room**.

Key: $: Under $10 / $$: $10–$20 / $$$: $20–$30 / $$$$: $30+. Area codes are 617 unless otherwise noted.

Map 1 · Beacon Hill / West End

75 Chestnut	75 Chestnut St	227-2175	$$$ Featuring a Sunday jazz brunch.
Cafe Podima	156 Cambridge St	227-4959	$ Sandwiches and such, frozen yogurt.
Federalist	15 Beacon St	670-2515	$$$$ A thoroughly top-end experience.
Figs	42 Charles St	742-3447	$$$ Beacon Hill branch of upscale pizza chain.
Harvard Gardens	316 Cambridge St	523-2727	$$ More for meeting and drinking than eating.
Hungry i	71 1/2 Charles St	227-3524	$$$$ French. Cozy spot for intimate meals.
King & I	145 Charles St	227-3320	$$ No-brainer for decent, inexpensive Thai.
Lala Rokh	97 Mt Vernon St	720-5511	$$$ Alluring Persian in a pleasant Beacon Hill townhouse.
Ma Soba	156 Cambridge St	973-6680	$$$ Sleek Asian fusion.
New York Soup Exchange	3 Center Plaza	973-6973	$ Good variety of hot and cold soups.
Panificio	144 Charles St	227-4340	$ Paninis, pastries. Try the formaggio.
Upper Crust	20 Charles St	723-9600	$$ Popular place for pizza pie.

Map 2 · North End / Faneuil Hall

Antico Forno	93 Salem St	723-6733	$$$ A home-style North End stand-out. Great pizza.
Billy Tse	240 Commercial St	227-9990	$$$ Pan-Asian near the waterfront.
Boston Sail Loft	80 Atlantic Ave	227-7280	$$ Serviceable seafood with a good view.
Bricco	241 Hanover St	248-6800	$$$ "Boutique Italian cuisine." Rather popular.
Caffe Paradiso	255 Hanover St	742-1768	$ Coffee and cannoli. Local landmark.
Daily Catch	323 Hanover St	523-8567	$$$ For those who can stand the heat in the kitchen.
Galleria Umberto	289 Hanover St	227-5709	$ Ideal for a tasty, cheap lunch.
Green Dragon Tavern	11 Marshall St	367-0055	$$ Pretend you're Sam Adams while having the same.
L'Osteria	104 Salem St	723-7847	$$$ Family-style red sauce joint.
La Famiglia Giorgio's	112 Salem St	367-6711	$$ Home-cooked Italian, student entree discounts.
La Summa	30 Fleet St	523-9503	$$$ More low-key than most North End places.

Lucca	226 Hanover St	742-9200	$$$$	Stylish Northern Italian.
Mamma Maria	3 North Sq	523-0077	$$$$	High-end Italian in a charming townhouse.
McCormick & Schmick's	Faneuil Hall Marketplace	720-5522	$$$$	Enormous fresh seafood selection in steakhouse atmosphere.
Pinang	Faneuil Hall Marketplace	227-6866	$$$	Not to be confused with Penang.
Pizzeria Regina	11 1/2 Thatcher St	227-0765	$	Original location of local landmark.
Prezza	24 Fleet St	227-1577	$$$	High-end Italian.
Sage	69 Prince St	248-8814	$$$$	Italian/American. Might trouble claustrophobics.
Sel de la Terre	255 State St	720-1300	$$$	A taste of Provence.
Taranta	210 Hanover St	720-0052	$$$$	Larger than most upscale North End spots.
Theo's Cozy Corner	162 Salem St	241-0202	$	Cozy diner. Killer hash browns.
Trattoria a Sacalinatella	253 Hanover St	742-8240	$$$$	Top-drawer Italian perched one story up.
Union Oyster House	41 Union St	227-2750	$$$	"Authentic New England" experience since 1826.

Map 3 • Downtown Crossing / Park Square / Bay Village

Aujourd'hui	200 Boylston St	351-2071	$$$$	French/American. Sublime.
Buddha's Delight	3 Beach St	451-2395	$$	All-vegetarian Asian.
Chacarero	426 Washington St	542-0392	$	Unique Chilean sandwich. Lunch, take-away only.
Davio's	75 Arlington St	357-4810	$$$	Refined Northern Italian in new Park Square location.
Dedo	69 Church St	338-9999	$$$	Rib-eye for the queer guy.
Dominic's	255 Tremont St	426-8769	$	Good for quick subs and pizza.
Emperor's Garden	690 Washington St	482-8898	$$$	Dim sum for the masses.
Finale	1 Columbus Ave	423-3184	$$	For the dessert fetishist.
Herrera's Mexican Grille	11 Temple Pl	426-2350	$	Good and cheap Cali-Mex.
Jacob Wirth	31-37 Stuart St	338-8586	$$	German-y. Local institution since 1868.
Krystal's Cafe	12 Church St	348-0012	$	Tiny, terrific. Breakfast, lunch. Bay Village's best secret.
Legal Sea Foods	25 Park Sq	426-4444	$$$	Fresh fish, famous chowder. Legal's sleekest space.
Locke-Ober	3 Winter Pl	542-1340	$$$$	Re-opened. Still has the Brahmin vibe.
Mantra	52 Temple Pl	542-8111	$$$$	French/Indian in a stylish former bank.
McCormick & Schmick's	34 Columbus Ave	482-3999	$$$$	$2 "social hour" bar menu—a great deal.
No 9 Park	9 Park St	742-9991	$$$$	Consistently rated among Boston's best.
Penang	685 Washington St	451-6373	$$$	Well-established Malaysian out of NYC.
Pho Pasteur	123 Stuart St	742-2436	$$	Reliable Vietnamese.
Pigalle	75 S Charles St	423-4944	$$$$	Modern French cuisine in an intimate setting.
Rock Bottom Brewery	115 Stuart St	742-2739	$$	Better food than most brewpubs.
Sam LaGrassa's	44 Province St	357-6861	$	Monster sandwiches. Try the pastrami.
Silvertone Bar & Grill	69 Bromfield St	338-7887	$$	Great after-work lounge with tasty home cooking.
Teatro	177 Tremont St	778-6841	$$$	Sleek Italian next to Loews.
Tequila Mexican Grill	55 Bromfield St	482-8822	$	Muy sabroso hole-in-the-wall.

Map 4 • Financial District / Chinatown

Chau Chow City	83 Essex St	338-8158	$$	Dim sum palace. Open late.
Cosi	53 State St	723-3369	$	Good sandwiches, but not cheap.
Country Life Vegetarian	200 High St	951-2534	$	Affordable option for legume lovers.
Good Life	28 Kingston St	451-2622	$$	For those channeling the Rat Pack.
J Pace & Son	2 Devonshire Pl	227-4949	$	Hot and cold Italian for take-away.
Julien	250 Franklin St	451-1900	$$$	Elegant French in the Langham hotel.
Les Zygomates	129 South St	542-5108	$$$	French bistro. Comprehensive wine list, pleasant bar.
Meritage	70 Rowes Wharf	439-3995	$$$$	Serious about pairing food with wine.
Milk Street Cafe	50 Milk St	542-3663	$	Dependable lunch option. Also in Post Office Square.
New Shanghai	21 Hudson St	338-6688	$$	Critically acclaimed Shanghainese.
News	150 Kneeland St	426-6397	$$	Terrific Leather District late-night spot.
Ocean Wealth	8 Tyler St	423-1338	$$	Cantonese seafood specialists.
Peach Farm	4 Tyler St	482-1116	$$	Family-style Cantonese. Cool seafood tanks.
Peking Tom's	25 Kingston St	482-6282	$$$	High-energy "Chinese."
Pho Hoa	17 Beach St	423-3934	$	Phat pho.
Radius	8 High St	426-1234	$$$$	A Financial District jewel. Expensive, worth it.
Sakurabana	57 Broad St	542-4311	$$	Good bet for low-key sushi.
Shabu-Zen	16 Tyler St	292-8828	$$	Japanese in Chinatown. Come with a group.
South Street Diner	178 Kneeland St	350-0028	$	Open all night.
Sultan's Kitchen	72 Broad St	338-7819	$	Terrific Turkish. A great lunch choice.
Taiwan Cafe	34 Oxford St	426-8181	$$	For opponents of the PRC's "one China" policy.
Vault	105 Water St	292-9966	$$$$	Take a client.

279

Arts & Entertainment · **Selected Restaurants**

Key: $: Under $10 / $$: $10–$20 / $$$: $20-$30 / $$$$: $30+. Area codes are 617 unless otherwise noted.

Map 5 · Back Bay (West) / Fenway (East)

Bangkok City	167 Massachusetts Ave	266-8884	$$$	Solid Thai served in a large, blue room.
Bangkok Cuisine	177A Massachusetts Ave	262-5377	$$$	Less fancy than Bangkok City, but just as tasty.
Betty's Wok & Noodle Diner	250 Huntington Ave	424-1950	$$	Reliable, if uninspiring, stir-fry joint.
Cactus Club	939 Boylston St	236-0200	$$	Loud, popular. There's better Tex-Mex nearby.
Cafe Jaffa	48 Gloucester St	536-0230	$	Affordable, delicious Mediterranean cafe.
Capital Grille	359 Newbury St	262-8900	$$$$	Arise, Sir Loin!
Ciao Bella	240A Newbury St	536-2626	$$$	Your server is the dish to admire here.
Clio	370A Commonwealth Ave	536-7200	$$$$	Sublime spot in the Eliot Hotel.
Island Hopper	91 Massachusetts Ave	266-1618	$$	Malaysian, Chinese, Thai.
L'Espalier	30 Gloucester St	262-3023	$$$$	One of Boston's best.
Legal Sea Foods	800 Boylston St	266-6800	$$$	Above the Kendall Square T stop.
Lir	903 Boylston St	778-0089	$$	"Upscale Irish." Large, handy for sports watchers.
Other Side Cosmic Cafe	407 Newbury St	536-9477	$	Good for a bite and beer on nice days.
Shanti: Taste of India	277B Huntington Ave	867-9700	$$$	Refined curry house behind Symphony Hall.
Sonsie	327 Newbury St	351-2500	$$$	People-watching mainstay. Nice French-doors street exposure.
Tapeo	266 Newbury St	267-4799	$$$	Tapas. Sip sangria outside on warm days.
Trident Booksellers and Cafe	338 Newbury St	267-8688	$	All-day breakfast in a cool bookstore.
Vinny T's	867 Boylston St	262-6699	$$$	Red sauce theme park. Count on leftovers.

Map 6 · Back Bay (East) / South End (Upper)

33	33 Stanhope St	572-3311	$$$$	Swanky. Big hit with major leaguers.
Abe & Louie's	793 Boylston St	536-6300	$$$$	Steak. Local riposte to Morton's and Capital Grille.
Bangkok Blue	651 Boylston St	266-1010	$$	Standard Thai. Some outdoor seating.
Bomboa	35 Stanhope St	236-6363	$$$	Brazilian hot-spot. Have a mojito or caipirinha.
Brasserie Jo	120 Huntington Ave	425-3240	$$$	French brasserie near Symphony Hall. Usually very busy.
Charlie's Sandwich Shoppe	429 Columbus Ave	536-7669	$	Been here forever. A good lunch choice.
Claremont Cafe	535 Columbus Ave	247-9001	$$	(Too) popular for weekend brunch. Good scones, though.
Fire & Ice	31 St James Ave	482-3473	$$	For when "fun" is more important than "food."
Geoffrey's Cafe Bar	160 Commonwealth Ave	266-1122	$$	A reliable spot, relocated from the South End.
George, An American Tavern	384 Boylston St	859-8555	$$	Handy Boylston Street meeting place. Relatively inexpensive.
Grill 23 & Bar	161 Berkeley St	542-2255	$$$$	Classic steakhouse. Ideal for business dinners.
Grillfish	162 Columbus Ave	357-1620	$$$	Self-explanatory. Check out the mural.
House of Siam	542 Columbus Ave	267-1755	$$	Solid Thai cuisine in pleasant surroundings.
Jae's	520 Columbus Ave	421-9405	$$$	Try the crispy Pad Thai. Sushi also.
Mistral	223 Columbus Ave	867-9300	$$$$	Superb. Great bar, too. Look sharp.
Osushi	10 Huntington Ave	266-2788	$$$	Sushi in the Westin Copley.
Pho Pasteur	119 Newbury St	262-8200	$$	Reliable Vietnamese.
Rouge	480 Columbus Ave	867-0600	$$$	For Delta delights.

Map 7 · South End (Lower)

Addis Red Sea	544 Tremont St	426-8727	$$	Ethiopian. Get jiggy with some injera.
Aquitaine	569 Tremont St	424-8577	$$$$	A solid French bistro.
B&G Oysters	550 Tremont St	423-0550	$$$	Stylish oyster shop. Good wine list.
Caffe Umbra	1395 Washington St	867-0707	$$$	Increasingly popular; justly so.
Delux Cafe	100 Chandler St	338-5258	$$	Small, hip spot with good eats, music.
Dish	253 Shawmut Ave	426-7866	$$$	Popular bistro. Outdoor seating.
Emilio's	536 Tremont St	423-4083	$	Solid choice for pizza and subs. Delivery.
flour bakery & cafe	1595 Washington St	267-4300	$	Flour Power.
Franklin Cafe	278 Shawmut Ave	350-0010	$$$	Delicious late-night option.

Garden of Eden	571 Tremont St	247-8377	$$	Popular bruncheonette. Associated with Lionette's next door.
Hamersley's Bistro	553 Tremont St	423-2700	$$$$	Outstanding. Deserves its reputation.
Joe V's	315 Shawmut Ave	338-5638	$$$	Casual, mostly pizza and pasta. Weekend brunch, too.
Masa	439 Tremont St	338-8884	$$$	Southwestern. A stylish South End secret.
Metropolis Cafe	584 Tremont St	247-2931	$$	A safe bet, but habitually crowded.
Mike's City Diner	1714 Washington St	267-9393	$	A trusty not-too-greasy spoon.
Morse Fish	1401 Washington St	262-9375	$$	The neighborhood's only fish shack.
Nicole's	639 Tremont St	266-0223	$	Pizza, sandwiches, and their ilk.
Nightingale	578 Tremont St	236-5658	$$$$	Chirpy, cheery newcomer.
On the Park	1 Union Park	426-0862	$$	Relatively unknown. Great food, pleasant room.
Perdix	560 Tremont St	338-8070	$$$	Newly relocated from Jamaica Plain. Yummy.
Pho Republique	1415 Washington St	262-0005	$$	Vietnamese gets the South End treatment.
Red Fez	1222 Washington St	338-6060	$$$	Open late. Red fez not required for entry.
Sister Sorel	645 Tremont St	266-4600	$$	Smaller, younger, cheaper sibling of Tremont 647.
Thai Village	592 Tremont St	536-6548	$$	Not as good as House of Siam.
Tremont 647	647 Tremont St	266-4600	$$$	One of the South End's best.
Union Bar and Grille	1357 Washington St	423-0555	$$$$	Newcomer with great food and feel. Worth checking out.

Map 8 • Charlestown

Brothers	156 Bunker Hill St	242-7333	$	Proudly serving "International Cuisine." They deliver.
Figs	67 Main St	242-2229	$$$	Charlestown branch of upscale pizza chain.
Ironside Grill	25 Park St	242-1384	$$$	Formerly managed by Raymond Burr.
Jenny's Pizza	320 Medford St	242-9474	$	Subs too. Nice view of the, erm, Autoport.
Meze Estiatorio	100 City Sq	242-6393	$$$	Greek newcomer in a well-windowed room.
Ninety Nine	29 Austin St	242-8999	$$	... bottles of beer on the wall ...
Olives	10 City Sq	242-1999	$$$$	Mediterranean mecca. Finally taking reservations.
Paolo's Trattoria	251 Main St	242-7229	$$$	Italian, including wood-oven-cooked pizzas.
Souper Salad	126 High St	542-3157	$	"Super Salad"? "Soup or Salad"? Well?
Tangierino	83 Main St	242-6009	$$$	Rockin' Moroccan.
Warren Tavern	2 Pleasant St	241-8142	$$	One of Paul Revere's favorite watering holes.

Map 9 • East Boston

Cafe Belo	254 Bennington St	561-0833	$	Brazilian cafeteria.
Cafe Italia	150 Meridian St	561-6480	$$	For enjoying jazz with coffee and dessert.
La Terraza	19 Bennington St	561-5200	$$	Straight-forward Colombian cooking. Try the flan.
Nana Cora's	295 Bennington St	569-1551	$$	Traditional Italian. Open Thursday through Saturday only.
Santarpio's Pizza	111 Cheslea St	567-9871	$	Thin and crispy. No need to dress up.
Topacio	120 Meridian St	567-9523	$$	Salvadoran. Try the seafood soup.
Uncle Pete's Hickory Ribs	309 Bennington St	569-7427	$$	East Boston's real deal.

Map 10 • South Boston (West) / Fort Point

Amrheins	80 W Broadway	268-6189	$$	Has been here since Southie was mostly German.
Baltic Deli & Cafe	632 Dorchester Ave	268-2435	$	Foods from the old country.
Barking Crab	88 Sleeper St	426-2722	$$	Make a mess while viewing the harbor skyline.
Boston Beer Garden	734 E Broadway	269-0990	$$	Had a makeover recently. Long wine list, too.
Cafe Porto Bello	672 E Broadway	269-7680	$$	Straight-forward, honest Italian.
Lucky's	355 Congress St	357-5825	$$	Well-liked retro cocktail lounge. Music most nights.
Playwright	658 E Broadway	269-2537	$$	For socializing and television watching.
Salsa's Mexican Grill	118 Dorchester St	269-7878	$$	Legit Mexican. Newly expanded.

Map 11 • South Boston (East)

Aura	1 Seaport Ln	385-4300	$$$$	In the Seaport Hotel.
Farragut House	149 P St	268-1212	$$	New England fare close to the bay.
No-Name Restaurant	15 Fish Pier Rd	338-7539	$$	Attracts tourists and waterfront workers alike.
Red's Eastside Grill	81 L St	269-0722	$$$	Dinner only. Decent wine list.

Key: $: Under $10 / $$: $10–$20 / $$$: $20-$30 / $$$$: $30+. Area codes are 617 unless otherwise noted.

Map 12 · Newmarket / Andrew Square

224 Boston Street	224 Boston St	265-1217	$$	A cut above its neighbors. New American.
Cafe Polonia	611 Dorchester Ave	269-0110	$	Polish. Small, inviting, authentic. Have a Zywiec.
Victoria	1024 Massachusetts Ave	442-5965	$$	Diner. Good choice before hitting the highway.

Map 13 · Roxbury

Bob the Chef's	604 Columbus Ave	536-6204	$$	For those needing a soul food fix.
Breezeway Bar and Grill	153 Blue Hill Ave	541-5400	$$	Decent American. Occasional live music.
Merengue	156 Blue Hill Ave	445-5403	$$	Dominican. Tropical vibe. Gets props from the Sox.

Map 14 · Jamaica Plain

Arbor	711 Centre St	522-1221	$$$	High-concept Mediterranean in a sleek space.
Bukhara	701 Centre St	522-2195	$$$	Well-liked Indian bistro.
Centre Street Cafe	699 Centre St	524-9217	$$	Groovy, particularly for brunch.
Doyle's Cafe	3484 Washington St	524-2345	$$	Reliable landmark. Serves decent pubgrub.
El Oriental de Cuba	416 Centre St	524-6464	$	A good place to lunch on a cubano.
Jake's Boss BBQ	3492 Washington St	983-3701	$	JP's top pig shack.
James's Gate	5 McBride St	983-2000	$$	Laid-back Irish gastropub.
JP Seafood Cafe	730 Centre St	983-5177	$$	Japanese-Korean.
Purple Cactus Burrito & Wrap	674 Centre St	522-7422	$	Satisfactory storefront.
Tacos El Charro	349 Centre St	983-9275	$$	Actual Mexican food.
Ten Tables	597 Centre St	524-8810	$$$	Short, precise, inspired menu.
Wonder Spice Cafe	697 Centre St	522-0200	$$	Tasty Cambodian/Thai. Well named.

Map 15 · Fenway (West) / Mission Hill

Brown Sugar Cafe	129 Jersey St	266-2928	$$	Thai. Very popular, deservedly so.
Buteco	130 Jersey St	247-9508	$$	Brazilian. Good for casual meat appreciation.
El Pelon Taqueria	92 Peterborough St	262-9090	$	Great value in a Fenway storefront.
Linwood Grill & BBQ	81 Kilmarnock St	247-8099	$$	Satisfactory barbecue. Live music in adjoining room.
Mississippi's	103 Terrace St	541-4411	$	Good for a hot lunch.
Rod Dee II	94 Peterborough St	859-0969	$	Ideal for Thai take-out.
Sorento's	86 Peterborough St	424-7070	$$	Darn good pasta and pizza.

Map 16 · Kenmore Square / Brookline (East)

Ankara Cafe	472 Commonwealth Ave	437-0404	$	Turkish place popular with student snackers.
Audubon Circle	838 Beacon St	421-1910	$$	Chill out with tasty bar food.
BB Wolf	109 Brookline Ave	247-2227	$$	Barbecue. Not related to Japanese band Guitar Wolf.
Boston Beer Works	61 Brookline Ave	536-2337	$$	Cavernous suds shop across from Fenway Park.
Cafe Belo	636 Beacon St	236-8666	$	Brazilian cafeteria.
Chef Chang's House	1004 Beacon St	277-4226	$$	Not exemplary, but not a bankbuster.
Great Bay	500 Commonwealth Ave	532-5000	$$$$	Elegant seafood newcomer.
India Quality	484 Commonwealth Ave	267-4499	$$	Quality Indian.
Sol Azteca	914A Beacon St	262-0909	$$$	Satisfying Mexican fusion. Try the mole.

Map 17 · Coolidge Corner / Brookline Hills

Anna's Taqueria	1412 Beacon St	739-7300	$	A cheap way to fill up.
B&D Deli	1653 Beacon St	232-3727	$$	Famous Jewish deli. A Brookline landmark.
Baja Betty's Burritos	3 Harvard Sq	277-8900	$	Tops taqueria.
Boca Grande	1294 Beacon St	739-3900	$	Lots of good taqueria fare. Consider ordering carnitas.
Cafe Mirror	362 Washington St	779-9662	$	Sandwiches and small bites.
Cafe St Petersburg	236 Washington St	277-7100	$$$	Boston's finest Russian restaurant. Na zdrov'e!
Fajitas & 'Ritas	48 Boylston St	566-1222	$$	Better crayon graffiti than Mexican food.
Fugakyu	1280 Beacon St	738-1268	$$$	Sushi, very popular. Be prepared to wait.
Lucy's	242 Harvard St	232-5829	$$	Low-fat focused. Try the "no fry French fries."
Matt Murphy's Pub	14 Harvard St	232-0188	$$	Well-liked Irish pub. Good food.

Pho Lemon Grass	239 Harvard St	731-8600	$$	Pho, Brookline-style.
Seoul Kitchen	349 Washington St	787-2822	$$	Japanese/Korean, with some sushi and Thai.
Soho	386 Market St	562-6000	$$$	Sleek, large dining spot-cum-nightclub.
Tsunami	10 Pleasant St	277-8008	$$$	Satisfactory sushi spot.
Village Fish	22 Harvard St	566-3474	$$	Neighborhood standby.
Village Smokehouse	1 Harvard St	566-3782	$$	Best barbecue in Brookline.
Washington Square Tavern	714 Washington St	231-8989	$$	Decent American food, slightly overpriced.

Map 18 · Brighton

Bamboo	1616 Commonwealth Ave	734-8192	$$	Very good Thai at Washington Street.
Bangkok Bistro	1952 Beacon St	739-7270	$$	Thai for the BC crowd.
Bluestone Bistro	1799 Commonwealth Ave	254-8309	$$	Pizza and pasta, small and hopping.
Devlin's	332 Washington St	779-8822	$$$	A little better than other places near here.
Harry's Bar & Grill	1430 Commonwealth Ave	738-9990	$$	Neighborhood pub replaces The Elbow Room.
Green Briar	304 Washington St	789-4100	$$	Pub with frequent live rock.
Jasmine Bistro	412 Market St	789-4676	$$	Hungarian-French-Lebanese. Somehow this works.
Tasca	1612 Commonwealth Ave	730-8002	$$	Tapas, Spanish wine.

Map 19 · Allston (South) / Brookline (North)

Anna's Taqueria	446 Harvard St	227-7111	$	A cheap way to fill up.
Brown Sugar Cafe	1033 Commonwealth Ave	787-4242	$$	Thai. Very popular, deservedly so.
Buddha's Delight	404 Harvard St	739-8830	$$	All-vegetarian Asian.
Cafe Belo	181 Brighton Ave	783-4858	$	Brazilian cafeteria.
Cafe Brazil	421 Cambridge St	789-5980	$$	Authentic, home-style Brazilian.
Coolidge Corner Clubhouse	307 Harvard St	566-4948	$$	"Sports bar" describes portions, food quality, ambiance.
El Cafetal	479 Cambridge St	789-4009	$$	Co-yum-bian.
Istanbul Cafe	1414 Commonwealth Ave	232-1700	$$$	Relocated from Beacon Hill, still excellent. Atatürk!
Rubin's	500 Harvard St	731-8787	$	Kosher. Tuck into some pastrami.
Saigon	431 Cambridge St	254-3373	$$	Vietnamese with a pleasant vibe. Good value.
Spike's Junkyard Dogs	108 Brighton Ave	254-7700	$	Vegetarian, as well as more traditional, hot dogs.
Sunset Grill & Tap	130 Brighton Ave	254-1331	$$	Live rock nightly. Showcases local bands.
V Majestic	164 Brighton Ave	782-6088	$	Perhaps Allston's best cheap Vietnamese.
Zaftigs Delicatessen	335 Harvard St	975-0075	$$	Popular deli with all-day breakfast.

Map 20 · Harvard Square / Allston (North)

9 Tastes	50 JFK St	547-6666	$$	Good Thai in a cheery basement.
Border Cafe	32 Church St	864-6100	$$	Feeding students quality Tex-Mex for many years.
Brother Jimmy's BBQ	96 Winthrop St	547-7427	$$	New York import in old House of Blues.
Caffe Paradiso	1 Eliot Sq	868-3240	$	For students getting their just desserts.
Cambridge, 1	27 Church St	576-1111	$$	Tasty pizzas, salads. Relaxed, stripped-down space.
Casablanca	40 Brattle St	876-0999	$$$	Still popular with the Harvard crowd.
Chez Henri	1 Shepard St	354-8980	$$$	French/Cuban bistro.
Finale	30 Dunster St	441-9797	$$	For the dessert fetishist.
Greenhouse Coffee Shop	3 Brattle St	354-3184	$	Affordable, old-style coffee shop.
Grendel's Den	89 Winthrop St	491-1050	$$	For the laid-back academic. Reasonable prices.
Harvest	44 Brattle St	868-2255	$$$$	Excellent. Nice garden terrace.
Hi-Rise Bread Company	56 Brattle St	492-3003	$	Tasty, but bring some extra cash.
John Harvard's Brew House	33 Dunster St	868-3585	$$	Large and loud, good for crowds.
Mr & Mrs Bartley's Burger Cottage	1246 Massachusetts Ave	354-6559	$	Campus-y burger joint across from the Yard.
Pho Pasteur	36 Dunster St	864-4100	$$	Reliable Vietnamese.
Rialto	1 Bennett St	661-5050	$$$$	Probably Cambridge's finest restaurant.
Shilla	57 JFK St	547-7971	$$	Quiet, subterranean Japanese/Korean.
UpStairs on the Square	91 Winthrop St	864-1933	$$$$	Neoclassical food in an expressionist room.
Veggie Planet	47 Palmer St	661-1513	$	At Club Passim. Mostly for pizzas, some vegan.

Arts & Entertainment · **Selected Restaurants**

Key: $: Under $10 / $$: $10–$20 / $$$: $20-$30 / $$$$: $30+. Area codes are 617 unless otherwise noted.

Map 21 • West Cambridge

Aspasia	377 Walden St	864-4745	$$$$	Mediterranean prepared with care.
Full Moon	344 Huron Ave	354-6699	$$	For a night out with the children.
Hi-Rise Bread Company	208 Concord Ave	876-8766	$	Tasty, but bring some extra cash.
Il Buongustaio	370 Huron Ave	491-3133	$	Very good pizzas, calzones, paninis.
Real Pizza	359 Huron Ave	497-4497	$$	Pizzeria associated with Hi-Rise Bread Company.
Tokyo	307 Fresh Pond Pkwy	876-6600	$$	Good for the lunch buffet.
Trattoria Pulcinella	147 Huron Ave	491-6336	$$$$	For those not going to the North End.

Map 22 • North Cambridge / West Somerville

Cafe Barada	2269 Massachusetts Ave	354-2112	$	Relaxed Middle Eastern.
Elephant Walk	2067 Massachusetts Ave	492-6900	$$$	French-Cambodian local legend.
Jasper White's Summer Shack	149 Alewife Brook Pkwy	520-9500	$$$	Seafood. More a hangar than a shack.
Jose's	131 Sherman St	354-0335	$$	So-so Mexican cantina.
Redbones	55 Chester St	628-2200	$$	Don't dig on swine? Then come for the beers.

Map 23 • Central Somerville / Porter Square

Anna's Taqueria	236 Elm St	666-3900	$	A cheap way to fill up.
Anna's Taqueria	822 Somerville Ave	661-8500	$	A cheap way to fill up.
Blue Fin	1815 Massachusetts Ave	497-8022	$$	Best sushi bang for your yen.
Christopher's	1920 Massachusetts Ave	876-9180	$$	Good for relaxing on a wet day.
Diva Indian Bistro	246 Elm St	629-4963	$$	Flashy and tasty, but pricy.
Kaya	1924 Massachusetts Ave	497-5656	$$$	Japanese/Korean. Decent food, uninspiring vibe.
Out of the Blue	382 Highland Ave	776-5020	$$	Good value for seafood, Italian. Colorful room.
RF O'Sullivan's	282 Beacon St	492-7773	$$	Quite possibly the best burgers in Boston.
Rosebud Diner	381 Summer St	666-6015	$$	Wise choice for a comfort food fix.
Savannah Grill	233 Elm St	666-4200	$$	Straight-forward, good-value Mediterranean.
Sound Bites	708 Broadway	623-8338	$	For filling breakfasts.

Map 24 • Winter Hill / Union Square

Neighborhood Restaurant & Bakery	25 Bow St	623-9710	$	Big, good breakfasts + patio = summer morning bliss.
Taqueria la Mexicana	247 Washington St	776-5232	$	The real deal. Terrific flautas.
Vinny's at Night	76 Broadway	628-1921	$$$	Quality home-style Italian tucked behind a deli.

Map 26 • East Cambridge / Kendall Square / MIT

Ajanta	145 First St	491-0075	$$	Good-value Indian enjoyed by proximate techies.
Black Sheep Cafe	350 Main St	577-1300	$$	In the Kendall Hotel. Go for breakfast.
The Blue Room	1 Kendall Sq	494-9034	$$$$	Terrific food, popular. Somehow elegant and casual.
Cheesecake Factory	100 Cambridgeside Pl	252-3810	$$$	Done shopping? Unsatisfied? Continue your consumption here.
Court House Seafood	498 Cambridge St	491-1213	$$	One step removed from bobbing for fish.
Davio's	5 Cambridge Pkwy	661-4810	$$$$	Good food, but it's about the river view.
El Coqui	561 Cambridge St	876-6500	$$	Puerto Rican newcomer.
Helmand	143 First St	492-4646	$$	Delightful, authentic. Family ties with Afghanistan's president.
Legal Sea Foods	5 Cambridge Ctr	864-3400	$$$	Above the Kendall T stop.
Second Street Cafe	89 Second St	661-1311	$$	Plenty of fresh, inexpensive choices.

Map 27 · Central Square / Cambridgeport

Asgard	350 Massachusetts Ave	577-9100	$$	Enormous "Celtic" gastropub.
Asmara	739 Massachusetts Ave	864-7447	$$	The only Ethiopian restaurant in Cambridge.
Brookline Lunch	9 Brookline St	354-2983	$	Popular diner. For food, not service.
Centro	720 Massachusetts Ave	868-2405	$$$$	Fancy Italian in sedate surroundings.
Dolphin Seafood	1105 Massachusetts Ave	661-2937	$$	Unpretentious fish house.
Green Street Grill	280 Green St	876-1655	$$$	Food with a slow burn. Live music.
Hi-Fi Pizza & Subs	496 Massachusetts Ave	492-4600	$	Soak up the beer you drank at T.T.'s.
India Pavilion	17 Central Sq	547-7463	$$	Reliable Indian. A decent value.
Johnny's Luncheonette	1105 Massachusetts Ave	495-0055	$$	All-day breakfast and other diner dishes.
La Groceria	853 Main St	497-4214	$$	Still there. Still good.
Mary Chung	464 Massachusetts Ave	864-1991	$$	Going strong.
Middle East	472 Massachusetts Ave	492-9181	$$	Venerable venue that gets high-profile music bookings.
Miracle of Science	321 Massachusetts Ave	868-2866	$$	Energetic neighborhood mainstay. Now serving breakfast!
Moody's Falafel Palace	25 Central Sq	864-0827	$	Located in what was once a White Tavern.
Picante Mexican Grill	735 Massachusetts Ave	576-6394	$	Cali-Mex. Pretty good salsas.
Salts	798 Main St	876-8444	$$$$	Small, upscale, and very tasty.
Sunny's Diner	7 Landsdowne St	491-9550	$	A reliable greasy spoon. Good for breakfast.
ZuZu!	474 Massachusetts Ave	492-9181	$$	Funky, colorful. Make a meal of maza.

Map 28 · Inman Square

1369	1369 Cambridge St	576-1369	$	Reliable, chill Inman Square coffee shop.
Amelia's Trattoria	111 Harvard St	868-7600	$$$	The best Italian in this area.
Argana	1287 Cambridge St	868-1247	$$$	Engaging North African.
Atasca	279 Broadway	354-4355	$$$	Prodigious Portuguese. Smaller sibling is around the corner.
B-Side Lounge	92 Hampshire St	354-0766	$$	Hip spot that deserves its reputation.
Dali	415 Washington St	661-3254	$$$	Fun taparia. Worth the wait.
East Coast Grill & Raw Bar	1271 Cambridge St	491-6568	$$$	Awesome seafood, barbecue. Try the Hell Sausage.
Emma's Pizzeria	40 Hampshire St	864-8534	$$	Design your own gourmet pie. Worth waiting.
EVOO	118 Beacon St	661-3866	$$$$	Creative cuisine. Possibly Somerville's best restaurant.
Koreana	154 Prospect St	576-8661	$$$	One of the area's better Korean restaurants.
Magnolia's	1193 Cambridge St	576-1971	$$$	Southern, Cajun. Try the fried chicken.
Oleana	134 Hampshire St	661-0505	$$$$	Top-notch Mediterranean. Patio seating in warm weather.
S&S Restaurant	1334 Cambridge St	357-0777	$$$	Serving deli, comfort food for eighty years.

If you're looking for books in Boston, you've got plenty of choices. If you want to pick up a coffee, CD, DVD, SUV, or condo while you shop for books, try one of the gigantic chain stores like **Barnes & Noble** or **Borders**. For the more discerning shopper, there are also a ton of specialty and used bookstores full of obscure titles, dusty out-of-print books, and Cambridge folk.

General New/Used

WordsWorth in Harvard Square is one of the best places to get a book and get out. Aside from free bookmarks, books are all they have. They more or less stock the same general books as the chain stores, are well organized, and reasonably priced. The **Avenue Victor Hugo Bookshop** on Newbury Street is an enjoyable, friendly place to get a used book. In Downtown Crossing, and not on Brattle Street in Cambridge where the name would make you think, there's the **Brattle Book Shop**, with its outdoor used book racks. Also worth checking out in Downtown Crossing is **Lame Duck Books**, a good place to look for first editions and rare books. If you're in Central Square and want to browse, stop into **Rodney's Bookstore**. **McIntyre & Moore** is worth a look if you're hanging out in Davis Square.

Specialty

In Downtown Crossing, the **Boston Globe Bookstore** offers historical Boston tomes. You can also pick up blown-up headline reprints such as the Titanic sinking/Fenway Park opening, the Patriots' 2002 Super Bowl win, and various close-ups of Larry Bird's mullet and mustache. Over on State Street is the **Rand McNally** shop, fulfilling all your travel needs.

Ars Libri has an exemplary collection of rare and out-of-print fine art books. The two GLBT bookstores in Boston are **We Think the World of You** (in the South End) and **Calamus** (near South Station). A big tip of the chapeau is due to **Schoenhof's Foreign Books** and its incredible selection. **Lucy Parsons Center** relocated from Cambridge to the South End a few years ago and continues to stock a wide variety of progressive titles.

In Allston, there's **Mister Music,** just in case you need the chord changes to "Stairway to Heaven." The best computer bookstore in town is Kendall Square's **Quantum Books**, which is suitably situated next to MIT.

There are also bookstores for the 4 million colleges in town, as well a bunch of **Buck A Books**, where most books are actually more than one dollar. Liars.

Harvard Square

Harvard Square has more than 25 bookstores—the greatest concentration of bookstores in the city (and perhaps the country). **WordsWorth** and **Harvard Book Store** (not affiliated with the university) are the two largest general stores in Harvard Square. Both are worth spending some quality time in. Don't overlook the **Harvard Coop**, which has plenty of books, magazines and maps along with its professor-assigned titles. **Globe Corner Bookstore** is also worth investigating. Grolier Poetry Book Shop, a national poetry landmark for many years, has closed.

Area codes are 617 unless otherwise noted

Map 1 • Beacon Hill / West End

Antiquarian Books Of Boston	310 Washington St	292-4700	Used
Barnes & Noble Booksellers	395 Washington St	426-5184	Chain–general
Suffolk University Bookstore	148 Cambridge St	227-4085	Books for their courses

Map 2 • North End / Faneuil Hall

Buck A Book	38 Court St	367-9419	

Map 3 • Downtown Crossing / Park Square / Bay Village

Borders Books & Music	10 School St	557-7188	Chain
Brattle Book Shop	9 West St	542-0210	Used
Children's Book Shop	237 Washington St	734-7323	Children's books
Commonwealth Books	134 Bolyston St	338-6328	Academic books
Cowley & Cathedral Bookstore	28 Temple Pl	423-4719	Religious books
Downtown Books	697 Washington St	426-7644	General

Emerson College Bookstore	80 Bolyston St	728-7700	Textbooks and some trade books
Fellowship Emanuel Bookstore	354 Tremont St	542-4342	General & Spanish books
James & Devon Gray Booksellers	12 Arrow St	868-0752	Antique books
Lame Duck Books	55 Temple Pl	542-2376	First editions
Massachusetts Bible Society Bookstore	41 Bromfield St	542-2224	Religious books
Suffolk Law School Book Store	110 Tremont St	227-8874	Law books
Tufts Medical Bookstore	136 Harrison Ave	636-6628	Medical, veterinary and dental

Map 4 • Financial District / Leather District / Chinatown

Barbara's Best Sellers	720 Atlantic Ave	443-0060	General
Calamus Bookstore	92 South St	338-1931	General
Central China Book Co	44 Kneeland St	426-0888	General
Cheetah Trading Co	75 Kneeland St	451-1309	General
F A Bernett	144 Lincoln St	350-7778	Art books
Kok Wa Co	8A Tyler St	695-3228	General
Rand McNally	84 State St	720-1125	Travel books

Map 5 • Back Bay (West) / Fenway (East)

Avenue Victor Hugo Book Shop	353 Newbury St	266-7746	Used–general
Barnes & Noble Booksellers	111 Huntington Ave	247-6959	Chain–general
Berklee College of Music Bookstore	1080 Boylston St	267-0023	Music books
Black Library Booksellers	325 Huntington Ave	442-2400	African American books
Christian Science Reading Room	175 Huntington Ave	247-6483	Christian Science
Christian Science Reading Room	194 Massachusetts Ave	247-6483	
Music Espresso	295 Huntington Ave	424-9322	Music books
Trident Booksellers	338 Newbury St	267-8688	General

Map 6 • Back Bay (East) / South End (Upper)

Brentano's	100 Huntington Ave	859-9511	Chain
Brentano's At Copley Place	100 Huntington Ave	859-9511	General
Bromer Booksellers	607 Boylston St	247-2818	Rare
Buddenbooks Fine & Rare Books	31 Newbury St	536-4433	Fine and rare books
Lucy Parsons Center	549 Columbus Ave	267-6272	Political books
Spencer's Mystery Bookshop	223 Newbury St	262-0880	New and used mysteries

Map 7 • South End (Lower)

Ars Libri	500 Harrison Ave	357-5212	Art and art history
Boston University Medical Center	700 Albany St	638-5496	Medical books
Grolier Poetry Book Shop Inc	6 Plympton St	547-4648	Poetry books
Red Book Store	549 Columbus Ave	267-6272	Political books
Seven Stars	731 Massachusetts Ave	547-1317	New age
We Think The World Of You Bookstore	540 Tremont St	574-5000	Travel Books

Map 9 • East Boston

| Pathfinder Books | 12 Bennington St | 569-9169 | Political books |

Map 12 • Newmarket / Andrew Square

Gardenias Bookstore	399 Dorchester St	268-6600	New Age pagan books
Kate's Mystery Books	2211 Massachusetts Ave	491-2660	New and used mysteries
Revolution Books	1156 Massachusetts Ave	492-5443	Political books

Map 14 • Jamaica Plain

Boston Book Co	705 Centre St	522-2100	Rare books
Jamaicaway Books & Gifts	676 Centre St	983-3204	General
Rhythm & Muse	470 Centre St	524-6622	General

Map 15 • Fenway (West) / Longwood / Mission Hill

Medical Center Coop	333 Longwood Ave	499-3300	Medical and general
Northeastern University Bookstore	360 Huntington Ave	373-2286	Academic–general
Roxbury Community College Bookstore	1234 Columbus Ave	442-8150	Books required for their courses
Simmons College Book Store	300 The Fenway	521-2054	Books for their courses

Map 16 • Kenmore Square / Brookline (East)

Barnes & Noble at Boston University	660 Beacon St	267-8484	Chain
Comicopia	464 Commonwealth Ave	266-4266	Comic books
Emmanuel College Bookstore	400 The Fenway	264-7697	Academic books

Map 19 • Allston (South) / Brookline (North)

Barnes & Noble Booksellers	325 Harvard St	232-0594	Chain
Brookline Booksmith	279 Harvard St	566-6660	General
Israel Book Shop	410 Harvard St	781-961-4989	Books about Israel
New England Comics	131 Harvard Ave	783-1848	Comic books
Russian Bookstore	1217A Commonwealth Ave	783-1590	Russian books

Map 20 • Harvard Square / Allston (North)

Curious George Goes to Wordsworth	1 JFK St	498-0062	
Globe Corner Bookstore	28 Church St	859-8008	General
Harvard Book Store	1256 Massachusetts Ave	661-1515	General
Harvard Coop	1400 Massachusetts Ave	499-2000	Academic–general
Schoenhof's Foreign Books	76A Mt Auburn St	547-8855	Foreign language books
Wordsworth	30 Brattle St	354-5201	General

Map 22 • North Cambridge / West Somerville / Davis Square

Sasuga Japanese Bookstore	7 Upland Rd	497-5460	Japanese books

Map 23 • Central Somerville / Porter Square

McIntyre & Moore Books	255 Elm St	629-4840	General

Map 25 • East Somerville / Sullivan Square

Borders Books & Music	100 Cambridgeside Pl	679-0887	Chain
MIT Coop	3 Cambridge Ctr	499-3200	Academic–general
Quantum Books	4 Cambridge Ctr	494-5042	Technical books

It's hard to believe that the lower end of Newbury Street was once considered down-market, but in the twenty-first century the whole span of Newbury offers something for the serious shopper (particularly those with a little extra cash). Downtown Crossing is Boston's once and future "high street," catering to people from all parts of Boston (i.e., not just those from Back Bay). As retail becomes increasingly dominated by big players, so too have Boston's urban malls (such as the Prudential Center, Copley Square, and Cambridgeside Galleria) become more popular and successful. We're not yet ready to declare Harvard Square a "mall."

Food

For splendid snacks, try **DeLuca's** and **Savenor's** on Beacon Hill, **The Butcher Shop** and **Lionette's** in the South End, **Cremaldi's** and **Cardullo's** in Cambridge, or any one of a few dozen shops in the North End. Among the major supermarket chains, **Trader Joe's** has the best frozen foods and bargains, **Whole Foods** has good fish and prepared foods but is overpriced for staples, and **Super 88** has all the cool Asian stuff. Both **Star Market** and **Shaw's** are owned by British behemoth J Sainsbury, but now that the new Shaw's is open on Huntington Avenue, they could be owned by Enron for all we care.

Area codes are 617 unless otherwise noted.

Clothing

There's more than just **Filene's Basement**, you know. Well-heeled Cantabrigians shopping for women's clothing should try **Tess**. In Downtown Crossing, **H & M** sells clothes that are both cheap and stylish. For a selection of "previously enjoyed" clothing, check out **Boomerangs**. If you need outdoors gear, check out **Hilton's Tent City**. Need running shoes, a ski hat, or a Speedo? Try **City Sports**. For vintage clothes, check out **The Garment District** (which stays open late during the Halloween season).

Shelter

Just moved? Need a few things for the apartment? **Economy Hardware** has carved out a little niche by selling inexpensive furniture along with all the nuts and bolts—they're slightly pricy but the people who went there tend to be yuppies. **Kitchen Arts** for fun gadgets. **Crate & Barrel** covers a lot of ground in both the kitchen and the rest of the home. Don't overlook **Home Depot** when shopping for home miscellany, even though neither the Somerville location nor the South Bay Mall location is convenient to the T.

Map 1 · Beacon Hill / West End

Black Ink	101 Charles St	723-3883	A blend of quirky and handy gifts.
DeLuca's Market	11 Charles St	523-4343	Good deli, pricy fruit, wine and beer downstairs.
Hilton's Tent City	272 Friend St	227-9242	Four floors of outdoors needs since 1947.
Savenor's Market	160 Charles St	723-6328	For a variety of gourmet goods.

Map 2 · North End / Faneuil Hall

Bova's Bakery	134 Salem St	523-5601	Pastries, also deli and pizza. Open 24 hours.
Dairy Fresh Candies	57 Salem St	742-2639	Big selection of candy imported from Italy.
Green Cross Pharmacy	393 Hanover St	227-3728	Old-world pharmacy. Also sells Italian sundries.
Holbrows Flowers	100 City Hall Plaza	227-8057	Convenient to Government Center T stop.
Maria's Pastry Shop	46 Cross St	523-1196	Sweet tooth heaven.
Mike's Pastry	300 Hanover St	742-3050	Another great North End Italian bakery.
Modern Pastry	257 Hanover St	523-3783	Boston's best cannoli? You decide.
Monica's Salumeria	130 Salem St	742-4101	Homemade takeout and Italian groceries.
Newbury Comics	1 Washington Mall	248-9992	Downtown location of successful music/novelties chain.
Rand McNally	84 State St	720-1125	All sorts of maps, guidebooks, and travel aids.
Salumeria Italiana	151 Richmond St	523-8743	Well-regarded Italian specialties store.
Salumeria Toscana	272 Hanover St	720-4243	Imported Italian specialties, heat-and-serve meals.

Map 3 · Downtown Crossing / Park Square / Bay Village

Beacon Hill Skate Shop	135 S Charles St	482-7400	Rentals available. Also has hockey gear.
Bromfield Camera & Video	10 Bromfield St	426-5230	Decent selection of new and used cameras.
City Sports	11 Bromfield St	423-2015	Covers all the basics in apparel and equipment.
Filene's	426 Washington St	357-2100	One of the two big downtown department stores.
Filene's Basement	426 Washington St	542-2011	Discount apparel since 1908.
H & M	350 Washington St	482-7001	Inexpensive sportswear from Swedish megamerchant.
HMV	24 Winter St	357-8444	For all your mainstream music needs.
Lotus Designs	482A Columbus Ave	262-7031	Flower shop.

Macy's	450 Washington St	357-3000	Once Jordan Marsh. The other big store downtown.
Marshall's	350 Washington St	338-6205	Discount clothing and other stuff.
Old Town Camera	226 Washington St	227-0202	Photo equipment, film developing.
Shreve, Crump & Low	330 Boylston St	267-9100	Boston jewelers since 1796.
Staples	25 Court St	367-1747	Printer ink and other more reasonably priced supplies.
TJ Maxx	350 Washington St	695-2424	Off-price apparel.

Map 4 • Financial District / Chinatown

Brooks Brothers	75 State St	261-9990	Branch of venerable Back Bay clothier.
Chinese American Company	38 Kneeland St	423-2264	For your martial arts and herbal medicine needs.

Map 5 • Back Bay (West) / Fenway (East)

Allston Beat	348 Newbury St	421-9555	For your next rave, club outing, etc.
Army Barracks	328 Newbury St	437-1657	Surplus store. Lots of coats, T-shirts.
Back Bay Bicycle	336 Commonwealth Ave	247-2336	Accurately monikered.
Blades Board & Skate	349A Newbury St	437-6300	Keeping local skaters stoked.
Boston Beat	279 Newbury St	247-2428	Focusing on dance music. Also has turntables, mixers.
CD Spins	324 Newbury St	267-5955	A good choice for selling back CDs.
Daddy's Junky Music	159 Massachusetts Ave	247-0909	Comprehensive store serving the Berklee community.
DeLuca's Market	239 Newbury St	262-5990	Good deli, pricy fruit, wine and beer downstairs.
Economy Hardware	219 Massachusetts Ave	536-4280	Hardware, household needs, cheap furniture. Very popular.
John Fluevog	306 Newbury St	266-1079	Buy your guy some nicer shoes.
Johnson Artist Materials	355 Newbury St	536-4065	Tony. Also a selection of stationery.
JP Licks	352 Newbury St	236-1666	Popular ice cream shop.
Mars Records	299 Newbury St	266-4270	Particularly strong in punk and jazz.
Matsu	259 Newbury St	266-9707	Gifts, accessories, good women's clothes.
Newbury Comics	332 Newbury St	247-8506	Original location of successful music/novelties chain.
Orpheus	362 Commonwealth Ave	247-7200	Focusing on classical music.
Saks Fifth Avenue	800 Boylston St	262-6000	Boston branch of New York playa.
Sweet & Nasty	90A Massachusetts Ave	262-7710	Erotic cakes and adult novelties.
Trident Booksellers and Cafe	338 Newbury St	267-8688	All-day breakfast in a cool bookstore.
Utrecht Art Supply Center	333 Massachusetts Ave	262-4948	Serious art store near Symphony Hall.
Virgin Megastore	360 Newbury St	896-0950	Soon to have condos on upper floors.

Map 6 • Back Bay (East) / South End (Upper)

Anthropologie	799 Boylston St	262-0545	Good for gifts and conversation pieces. Some clothes.
Brooks Brothers	46 Newbury St	267-2600	Flagship store of company operating since 1818.
Chocolate Truffle	31 St James Ave	423-9400	For that funny valentine of yours.
City Sports	480 Boylston St	267-3900	Covers all the basics in apparel and equipment.
Crate & Barrel	777 Boylston St	262-8700	Back Bay location of Chicago behemoth.
E6 Apothecary	167 Newbury St	236-8138	Cosmetics. Service and selection attract a devoted clientele.
Hempest	207 Newbury St	421-9944	Don't ask if they sell screens.
International Poster Gallery	205 Newbury St	375-0076	Prints and posters from around the world.
Kitchen Arts	161 Newbury St	266-8701	Broad range of kitchen needs and esoterica.
Lindt Master Chocolatier	704 Boylston St	236-0571	Nifty gifts for your Swiss miss.
Lord & Taylor	760 Boylston St	262-6000	Might not be here for much longer.
Louis Boston	234 Berkeley St	262-6100	High-end men's and women's designer clothing.
Marshall's	500 Boylston St	262-6066	Discount clothing and other stuff.
Neiman Marcus	5 Copley Pl	536-3660	Needless Markup?
Tannery	400 Boylston St	267-0899	Boots, leather, coats, sneakers. Hit-or-miss service.
Teuscher Chocolates of Switzerland	230 Newbury St	536-1922	For the chocoholic.
Tweeter Etc	350 Boylston St	262-2299	Audio and video equipment.
Winston Flowers	131 Newbury St	442-0660	Well-established high-end flower shop.

Map 7 · South End (Lower)

Aunt Sadie's	18 Union Park St	357-7117	Fabulous candles, other gifts.
Community Bicycle Supply	496 Tremont St	542-8623	South End bike shop.
Earthbound	607A Tremont St	424-1881	An "urban garden center."
Lionette's	577 Tremont St	778-0360	Food shop associated with Garden of Eden.
Posh	557 Tremont St	437-1970	Gifts, home furnishings, and accessories.
The Butcher Shop	552 Tremont St	423-4800	Sweet meats. Also a wine bar serving specialties.
Tommy Tish	102 Waltham St	482-1111	Tiny shop with cards and gifts.

Map 11 · South Boston (East)

Miller's Market	336 K St	268-2526	Apparently, the coldest beer in town.

Map 14 · Jamaica Plain

Boomerangs	716 Centre St	524-5120	Used clothing.
CD Spins	668 Centre St	524-4800	A good choice for selling back CDs.
Ferris Wheels Bicycle Shop	64 South St	522-7082	JP bike shop.
JP Licks	659 Centre St	524-6740	Popular ice cream shop.
LJ Peretti	2 1/2 Park Sq	482-0218	Oldest family-run tobacconist in the country.

Map 16 · Kenmore Square / Brookline (East)

Bed Bath & Beyond	401 Park Dr	536-1090	For when holes are growing in your towels.
Boston Bicycle	842 Beacon St	236-0752	Kenmore Square bike shop.
Economy Hardware	1012 Beacon St	277-8811	Hardware, household needs, cheap furniture. Very popular.
Guitar Center	750 Commonwealth Ave	738-5958	Also has drums, keys, etc.
Nuggets	486 Commonwealth Ave	536-0679	Sells only used recordings. Quite fun to browse.
Ski Market	860 Commonwealth Ave	731-6100	Snowboards downstairs in Underground.
Staples	401 Park Dr	638-3292	Printer ink and other more reasonably priced supplies.
Tweeter Etc	874 Commonwealth Ave	738-4411	Audio and video equipment.

Map 17 · Coolidge Corner / Brookline Hills

Flip Side Records	1410 Beacon St	739-8622	Also runs an online store.

Map 18 · Brighton

CompUSA	205 Market St	783-1900	Has the basics, but service could be sharper.
Staples	1660 Soldiers Field Rd	254-4822	Printer ink and other more reasonably priced supplies.

Map 19 · Allston (South) / Brookline (North)

Berezka International Food Store	1215 Commonwealth Ave	787-2837	For the slavophile.
Bob Smith's Wilderness House	1048 Commonwealth Ave	277-5858	Outdoors gear, including skis.
CD Spins	187 Harvard Ave	787-7860	A good choice for selling back CDs.
City Sports	1035 Commonwealth Ave	782-5121	Covers all the basics in apparel and equipment.
Economy Hardware	140 Harvard Ave	789-5552	Hardware, household needs, cheap furniture. Very popular.
Herrell's Ice Cream	155 Brighton Ave	782-9599	Try the hot fudge.
In Your Ear	957 Commonwealth Ave	787-9755	Good selection of independent, experimental music.
International Bicycle Center	89 Brighton Ave	783-5804	Allston bike shop.
JP Licks	311A Harvard Ave	738-8252	Popular ice cream shop.

Map 20 · Harvard Square / Allston (North)

Alpha Omega	57 JFK St	864-1227	Jewelry, large selection of watches.
Black Ink	5 Brattle St	497-1221	A blend of quirky and handy gifts.
Bob Slate	1288 Massachusetts Ave	547-1230	Well-liked stationery store. Art supplies too.
Cardullo's Gourmet Shoppe	6 Brattle St	491-8888	Going for more than sixty years. Expensive, recommended.

City Sports	16 Dunster St	868-9232	Covers all the basics in apparel and equipment.
Crate & Barrel	48 Brattle St	876-6300	Harvard Square location of Chicago behemoth.
Harvard Coop	1400 Massachusetts Ave	499-2000	Good for books, maps, school stuff.
Herrell's Ice Cream	15 Dunster St	497-2179	Try the hot fudge.
Leavitt & Pierce	1316 Massachusetts Ave	547-0576	Best tobacconist in Cambridge. Chess sets too.
Newbury Comics	36 JFK St	491-0337	A zoo on weekends.
Nini's Corner	1394 Massachusetts Ave	547-3558	What are sundries? This place sells sundries.
Nomad	1741 Massachusetts Ave	497-6667	Cool stuff from all over.
Out of Town News	0 Harvard Sq	354-7777	The sensible Harvard Square rendezvous spot.
Planet Records	54B JFK St	353-0693	CDs, some vinyl. Grab a $1 "mystery bag."
Staples	57 JFK St	491-1166	Printer ink and other more reasonably priced supplies.
Stereo Jack's	1686 Massachusetts Ave	497-9447	Specializing in jazz, blues, and the like.
Tannery	11A Brattle St	491-0810	Boots, leather, coat, sneakers. Hit-or-miss service.
Tess	20 Brattle St	864-8377	Chi-chi clothes.
Tweeter Etc	104 Mt Auburn St	492-4411	Audio and video equipment.
Twisted Village	12B Eliot St	354-6898	Focusing on experimental, modern psychedelic music.

Map 22 · North Cambridge / West Somerville

Bicycle Exchange	2067 Massachusetts Ave	864-1300	Porter Square bike shop.
Daddy's Junky Music	2238 Massachusetts Ave	497-1556	Comprehensive store serving Cambridge musicians.

Map 23 · Central Somerville / Porter Square

Ace Wheelworks	145 Elm St	776-2100	Davis Square bike shop.
Bob Slate	1975 Massachusetts Ave	547-8624	Well-liked stationery store. Art supplies too.
CD Spins	235 Elm St	666-8080	A good choice for selling back CDs.
City Sports	1815 Massachusetts Ave	661-1666	Covers all the basics in apparel and equipment.
Disc Diggers	401 Highland Ave	776-7560	New and used CDs, videos.
Nuggets	46 White St	623-1001	Sells only used recordings. Quite fun to browse.

Map 26 · East Cambridge / Kendall Square/MIT

Apple Store	100 Cambridgeside Pl	225-0442	Mac heaven in the Galleria.
Best Buy	100 Cambridgeside Pl	577-8866	Big box electronics retailer in the Galleria.
Cambridge Antique Market	201 Monsignor O'Brien Hwy	868-9655	Five floors to keep you busy.
Chocolate Truffle	2 Cambridge Ctr	374-8888	For that funny valentine of yours.
Haviland Candy	134 Cambridge St	498-0500	Bulk candy straight from the factory.
Mayflower Poultry	621 Cambridge St	547-9191	Live poultry, fresh killed.

Map 27 · Central Square / Cambridgeport

Cambridge Bicycle	259 Massachusetts Ave	876-6555	Bike shop near MIT.
Cheapo Records	645 Massachusetts Ave	354-4455	A treasure trove of older tunes.
Cremaldi's	31 Putnam Ave	354-7969	Gourmet shop behind Central Square.
Economy Hardware	438 Massachusetts Ave	864-3300	Hardware, household needs, cheap furniture. Very popular.
Hubba Hubba	534 Massachusetts Ave	492-9082	Focusing on the naughty bits.
Looney Tunes	1001 Massachusetts Ave	876-5624	Records covered with the finest dust.
Mass Army Navy Store	698 Massachusetts Ave	497-1250	Surplus store.
Micro Center	727 Memorial Dr	264-6400	Computer have-it-all. Avoid going on Saturdays.
Mojo Music	904 Massachusetts Ave	547-9976	A little bit of everything here.
Pearl Art & Craft Supplies	597 Massachusetts Ave	547-6600	Arts and crafts, Central Square style.
Sadye & Company	182 Massachusetts Ave	547-4424	Good antiques store.
Second Coming Records	1105 Massachusetts Ave	576-6400	Focusing on rock. Plenty of vinyl.
Skippy White's	538 Massachusetts Ave	491-3345	Mostly R&B, soul, Motown, other oldies.
Toscanini's	899 Main St	491-5877	In our opinion, Boston's best ice cream.
University Stationery	311 Massachusetts Ave	547-6650	A friendly little shop near MIT.

Map 28 · Inman Square

Garment District	200 Broadway	876-5230	Vintage threads, costumes, clothing by-the-pound.
Target	180 Somerville Ave	776-4036	Oh, you know.

Arts & Entertainment · **Theaters**

In addition to the **Wang Center for the Performing Arts** and the **Shubert Theatre** (see pages 277 and 275, respectively), the Theater District is home to the **Cutler Majestic Theatre** (owned by Emerson College) and the **Colonial Theatre** (which nabbed *The Producers* when it came through town after its successful Broadway run). Both the delightful *Blue Man Group* and the "fun" *Shear Madness* are in very extended runs at the **Charles Playhouse** (on Warrenton Street behind the Shubert Theatre).

There's always a little bit of drama going on in the South End, but if you prefer your drama to be a little more structured and professional, check out what's on at the Boston Center for the Arts, which is home to the **BCA Theater**, the **Black Box Theater** and the **Leland Center**. The BCA is currently the home of four in-residence companies: Sugan (focusing on

contemporary Irish/Celtic plays), Theater Offensive (queer theater), Pilgrim Theater (a "research and performance collaborative") and SpeakEasy Stage.

For laughs, try one of Boston's improv companies—two of the better known are **ImprovBoston** in Inman Square and **Improv Asylum** in the North End. **Jimmy Tingle's Off-Broadway** in Davis Square is an intimate place to see a show, featuring occasional stand-up performances from Mr. Tingle himself. **The Publick Theatre** in Brighton puts on free outdoor Shakespeare in the summer.

If you're more of a choir and orchestra person, keep your eye on what's playing at the **Sanders Theatre**, located in Harvard's Memorial Hall. This theater, which was built to offer a 180-degree perspective for the audience and was inspired by a Christopher Wren design, offers terrific acoustics and a classic interior.

Theater	Address	Phone	Map
ImprovAsylum	216 Hanover St	617-263-6887	2
Charles Playhouse	74 Warrenton St	617-426-6912	3
Colonial Theatre	106 Boylston St	617-426-9366	3
Cutler Majestic Theatre at Emerson College	219 Tremont St	617-824-8000	3
Orpheum Theatre	Hamilton Pl	617-679-0810	3
Shubert Theatre	265 Tremont St	617-482-9393	3
Stuart Street Playhouse	200 Stuart St	617-426-4499	3
Tremont Theater	276 Tremont St	617-542-4599	3
Wang Theatre	270 Tremont St	617-482-9393	3
Wilbur Theatre	246 Tremont St	617-423-4008	3
Actors Workshop	327 Summer St	617-423-7313	4
Berklee Performance Center	136 Massachusetts Ave	617-747-2261	5
Boston Children's Theater	321 Columbus Ave	617-424-6634	5
Boston Conservatory Theater	31 Hemenway St	617-536-3063	5
Boston Playwrights' Theatre	949 Commonwealth Ave	617-353-5443	5
Huntington Theatre Company	264 Huntington Ave	617-266-0800	5
Symphony Hall	301 Massachusetts Ave	617-266-1492	5
Lyric Stage Company	140 Clarendon St	617-437-7172	6
BCA Theater	539 Tremont St	617-426-5000	7
Black Box Theater	539 Tremont St	617-426-5000	7
Leland Center	539 Tremont St	617-426-5000	7
Footlight Club	7A Eliot St	617-524-3200	14
Blackman Auditorium/Studio Theatre	360 Huntington Ave	617-373-2247	15
Remis Auditorium	465 Huntington Ave	617-369-3770	15
Tower Auditorium	621 Huntington Ave	617-879-7000	15
Lansdowne Street Playhouse	41 Lansdowne St	617-536-2100	16
Wheelock Family Theatre	180 The Riverway	617-879-2000	16
The Publick Theatre	1400 Soldiers Field Rd	617-782-5425	19
Hasty Pudding Theatre	12 Holyoke St	617-495-5205	20
Loeb Drama Center	64 Brattle St	617-547-8300	20
Sanders Theatre	45 Quincy St	617-482-6661	20
Somerville Theatre	55 Davis Sq	617-625-5700	22
Jimmy Tingle's Off Broadway	255 Elm St	617-591-1616	23
Improv Boston	1253 Cambridge St	617-576-1253	28

The Arts and Entertainment Authority.

Every week the *Phoenix* arts and entertainment coverage rises above the media clutter. With more than 1000 places to go and things to do, the *Phoenix* offers the area's most sophisticated and useful listings. In the 8 Days a Week section you'll find smart – as well as quirky – picks of the hottest and most interesting happenings. You may agree or disagree with what *Phoenix* writers and critics have to say, but you'll never be bored. Odds are, you'll be challenged. Whether it's a review of a hot new film, like *The Matrix Reloaded*, or a report on classical maestro Pierre Boulez's recent visit to Harvard, or opinions on local bands and national releases from bands as varied as The White Stripes, Uncle Tupelo, and Powerman 5000, you'll be engaged. The *Phoenix*. Free everywhere and online at thephoenix.com.

THE

Phoenix

BOSTON · PROVIDENCE · PORTLAND

Don't you have better things to do?

City Schleppers runs your errands and provides you with that extra hand when you're at work, away on vacation or simply "because." You can be at two places at once with a little help from City Schleppers...the newest, most unbelievable errand service!

(888) 843-2662
www.cityschleppers.com
505 Boylston St., Boston, MA 02116

Because you have better things to do.™

Allston

Street		
Adamson St	19	A1
Adella Pl	19	A1
Alcorn St	19	A2
Alcott St	19	A1
Aldie St	19	A1
Allston St (1-399)	19	B1/A1
Almy St	19	A2
Amboy St	19	A2
Appian Way (1-99)	19	A1
Arden St	19	A1
Armington St	19	A1
Ashford Ct	19	A1
Ashford St	19	A1/A2
Ashford Ter	19	A2
Athol St	19	A1
Bagnal St	19	A1
Balliol St	19	A1
Barrows St	19	A1
Barstow St	18	A2
Bayard St	19	A1
Bertram St	19	A1
Blaine St	19	A1
Boston University Brg	16	A1
Boulevard Ter	19	B1
Bradbury St (1-99)	19	A1
Brainerd Rd	19	B1
Braintree St	19	A1
Brentwood St	19	
Brighton Ave	19	A1/A2
Callahan Pl	20	B1
Cambridge St (1-567)	19	A1/A2
Cambridge St (589-799)	18	B2/A2
Cambridge Ter (1-99)	19	
Chester St (1-199)	19	A1
City View Rd	19	B1
Clevemont Ave	19	A1
Colerain St	19	A1
Commonwealth Ave (883-1520)	19	B1/B2/A2
Coolidge Rd	19	
Craftsman St	19	A1
Denby Rd	19	A1
Easton St	19	A1
Eatonia St	19	A2
Eleanor St	18	A2
Eliot Brg	20	B1
Emery Rd	19	A1
Empire St	19	A2
Eric Rd	19	A1
Everett Sq	19	A1
Everett St (1-266)	19	A1
Everett St (301-399)	20	B1
Farrington Ave	19	A1
Feneno Ter	19	B1
Fern St (1-99)	19	A1
Fiske Ter	19	B1
Fordham Rd	19	B1
Franklin St (1-199)	19	A1
Fuller St	19	B2/B1
Gardner St (1-299)	19	A1/A2
Gardner Ter	19	A2
Glenville Ave	19	B1
Glenville Ter	19	B1
Gordon St (1-199)	19	A1/B1
Gorham St (1-99)	19	B1
Greylock Rd	19	B1
Griggs Pl	19	B1
Griggs St	19	B1
Hano St	19	A1
Hartley Ter	19	A2
Harvard Ave (1-387)	19	A1/B1
Harvard St	19	A1
Harvard Way	20	B1
Harvester St	19	A1

Street		
Harvey Steel Rd	19	A1
Haskell St (1-99)	19	A1
Hefferan St	20	B1
Higgins St	19	A1
High Rock Way	19	B1
Highgate St	19	A1
Hollis Pl	19	B1
Holman St	19	A1
Holmes St	19	A1
Hooker St	19	A1/A2
Hopedale St	19	A2
Imrie Rd	19	A1/B1
Islington St	19	A1
Islington Ter	19	A1
Kelton St	19	B1
Kingsley St	19	A1
Linden St (1-199)	19	A1
Long Ave	19	B1
Lorraine Ter	19	B1
Malvern St	19	A2
Mansfield St	19	A1
Manton Ter	19	B1
McDonald Ave	19	A1
Mead St (1-99)	19	A1
Myrick St	19	B1
N Beacon St (1-58)	19	A1
N Harvard St (1-203)	20	B1
N Harvard St (207-399)	19	A1/A2
Oxford St (1-99)	19	
Parkvale Ave	19	
Penniman Rd	19	A1
Pomeroy St (1-3)	19	A1
Pomeroy St (20-99)	18	A2
Pratt St	19	A2
Prescott Pl	19	A1
President Ter	19	A1
Price Rd	19	B1
Quint Ave	19	B1
Radcliffe Rd (1-99)	19	B1
Raymond St (1-99)	19	A1
Redford St	19	B1
Reedsdale St	19	
Rena St	19	A1
Ridgemont St	18	A2
River Street Brg	19	A2
Rotterdam St	19	A1
Royal St	19	A1
Royce Rd	19	B1
Rugg Rd	19	A1
Saunders St	18	A2
Sawyer Ter	19	A2
Scottfield Rd	19	B1
Seattle St	19	B1
Seven Pine Rd	19	A1
Sinclair Rd	19	A1
Soldiers Field Rd (1-1200)	20	B1
Sorrento St	19	A2
Speedway Ave	19	A2
Spofford Rd	19	B1
St Lukes Rd	19	
Stadium Way	20	B1
State Highway 30	19	B1/A2/B2
Thor Ter	19	A1
Thorndike St (1-187)	19	B2/B1
Travis St	19	
W Alcorn St	19	
W Sorrento St	19	A2
Wadsworth St (1-62)	19	A2
Walbridge St	19	B1
Webley St	19	
Weitz St	19	A1
Westford Pl	19	A1
Westford St	19	A1
Wilton St (1-99)	19	A1
Wilton Ter	19	A1
Windom St (1-199)	19	A2

Boston

Street		
3rd Pl	10	B2
4th Street Pl (1-99)	10	B2
A St (1-13)	12	A2
A St (20-399)	10	A1
Abbotsford St	13	B1
Aberdeen St	16	A2
Academy Ct	13	B1
Academy Rd	13	B1
Academy Ter	13	B1
Acadia St	11	B2
Access Rd	12	A1
Accolyn Way	1	A2
Achorn Cir	14	B1
Ackley Pl	14	B2
Acorn St (1-99)	1	B1
Adams Pl (1-99)	1	B1
Adams Pl (1-99)	10	B1
Adams St (1-99)	13	A2
Adelaide St	14	A2
Adelaide Ter	14	A2
Adrain St	13	B2
Agassiz Park	14	B1
Agassiz Rd	15	A2
Aguadilla St	7	A1
Akron Pl	13	B1
Akron St (1-99)	13	B1
Akron St (1-99)	27	A1
Al St	7	A1
Alaska St	13	A1
Albany St (169-798)	7	B1/B2/A2
Albany St (791-999)	13	A2
Albemarle Ct	5	B2
Albemarle St	5	B2
Albemarle Ter	5	B2
Aldine St	4	A2
Aldworth St	14	B1
Alfred St (1-99)	14	B2
Alger St	12	A2
Alleghany St	15	B1/B2
Allerton St (1-19)	13	A2
Allerton St (32-99)	12	B1
Alley 516	7	A1
Allstate Rd	12	B1
Alna Pl	9	B1
Alpine Pl	13	B1
Alpine St (1-99)	13	B1
Alther St	13	A2
Alton Ct (1-47)	15	B2
Alvah Kittredge Park	13	A1
Alveston St	14	B2
Alveston Ter	14	B2
Ambrose St	13	A2
Amory Ave	14	A2
Amory St (1-599)	14	A2/B2
Amory Ter	14	A2
Amy Ct	1	A2
Anchor Way	11	A2
Anderson Pl	1	B1
Anderson St	1	B1
Andrew Sq	12	B2
Andrews Pl	7	B2
Andrews St	7	B2
Anita Ter	13	A1
Annunciation Rd	15	A2
Anson St	14	B1
Anthony J Grieco Ter	9	B1
Anthony Pl	2	B1
Appian Pl	9	A1
Appleton St (1-129)	7	A1/A2
Aquadilla St	7	A1
Aramon St	9	B2
Arborway	14	B1
Arborway Ter	14	B1

Street Index

Street Index

Street Index

Street Index